Save yourself the time and trouble of manual file entry ...

Order the
Fractal Programming in C disk!

This optional disk contains all the individual programs listed in the book. Source code for over 100 black and white pictures and over 50 color pictures are provided, allowing you to reproduce them. MS-DOS format. Requires PC or clone with EGA or VGA and color monitor; Turbo C, Quick C or Microsoft C compiler.

To order, return this postage-paid card with your payment to: **M&T Books**, 501 Galveston Drive, Redwood City, CA 94063-4728. Or, call TOLL-FREE 1-800-533-4372 (In CA 1-800-356-2002).

YES! Please rush me *Fractal Programming in C* program disk for $20 _____

CA residents add applicable sales tax _____ % _____

TOTAL _____

Check enclosed. Make payable to **M&T Books**.

Charge my: _____ VISA _____ MasterCard _____ American Express

Card # _____ Exp. date _____

Name _____

Address _____

City _____ State _____ Zip _____

7032

BUSINESS REPLY MAIL
FIRST CLASS PERMIT 871 REDWOOD CITY CA

POSTAGE WILL BE PAID BY ADDRESSEE

M&T BOOKS
501 Galveston Drive
Redwood City CA 94063-9925

PLEASE FOLD ALONG LINE AND TAPE CLOSED

Fractal
Programming in C

M&T BOOKS

Fractal
Programming in C

Roger T. Stevens

M&T BOOKS

M&T Publishing, Inc.
Redwood City, California

M&T Books
A Division of M&T Publishing, Inc.
501 Galveston Drive
Redwood City, CA 94063

M&T Books
General Manager, Ellen Ablow
Operations Manager, Michelle Hudun
Project Editor, David Rosenthal
Technical Editor, Alan Norman
Editorial Assistant, Kurt Rosenthal
Cover Art Director, Michael Hollister
Cover Designer, Theresa Tomlin

Library of Congress Cataloging in Publication Data

Stevens, Roger T., 1927–
    Fractal programming in C / Roger T. Stevens. -- 1st ed.
        p. cm.
    Includes bibliographical references.
        1. Fractals--Computer programs. 2. C (Computer program language)
I. Title.
QA614.86.S74   1989
516--dc20

ISBN 1-55851-038-9   (book/disk) $39.95
ISBN 1-55851-037-0   (book) $24.95
ISBN 1-55851-039-7   (disk) $20.00

93 92 91 90 89   5 4 3 2 1

For My Wife Barbara

Writing a book requires large amounts of time and concentration which do not necessarily make the author the easiest person in the world to live with. Without her understanding and love and encouragement, this book would soon have become a drag and probably would never have been finished.

Acknowledgments

All of the software in this book was written in Turbo C version 2.0 furnished by Borland International, 4385 Scotts Valley Drive, Scotts Valley, CA 95066. The software was also checked with Microsoft C 5.0 furnished by Microsoft Corp., 16011 NE 36th Way, Redmond, WA 98073.

Valuable technical information on the format of .PCX files and a copy of PC Paintbrush were supplied by Shannon of Z-Soft Corporation, 1950 Spectrum Circle, Marietta, GA 30067. Dr. Michael Batty of the University of Wales Institute of Science and Technology was kind enough to send me several reprints of his publications and direct me to his book *Microcomputer Graphics*, which contains much useful information.

All software was checked out on a computer with a Vega VGA card furnished by Video Seven, Inc., 46335 Landing Parkway, Fremont, CA 94538, and a NEC Multisync Plus Color Monitor furnished by NEC Home Electronics (U. S. A.) Inc.

Limits of Liability
and Disclaimer of Warranty

The Author and Publisher of this book have used their best efforts in preparing the book and the programs contained in it. These efforts include the development, research, and testing of the theories and programs to determine their effectiveness.

The Author and Publisher make no warranty of any kind, expressed or implied, with regard to these programs or the documentation contained in this book. The Author and Publisher shall not be liable in any event for incidental or consequential damages in connection with, or arising out of, the furnishing, performance, or use of these programs.

How to Order
the Accompanying Disk

Fractal Programming in C is a comprehensive "how to" book written for programmers interested in fractals. Learn about reproducing those developments that have changed our thinking about the physical sciences, and in creating pictures that have both beauty and an underlying mathematical meaning. Included are more than 100 black and white pictures and 32 color pictures. All source code to reproduce these pictures is provided on disk, in MS-DOS format. It requires a PC or clone with an EGA or VGA card and a color monitor; and a Turbo C, Quick C, or Microsoft C compiler.

The disk is $20, plus sales tax if you are a California resident. Order by sending a check, or credit card number and expiration date, to:

Fractal Programming in C Disk
M&T Books
501 Galveston Drive
Redwood City, CA 94063

Or, you may order by calling our toll-free number between 8 A.M. and 5:00 P.M. Pacific Standard Time: 800/533-4372 (800/356-2002 in California). Ask for **Item #039-7**.

Contents

1
Introduction

Alfred North Whitehead, the American mathematician and philosopher, was fond of relating how physicists, at the end of the nineteenth century, considered physics to be essentially a closed book. Everything of any importance in the field was already known. All that needed to be done was to clean up a few loose ends and the volume could be marked "COMPLETE" and closed forever. Then, in the course of cleaning up the loose ends, Schrödinger discovered quantum mechanics and Einstein created the theory of relativity and physics was in a state of revolution, with more unanswered questions than ever before. To Whitehead, one of the most significant aspects of this revolution was its effect upon the philosophical outlook of physicists. Never again would they take the smug, self-contained approach that everything was known and complete. Instead, their minds would always be open to the myriad of possibilities of the unknown.

By 1980, however, things had gone full circle. The cosmologist extraordinaire Stephen Hawking presented a lecture, "Is the End in Sight for Theoretical Physics?", in which he postulated that we already know everything about physics that is important in daily life, and that future discoveries would require huge sums of money and large machines to discover insignificant refinements. While Hawking was closing out physics, a revolution in scientific thinking had already begun that would cut across disciplinary boundaries so that physics, as well as other sciences, would never be the same again. The name of this revolution is *Chaos*.

For centuries, mathematicians were comfortable with an intuitive feeling for what might happen when they wrote down systems of equations. A simple set of equations would produce simple results. In most cases, the end result would be a simple, stable expression that represented the end state of the system. If things got a little more complicated, the equation might blow up, meaning that there were unfortunate sets of inputs for which the result would go off toward infinity. In other situations, the result might be a periodic function, which would never reach an end value, but would at least settle down to a regular repeating function that could be easily predicted. In the real world, situations existed where the state of a system could not be predicted at any given time. Mathematicians got around this problem by representing the system state through the selection of random numbers. They often referred to the system as *noisy*, where noise was a function that took on completely random values, over a given range, through time. The intuitive feeling was that noise represented the results of some regular functions that we did not yet know how to define and measure and that as soon as our understanding and methods improved a little more, we could fully understand, characterize, and eliminate (if necessary) the effects of noise.

"Monster" Curves

The first cracks in this structure began to appear in the late nineteenth and early twentieth century, when mathematicians such as Cantor, von Koch, and Peano began to draw curves quite unlike those that mathematicians had ever seen before. They were often undifferentiable. They were usually self-similar (the shape of each small segment of the curve was the same as the shape of a much larger segment), their length could not easily be measured or defined, and their dimension appeared to differ from the traditional dimension of one for a line and to perhaps be somewhere between a line and a plane.

Traditional mathematicians called these curves "monsters" and "pathological" and refused to deal with them at all. Lacking the tools of modern computers, not much progress was made in studying these curves for many years. In chapters 8, 9, 10, and 11, we shall look at some of these curves in considerable detail and provide software for drawing and investigating them.

Strange Attractors

The chaos revolution really began in about 1961. Edward Lorenz, at the Massachusetts Institute of Technology, was attempting to develop a model for weather systems that would make improved weather forecasting possible. His model appeared to be a fairly good representation of weather patterns, which when run produced results similar to the kind of weather that actually occurred.

One day, Lorenz wanted to pick up from the middle of a previous computer run and examine a sequence in greater detail. He typed in his intermediate data and started the computer going again. To his dismay, the new computer run started by duplicating the results of the previous one, but then began to diverge farther and farther. Lorenz satisfied himself that these results were not due to a faulty computer, and ultimately determined that the cause was that he had typed in the intermediate results to only three decimal places, whereas the computer had originally stored them to six decimal places.

This appeared to be bad news for weather forecasters; if over a period of weeks weather patterns could be completely different due to differences in the fourth or higher decimal places of input data, there appeared to be little possibility that forecasters could collect accurate enough data to make accurate long-range forecasting possible. Lorenz eventually reduced his model to three simple differential equations, which also happened to represent fluid flow or the action of a particular type of water wheel. The result of these equations, over time, was not a single stable result or a periodic function. But it was not random noise, either. Instead, a curve appeared that was ordered and predictable, but never the same. Basically, regardless of input, this set of equations settled down to values from within a family of curves. Fortunately, the curves took on a set of predictable values; unfortunately, the curves continued on to infinity without ever repeating themselves. These curves became known as the *Lorenz attractor*. It was the first of the strange attractors.

The Lorenz equations, a program for graphing the Lorenz attractor, and equations and software for other strange attractors are given in Chapter 6.

Population Curves and Bifurcation Diagrams

In the early 1970s, Robert May, at the Institute for Advanced Studies at Princeton, was looking at the mathematics of population growth. The critical equation was:

$$x_n = rx_{n-1}(1-x_{n-1}) \qquad \text{(Equation 1-1)}$$

This simple equation had been assumed to have two outcomes: either a population achieved a stable equilibrium value or it tapered off to extinction.

As May experimented with different values of the parameter r, however, a strange phenomena occurred. As the parameter grew larger, the result ceased to achieve a stable equilibrium and instead began to oscillate between two different values. A little larger value of the parameter and there were four alternating stable states, then eight, and so forth until the behavior became chaotic and didn't settle down to any value at all. But then, as the parameter increased some more, a stable window was found in the middle of chaos, with three alternating states that then increased to six, twelve, and finally back to chaos again. Another window, farther on, began with seven alternating states.

May's friend James Yorke, at the Institute for Physical Science and Technology at the University of Maryland, did a rigorous mathematical analysis of the behavior of this equation and proved that if a regular cycle of period three ever occurs in any one dimensional system, then the same system will also display regular cycles of every other possible length and various completely chaotic cycles as well. Yorke and Tien-Yien Li wrote a paper on this, which was mischievously called *Period Three Implies Chaos*. This is the origin for the name *chaos* in this new field of science.

A few years later, Mitchell Feigenbaum was studying the same equation at the Los Alamos National Laboratory. He observed a regularity in the period doubling effect, which had a ratio of 4.6692016090, now known as the *Feigenbaum number*. Strangely enough, this same ratio applies to period doubling in a wide variety of iterated equations; almost any iterated equation for which the basic equation produces a curve with a hump. Software to produce bifurcation diagrams and investigate the Feigenbaum number is found in Chapter 7.

Mandelbrot and Julia Sets

At about this same time, Benoit Mandelbrot at IBM's Thomas J. Watson Research Center, was taking a closer look at the von Koch and Peano curves. A technique had been developed years before for assigning a dimension greater than the standard Euclidian dimension to such curves. This dimension is known as the *Hausdorff-Besicovitch dimension.* Mandelbrot coined the term "fractals" to describe all curves whose Hausdorff-Besicovitch dimension is greater than their Euclidian dimension. Mandelbrot was also looking at the characteristics of Julia sets, an intriguing variety of curves based upon mapping the function:

$$z_n = z_{n-1}^2 + c \qquad\qquad \text{(Equation 1-2)}$$

where z and c are complex numbers. Mandelbrot developed a new way of mapping this equation: the *Mandelbrot set.* This set also turns out to be a kind of catalog of all possible Julia sets, from which particularly interesting Julia set parameters may be selected for mapping. Mandelbrot was beginning to discover the same characteristic discovered by Lorenz; that very simple mathematical expressions can result in chaotic nonperiodic functions, which nonetheless do have a very rigid kind of order that is completely specified by the original equations. A complete discussion of the Mandelbrot set, together with software for plotting and investigating it, is given in Chapter 14.

Chapter 15 describes in detail how to create displays of the Julia sets. Mandelbrot began to develop an intuition, which has proved to be right in many cases, that fractals are the natural way of representing many of the shapes in nature. Thus, just as Euclidian geometry is the natural way of describing man-made shapes such as squares, triangles, or cubes, fractals are the natural language for describing clouds, trees, leaves, and other natural objects. This seems to make sense, since we know that apparently very complex natural objects often are generated from rather limited genetic codes.

Iterated Function Systems

Michael Barnsley, a mathematics professor at Georgia Tech, investigated Julia sets, looking for ways to produce even more variability and, perhaps, to generate patterns that matched those of living things. Barnsley discovered what he called *iterated function systems.*

Basically, such a system consisted of several sets of equations, each of which represented a rotation, a translation, and a scaling. By starting with a point and randomly applying one of his sets of equations, according to specified probability rules, Barnsley could generate classic fractals, and he soon discovered how to make the rules for generating ferns and other shapes from nature. Chapter 22 provides a description of this technique and some software for generating various shapes.

The State of Science

Until scientists equipped with the capabilities of modern computers began investigating the characteristics of iterated equations, it was assumed that a simple equation produced a simple result and a more complex equation produced a more complex result. Investigators delving into either mathematics or physical sciences looked for well-behaved functions and tended to ignore or bypass nonlinear effects. The idea that a very simple expression could produce complex, nonperiodic, but regular behavior had not been conceived. Evidences of these effects were passed off as "noise" or as "experimental error."

Today, the effects of investigation into chaos and the application of fractals are changing the way we think about many aspects of the physical sciences and are opening up new areas in mathematics. The news for science is good and bad. The bad news is that things are much more complicated than we thought. The good news is that things are much simpler than we thought. To expand that thought, the good news is that many very complex structures and very complex behaviors can be expressed by very simple iterated equations. The bad news is that the structures and behaviors are aperiodic and that portions of the curve that ultimately diverge widely can, at some point, be physically located so close together that absolutely precise knowledge of coordinates is necessary to know which portion of the curve we are on. We can only predict the future of the curve accurately, if we know exactly where we are on it, and this requires more precise measurement of our present position than we are capable of making.

Why this Book is Different

One might guess, from the brief summary given above, that the introduction of the new field of chaos into the sciences was not greeted with tremendous enthusiasm by many scientists. There is a myth that scientists are totally objective, impassionately conducting experiments and using the results to discover truth. Actually, scientists are persons, not unlike you and me. Their investigations and theories are often directed by prejudice, and the "truth" that they come up with is often only one truth from many, and that truth is the one which their predisposition has led them to discover. The result, as far as chaos is concerned, is that those who were pioneers in the field tended to be a particular type of person. They needed to be a unique combination of scientist, philosopher, and artist, with a reasonable amount of stubbornness and a little eccentricity thrown in. The result is that many of the books which are currently available on fractals bear some resemblance to treatises on medieval alchemy.

These books are filled with esoteric equations and beautiful illustrations of results, but the mechanics of how to get from one to the other is slighted or missing altogether. This book is taking a completely different approach. Its purpose is to provide you with software that you can use to duplicate many of the fractal pictures and basic diagrams of chaos and to proceed from there to easily modify the software to whatever new results come from your own ideas. If you have seen some of the beautiful pictures produced by fractal programs and want to produce the same kind of pictures on your IBM PC (or clone) or perhaps create new and interesting pictures, or if you are interested in using the basic tools to apply fractals to problems in the physical sciences, then this book is for you. It discusses all of the well-known types of fractal curves and provides C language programs (that will work with Microsoft C or Turbo C) to reproduce all of the pictures that are shown in this book.

Hints are given on how to modify parameters to create your own original pictures. These are the tools; how you use them depends strictly on your skill and imagination. The whole field of chaos is still new. There is plenty of room for new discoveries or new art. Good luck!

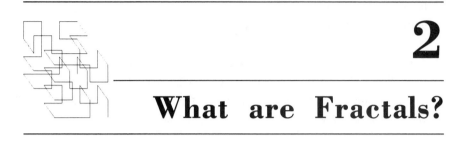

2

What are Fractals?

When I tell people that I have been writing a book on fractals, they usually respond with two questions. The first is "What are fractals?" and the second is "What are fractals good for?" If I am feeling ornery, I respond to the first question with Mandelbrot's classical definition: "A fractal is a curve whose Hausdorff-Besicovitch dimension is larger than its Euclidian dimension." But more is really required in explaining fractals, so let's start at the beginning.

The Beginning of Fractal Curves

Draw a line on a sheet of paper. Euclidean geometry tells us that this is a figure of one dimension, namely length. Now extend the line. Make it wind around and around, back and forth, without crossing itself, until it fills the entire sheet of paper. Euclidean geometry says that this is still a line, a figure of one dimension. But our intuition strongly tells us that if the line completely fills the entire plane, it must be two dimensional.

Such thinking started a revolution in mathematics about a hundred years ago. Mathematicians such as Cantor, von Koch, Peano, Hausdorff, and Besicovitch drew curves that were called "monsters," "psychotic," and "pathological" by traditional mathematicians. A new type of dimensioning was proposed, in which a curve could have a fractional dimension, not just an integer one. Recursive techniques and iterated expressions were found that could describe curves that have fractional dimensions. But without high-speed digital computers, the actual drawing of such curves was a long and tedious process. So little progress occurred in this unusual field for nearly a hundred years.

The advent of digital computers made the investigation of such curves a fruitful field. From the early investigations, we could understand what we were trying to do. We wanted to draw curves that appeared to have more complex dimensional characteristics than were explained by traditional geometry.

Computers were turned loose on very simple mathematical iterated expressions in which the next state of a parameter depended solely on a simple relationship to the current state of the parameter. The iteration was performed many times and the resulting location of the parameter at each state was plotted. The resulting plots turned out to have many interesting characteristics. For one thing, they never repeated themselves. Furthermore, they tended to have the characteristic of self-similarity. In other words, if a small portion of the plot was enlarged, its shape was very much like a large portion of the original plot. The plots turned out to have shapes of great interest and extreme beauty.

The curves still didn't make much sense in terms of traditional mathematics, and consequently remained an anathema to traditional mathematicians. Dr. Benoit Mandelbrot was the first person to make use of a digital computer to investigate fractals in depth, and his results were not welcomed warmly by traditional mathematicians.

How are Fractals Used?

Now we have explained what a fractal is, but explaining how a fractal is used is a little more difficult. Mandelbrot contends that just as the shapes of traditional geometry are the natural way of representing man-made objects (squares, circles, triangles, etc.), fractal curves are the natural way of representing objects that occur in nature. Thus, fractals have a value both as art objects and as a means of representing natural scenes. Moreover, fractals occur naturally in the expressions for mathematical phenomena as varied as the prediction of weather systems, the describing of turbulent flow of liquid, and the growth and decline of populations. Fractals are also useful in dimensional transformations that can be used for expressing and compressing graphical data. Ignoring the artistic value, the best an-swer to the question "What are fractals good for?" is the reply "Fractals appear to provide solutions to many previously unanswered questions at the frontiers of the physical sciences." Consequently, to work at the frontiers of science, one needs to understand what fractals are and how to work with them.

In the later chapters of this book, we shall attempt to do our own experimenting with the creation and modification of fractal curves. We shall not spend too much time worrying about the uses of fractals in the sciences, but will concen-trate on understanding as many different types of fractal curves as possible and developing computer programs to generate these curves. Then, when we en-counter a physical problem that requires a fractal solution, we will know what to do and how to do it.

Basic Considerations

Let's establish some points of orientation that will be useful in practical investi-gations of the chaotic field of fractals:

1) Intuition leads us to believe that fractal curves should have a dimension greater than their traditional geometric dimension.

2) There is now sound mathematical grounding for accepting this premise.

3) Fractal curves are associated with many physical and natural phenomena.

4) Fractals often possess a rare and unusual beauty. No doubt, this is partly true because fractals correspond to the way in which nature produces those shapes that we are most familiar with and that basically define our ideas of "the beautiful."

5) Fractals have the unusual characteristic that they can be defined totally by relatively simple mathematical equations, yet they are not periodic. Thus, the progression of the fractal curve may differ widely if we start at just slightly different points in space, so unless we can measure where we are

with absolute precision we cannot be sure just what the progression of the curve will look like. This is in spite of the fact that the curve is defined through all of its wanderings by very simple iterated expressions.

6) Most fractals are self-similar, so that the shape that we identify in the plot of a fractal curve repeats itself on a smaller and smaller scale as we enlarge the image further and further.

Fractal Dimensions

Let's return to the statement made at the beginning of this chapter that a fractal is a curve whose Hausdorff-Besicovitch dimension is greater than its Euclidian dimension. We now have some idea of the nature of fractal curves and of what this new definition of dimension means, but that doesn't help much unless we can actually come up with some meaningful dimensional numbers. A rigorous definition of the Hausdorff-Besicovitch dimension is a rather lengthy mathematical process, and for many fractals it is almost impossible to determine this dimension. However, for a large class of self-similar fractals, which we will discuss in chapters 8, 9, and 10, the fractal dimension is easily obtained. Suppose that we start with an initiator that is some simple geometric figure consisting of a number of connected line segments. It may be a triangle or a square or even just a straight line. We now define a generator. This generator is is a series of line segments that is going to replace every line segment of the initiator. The generator consists of N line segments, each of length r, where r is a fraction of the line segment being replaced. The arrangement of the N line segments is such that the distance from the beginning of the generator to its end is the same as the length of the line segment being replaced. The replacement process repeats an infinite number of times, each time replacing each line segment of the previous level curve with a scaled-down replica of the generator. It can then be shown that the Hausdorff-Besicovitch dimension of the resulting fractal curve is:

$$D = \log N\ /\ \log(1/r) \hspace{4cm} \text{(Equation 2-1)}$$

Comparing this dimension with the Euclidian dimension gives us some idea of the properties of a fractal. For example, a D of 1.0 is simply an ordinary line, whereas a D of 2.0 means that the curve completely fills the plane.

Background Material

With this background in mind, let's begin looking at fractal curves and creating software to view them and work with them on our IBM PC computers. But first, we need to get some basic considerations out of the way. We need to talk a little bit about what hardware is required to do a good job of investigating fractals. We need to define the software tools that we will use to generate our graphic images. And we need to have techniques for saving the images of fractals on disk files and recalling them when we need to view them.

3

Hardware Requirements

With the wide variety of PC clones that are now available, including some that use 80286 microprocessors at speeds far faster than anything envisioned by IBM, there is no telling when some strange glitch is going to wreak havoc with your program. To attempt to minimize that kind of problem, I have attempted to run most of the programs described in this book on three different systems. One consists of the following:

Motherboard: Bullet-286E from Wave Mate, Inc., Torrance, CA. This board is a drop-in replacement for the PC XT motherboard. It uses an 80286 and has 1MB of on-board 0 wait state memory. The memory from 640K to 1MB is used as a hard disk cache. An 80287-10 math coprocessor was used.

Floppy Disk Controller: MCT-FDC-1.2 from JDR Microdevices, Los Gatos, CA. This board supports 360K or 1.2MB disk drives.

Floppy Disk Drives: 1 Fujitsu 1.2MB disk drive.
1 Mitsubishi 360K floppy disk drive.

I/O Board: MCT-IO from JDR Microdevices.

Hard Disk Controller: MCT-RLL from JDR Microdevices.

Hard Disk Drive: LaPine LT300 30MB from Advanced Computer Products, Santa Ana, CA.

Keyboard: Surplus Honeywell keyboard from B. G. Micro, Dallas, TX.

EGA Card: MCT-EGA from JDR Microdevices.

EGA Monitor: Casper EGA Monitor from JDR Microdevices.

The second system consists of:

Motherboard: DTK Baby AT with 80286. Speeds 8 and 12 MHz. 1MB memory on-board, running with 1 wait state. from U. S. Turbo Systems, South El Monte, CA.

Floppy Disk Controller: KW 530-D from Mica Computer Center, Santa Fe Springs, CA.

Floppy Disk Drives: One Fujitsu 1.2MB from Gems Computer and one 360K Qume from Jade Computer, Hawthorne, CA.

VGA Card: Vega VGA from Video Seven, Fremont, CA.

VGA Monitor: NEC Multisync Plus.

Some cards were occasionally swapped between the two systems described above. In addition, text was printed out on a Hewlett-Packard DeskJet Printer, with 128K added memory and Soft Fonts, and color pictures were printed out on a Hewlett-Packard PaintJet Printer.

The third system was a standard IBM PC AT with math coprocessor and a Plus Passport 40MB hard disk.

Programs that work satisfactorily on such a wide variety of systems as this should have a good chance of working on your system, too. If you encounter problems, try to identify how your system differs from the three described above.

Display Considerations

I highly recommend that if you are going to get serious about fractals, you should buy an EGA or VGA display. Much of the beauty and power of fractal displays comes from manipulating the colors to match the conceptions of the programmer/artist. You will find a number of black and white illustrations of fractal curve results throughout this book. If you must work with a Hercules Graphics Card or compatible monochrome display, you can reproduce these illustrations. You will find full details on how to use the Hercules Graphics mode in my book *Graphics Programming in C* (M&T Books, 1989). Not all of the fractal programs in this book will work in monochrome; those that will, and the program changes needed, are listed in Appendix B. All of the color illustrations in the book were done using color mode 16 (which is high resolution, 16 colors, and is common to the EGA and VGA).

You can duplicate all of the color programs using this mode, and if you have a VGA, you can go to mode 18 and with a few minor changes obtain greater vertical resolution. The VGA also permits you to select the 16 color palettes used in modes 16 or 18 from 256K shades of color instead of the 64 available with the EGA. In most cases, however, you are going to find that the EGA gives you plenty of color capability.

I don't recommend using the CGA color monitor for fractal displays. The resolution is just not adequate for the detail needed to produce interesting fractals. If you have a VGA, mode 19 has the same resolution as the CGA, but permits you to display 256 different colors simultaneously. You're welcome to experiment with that, but I think you will find that the additional picture detail is much to be preferred over the additional color shades.

Processor Speed

As you get into the more complicated fractal displays, such as the Mandelbrot and Julia sets, you are going to find that processor speed becomes more and more of a problem. Even on a fairly fast machine, many of the more interesting displays take days to generate. How can this be resolved? First, code needs to be optimized so that the loops that are iterated most have simple procedures.

More will be said about this later. Next, if you have one of the fast 286 clones, make sure you have fast enough memory so that you can run the programs at the highest available clock speed and preferably with no wait states. Finally, get a math coprocessor chip. Steve Ciarcia wrote in the December 1988 issue of *Byte* magazine that tests he ran show that the coprocessor runs the Mandelbrot set program eight times faster that with the math routines emulated in the C language. Either Microsoft or Turbo C can be used without modification with the coprocessor. Turbo C automatically makes use of the coprocessor if it is available, and also permits you to compile in a coprocessor-only mode, which may give a little extra speed.

If you do not have a coprocessor, an attractive alternative might appear to be generating your own assembly language routines to perform the special math processing that uses most of the time in generating the Mandelbrot sets and similar programs. This, however, turns out not only to be difficult, but also to be less timesaving than one might think. The programmers who wrote the math routines for the most popular versions of the C language spent a lot of time making these routines as fast and efficient as possible.

You are not likely to come up with anything faster for a particular operation, and if you try to save by reducing the precision of the routines, you will probably find that your display looks inferior compared to ones generated by more conventional means. The remaining timesaving that you might achieve is by holding results in registers and doing all of the iterations without transferring to memory, but this will require a lot of register manipulation for 8086 or 80286 machines, which probably isn't worth it.

There are a couple of exceptions to the above. If you have an 80386-based machine, the internal 32-bit registers provide sufficient precision to perform good fractal computations. H. W. Stockman, in the September–October 1988 issue of *Micro Cornucopia*, describes how to write 386 assembly language code to compute the Mandelbrot set directly on the microprocessor's internal registers. He claims that his program is 100 times faster than using floating point math. Once you understand his assembly language code, you should be able to adapt it for generating fast Julia sets, dragons, or phoenixes.

Another approach was used by Steve Ciarcia in the October, November, and December 1988 issues of *Byte*. Ciarcia built a parallel processor that uses 64 Intel 8051 microprocessors in parallel in a special Mandelbrot set generating computer. The cost of this monster, in addition to its PC driver, runs around $6,000. Steve found that it about matched the AT with coprocessor when he used fifteen of the 8051's and was many times faster with 64 parallel processors. And, of course, there is nothing to prevent you from stopping there. In the extreme, you could have one 8051 for each pixel on the display, all working simultaneously and limited only by the time required to dump the results to the display. If you're going to take either of the above routes, you need some real dedication; in most cases, an AT type machine with an EGA display and a math coprocessor will generate all of the fractal displays you will ever need or want without delays that are objectionably long.

Where Do We Go from Here

I've told you what you need in the way of hardware to delve deeply into fractals, but what if you've already purchased the book and don't have the recommended hardware. What can you do, other than save your pennies for an upgrade? Don't despair. While you're saving, you can begin producing some of the simpler monochrome displays. Indeed, some of the most interesting areas for investigating the progress of the new science of Chaos and the applications of fractals to it are found in some of the more simple displays. If you have a computer that is IBM compatible, but takes a long long time to generate a fractal display, there is hope for you, also. In Chapter 4, we will describe techniques for saving a screen (even if only partially completed) to a disk file and then picking up where we left off to finish the display at a later date. So if you're halfway through a fractal display and find that you must have your computer now for a higher priority task, you need not lose everything that you've done so far.

4

Saving and Compressing Display Data

As many as three days may be required to draw some of the fractal pictures that will be discussed in the following chapters, particularly if you do not have a math coprocessor. Since we don't want to spend another three days of drawing time whenever we want to display one of these pictures, it is essential that we have a quick, simple means of saving a picture that is on the screen to a disk file and then quickly restoring it to the screen whenever we need it. There are two instances, in particular, where we need this feature:

1. When we are investigating deep within the Mandelbrot set or a similar set, and wish to start with a set that we have already generated and create an expansion of a particular part of it, we need to quickly display the last set generated from a saved disk file, and then use the cursor to select the portion of it from which a new picture is to be created.

2. When we are in the process of drawing a lengthy picture and discover that we need our computer for something else, we need the capability to save the partially drawn picture to a disk file so that we can later recover it and proceed from where we left off, rather than having to begin the drawing process all over again.

Format for Saving a Screen File

The format chosen for the file that results from saving a screen is that of the .PCX file developed by ZSoft and used with their PC Paintbrush and other drawing programs. This format is widely used and permits your screens to be edited with PC Paintbrush. Also, ImageSet Corp. in San Francisco, CA has programs available that can convert these files directly to slides or photographic artwork suitable for publication. ZSoft is extremely cooperative in making information on this format available to those who want to write compatible software to use it. Shannon, of ZSoft's technical support group, provided me with a pamphlet giving full technical details on the .PCX format. Functions will be listed below that permit you to save a screen to a disk file using the .PCX format and also to read the file back from disk to your display.

In addition, there is an excellent public-domain program called *ZS* which can be used to display any one or all of your EGA .PCX files or run a slide show of them. This program is available on bulletin boards or may be obtained directly by sending $10.00 to:

> Bob Montgomery
> 132 Parsons Rd.
> Longwood, FL 32779

The file starts with a 128 byte header, the contents of which are shown in Figure 4-1. Except for the color map, most of the header contents are self-evident. The floating point numbers for *XMax, XMin, YMax, YMin, Pval,* and *Qval* are not part of the original ZSoft format. They are needed when we save files for Mandelbrot sets and similar displays to preserve data required to define the figure. They are transferred to and from the disk file as four characters, each through the use of the union statement:

```
union LIMIT
{
    float f;
    unsigned char c[4];
};
```

Since that part of the ZSoft header which contains XMax, XMin, YMax, YMin, Pval, and Qval is normally empty, using any other ZSoft compatible program with these files should not present a problem. If the file is read by one of the programs described in the later chapters of this book, the values will be extracted and used as needed. If the file is read by another program, the values will be ignored.

Figure 4-2 shows the contents of a palette register for the EGA color system.

Figure 4-1: Header Data for .PCX Screen File

	Size		
HEADER DATA			
Byte	**(bytes)**	**Name**	**Description**
0	1	Password	0AH designates ZSoft.PCX files.
1	1	Version	versions of PC Paintbrush 0 = vers 2.5 2 = vers 2.8 w/palette info 3 = vers 2.8 w/o palette information 5 = vers 3.0
2	1	Encoding	Encoding scheme used 1 = .PCX run length en- coding.
3	1	Bits per pixel	No. of bits required to store data for 1 pixel from 1 plane. = 1 for EGA, VGA or Hercules = 2 for CGA
4	8	Window dimensions	4 integers (2 bytes each) giving top left and bottom right corners of display in the order x1, y1, x2, y2.
12	2	Horizontal Resolution	Horizontal resolution of display device = 640 for EGA or VGA = 320 for CGA = 720 for Hercules

(continued on next page)

Byte	Size (bytes)	Name	Description
14	2	Vertical Resolution	Vertical resolution of display device (lines) = 480 for VGA = 350 for EGA = 200 for CGA = 348 for Hercules
16	48	Color Map	Information on color palette settings. See following figures for details.
64	1	Reserved	
65	1	Number of planes	Number of color planes in the original image = 1 for CGA, Hercules = 4 for EGA, VGA
66	2	Bytes per line	Number of bytes per scan line in the image
68	2	Palette Information	How to interpret palette. 1 = color/monochrome 2 = grayscale
70	16	Picture limits	Four floating point numbers giving the bounds for the set computation. The order is XMax, XMin, YMax, YMin. This section is not used in original ZSoft format.
86	8	Iteration	Values for 'P' and 'Q' used Parameters for fractal computation. This section is not used in original ZSoft format.
94	32	Not used	Fill to end of header block.

Six bits are used, with two each for the primary colors red, green, and blue. The capital letters represent colors of 75 percent amplitude; the small letters colors of 25 percent amplitude. Thus for each primary colors, four levels are available: 0 (none of that color), 25 percent amplitude, 75 percent amplitude, and 100 percent amplitude (both capital and small letter bits are one). The color map in the file header contains 16 sets of triples, one for each EGA palette. For the first byte of a triple, the values of the capital and small letter position for red are extracted and combined to produce a number from one to three. This number is multiplied by 85 and stored in the header. The same procedure takes place for the second byte of the triple for green and the third byte for blue. The process is repeated sixteen times, once for each palette. Note that when we set the palette registers on the EGA, we are setting a write-only register, so that we can never recover the contents if we want to know later what the setting was.

Consequently, our *setEGApalette* function saves the palette register information in a global array *PALETTE[16]*. It is this data that we use to write the color map in the header when we are saving a screen. Figure 4-3 shows the color map data for the EGA and VGA.

Figure 4-2: Contents of EGA Palette Register

Byte 7	Byte 6	Byte 5	Byte 4	Byte 3	Byte 2	Byte 1	Byte 0
		r (25%)	g (25%)	b (25%)	R (75%)	G (75%)	B (75%)

The VGA is quite different in the way that it handles colors. With the VGA, each palette register contains the number of a color register. The color register contains six bits for each primary, permitting 64 shades of that color. With the VGA we can read each palette register to determine which of the 64 color registers has been selected and then read the selected color register to determine the selected one of 64 shades each of red, green, and blue that make up the color.

For all but 18, we create the .PCX color map by reading the palette register and then the color register pointed to by the palette register.and in the color registers. We then multiply the red, green, and blue values by four and store the results in the triple associated with that palette. Note that when we restore a screen, we may not assign a color value to the same color register that it was obtained from originally, and that the palette registers may not select the same color registers. However, the net result is the same, because each palette register points to a color register that contains the same color information that was contained in the original screen.

The VGA also has color modes in which 256 different colors may be displayed simultaneously. Since this is at a lower resolution (the same resolution as the

CGA display), we won't be using it in our screen-saving and restoring functions. For reference, the format is the same as that used to display the 16-color palette, but due to the 256 colors, the palette information is much longer. It is appended at the end of the .PCX file.

To access this information, you must first ascertain that the version number data in the header (byte 1) is *5* (version 3.0). Then read to the end of the file and count back 769 bytes. If the value in this byte position is *0CH* (12 decimal), the succeeding information is 256-color palette data.

Figure 4-3: Contents of .PCX File Color Map

Byte	Palette	Color	Description
16	0	Red	For the EGA, the values of each
17	0	Green	color of each byte of each
18	0	Blue	triple are:
19	1	Red	
20	1	Green	00H to 54H = 0%
21	1	Blue	55H to A9H = 25%
22	2	Red	AAH to FEH = 75%
23	2	Green	
24	2	Blue	
25	3	Red	
26	3	Green	For the VGA, the value of each
27	3	Blue	byte is the value of the six-
28	4	Red	bit color value from the color
29	4	Green	register pointed to by the
30	4	Blue	appropriate palette register
31	5	Red	for each color of the triple,
32	5	Green	multiplied by four.
33	5	Blue	
34	6	Red	
35	6	Green	
36	6	Blue	
37	7	Red	
38	7	Green	
39	7	Blue	
40	8	Red	
41	8	Green	
42	8	Blue	

(continued on next page)

Byte	Palette	Color	Description
43	9	Red	
44	9	Green	
45	9	Blue	
46	10	Red	
47	10	Green	
48	10	Blue	
49	11	Red	
50	11	Green	
51	11	Blue	
52	12	Red	
53	12	Green	
54	12	Blue	
55	13	Red	
56	13	Green	
57	13	Blue	
58	14	Red	
59	14	Green	
60	14	Blue	
61	15	Red	
62	15	Green	
63	15	Blue	

Data is read from the screen, horizontally from left to right, starting at the pixel position for the upper left corner. For EGA and VGA, which have multiple memory planes, a line is read of the color red (to the end of the window boundary, then the green information for the same line is read, and finally the blue.

The functions that we will develop below only work if the horizontal pixel boundaries are at a byte interface (the column number must be divisible by eight.) Data is run length encoded in the following manner: If the byte is unlike the ones on either side of it, and if its two most significant bits are not *11*, it is written to the file. Otherwise, a count is made of the number of like bytes (up to 63) and this count is ANDed with *C0H* and the result written to the file, followed by the value of the byte. If there are more that 63 successive bytes, the count for 63 and the byte are written and then the count begins all over again. (Note that the case for a singular byte having the two most significant bits 1 is handled by writing a count of one followed by the byte value.)

Function to Save a Screen

Figure 4-4 lists a function to save the EGA screen. The parameters passed to this function are the coordinates of the upper left corner of the window to be saved, the coordinates of the lower right corner, and the name of the file in which the screen data is to be stored. No protection is afforded for values that are outside the screen limits; the programmer must provide this in the calling program. Also, although any pixel location on the screen may be specified, the x value of each corner, as used by the program, is set up to be a byte boundary, which may be as much as seven pixels off from the specified value. Normally, this will not cause a problem; if it does, the programmer should assure that the x values are divisible by eight. The program assumes that the file name, which is passed to it as a parameter, consists of six letters followed by two numbers.

The program begins by trying to open the file in the read mode with the given file name. If the file can be opened (meaning that the file does indeed exist), the program assumes that the file already contains valuable data and therefore increments the two-digit ending and tries again. The loop continues until a file name is generated that cannot be opened, indicating that the file does not exist. This file is then opened in the write mode for saving of the current screen. Note that if the two digits get to *99* without a nonexistent file being found, the loop gives up. Your file will then not be saved.

The function then continues by initiating a sound that continues until the function has completed its work of generating the screen file. Next, the appropriate header information is stored, including the palette information, which is generated as described above. Just preceding the function is shown the global *PALETTE* array, which is initialized with the default palette values for the EGA. Whenever the *setEGApalette* function is called, in addition to resetting the appropriate palette register, it also stores the information in a member of this array, so that it is available for transfer to the .PCX file. The floating point x and y limits and P and Q values for Mandelbrot or other sets are also stored. This data is stored in a set of global coordinates, which are defined by the union LIMIT statement defined above, which permits the limits to be treated as floating point numbers by the original program and yet read from and written to the disk file as sets of four

characters. This alleviates any need for conversion in the process of transferring
to and from the disk.

Figure 4-4: Function to Save an EGA Screen to a Disk File

```
        save_screen() = save screen to disk file
```

```
#include "tools.h"
#include <stdio.h>

void save_screen(int x1, int y1, int x2, int y2,
    char file_name[])
{
    extern union LIMIT XMax,XMin,YMax,YMin,Pval,Qval;
    extern unsigned char PALETTE[16];
    int i,j,k,add1,add2,number,num_out, line_length, end,
        start_line, end_line;
    unsigned char ch,ch1,old_ch,red,green,blue;
    FILE *fsave;
    sound (256);
    while (file_name[6] < 0x3A)
    {
        if ((fsave = fopen (file_name,"rb")) != NULL)
        {
            file_name[7]++;
            if (file_name[7] >= 0x3A)
            {
                file_name[7] = 0x30;
                file_name[6]++;
            }
            fclose(fsave);
        }
        else
        {
            fclose(fsave);
            fsave = fopen(file_name,"wb");
            fputc(0x0A,fsave);
            fputc(0x05,fsave);
            fputc(0x01,fsave);
            fputc(0x04,fsave);
            putw(x1,fsave);
            putw(y1,fsave);
            putw(x2,fsave);
            putw(y2,fsave);
            putw(640,fsave);
            putw(350,fsave);
            ch = 0x00;
```

```
for (i=0; i<16; i++)
{
    red = ((((PALETTE[i] & 0x20) >> 5) |
        ((PALETTE[i] & 0x04) >> 1)) * 85;
    green = ((((PALETTE[i] & 0x10) >> 4) |
        (PALETTE[i] & 0x02)) * 85;
    blue = ((((PALETTE[i] & 0x08) >> 3) |
        ((PALETTE[i] & 0x01) << 1)) * 85;
    fputc(red,fsave);
    fputc(green,fsave);
    fputc(blue,fsave);
}
fputc(0x00,fsave);
fputc(0x04,fsave);
start_line = x1/8;
end_line = x2/8 + 1;
line_length = end_line - start_line;
end = start_line + line_length * 4 + 1;
putw(line_length,fsave);
putw(1,fsave);
for (i=0; i<4; i++)
    fputc(XMax.c[i],fsave);
for (i=0; i<4; i++)
    fputc(XMin.c[i],fsave);
for (i=0; i<4; i++)
    fputc(YMax.c[i],fsave);
for (i=0; i<4; i++)
    fputc(YMin.c[i],fsave);
for (i=0; i<4; i++)
    fputc(Pval.c[i],fsave);
for (i=0; i<4; i++)
    fputc(Qval.c[i],fsave);
for (i=94; i<128; i++)
    fputc(' ',fsave);
for (k=y1; k<y2; k++)
{
    add1 = 80*k;
    number = 1;
    j = 0;
    add2 = (start_line);
    old_ch = read_screen(add1 + add2++,0);
    for (i=add2; i<end; i++)
    {
        if (i == end - 1)
            ch = old_ch - 1;
        else
        {
            if ((add2) == end_line)
            {
                j++;
                add2 = (start_line);
```

```
            }
        ch = read_screen(add1 + add2,
                j);
        }
        if ((ch == old_ch) && number < 63)
            number++;
        else
        {
            num_out = ((unsigned char)
                number | 0xC0);
            if ((number != 1) ||
                ((old_ch & 0xC0) ==
                0xC0))
                fputc(num_out,fsave);
            fputc(old_ch,fsave);
            old_ch = ch;
            number = 1;
        }
        add2++;
        }
    }
    fclose(fsave);
    break;
    }
    }
    nosound();
}
```

The function initializes some address variables and then starts a loop that reiter-
ates for every line of the display from the first one specified by *y1*, to the last
one, specified by *y2*. At the beginning of this loop, the function gets the first
byte of eight pixels from the first plane of the EGA screen. This is stored in
old_ch. Next, another *for* loop is begun, which reads one byte at a time from the
beginning to the end of the line for each of the four memory planes.

After each read, action is taken based upon comparing the read character with the
previous character, which was stored in *old_ch*. For the very last pass through
the loop, instead of reading a byte (which wouldn't be there anyway, since we
have already finished the line), we create an artificial character that is always different from *old_ch*, which forces a write out to the file of the previous data. On
each pass through the loop, we check the value of the address variable *add2*
(which is incremented at the end of each pass). If it is equal to the value representing the end of the line, we reset it to the starting value and also increment *j*,
which determines which memory plane is read.

After the character is read, we check it against the previous character value; if it is the same and if *number*—which stores the number of like characters so far encountered—is less than 63, we simply increment *number* and return for the next pass through the loop. If *number* had reached 63, or if the character read differs from the previous character, we write out to the file. If *number* is one, indicating that the previous character is unlike those on either side of it, and if the value in *old_ch* does not have its two most significant bits equal to one, we simply write this value out to the file. If the value in *old_ch* was repeated, or if its two most significant bits are ones, we first write out the value of *number* with its two most significant bits set to one. We then write out the value in *old_ch*. We then reset *number* to one and are ready for another pass through the loop. When this loop and the display line loop have been completed, the disk file is closed and the sound is turned off.

The function to save a VGA screen is quite similar, except for the way the palette data is treated. The number of lines for a full screen is different from the EGA, but since the number of lines is determined by the values of *y1* and *y2* passed to the function, this does not require any change in the coding.

Figure 4-5 shows the code that is used to save the color information for the VGA.

Figure 4-5: Code to Save VGA Color Information

```
int i,palette,red,green,blue;

for (i=0; i<16; i++)
{
    palette = getVGApalette();
    readColorReg(palette,&red,&green,&blue);
    fputc(red*4);
    fputc(green*4);
    fputc(blue*4);
}
```

Function to Restore an EGA Screen

Figure 4-6 lists a function to restore the screen saved by the save-screen function just described. It will also display any EGA mode 16 screen saved in .PCX format, although it won't have values for *XMax*, *XMin*, *YMax*, *YMin*, *Pval*, or *Qval*. The function begins by attempting to open the file whose designation is passed through the parameter *file_name*. If the file does not exist, the function displays *Cannot find 'file_name*, where *file_name* is the designated name, and then returns a value of 0. If the file does exist, the first character of the header is read. If it is not the password character *0AH* for .PCX files, the function displays *file_name is not a valid ZSoft file* and then returns a value of 0. If the file appears to be a valid one, the computer is set to EGA display mode 16 and the screen is cleared to a black background.

The function then begins to read the header information. The window top left and bottom right coordinates are read and stored. The color data for each palette is read from each triple and converted to an IBM EGA format color word, which is sent to the appropriate palette. The limits and *P* and *Q* values for Mandelbrot and similar sets are read. Dummy reads then take place to get to the end of the header block. The function then sends data to set up the registers of the EGA for reception of color data.

Next, a *for* loop is begun for reading and displaying data for each line of the display from the top to the bottom of the window. Parameters are set up for the initial address at screen memory and for the address of the end of the current line. The parameter *j* is set to zero so that data will be sent to the first memory plane. The function then begins a *while* loop that reads data from the disk file, character by character. If the character does not have its two most significant bits set to one, it is simply sent to display memory and the memory address incremented. If the first two bits are one, these are stripped and the remainder of the byte is used as a counter.

Figure 4-6: Function to Display an EGA Screen from Disk

```
restore_screen() = paint screen from disk data
```

```c
#include <stdiio.h>
#include <stalib.h>
#include "tools.h"
extern union LIMIT XMax, XMin, YMax, YMin, Pval, Qval;
int restore_screen(char file_name[])
{
    #include <dos.h>
    #define graph_out (index, val)
    {outp (0x3CE,index);\ outp (0x3CF, val);}
    FILE *fsave;
    unsigned char ch,ch1,red,green,blue,color,
        line_length,end;
    int line_end,i,j,k,m,pass,x1,y1,x2,y2;
    if ((fsave = fopen(file_name,"rb")) == NULL)
    {
        printf("\nCan't find %s.\n",file_name);
        return(0);
    }
    else
    {
        ch = fgetc(fsave);
        if (ch != 0x0A)
        {
            printf("\n%s is not a valid ZSoft file.\n",
            file_name);
            fclose(fsave);
            return(0);
        }
    }
    setMode(16);
    cls(0);

    for (i=1; i<4; i++)
        ch = fgetc(fsave);
    x1 = getw(fsave);
    y1 = getw(fsave);
    x2 = getw(fsave);
    y2 = getw(fsave);
    for (i=12; i<16; i++)
        ch = fgetc(fsave);
    for (i=0; i<16; i++)
    {
        red = fgetc(fsave)/85;
        green = fgetc(fsave)/85;
```

```
    blue = fgetc(fsave)/85;
    color = ((red & 0x01) << 5) | ((red & 0x02)
        << 1) | ((green & 0x01) << 4) | (green
        & 0x02) | ((blue & 0x01) << 3) | ((blue &
        0x02) >> 1);
    setEGApalette(i,color);
}

for (i=64; i<70; i++)
    ch = fgetc(fsave);
for (i=0; i<4; i++)
    XMax.c[i] = fgetc(fsave);
for (i=0; i<4; i++)
    XMin.c[i] = fgetc(fsave);
for (i=0; i<4; i++)
    YMax.c[i] = fgetc(fsave);
for (i=0; i<4; i++)
    YMin.c[i] = fgetc(fsave);
for (i=0; i<4; i++)
    Pval.c[i] = fgetc(fsave);
for (i=0; i<4; i++)
    Qval.c[i] = fgetc(fsave);
for (i=94; i<128; i++)
    ch = fgetc(fsave);

graph_out(8,0xFF);
graph_out(3,0x10);
for (k=y1; k<y2; k++)
{
    i = k*80 + (x1/8);
    line_end = k* 80 + (x2/8)+1;
    j = 0;
    while (j < 4)
    {
        ch1 = fgetc(fsave);
        if ((ch1 & 0xC0) != 0xC0)
        {
            display(i, j, ch1);
            i++;
            if (i >= line_end)
            {
                j++;
                i = k*80 + (x1/8);
            }
        }
        else
        {
            ch1 &= 0x3F;
            pass = ch1;
            ch = fgetc(fsave);
            for (m=0; m<pass; m++)
```

```
            {
                display(i, j, ch);
                i++;
                if (i >= line_end)
                {
                    j++;
                    i = k*80 + (x1/8);
                }
            }
        }
    }
    graph_out(3,0);
    graph_out(8,0xFF);
    fclose(fsave);
    return(x2);
}
```

The next character is read from disk and repeatedly sent to display memory and the memory address incremented and the counter decremented each time until the counter reaches zero. After each incrementing of the memory address, the address is checked against the value for line end and if that value has been reached, the memory address is reset to the beginning of the line and the memory plane indicator is incremented. When this indicator reaches 4, all memory planes have been completed for the designated line, so the *while* loop is terminated. When all lines have been completed, the *for* loop terminates, the EGA registers are reset, the disk file is closed, and the function returns with a value of x2 (the end of the horizontal dimension of the window). This value of x2 is used as a starting point for continued operations if an incomplete display was saved.

Function to Restore a VGA Screen

The function to restore the VGA screen is just the same as that listed in Figure 4-6 except for the way the palette and color data is treated. Figure 4-7 shows the code for this section of the VGA function. Note that we do not try to determine what palette numbers the original color information was associated with, but simply determine the color register currently associated with each of the sixteen palettes that are being displayed and send it the appropriate color data from the disk file.

Figure 4-7: Code for Setting VGA Color Register Data

```
int palette,red,green,blue;

for (i=0; i<16; i++)
{
    palette = getVGApalette();
    writeColorReg(palette,red*4,green*4,blue*4);
}
```

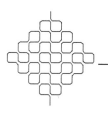

5

Tools for Graphics
Display Generation

Most C Languages now contain a reasonably good assortment of tools for graphics display generation. Furthermore, my book *Graphics Programming in C* contains an extensive graphics library with a full explanation of every function. Why then do we propose to describe a separate graphics library for fractal generation in this chapter?

The first answer to this question is that the individual graphics libraries for each version of C are not usually compatible, so that a program written using one set of routines is not transferable to another C compiler. It would be ideal if the producers of the different C language compilers would get together and establish a standard set of graphics routines that were transferable from one compiler to another. Until they do this, we'll try the next best thing and give a toolbox of routines here that may be used with either Turbo C or Microsoft and Quick C.

Another consideration is that some of the functions provided in this chapter are a little unusual because they are tailored especially for the fractal curve generating programs that appear in later chapters or because they offer some unique capabilities that would not usually be included in a generic package.

We will list in this chapter all of the programs and functions that are included in the *tools* library of the program disk that accompanies this book. We won't go into any detailed description of those routines that are simply duplications of those described in detail in *Graphics Programming in C*.

We will also avoid a detailed description of how to assemble these functions in a library; this is fully described in the previous book and also is now described in the documentation for both Turbo C and Microsoft C.

Setting the Display Mode

Before running a graphics program, the system must be set for a display mode. These modes are fully described in *Graphics Programming in C* in which functions are provided for setting up display modes for the CGA, EGA, VGA, and Hercules Graphics Card. The function listed in Figure 5-1 is the mode setting function for CGA, EGA, and VGA. It cannot be used with the Hercules Graphics Card. We are primarily going to be interested only in mode 16 (10H), which sets the display for a 640 x 350 pixel display having 16 colors. If you have a VGA, you can experiment with mode 18, which gives higher vertical resolution, but you will have to modify the programs to run properly.

These colors are set to default values, but can be changed to any of 64 different values for the EGA using the *setEGApalette* function or 256K values for the VGA using the *setEGApalette* function to set the palettes and a function of your own design to set the VGA color registers. (If we're going to save some unusual VGA colors (other than the default colors) to a disk file, we need to define how we're going to retrieve and record color register data. At present, not all VGA cards do things exactly the way IBM specifies that they should be done in this area, so you need to experiment to determine whether your card can really retrieve color register data or whether you need to save it in a separate buffer when you're changing color register values.)

Figure 5-1: Function to Set Display Mode

```
                    setMode() = sets video mode
```

```
#include "tools.h"

void setMode(int mode)
{
```

```
#include <dos.h>

union REGS reg;

reg.h.ah = 0;
reg.h.al = mode;
int86 (0x10,&reg,&reg);
}
```

Setting the EGA Palettes

The EGA is capable of displaying sixteen different colors at one time in high resolution mode 16. This function permits us to set each of the sixteen different colors (referred to as *palettes*) to any of the 64 color shades available with the EGA. Figure 5-2 shows the way in which a color number sent to the EGA by this function controls the color content for that palette on the display. With one exception, the palettes are set to a color number matching the palette number in the default state. Thus, the low intensity set of colors corresponds to a 75 percent level of the colors specified by the bits set. The high intensity colors represent both the 75 percent and 25 percent bits for the selected colors, giving 100 percent level of that color. The exception is low intensity yellow (brown) which is palette number 6, but is set to 20H, which sets g een to 25 percent and red to 75 percent.

Figure 5-2: Contents of Color Byte Sent to Palette Register

Bit	7	6	5	4	3	2	1	0
			25% Red	25% Green	25% Blue	75% Red	75% Green	75% Blue

The VGA operates in a different fashion, but for mode 16 it can be quite transparent and appear to be the same as the EGA. The VGA has 256 color registers, each of which can be set to 256K color hues. These registers are broken up into four sets of 64 registers. Any one of these four sets can be used to define the 64 colors from which the display selects the 16 palettes. When you send a number from 0 to 63 to the *setEGApalette* function while using the VGA, you are actually selecting one of the 64 registers from which the VGA takes the designated color hue. In the default condition, however, one set of 64 registers is always selected, and that set contains the same 64 shades of color that are designated by the numbers 0 to 63 by the EGA.

Therefore, although the mechanism is quite different, sending a number to the *setEGApalette* function for the VGA results in the same color that is called up by using that function with the EGA. You can develop functions that choose a different set of 64 registers to define the colors and that change the color shadings of the registers from the default values, which makes it possible for you to access the highly increased number of color hues available on the VGA. Note, however, that for mode 16 you are always limited to 16 different colors on a display at one time.

Figure 5-3 shows the function which sets the EGA palettes. It makes use of the ROM BIOS services to perform this task. Note that whatever value is sent to a palette register is also stored in the global array *PALETTE*. This permits us to keep track of which colors have been set into the palette registers, since this data is not recoverable from the EGA hardware.

Thus we can use the contents of *PALETTE* to obtain color data to store in a file when we are saving a display and be able to regenerate the display with the same colors that were originally specified. Note, however, that the price we pay for this is that we must include *PALETTE* as a global array in each of our programs that make use of the *setEGApalette* function. If we don't do this, we will not be able to compile and run the program properly. Furthermore, if we are going to use the *save_screen* function, we must initialize the *PALETTE* array with the proper default colors in order to have the correct color information saved to the file. The only exception to this initialization requirement is when we are going to set every one of the sixteen EGA palettes to a new color.

Figure 5-3: Function to Set EGA/VGA Palettes

```
    setEGApalette() = sets the color for an EGA palette number
```

```
#include "tools.h"

extern unsigned char PALETTE[16];
```

```
void setEGApalette(int palette, int color)
{
    #include <dos.h>

    union REGS reg;

    PALETTE[palette] = color;
    reg.h.ah = 0x10;
    reg.h.al = 0;
    reg.h.bh = color;
    reg.h.bl = palette;
    int86(0x10,&reg,&reg);
}
```

Clearing the Screen

Figure 5-4 is a function to clear the screen and leave it with a designated back-ground color. This function makes use of the ROM BIOS window scrolling service to fill the screen with a designated color. The service shown here is for use with mode 16. If you are going to use VGA mode 17 or VGA mode 18, you need to change the value put into register d from *0x184F* to *0x1D4F* to fill the extra lines provided by the higher vertical resolution of these modes.

Figure 5-4: Function to Clear the Screen

```
cls() = clears the screen
```

```
#include "tools.h"

void cls(int color)
{
    #include <dos.h>
    union REGS reg;

    reg.x.ax = 0x0600;
    reg.x.cx = 0;
    reg.x.dx = 0x184F;
    reg.h.bh = color;
    int86(0x10,&reg,&reg)
}
```

Plotting a Point on the Screen

Figure 5-5 is a function to plot a point on the EGA or VGA screen. The function makes use of in-line assembly language and therefore, if compiled with Turbo C, must be compiled using the on-line compile command *tcc* since compilation of assembly language from within the integrated environment package is not permitted. If you are going to attempt to compile this from Microsoft C, you will need to refer to MicroSoft's documentation for instructions on how to proceed. Alternately, you can use the function shown in Figure 5-6, which is basically the same procedure, but will be much slower due to the additional conversions which take place when working entirely through a higher level language.

Figure 5-5: Function to Plot a Point on the Screen

```
        plot() = plots a point at (x,y) in color
                 for EGA, using assembly
                 language at critical points
```

```c
#include "tools.h"

void plot(int x, int y, int color)
{
    #include <dos.h>

    unsigned int offset;
    int mask;

    offset = (long)y * 80L + ((long)x / 8L);
    mask = 0x80 >> (x % 8);
    _ES = 0xA000;
    _BX = offset;
    _CX = color;
    _AX = mask;
    asm MOV     AH,AL
    asm MOV     AL,08
    asm MOV     DX,03CEH
    asm OUT     DX,AX
    asm MOV     AX, 0FF02H
    asm MOV     DL, 0C4H
    asm OUT     DX,AX
    asm OR      ES:[BX],CH
    asm MOV     BYTE PTR ES: [BX],00H
    asm MOV     AH,CL
```

```
asm OUT     DX,AX
asm MOV     BYTE PTR ES: [BX],OFFH
asm MOV     AH,OFFH
asm OUT     DX,AX
asm MOV     DL,OCEH
asm MOV     AX,0003
asm OUT     DX,AX
asm MOV     AX,OFF08H
asm OUT     DX,AX
}
```

Figure 5-6: Function to Plot a Point on the Screen
Without Using Assembly Language

```
            plot() = plots a point at (x,y) in color
                     for EGA, using assembly
                     language at critical points
```

```c
#include "tools.h"

void plot(int x, int y, int color)
{
    #include <dos.h>

    #define seq_out(index,val)      {outp(0x3C4, index);\
                                     outp(0x3C5, val);}
    #define graph_out(index,val)    {outp(0x3CE,index);\
                                     outp(0x3CF, val);}
    unsigned int offset;
    int dummy,mask;

    offset = (long)y * 80L + ((long)x / 8L);
    mem_address = (char far *) 0xA0000000L + offset;
    mask = 0x80 >> (x % 8);
    graph_out(8,mask);
    graph_out(3,0x00);
    seq_out(2,0x0F);
    dummy = *mem_address;
    *mem_address = 0;
    seq_out(2,color);
    *mem_address = 0xFF;
    seq_out(2,0x0F);
    graph_out(3,0);
    graph_out(8,0xFF);
}
```

Displaying a Byte on the Screen

Figure 5-7 is a function that is used to display data on the screen where we have a byte representing the condition of eight consecutive points on the screen for a single color plane. This kind of data is available when we are restoring a screen from a disk file. Having data collected in bytes and isolated by color plane makes it possible to display it with a much simpler and faster function than if we had to plot it point by point using the *plot* function.

Figure 5-7: Displaying a Byte on the Screen

```
            display() = displays byte on the screen
```

```
#include "tools.h"

void display(unsigned long int address, int color_plane,
    unsigned char ch)
{
    #include <dos.h>

    #define seq_out(index,val)  {outp(0x3C4,index);\
                 outp(0x3C5,val);}
    char far * mem_address;
    char dummy;

    mem_address = (char far *) 0xA0000000L + address;
    dummy = *mem_address;
    seq_out(2,(0x01 << color_plane));
    *mem_address = ch;
}
```

Reading a Pixel from the Screen

Figure 5-8 is a function that uses the ROM BIOS video services to read a pixel from the screen. This function is rather slow, but fortunately we don't need to use it nearly as much as its inverse, which plots a point to the screen.

Figure 5-8: Function to Read a Pixel from the Screen

```
                readPixel = reads a pixel from the screen
```

```
#include "tools.h"

int readPixel(int x, int y)
{
    #include <dos.h>

    union REGS reg;

    reg.h.ah = 0x0D;
    reg.x.cx = x;
    reg.x.dx = y;
    int86 (0x10,&reg,&reg);
    return (reg.h.al);
}
```

Reading a Byte from a Color Plane

This function bears the same relation to the *read_pixel* function that *display* does to the *plot* function. In other words, instead of reading a single pixel, it reads information on eight adjacent pixels from one color plane only. It is used in saving a screen to a disk file. The function is listed in Figure 5-9.

Figure 5-9: Function to Read a Byte from a Color Plane

```
            read_screen() = reads a byte from the screen
```

```
#include "tools.h"

unsigned char read_screen(unsigned long int address,
    int color_plane)
{

    #include <dos.h>
    #define graph_out(index,val)   {outp(0x3CE,index);\
                    outp(0x3CF,val);}
    char far * mem_address;
```

```
    unsigned char pixel_data;

    mem_address = (char far *) 0xA0000000L + address;
    graph_out(4,color_plane);
    graph_out(5,0);
    pixel_data = *mem_address;
    return (pixel_data);
}
```

Drawing a Line

Figure 5-10 is a function for drawing a line on the screen. This function, which makes use of Bresenham's algorithm, is fully described in my book *Graphics Programming in C*.

Figure 5-10: Function to Draw a Line on the Screen

```
        drawLine() = draws a line from one set of coordinates
                     to another in a designated color
```

```
#include "tools.h"

void drawLine(int x1, int y1, int x2, int y2, int color)
{
    #include <dos.h>

    extern int LINEWIDTH;
    extern unsigned long int PATTERN;
    union REGS reg;

    #define sign(x) ((x) > 0 ? 1:  ((x) == 0 ? 0:  (-1)))

    int dx, dy, dxabs, dyabs, i, j, px, py, sdx, sdy, x, y;
    unsigned long int mask=0x80000000;

    x1   += 320;
    y1 = 175 - ((y1*93) >> 7);
    x2   += 320;
    y2 = 175 - ((y2*93) >> 7);
    dx = x2 - x1;
    dy = y2 - y1;
    sdx = sign(dx);
    sdy = sign(dy);
```

```
        dxabs = abs(dx);
        dyabs = abs(dy);
        x = 0;
        y = 0;
        px = x1;
        py = y1;
        if (dxabs >= dyabs)
        {
            for (i=0; i<dxabs; i++)
            {
                mask = mask ? mask : 0x80000000;
                y += dyabs;
                if (y>=dxabs)
                {
                    y -= dxabs;
                    py += sdy;
                }
                px += sdx;
                if (PATTERN & mask)
                    {
                    for (j=-LINEWIDTH/2; j<=LINEWIDTH/2; j++)
                        plot(px,py+j,color);
                    }
                mask >>= 1;
            }
        }
        else
        {
            for (i=0; i<dyabs; i++)
            {
                mask = mask ? mask : 0x80000000;
                x += dxabs;
                if (x>=dyabs)
                {
                    x -= dyabs;
                    px += sdx;
                }
                py += sdy;
                if (PATTERN & mask)
                {
                    for (j=-LINEWIDTH/2; j<=LINEWIDTH/2; j++)
                        plot(px+j,py,color);
                }
                mask >>= 1;
            }
        }
    }
```

Filling a Triangle

Filling a triangle with a designated color is a function that occurs repeatedly when we are attempting to create fractal landscapes using the midpoint displacement method as described in Chapter 21. *Graphics Programming in C* provides a generalized function for filling polygons that will fill triangles, but is somewhat complex for the triangle, which is a very simple form of polygon.

The function described here is a lot simpler and faster, but is confined to the one case of triangles. It is listed in Figure 5-11. The function uses the same technique as the line drawing algorithm listed above, but instead of plotting each point on each of the three lines that make up the triangle, it saves the *x* and *y* values of each point in an array of coordinates.

The algorithm is set up so that the coordinate pairs are ordered from the lowest to the highest values of *y*, with the *x*'s in order from low to high for each *y*. All values are then changed, if necessary, to be within the bounds of the display. Finally, lines are drawn along each *y* coordinate from the beginning to the ending *x* values. The function assumes that once you have ordered all of the coordinate pairs on the three triangle lines, there can only be two values of *x* for any *y*, the first of which marks the beginning of the fill line, and the second marks the end of the line. Draw a few differently oriented triangles and you can verify that this is true.

Figure 5-11: Function to Fill a Triangle

```
            fillTriangle() = fills a triangle in a specified color
```

```
#include "tools.h"

void fillTriangle (int x1, int y1, int x2, int y2, int x3,
     int y3, int color)
{

    #define sign(x) ((x) > 0 ? 1:  ((x) == 0 ? 0:  (-1)))

    int dx, dy, dxabs, dyabs, i, j, k, px, py, sdx, sdy, x, y,
        xpoint[4], ypoint[4], xa[350],xb[350],
```

```
    start,end;
    long int check;
int x_coord[350], y_coord[350];

for (i=0; i<350; i++)
{
    xa[i] = 640;
    xb[i] = 0;
}
xpoint[0] = x1 + 320;
ypoint[0] = 175 - ((y1*93L) >> 7);
xpoint[1] = x2 + 320;
ypoint[1] = 175 - ((y2*93L) >> 7);
xpoint[2] = x3 + 320;
ypoint[2] = 175 - ((y3*93L) >> 7);
xpoint[3] = xpoint[0];
ypoint[3] = ypoint[0];
px = xpoint[0];
py = ypoint[0];
for (j=0; j<3; j++)
{
    dx = xpoint[j+1] - xpoint[j];
    dy = ypoint[j+1] - ypoint[j];
    sdx = sign(dx);
    sdy = sign(dy);
    dxabs = abs(dx);
    dyabs = abs(dy);
    x = 0;
    y = 0;
    if (dxabs >= dyabs)
    {
        for (k=0; k<dxabs; k++)
        {
            y += dyabs;
            px += sdx;
            if (y>=dxabs)
            {
                y -= dxabs;
                py += sdy;
            }
            if ((py>=0) && (py<=349))
            {
                if (px < xa[py])
                    xa[py] = px;
                if (px > xb[py])
                    xb[py] = px;
            }
        }
    }
    else
    {
```

```
        for (k=0; k<dyabs; k++)
        {
            py += sdy;
            x += dxabs;
            if (x>=dyabs)
            {
                x -= dyabs;
                px += sdx;
            }
            if ((py>=0) && (py<=349))
            {
                if (px < xa[py])
                    xa[py] = px;
                if (px > xb[py])
                    xb[py] = px;
            }
        }
    }
}
if (ypoint[0] < ypoint[1])
{
    start = ypoint[0];
    end = ypoint[1];
}
else
{
    start = ypoint[1];
    end = ypoint[0];
}
for (i=0; i<350; i++)
{
    if (xa[i] < 0)
        xa[i] = 0;
    if (xb[i] > 639)
        xb[i] = 639;
}
if (ypoint[2] < start)
    start = ypoint[2];
if (ypoint[2] > end)
    end = ypoint[2];
if (start < 0)
    start = 0;
if (end > 349)
    end = 349;
for (i=start; i<=end; i++)
{
    for (j=xa[i]; j<=xb[i]; j++)
        plot(j,i,color);
}

}
```

Filling an Oval

We are going to be filling a lot of circles and ovals. The function listed in Figure 5-12 will perform this task. It is quite an improvement over the function given in *Graphics Programming in C* as far as simplicity is concerned and it is just as fast as the previous function. The original function used Bresenham's algorithm to generate a circle, simultaneously plotting points in four quadrants. Then a line was drawn from the point determined for the radius minus *y* coordinate to the corresponding point for the radius plus quadrant. The algorithm used here scans each point within a rectangle bounding the specified oval, and if the point is found to be inside the oval plots it on the screen.

Figure 5-12: Function to Fill an Oval

```
fillOval() = draws an oval centered at (x,y) with
             radius in y direction of 'b' with
             aspect ratio 'aspect' and fills it
             with color 'color'
```

```c
#include "tools.h"
#include <stdio.h>

void fillOval(float x_cen, float y_cen, float radius,
    int color, float aspect)
{
    #include <dos.h>

    union REGS reg;

    #define seq_out(index,val)   {outp(0x3C4,index);\
                  outp(0x3C5,val);}
    #define graph_out(index,val)  {outp(0x3CE,index);\
                  outp(0x3CF,val);}

    unsigned int offset;
    char far * mem_address;
    float a,b,aspect_square;
    long x,y,col,row,dummy,mask,start_x, start_y,end_x,end_y;
    float a_square,b_square,b_test;

    a = radius/aspect;
    a_square = a*a;
    b = .729*radius;
```

```
b_square = b*b;
x = x_cen + 319;
y = 175 - (.729*y_cen);
start_x = max(0,x-a);
end_x = min (639,x+a);
start_y = max(0,y-b);
end_y = min(349,y+b);

for (col=start_x; col<=end_x; col++)
{
    b_test = b_square - (b_square*(col-x)*(col-x))/a_square;
    mask = 0x80 >> ((col) % 8);
    graph_out(8,mask);
    seq_out(2,0x0F);
    for (row=start_y; row<=end_y; row++)
        if ((long)(row-y)*(row-y) <= b_test)
        {
            offset = (long)row*80L + ((long)(col)/8L);
            mem_address = (char far *) 0xA0000000L +
                offset;
            dummy = *mem_address;
            *mem_address = 0;
            seq_out(2,color);
            *mem_address = 0xFF;
            seq_out(2,0x0F);
        }
}
graph_out(3,0);
graph_out(8,0xFF);
}
```

Turtle Graphics

Turtle Graphics was first developed for the LOGO language, which was supposed to simplify programming for children. It consisted of a "turtle," which was displayed on the graphics screen and could be pointed and moved by simple commands. A variation of turtle graphics has been found to be useful for generating von Koch and other fractal curves. We have global variables that tell us the direction that the turtle is pointing, its coordinates, and the size for a step of turtle movement. There are only three functions that we use. They are described below.

Point

The input parameters to the function *point* are the coordinates of the beginning
and end points of a line. The function determines the *turtle* angle in relation to
the *x* axis if the turtle is facing in the direction of the line defined by the input
points. This angle, in degrees, is returned by the function. The function is listed
in Figure 5-13.

Figure 5-13: Point Function

```
          point() = sets the beginning angle for turtle
                    in tenths of a degree
```

```c
#include "tools.h"
#include <math.h>

float point(float x1, float y-one, float x2, float y2)
{
    #include <math.h>

    float theta;
    if ((x2 - x1) == 0)
        if (y2 > y-one)
            theta = 90;
        else
            theta = 270;
    else
        theta = atan((y2-y-one)/(x2-x1))*57.295779;
    if (x1>x2)
        theta += 180;
    return(theta);
}
```

Turn

For this function, you specify an angle through which you want the *turtle* to
turn. Positive angles are counter-clockwise and negative angles are clockwise.
The function adds the specified angle to the global variable that defines the current
turtle angle. The function is listed in Figure 5-14.

Figure 5-14: Turn Function

```
turn() = changes turtle pointing direction
```

```
#include "tools.h"

void turn(float angle)
{
    extern float turtle_theta;

    turtle_theta += angle;
}
```

Step

This function moves the *turtle* position by one step. The step length is defined by the parameter *turtle_r*. The function makes use of the current *turtle* position coordinates *turtle_x* and *turtle_y* and the *turtle* direction angle *turtle_theta* to determine the new position coordinates after the step has been taken. The function is listed in Figure 5-15.

Figure 5-15: Step Function

```
step() = advances turtle by step r in current direction
```

```
#include "tools.h"

void step (void)
{
    #include <math.h>
    extern float turtle_x;
    extern float turtle_y;
    extern float turtle_r;
    extern float turtle_theta;

    turtle_x += turtle_r*cos(turtle_theta*.017453292);
    turtle_y += turtle_r*sin(turtle_theta*.017453292);
}
```

Function to Display and Move Cursor

The improved Mandelbrot set program, as well as the programs for generating similar sets for dragon and phoenix functions, which will be listed later, all make use of the *move_cursor* function to position a cursor on the screen and/or use it to select the limits for a rectangle that defines the limits of the next screen to be generated. Figure 5-16 lists the *move_cursor* function. The parameters that are passed to this function are a type number, a number for the color of the cursor, and the minimum column and row positions.

Figure 5-16: Function to Display and Move Cursor

```
             move_cursor( ) = moves cursor and saves position
```

```
#include <stdio.h>
#include "tools.h"

void move_cursor(int type,int color,int min_col, int min_row)
{
    #include <dos.h>

    extern int CURSOR_X,CURSOR_Y;
    extern union LIMIT XMax,YMax,XMin,YMin,Pval,Qval;
    extern float TXMax,TXMin,TYMax,TYMin;
    union REGS reg;

    unsigned int mask;
    int i,j,image,image_store[256],index,ch,temp,limit[7];
    char far *base;

    limit[0] = 11;
    limit[1] = 9;
    limit[2] = 10;
    limit[3] = 10;
    limit[4] = 12;
    limit[5] = 14;
    limit[6] = 14;
    do
    {
        index = 0;
        switch(type)
        {
            case 0:
                for (i=0; i<16; i++)
```

```
                    image_store[index++] = plot_point
                        (CURSOR_X+i,CURSOR_Y,
                        color);
                for (i=1; i<16; i++)
                    image_store[index++] = plot_point
                        (CURSOR_X,CURSOR_Y+i,
                        color);
            break;
        case 1:
            for (i=0; i<16; i++)
                image_store[index++] = plot_point
                    (CURSOR_X+15,CURSOR_Y+i,
                    color);
            for (i=0; i<15; i++)
                image_store[index++] = plot_point
                    (CURSOR_X+i,CURSOR_Y+15,
                    color);
            break;
        case 2:
            for (j=0; j<7; j++)
            {
                for(i=j; i<limit[j]; i++)
                {
                    if((i==8) && (j ==5))
                        i=10;
                    if((i==8) && (j ==6))
                        i=12;
                    image_store[index++] = plot_point
                        (CURSOR_X+j,CURSOR_Y+i,
                        color);
                }
            }
            image_store[index++] = plot_point(CURSOR_X+7,
                CURSOR_Y+7,color);
    }
    ch = getch();
    if (ch != 0x0D)
    {
        if (ch == 0)
            ch = getch() + 256;
        index = 0;
        switch(type)
        {
            case 0:
                for (i=0; i<16; i++)
                    plot_point(CURSOR_X+i,CURSOR_Y,
                        image_store[index++]);
                for (i=1; i<16; i++)
                    plot_point(CURSOR_X,CURSOR_Y+i,
                        image_store[index++]);
                break;
```

```
    case 1:
        for (i=0; i<16; i++)
            plot_point(CURSOR_X+15,CURSOR_Y+i,
                image_store[index++]);
        for (i=0; i<15; i++)
            plot_point(CURSOR_X+i,CURSOR_Y+15,
                image_store[index++]);
        break;
    case 2:
        for (j=0; j<7; j++)
        {
            for(i=j; i<limit[j]; i++)
            {
                if((i==8) && (j ==5))
                    i=10;
                if((i==8) && (j ==6))
                    i=12;
                plot(CURSOR_X+j,CURSOR_Y+i,
                    image_store[index++]);
            }
        }
        plot(CURSOR_X+7,CURSOR_Y+7,
            image_store[index++]);
    }
reg.h.ah = 2;
int86(0x16,&reg,&reg);
if ((reg.h.al & 0x03) != 0)
{
    switch(ch)
    {
        case 56:
            if (CURSOR_Y > min_row)
                CURSOR_Y -= 10;
            break;
        case 52:
            if (CURSOR_X > min_col)
                CURSOR_X -= 10;
            break;
        case 54:
            if (CURSOR_X < 629)
                CURSOR_X += 10;
            break;
        case 50:
            if (CURSOR_Y < 329)
                CURSOR_Y += 10;
    }
}
else
{
    switch(ch)
    {
```

```
                    case 333:
                        if (CURSOR_X < 639)
                            CURSOR_X++;
                        break;
                    case 331:
                        if (CURSOR_X > min_col)
                            CURSOR_X--;
                        break;
                    case 328:
                        if (CURSOR_Y > min_row)
                            CURSOR_Y--;
                        break;
                    case 336:
                        if (CURSOR_Y < 335)
                            CURSOR_Y++;
                        break;
                }
            }
            switch(type)
            {
                case 0:

                    TXMin = XMin.f + (XMax.f - XMin.f)/
                        639*(CURSOR_X);
                    TYMax = YMax.f - (YMax.f - YMin.f)/
                        349*CURSOR_Y;
                    gotoxy(5,24);
                    printf("XMin= %f   YMax= %f",TXMin,TYMax);
                    break;
                case 1:
                    TXMax = XMin.f + (XMax.f - XMin.f)/
                        639*(CURSOR_X + 16);
                    TYMin = YMax.f - (YMax.f - YMin.f)/
                        349*(CURSOR_Y + 16);
                    gotoxy(41,24);
                    printf("  XMax= %f   YMin= %f",TXMax,TYMin);
                    break;

                case 2:
                    Pval.f = XMin.f + (XMax.f - XMin.f)/639*
                        CURSOR_X;
                    Qval.f = YMax.f - (YMax.f - YMin.f)/
                        349*CURSOR_Y;
                    gotoxy(5,24);
                    printf("  P= %f    Q= %f     ",Pval.f,Qval.f);
            }
        }
    }
    while (ch != 0x0D);
}
```

```
        plot_point() = plots a point at (x,y) in color
                       for EGA, using Turbo C port
                       output functions and returns
                       original point color
```

```c
int plot_point(int x, int y, int color)
{
    #define seq_out(index,val)   {outp(0x3C4,index);\
                    outp(0x3C5,val);}
    #define graph_out(index,val)   {outp(0x3CE,index);\
                    outp(0x3CF,val);}
    #define EGAaddress 0xA0000000L

    int index,old_color=0;
    unsigned char mask, dummy,exist_color;
    char far *mem_address;

    mem_address = (char far *) (EGAaddress +
        ((long)y * 80L + ((long)x / 8L)));
    mask = 0x80 >> (x % 8);
    for (index = 0; index<4; index++)
    {
        graph_out(4,index);
        graph_out(5,0);
        exist_color = *mem_address & mask;
        if (exist_color != 0)
            old_color |=(0x01<<index);
    }
    graph_out(8,mask);
    seq_out(2,0x0F);
    dummy = *mem_address;
    *mem_address = 0;
    seq_out(2,color);
    *mem_address = 0xFF;
    seq_out(2,0x0F);
    graph_out(3,0);
    graph_out(8,0xFF);
    return(old_color);
}
```

The initial cursor position is established by the global parameters CURSOR_X and CURSOR_Y, which are in display coordinates (0,0 is at the top left corner of the screen; for the EGA, the maximum column is 639 and the maximum row is 349). The *move_cursor* function makes use of the function *plot_point*, which is similar to the *plot* function except that it has the capability to read a pixel from the screen, as well as plotting one.

When this function is called, if the parameter *image* is zero, the pixel color at location (CURSOR_X, CURSOR_Y) is read and returned by the function. When *image* is not zero, the pixel color is read and then a new pixel of the color *color* is written. Now, looking at *move_cursor* you will note that for each type of cursor that is to be plotted, we plot points to the screen to generate the desired cursor pattern and at the same time read the original screen contents of those points into an array. The function then goes into a loop, processing keystrokes until an *Ent* is encountered (0x0D), whereupon the loop is terminated.

The only other keystrokes that are recognized are the shifted and unshifted arrow keys. We can read the keystrokes in normal fashion for the unshifted arrow keys. We expect a first character of 0x00; if that occurs, the function automatically reads another character and adds 256 to it to give a unique indication. If one of the arrow keys is hit, the cursor is moved one pixel in that direction if there is sufficient space for the movement. The shifted arrow keys look just like ordinary numbers so we have to call one of the ROM BIOS services to determine if the *Shift* key was also activated. If a shifted arrow is encountered, the cursor is moved ten pixels in the arrow direction if enough space exists.

After each keystroke, the saved background is rewritten at the old cursor position. The cursor is then redrawn at the new position. For type *0*, the ultimate cursor position defines the values of XMin and YMax that are used in future display generation. Type *1* operation is the same, except that the cursor is in the lower right corner and the values stored and displayed are XMax and YMin. Usually on the second *move_cursor* call (type *1*), the limiting values for the upper and right positions of the cursor are the final values stored by the first *move_cursor* call. Thus, the lower right corner of the rectangle is prohibited from ever moving to the left or above the upper left corner.

For type *2*, the cursor is an arrow, which is used in such cases as to select the *P* and *Q* parameter locations on a map of the Mandelbrot set in order to generate a Julia set (more about this later). The position values that are displayed and stored are for *P* and *Q*. The values for these various parameters are calculated within the *move_cursor* function and displayed at the bottom of the screen.

When the *do* loop finally encounters an *Ent* keystroke, it terminates; the values of CURSOR_X and CURSOR_Y are preserved in the global variables and must be processed as needed by the calling program.

Bounds Program

The values of some or all of *XMax, YMax, XMin, YMin, P*, and *Q* are essential in proceeding from one of the Mandelbrot sets or similar figures to another more expanded one, in completing a partially generated figure that has been saved on disk, and in generating one of the Julia or similar sets from the appropriate map figure. We also would like to know at times the actual color values used in generating a figure. All of this information is stored on the disk file that stores the figure for future use.

The program *Bounds* asks for a figure file name and then displays that file on the screen. It then overwrites on it the parameters given above and all of the color palette values. The figure is not displayed primarily for use at this time, but simply to give you an opportunity to assure that you asked for the right file name. Thus it doesn't matter much if it gets partially covered up. By then, you have already identified the figure, and after *Bounds* is done there is usually enough of the figure left displayed for satisfactory identification. Figure 5-17 lists the *Bounds* program.

Figure 5-17: Function to Show Figure Parameters

```
            bounds = program to get saved screen parameters
```

```c
#include <stdio.h>
#include <stdlib.h>
#include <math.h>
#include <dos.h>
#include <process.h>
#include "tools.h"

int LINEWIDTH=1, OPERATOR=0x00, ANGLE, XCENTER, YCENTER;
unsigned long int PATTERN=0xFFFFFFFF;
unsigned char PALETTE[16]={0,1,2,3,4,5,20,7,56,57,58,59,60,
```

```
    61,62,63};
union LIMIT XMax,YMax,XMin,YMin;

char file_name[13];
FILE *f1;

main()
{
    int i,color, row, col,error,response,repeat=0x30,start_col;

    printf("Enter file name: ");
    scanf("%s",file_name);
    error = restore_screen(file_name);
    if (error == 0)
    {
        printf("\nCannot find %s.  Hit any key to exit",
            file_name);
        exit(0);
    }
    else
    {
        for (i=0; i<16; i++)
            printf("\nPalette #%d = %d",i,PALETTE[i]);
        printf("\n XMax = %f",XMax.f);
        printf("\n XMin = %f",XMin.f);
        printf("\n YMax = %f",YMax.f);
        printf("\n YMin = %f",YMin.f);
        printf("\n P = %f",Pval);
        printf("\n Q = %f",Qval);
        getch();
    }
}
```

Selecting Colors

Sometimes, the best laid plans for creating beautiful colors go astray, and the resulting figure is horribly different from what you anticipated. Of course, you could go back to the original program, change the *setEGApalette* statements or in some other way modify the way in which you specify that colors be generated. The program described in this section provides an easier method. It will display a selected screen file on the screen and allow you to change each of the sixteen palettes to any of the 64 shades available with the EGA. When you are done, it will save the display together with the new color designations in a new disk file.

The program *colors* is listed in Figure 5-18. At the beginning, the program asks you for a file name. It can read in any *.pcx* file on which you have stored a display. It then permits you to change all of the display colors. Once you start changing colors with the left and right cursor arrows, a legend will appear at the bottom of the screen giving the current palette number and color number. Don't be dismayed; when you are finished changing colors, the display will be redrawn so that the legend will not appear in your new display file.

Figure 5-18: Function to Change Display Colors

```
         colors = program to change colors of a display
```

```c
#include <stdio.h>
#include <math.h>
#include <dos.h>
#include <process.h>
#include "tools.h"

int readPixel(int x, int y);

int LINEWIDTH=1, OPERATOR=0x00;
unsigned long int PATTERN=0xFFFFFFFF;
unsigned char PALETTE[16]={0,1,2,3,4,5,20,7,56,57,58,59,60,61,
    62,63};
unsigned char SAVER[16];
char file_name[13],file_name2[13] = {"colors00.pcx"};
int ch,i;
int error,color;
int palette_register;

FILE *f1;

union LIMIT XMax, YMax, XMin, YMin, Pval, Qval;

main()
{
    printf("Enter file name: ");
    scanf("%s",&file_name);
    error = restore_screen(file_name);
    if (error == 0)
        exit(0);
    for (;;)
    {
        ch = 0;
        cscanf("%d",&palette_register);
```

```
        if (palette_register > 15)
            break;
        color = PALETTE[palette_register];
        for (;;)
        {
            ch = getch();
            if (ch == 0x0D)
                break;
            if (ch == 0)
                ch = getch() + 256;
            if (ch == 333)
                color++;
            if (ch == 331)
                color--;
            if (color > 63)
                color = 0;
            else
                if (color < 0)
                    color = 63;
            gotoxy(10,23);
            printf("Palette: %d   ",palette_register);
            gotoxy(10,24);
            printf("Color #: %d   ",color);
            setEGApalette(palette_register,color);
        }
    }
    for (i=0; i<16; i++)
        SAVER[i] = PALETTE[i];
    error = restore_screen(file_name);
    for (i=0; i<16; i++)
        PALETTE[i] = SAVER[i];
    save_screen(0,0,639,349,file_name2);
}
```

You begin the process by entering a palette number (between 0 and 15), followed by hitting the *Ent* key. The color number will be automatically set to that of the current color shade for the selected palette.

You can change the color number by hitting the right or left arrow keys. Each time you hit the right arrow, the color number will increase by one and the color of the selected palette on the display will change accordingly. Each time you hit the left arrow, the color number will decrease by one and the color of the selected palette on the display will change accordingly. If you are holding down an arrow key to scan through color changes and you go too far, you can reverse direction by using the other arrow key.

Have no fear, you cannot get out of the permissible color range of 0 to 63; if you go beyond 63, the color number returns to 0, and if you go below zero, the color number returns to 63. Once you find the color shade that you like, hitting *Ent* freezes that color into the selected palette. You are then ready to enter another palette number.

When you have the picture colored exactly as you want it, entering a palette number greater than 15 terminates the program. The screen is rewritten to get rid of the legend at the bottom. The rewritten screen appears in the original colors, but your color modifications are saved and will permanently become part of the new file.

The new display will be saved in a file called *colorsnn.pcx*, where nn is a pair of digits from *00* to *99*. The program will automatically start out with *00* and search sequentially for a pair of digits that you have not used yet. When it finds them, they will be used for the file that is currently being saved.

6

The Lorenz and Other Strange Attractors

In 1962, Edward Lorenz was attempting to develop a model of the weather when he observed some strange discrepancies in the behavior of his model. When he attempted to restart the model at a point partway through the original computer run, the results, although apparently starting at the same point, diverged farther and farther from the original run as time went on. He verified that this was not a computer error, but rather was caused by the fact that he had reentered the data to only three decimal place accuracy, whereas the computer data at that point in the original computer run was saved to six decimal places. Lorenz simplified his model until it consisted of only three differential equations, which, in addition to being a simplified weather model, also described the flow of fluid in a layer of fluid having a uniform depth and a constant temperature difference between the upper and lower surfaces. The equations are:

```
dx/dt = 10(y - x)              (Equation 6-1)
dy/dt = xz + 28x -y            (Equation 6-2)
dz/dt = xy - (8/3)z            (Equation 6-3)
```

When Lorenz laboriously calculated a number of values for these equations on a primitive computer, he discovered the first of the strange attractors, and created the foundation for the discipline of "Chaos," which is creating drastic changes in all fields of science, and of which the principle drawing tools are fractals.

Strange Attractors

What is a strange attractor? To answer this question, we must first plot a candidate set of equations in phase space—a space of enough dimensions to permit representing each solution of the equation set at a given time as a single point. For the Lorenz equations given above, a three-dimensional phase space is needed. If the solution to this set of equations was constant throughout time, it would converge in phase space to a single point, the attractor, no matter what the initial conditions had been. If the solution converged to a periodic function, which repeated over and over after fixed interval of time, the result in phase space would be some form of closed curve, the periodic attractor or limit cycle. If neither of these cases is true, yet the equation has a fully determined path through phase space, which never recurs, the resulting curve is called a *strange attractor*. No matter what initial conditions are specified, the solution always converges quickly to a point on this curve and continues to follow the path of the curve from there on.

The Lorenz Attractor

It's time to take a close look at the Lorenz attractor. Plate 1 shows it projected upon the YZ plane. Note, however, that without most of the traditional cues that help our senses to convert a two-dimensional drawing to three dimensions, it is not too easy to understand the exact dimensional qualities of the Lorenz attractor, no matter what kind of projection we use. The color in the color scheme is changed each time the value of the x coordinate crosses zero. The curves represent 4,000 iterations of the equation with a time step of 0.01. Unfortunately, the resolution of the display screen has proven inadequate to the task of separating out adjacent portions of the curve. However, no matter how good the resolution of your display, the curves will exceed the resolution capability if enough iterations are run.

These curves are a sort of encapsulation of what this new science of Chaos is all about, both in its good and its bad features. You need to watch the curve being drawn and understand that although the curve seems to intersect with itself in the projections, it never does touch itself in actual three-dimensional space.

The good aspect of Chaos is that this simple set of equations can completely describe a very rich and complex nonperiodic behavior. Prior to investigating this kind of equation system with modern high-speed computers, scientists postulated that such complex behavior must be the result of very complex systems of equations containing many parameters and variables, with possibly a number of random variables thrown in. Now it is known that complex behavior may often be represented in a very simple manner. The bad aspect can be discovered in the following manner: select a starting point somewhere on the very crowded part of the curve; attempt to trace the path from there on.

We already pointed out that the display has inadequate resolution, so that a couple of different portions of the curve double up at the most crowded places. Thus, you can't be sure that you are tracing the right path, since as the adjacent curves begin to diverge, your selected path will break in two and you can't be sure which path to follow. How does this apply in the real case? There is no overlapping on the infinite resolution display; each set of initial values determines one and only one path to be followed. But there are an infinite number of paths in the vicinity of the starting point you selected, and which one will be followed depends upon how precisely you specified your initial coordinates.

If you selected x = 3.15678, for example, you would travel a totally different path than if you had selected x = 3.15679. And you must remember that x = 3.15678 is actually x = 3.15678000..., so that by adding another decimal place with a value other than zero, you can always diverge to a different path altogether. This means that no matter how accurately you select the initial coordinates, if they are *at all* different from the real values that might exist for a natural phenomena, the value that you predict will diverge farther and farther from the *real* value as time progresses. This is bad news for those who wish to measure some initial conditions and use them to predict long-term results. Note that measuring more precisely, so as to come closer to the correct long-term values, does not work because the amount of divergence is not a function of the size of the error, but can differ widely and unpredictably.

Runge Kutta Integration

In order to solve the system of differential equations given above, we must use some numerical technique that comes up with an accurate value for x, y, and z as we integrate over time. We have chosen a time step of 0.01. Lorenz, in his original paper, used a double approximation integration technique. However, with more sophisticated computers at our disposal, we can use a more complicated integration method to produce greater accuracy. The method that will be used is the fourth order Runge Kutta technique. This method is a one-step procedure that uses only first-order derivatives to achieve the same accuracy obtainable with an equivalent order Taylor expansion using higher order derivatives. There are many different sets of coefficients that can be used with the Runge Kutta integration method; the coefficients that we have selected were chosen to minimize the computer time required for each iteration. Given a differential equation:

$$dy/dt = f(t,y) \qquad \text{(Equation 6-4)}$$

once the initial condition is established, at each time step, we have:

$$y_{n+1} = y_n + k_0/6 + k_1/3 + k_2/3 + k_3/6 \quad \text{(Equation 6-5)}$$

where:

$$k_0 = h \; f(t_n, \; y_n) \qquad \text{(Equation 6-6)}$$

$$k_1 = h \; f(t_n + h/2, \; y_n + k_0/2) \qquad \text{(Equation 6-7)}$$

$$k_2 = h \; f(t_n + h/2, \; y_n + k_1/2) \qquad \text{(Equation 6-8)}$$

$$k_3 = h \; f(t_n + h, \; y_n + k_2) \qquad \text{(Equation 6-9)}$$

and h is the time step (0.01).

You will find this integration technique in the middle of the Lorenz attractor program. Note that in determining each k, the equation has to be solved for the appropriate values of t and y.

Programming the Lorenz Attractor

Figure 6-1 lists the program to generate the Lorenz attractor. Three loops are made through the program; one to plot the projection on the YZ plane, one to plot the projection on the XY plane, and one to provide the three-dimensional projection. As mentioned above, the color scheme used is to change the color each time that the curve crosses the x axis. You may want to try some other color technique. For example, you could use different colors to represent the position of the curve. The program generates one projection of the curve and then stops until you hit a key. It then generates the next projection, waits for another key input and finally generates the three-dimensional projection. You can insert different angles to change the viewing direction of the three-dimensional projection, but you may also have to do some additional modification of the dimensioning to keep part of the curve from falling off of the edge of the display.

Figure 6-1: Program to Generate Lorenz Attractors

```
            lorenz = program to plot Lorenz Attractor
```

```
#include <dos.h>
#include <stdio.h>
#include <math.h>
#include "tools.h"

float (radians_to_degrees(float degrees);;

const int maxcol = 639;
const int maxrow = 349;

int LINEWIDTH = 3, OPERATOR = 0;
int color = 15;
unsigned long int PATTERN = 0xFFFFFFFF;
unsigned char PALETTE[16]={0,1,2,3,4,5,20,7,56,57,58,59,60,61,62,63};
float rad_per_degree=0.0174533,x_angle=45,y_angle=0,z_angle=90;
union LIMIT XMax,YMax,XMin,YMin,Pval,Qval;
char file_name[13] = {"lorenz00.pcx"};

main()
{
    double x,y,z,d0_x,d0_y,d0_z,d1_x,d1_y,d1_z,d2_x,d2_y,d2_z,
        d3_x,d3_y,d3_z,xt,yt,zt,dt,dt2,third=0.333333333,
        sx,sy,sz,cx,cy,cz,temp_x,temp_y,old_y;
```

```
int i, j, row, col, old_row, old_col;

x_angle = radians_to_degrees(x_angle);
sx = sin(x_angle);
cx = cos(x_angle);
y_angle = radians_to_degrees(y_angle);
sy = sin(y_angle);
cy = cos(y_angle);
z_angle = radians_to_degrees(z_angle);
sz = sin(z_angle);
cz = cos(z_angle);
for (j=0; j<3; j++)
{
    color = 4;
    LINEWIDTH = 3;
    x = 0;
    y = 1;
    z = 0;
    setMode(16);
    if (j == 0)
    {
        old_col = y*9;
        old_row = 9*z - 240;
        drawLine(-320,-238,319,-238,15);
        drawLine(0,-238,0,239,15);
        gotoxy(79,24);
        printf("Y");
        gotoxy(42,1);
        printf("Z");
    }
    if (j == 1)
    {
        old_col = y*10;
        old_row = 10*x;
        drawLine(-320,0,319,0,15);
        drawLine(0,-238,0,238,15);
        gotoxy(79,12);
        printf("Y");
        gotoxy(42,1);
        printf("X");
    }
    if (j == 2)
    {
        old_col = y*9;
        old_row = 9*z - 240;
        drawLine(-320,-238,319,-238,15);
        drawLine(0,-238,0,239,15);
        drawLine(0,-238,319,82,15);
        gotoxy(79,24);
        printf("Y");
        gotoxy(42,1);
```

```
    printf("Z");
    gotoxy(79,8);
    printf("X");
}
LINEWIDTH = 1;
dt = 0.01;
dt2 = dt/2;
for (i=0; i<8000; i++)
{
    d0_x = 10*(y-x)*dt2;
    d0_y = (-x*z + 28*x - y)*dt2;
    d0_z = (x*y - 8*z/3)*dt2;
    xt = x + d0_x;
    yt = y + d0_y;
    zt = z + d0_z;
    d1_x = (10*(yt-xt))*dt2;
    d1_y = (-xt*zt + 28*xt - yt)*dt2;
    d1_z =(xt*yt - 8*zt/3)*dt2;
    xt = x + d1_x;
    yt = y + d1_y;
    zt = z + d1_z;
    d2_x = (10*(yt-xt))*dt;
    d2_y = (-xt*zt + 28*xt - yt)*dt;
    d2_z =(xt*yt - 8*zt/3)*dt;
    xt = x + d2_x;
    yt = y + d2_y;
    zt = z + d2_z;
    d3_x = (10*(yt - xt))*dt2;
    d3_y = (-xt*zt + 28*xt - yt)*dt2;
    d3_z = (xt*yt - 8*zt/3)*dt2;
    old_y = y;
    x += (d0_x + d1_x + d1_x + d2_x + d3_x) * third;
    y += (d0_y + d1_y + d1_y + d2_y + d3_y) * third;
    z += (d0_z + d1_z + d1_z + d2_z + d3_z) * third;
    if (j == 0)
    {
        col = y*9;
        row = 9*z - 240;
        if (((col<0) && (old_col >= 0)) || ((col > 0)
            && (old_col <= 0)))
            color++;
    }
    if (j == 1)
    {
        col = y*10;
        row = 10*x;
        if (((col<0) && (old_col >= 0)) || ((col > 0)
            && (old_col <= 0)))
            color++;
    }
    if (j == 2)
```

```
            {
                if (((y<0) && (old_y >=0)) || ((y > 0)
                    && (old_y <=0)))
                    color++;
                temp_x = x*cx + y*cy + z*cz;
                temp_y = x*sx + y*sy + z*sz;
                col = temp_x*8;
                row = temp_y*7-240;
            }
            drawLine(old_col,old_row,col,row,color);
            old_row = row;
            old_col = col;
        }
        save_screen(0,0,639,349,file_name);
        getch();
    }
}


float radians_to_degrees(float degrees);
{
    float angle;

    while (degrees >= 360)
        degrees -= 360;
    while (degrees < 0)
        degrees += 360;
    angle = rad_per_degree*degrees;
    return angle;
}
```

Another thing that you might like to investigate is the number of iterations of the inner loop. You can reduce or increase it and obtain different amounts of detail in the displays. Finally, just before the *drawLine* function, you can insert an *if* statement similar to this:

```
    if ((i>= 1400) && (i <= 1900)
```

This statement will cause only the iterations between 1400 and 1900 to be displayed. This is the section of the curve that Lorenz used to illustrate his original paper. You can, if you wish to speed up the program, use an *if* statement like:

```
    if (i >= 1400)
```

and change the upper limit of the *for* loop to 1900 to achieve the same result. You cannot change the starting value of the *for* loop to 1400, since you will not then know what the initial values are for x, y, and z.

Other Strange Attractors

The Lorenz attractor proceeds in an orderly fashion from one point to the next as time increases, so that we can draw a good picture of it by drawing lines that connect each pair of adjacent points. Now let's consider a different kind of strange attractor. This one is a dynamical system first reported by Clifford A. Pickover. It consists of the system of equations:

$x_{n+1} = \sin(ay_n) - z_n\cos(bx_n)$ (Equation 6-10)

$y_{n+1} = z_n\sin(cx_n) - \cos(dy_n)$ (Equation 6-11)

$z_{n+1} = \sin(x_n)$ (Equation 6-12)

There is no time step here. Moreover, the point in phase space described by the equations jumps about in what appears to be a totally random fashion. However, when the points for a large number of iterations are plotted, it becomes evident that there is a finite set of positions that the point described by the function can occupy, and that the point ultimately goes to this attractor irrespective of the initial conditions. Figure 6-2 lists a program for generating this strange attractor for a specific set of the parameters a, b, c, d, and e and displaying it projected on first the XY and then the YZ planes. The resulting displays are shown in Figures 6-3 and 6-4, respectively.

Figure 6-2: Program to Generate a Strange Attractor

```
         strange = program to generate strange attractor
```

```c
#include <stdio.h>
#include <math.h>
#include <dos.h>
#include "tools.h"
```

```
float Xmax = 2.8,Xmin = -2.8,Ymax = 2,Ymin = -2, X = 0, Y = 0,
    Z = 0;
float deltaX,deltaY,Xtemp,Ytemp,Ztemp;
int col,row,j,max_row = 349, max_col = 639,color;
float a = 2.24, b = .43, c = -.65, d = -2.43, e = 1;
long int max_iterations=50000,i;
int OPERATOR = 0;
char ch;
main()
{
    setMode(16);
    deltaX = max_col/(Xmax - Xmin);
    deltaY = max_row/(Ymax - Ymin);
    for (j=0; j<2; j++)
    {
        cls(0);
        for (i=0; i<max_iterations; i++)
        {
            Xtemp = sin(a*Y) - Z*cos(b*X);
            Ytemp = Z*sin(c*X) - cos(d*Y);
            Z = e*sin(X);
            X = Xtemp;
            Y = Ytemp;
            if (j==0)
            {
                col = (X - Xmin)*deltaX;
                row = (Y - Ymin)*deltaY;
            }
            else
            {
                col = (Y - Xmin)*deltaX;
                row = (Z - Ymin)*deltaY;
            }
            if ((col>0) && (col<=max_col) &&
                (row>0) && (row<=max_row))
            {
                color = readPixel(col,row);
                color = (++color) %15+1;
                plot(col,row,color);
            }
        }
    getch();
    }
}
```

Figure 6-3: Strange Attractor Projected on XY Plane

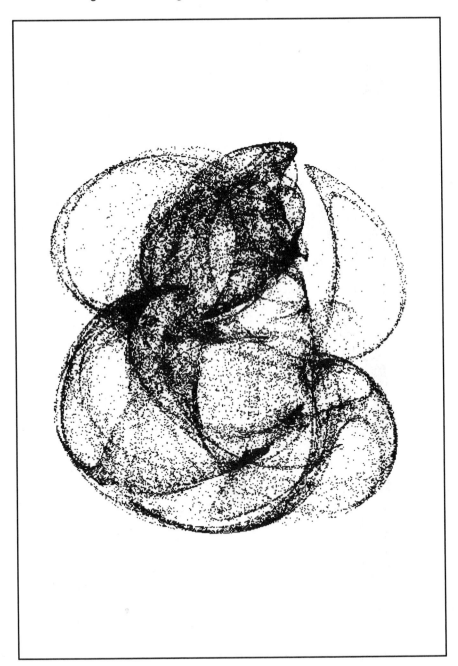

Figure 6-4: Strange Attractor Projected on YZ Plane

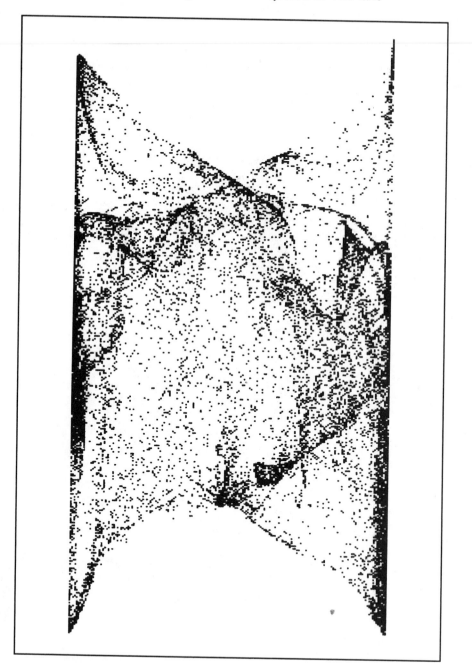

7

The Population Equation and Bifurcation Diagrams

It was in 1798 that Thomas Malthus made the first well-known attempt to apply mathematics to the growth and decline of populations. In his paper "An Essay on the Principle of Population As It Affects the Future Improvement of Society," Malthus presented the proposition that population, if unchecked, grows in a geometric manner while the growth of available food supplies is arithmetic.

Consequently, unless strict birth control measures were introduced, Malthus foresaw extended calamity and widespread starvation. Fortunately for us, and unfortunately for the validity of Malthus' theory, improvements in food production techniques kept pace with population growth and the disaster never occurred. Consequently Malthus' theory has been out of favor for a number of years. Just a few years ago, however, the Club of Rome commissioned the development of a massive computer model to model the future of the world. Its first runs predicted that population increases will reach the limit of earthly resources and cause, by the year 2000, the kind of catastrophes that Malthus predicted. Whether one accepts these results at face value or not, the Malthusian predictions have certainly gained a new lease on life.

The Population Equation

By the early 1950s, a simplified equation for population growth was being regularly used by ecologists. The equation is:

$$x_{n+1} = rx_n(1 - x_n) \qquad \text{(Equation 7-1)}$$

Rather than simply allow the population to grow at an uncontrolled rate, the use of the *(1 - x)* factor implies that the larger the population becomes, the more forces are applied to reduce growth. Generally speaking, using this equation (particularly if the parameter *r* is less than one) causes the population to reach a maximum when *x* is equal to 0.5. If the population dies out (*x* decreases to zero), it, of course, never recovers and the species is extinct.

On the other hand, the population will also die out if such tremendous over-growth occurs that the value of *x* reaches one. Strangely enough, everyone assumed that this equation was well-behaved, and for a long time, no one discovered the chaotic behavior that could occur when *r* took on larger values. This is one of those things that common sense makes obvious once the facts are discovered. We have things like the seven-year locusts, which have a tremendous population explosion every seven years. Surely such examples should have made us suspect that a population value could achieve a stability with more than one stable value and shift back and forth between these values in successive iterations. But it was not until 1971 that Robert May, at the Institute for Advanced Study at Princeton, studied this equation in detail for a wide range of values of *r* and at last began to come to an understanding of the complicated behavior that was hidden in the simple expression.

Bifurcation Diagrams

The best way to make sense of the really complicated behavior of the simple equation given above is through the use of a graph. These graphs are usually referred to as *bifurcation diagrams*. What we are going to do is travel through a range of values of *r*, sampling at intervals close enough so that we won't miss anything. For each *r*, we will start with the nominal value of 0.5 for *x* and do 256 iterations. After 64 iterations, *x* should have settled down to its final steady state conditions. We then plot the values of *x* associated with this *r* from 64 to 256 iterations. For the smaller values of *r*, where everything is well-behaved, we find that *x* has settled to a single value. But at some point, there are two final values for *x*, then 4, then 8 and so forth. Figure 7-1 is the listing for the program to generate our bifurcation diagrams for the population equation.

Figure 7-1: Program to Plot Bifurcation Diagrams

```c
#include <conio.h>
#include <stdio.h>
#include <dos.h>
#include <math.h>
#include "tools.h"

char ch;
int LINEWIDTH = 1;
unsigned long int PATTERN = 0xFFFFFFFF;

void main()
{
    float r=.95,x,delta_r;
    int i,j, row, col;

    setMode(16);

    for (j=0; j<2; j++)
    {
        delta_r = 0.005;
        if (j == 1)
        {
            cls(0);
            r = 3.55;
            delta_r = 0.0005;
        }
        for (col=0; col<639; col++)
        {
            x = .5;
            r += delta_r;
            for (i=0; i<256; i++)
            {
                x = r*x*(1-x);
                if ((x>1000000) || (x<-1000000))
                    break;
/*COMPUTATION FOR rx(x-1)*/
                row = 349 -(x*350);
/*COMPUTATION FOR x(1-x)
                row = 349 - ((x/r)*700);
*/
                if ((i>64) && (row<349) && (row>=0) &&
                    (col>=0) && (col<639))
                {
                    plot(col,row,15);
                }
            }
        }
        getch();
    }
}
```

Figure 7-2: Bifurcation Diagram for Population Equation

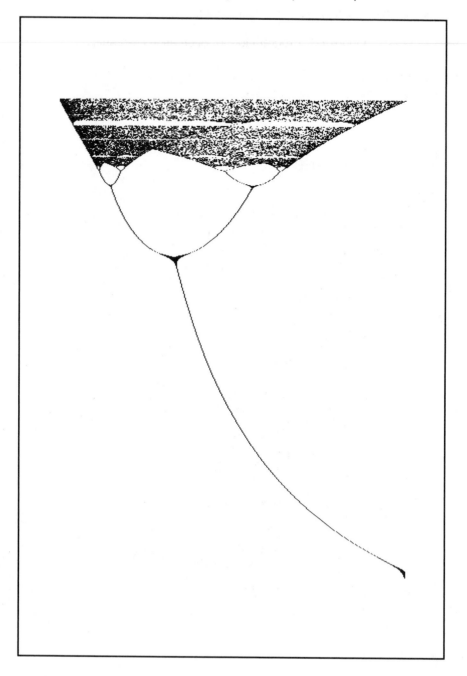

Figure 7-3: Expansion of the Bifurcation Diagram

We loop through two iterations; the first steps r in steps of 0.005, beginning at 0.95. The resulting diagram is shown in Figure 7-2. The second pass through the loop does an expansion in the area of period three. It begins with an r of 3.55 and steps in 0.0005 increments. The resulting diagram appears in Figure 7-3.

Now lets take a close look at these diagrams. Beginning at an r value of about one, the system settles down to a single value greater than zero, which remains the same no matter how many additional iterations we perform. This stable value increases as r is increased until at an r in the neighborhood of three there is a split into two stable values that alternate with each iteration. Next there is another split and there are now four stable values between which the iterations cycle. The four then become eight, then sixteen, and so forth, until we reach a state of chaos in which there are so many values that we never see the repetition with the tools that we have. Although this is normally called the chaotic region, one must be careful to remember that the period doubling scenario that we have seen thus far may be continuing. There may be a repetition, but since there are 2 to a very high power different values before the cycle repeats, we are unlikely to find it.

If you like scanning tables of numbers, you can develop a program to print out a large number of values of this function and scan them to see if you can find any traces of order in the chaos. Interestingly enough, as you can see from Figure 7-3, there are windows in this chaotic behavior. At one of these, the function reverts to cycling between three stable states, then bifurcates to six, then to twelve, and so forth.

"Period Three Implies Chaos"

Robert May's friend James Yorke did a rigorous mathematical analysis of the behavior of the population equation and in December 1975, together with Tien-Yien Li, published a paper called "Period Three Implies Chaos." What Yorke and Li were able to show is that, if a function similar to the population equation has a period of three, then it has periods of every other number, n. Thus it is rigorously established that there is an infinitely rich spectrum of results for this type of equation.

The Feigenbaum Number

If Mitchell Feigenbaum had known of the work of Robert May and James Yorke, or if he had been able to view May's bifurcation diagrams, he might never have made his significant discovery. But, in 1976, Feigenbaum was looking at the population equation from a different point of view. Consider for a moment just part of the equation:

$$y = x(1 - x) \qquad \text{(Equation 7-2)}$$

This equation has a maximum at $x = 0.5$. In fact, for the original population equation, in each set of bifurcations there is a value of r at which y of equation 7-2 achieves its maximum of 0.5. If Feigenbaum had been into bifurcation diagrams, he could have produced something like Figure 7-4 or the expanded version of Figure 7-5, where for each value of r we plot $x(1 - x)$ instead of $rx(1 - x)$. In these figures it becomes very clear that each set of bifurcations has one or more values of r at which y achieves its maximum.

Feigenbaum was trying to determine the values of the r at which the maximum is reached for each set of bifurcations. If we start with the maximum value of x and perform 2^n iterations, where n is the number of bifurcations, we should cycle through all of the bifurcated values of x and be back to the maximum again. Thus we have the general expression:

$$x_{max} = (r_n f)^{2m^n} (x_{max}) \qquad \text{(Equation 7-3)}$$

which for the population equation is:

$$x_{max} = [r_n x_{max}(1 - x_{max})]^{2m^n} \qquad \text{(Equation 7-4)}$$

This equation can be solved easily for x_0 and with more difficulty for x_1, but it very quickly gets so complicated and has so many roots that a solution becomes nearly impossible.

Figure 7-4: Bifurcation Diagram of *x(1 - x)*

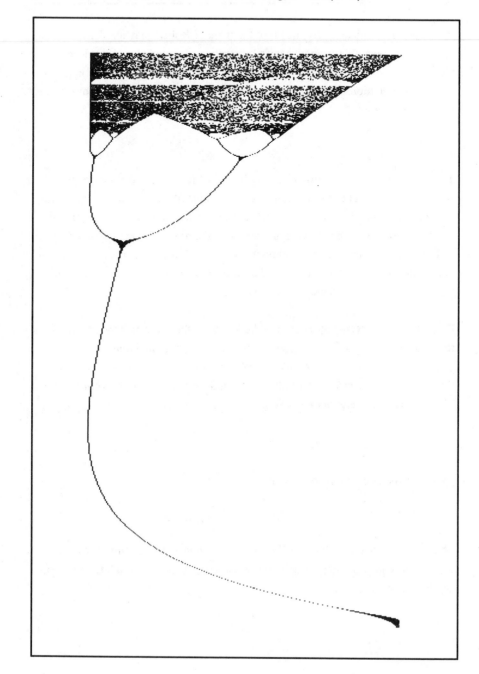

Figure 7-5: Expansion of the Bifurcation Diagram of *x(1 - x)*

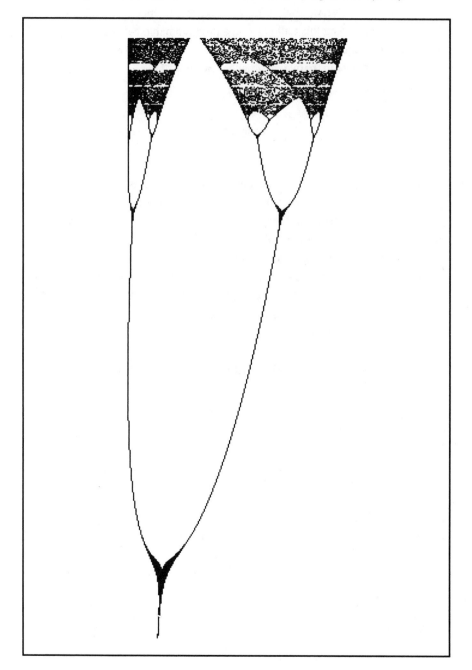

The best method of solution is to start with a value for x below the first known root and increase it very slowly until the next root is encountered and so forth. Feigenbaum was doing this tediously on a programmable calculator. In looking for a way to reduce the number of calculations, he discovered a remarkable universal relationship between adjacent roots. This is expressed as the *Feigenbaum number*:

$$\frac{r_n - r_{n-1}}{r_{n+1} - r_n} = 4.6692016091029\dots \quad \text{(Equation 7-5)}$$

To be mathematically precise, the Feigenbaum number is the value that this constant reaches as n approaches infinity, so that the first few values, especially, differ by a considerable error. Feigenbaum later discovered that this universal ratio applies to every kind of iterated function that is characterized by having a single differentiable maximum. This includes many different kinds of algebraic equations as well as trigonometric equations that make use of only a single hump of the curve. Figure 7-6 lists a program to generate the first 19 r_n values for the population equation. It makes use of the maximum precision available from the IBM PC using Turbo C or MicroSoft C.

Figure 7-6: Program to Generate Roots of Population Equation

```c
#include <stdio.h>
#include <stalib.h>
#include <math.h>
#include "tools.h"

long double x,lambda,f,step_size,old_x,test,lambda_1,lambda_2,
    delta,init_step, old_lambda;
double iterations;
double new_step, old_step;
long int i, iterations;
int j,sign;

main()
{

    setMode(3);
    lambda = 3.0;
    printf("\n n          Lambda              Delta\n");
    init_step = 1;
    for (j=1; j<20; j++)
```

```
{
    if (j%2 == 0)
        sign = -1;
    else
        sign = 1;
    gotoxy(0,15+j);;
        init_step /= 4.67;
    step_size = init_step;
    iterations = pow(2,j);
    old_x = 0.5;
    lambda+=step_size;
    for(;;)
    {
        x = old_x;
        for (i=0; i<iterations; i++)
            x = lambda*x*(1-x);
        test = (x - old_x)*sign;
        if (test < 0)
        {
            lambda -= step_size;
            step_size = step_size/2;
            old_lambda = lambda;
        }
    if (old_lambda > = lambda) break;
    gotoxy(1,j+3);
    printf(" %2d    %18.15Lf",j,lambda);
    }
    if (j > 2)
    {
        delta = (lambda_1 - lambda_2)/(lambda - lambda_1);
        printf("    %20.17Lf",delta);
    }
    lambda_2 = lambda_1;
    lambda_1 = lambda;
    }
}
```

Unfortunately, you will note that the precision of the Feigenbaum number reaches its peak at around the 15th and 16th values and after that, the computer does not have enough precision to give highly accurate values. Figure 7-7 is a table of the values obtained by the program of Figure 7-6. The program starts with a value of x and a step size. The equation is solved with the proper number of iterations to return to the maximized root, and then the result is compared with the value of x_{max}. Initially, x is approaching x_{max} from below, so that if the value hasn't been reached yet, we add the step and try again. We keep looping and doing this until we do exceed x_{max} and then we subtract one step value, reduce the step size, and try again. We keep on with this looping until the step is less than the minimum value that we can handle with the computer. The next root is approached decreasing from above, so that we have to reverse our test against x_{max} and reduce step size when we get below instead of above. Finally, as we proceed to higher roots, we need to be careful to assure that the initial step size is not so large that we jump right over several adjacent roots, and the roots are getting closer together all the time. Consequently we begin reducing the initial step size by dividing it by 4.7 at each iteration. You will recognize this as a crude round-off of the Feigenbaum number.

Figure 7-7: Values of Roots and Feigenbaum Number

n	r	delta
1	3.23606797749978969	
2	3.49856169932770152	
3	3.55464086276882486	4.68077099801069546
4	3.56666737985626851	4.66295961111410222
5	3.56924353163711033	4.66840392591840145
6	3.56979529374994462	4.66895374096762252
7	3.56991346542234851	4.66915718132887754
8	3.56993877423330548	4.66919100248498318
9	3.56994419460806493	4.66919947054711264
10	3.56994535548646858	4.66920113460536986
11	3.56994560411107844	4.66920150943092950
12	3.56994565735885649	4.66920158824756554
13	3.56994566876289996	4.66920160286821290
14	3.56994567120529684	4.66920162588405047
15	3.56994567172838347	4.66920155028815866
16	3.56994567184041260	4.66920176639898966
17	3.56994567186440580	4.66920254147147496
18	3.56994567186954440	4.66921926366696325
19	3.56994567187064489	4.66934028643927598

8

The Snowflake and Other von Koch Curves

The next few chapters will discuss fractals that are generated using a recursive initiator/generator technique that results in complete self-similarity. Their similarity dimension is the same as their fractal and Hausdorff-Besicovitch dimensions and is easily defined as discussed in Chapter 2. Such curves are constructed using the following technique.

We start with an initiator, which may be a straight line or a polygon. Each side of the initiator is then replaced by a generator, which is a connected set of straight lines that form a path from the beginning to the end of the line being replaced. (Usually the points of the generator are on a square grid or a grid made up of equilateral triangles.) Then, each straight line segment of the new figure is replaced by a scaled-down version of the generator. This process continues indefinitely. Of course, in reality, we cannot continue the process an infinite number of times, and even if we did, the result would not be interesting since the detail would be far beyond the resolution of our computer monitor. In practice, we perform from two to sixteen repetitions.

The von Koch Snowflake

This figure was first constructed by the mathematician Helge von Koch in 1904. The initiator, shown in Figure 8-1(a), is an equilateral triangle. The generator, shown in Figure 8-1(b), divides each line segment into three equal parts. Each segment of the generator has a length (r) of 1/3. The first segment of the generator follows the original line segment. The next two segments form the two sides of an equilateral triangle, the base of which is the second third of the original line. Finally, the fourth segment is identical with the final third of the original line. Thus the number of segments of the generator, N, is four. From equation 2.1 of Chapter 2, we find the fractal (or similarity) dimension of the snowflake to be:

```
D = log N / log (1/r) = log 4 / log 3 = 1.2618     (Equation 6.1)
```

Figure 8-2 shows the resulting snowflake for 2, 3, 4, and 6 levels.

Figure 8-1: Initiator and Generator for Snowflake

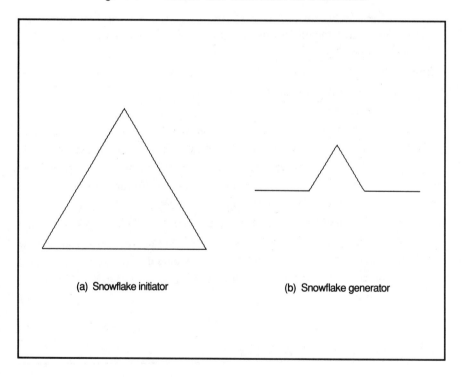

(a) Snowflake initiator   (b) Snowflake generator

Figure 8-2 (a, b, c, d): von Koch Snowflakes with 2, 3, 4, and 6 Levels

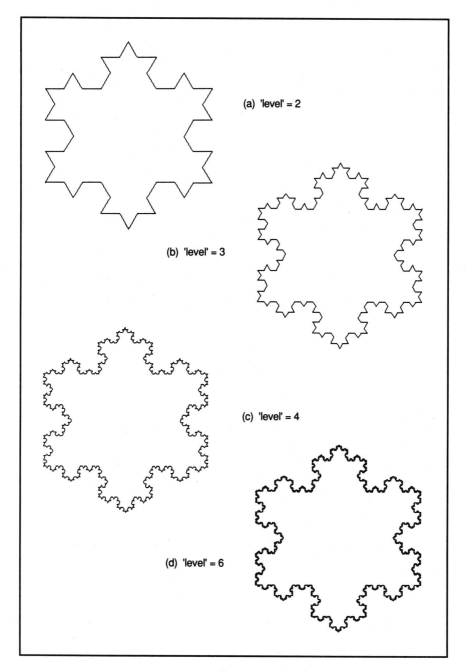

(a) 'level' = 2

(b) 'level' = 3

(c) 'level' = 4

(d) 'level' = 6

Generic Initiator/Generator Program

Figure 8-3 is a program to generate the von Koch snowflake. It can be considered as a somewhat generic program for creating this type of curve. As we progress through the next few chapters, we will encounter various complications as the generators become more complex, and we will learn how to deal with them.

Figure 8-3: Program to Generate von Koch Snowflake

```
            snoflake = program to generate von Koch snowflake
```

```c
#include <stdio.h>
#include <math.h>
#include <dos.h>
#include "tools.h"

void generate (float X1, float Y1, float X2, float Y2,
    int level);

int combination = 0,LINEWIDTH=1, operator=0:
unsigned long int PATTERN=0xFFFFFFFF;
float turtle_theta;
int i;
int generator_size = 5;
int level;
int init_size = 3;
int initiator_x1[10] = {-150,0,150},initiator_x2[10]={0,
    150,-150},initiator_y1[10]={-75,185,-75},
    initiator_y2[10]={185,-75,-75};
float Xpoints[25], Ypoints[25];
float turtle_x,turtle_y,turtle_r;

main()
{
    printf("\nEnter level (1 - 8): ");
    scanf("%d",&level);
    if (level < 1)
        level = 1;
    setMode(16);
    cls(0);
    for (i=0; i<init_size; i++)
    {
        generate(initiator_x1[i], initiator_y1[i],
            initiator_x2[i], initiator_y2[i], level);
```

```
    }
    getch();
}
```

```
generate() = generates curve
```

```
void generate (float X1, float Y1, float X2, float Y2,
    int level)
{
    int j,k,line;
    float a, b, Xpoints[25], Ypoints[25];
    level--;
    turtle_r = (sqrt((X2 - X1)*(X2 - X1) + (Y2 - Y1)*(Y2 -
        Y1)))/3.0;
    Xpoints[0] = X1;
    Ypoints[0] = Y1;
    Xpoints[4] = X2;
    Ypoints[4] = Y2;
    turtle_theta = point(X1,Y1,X2,Y2);
    turtle_x = X1;
    turtle_y = Y1;
    step();
    Xpoints[1] = turtle_x;
    Ypoints[1] = turtle_y;
    turn(60);
    step();
    Xpoints[2] = turtle_x;
    Ypoints[2] = turtle_y;
    turn(-120);
    step();
    Xpoints[3] = turtle_x;
    Ypoints[3] = turtle_y;
    if (level > 0)
    {
        for (j=0; j<generator_size-1; j++)
        {
            X1 = Xpoints[j];
            X2 = Xpoints[j+1];
            Y1 = Ypoints[j];
            Y2 = Ypoints[j+1];
            generate (X1,Y1,X2,Y2,level);
        }
    }
    else
    {
        for (k=0; k<generator_size-1; k++)
        {
            drawLine(Xpoints[k],Ypoints[k],
```

```
                              Xpoints[k+1],Ypoints[k+1],15);
        }
     }
  }
```

For each time that we replace a line segment by the generator, we are going to create an array of coordinate locations (stored in the array *Xpoints* for the *x* coordinates, and in the array *Ypoints* for the *y* coordinates) and then draw a line from the first set of coordinates to the second, from the second to the third, and so forth until we have drawn as many line segments as are specified by the parameter *generator_size*. To generate these coordinate pairs, we will make use of the modified turtle graphics commands which were developed in Chapter 4.

We first identify the beginning and end of the line segment and store the coordinates of each as the beginning and end points of our coordinate arrays. Then we insert these values into the function *point* which sets the turtle direction (*turtle_theta*) along the original line segment. The step size for turtle movement (*turtle_r*) is determined by measuring the length of the line segment and dividing by the proper divisor to get *r*. Note that for the snowflake, this divisior is 3; we will see later that it can take on other values for other curves. Next, we use *turn*, if necessary, to properly position the turtle. We then use *step* to advance the turtle and record its new position in the position arrays. At any time in the process of stepping through the pattern for the generator, we can record the turtle position in any set of members of the coordinate arrays. Thus, the turtle does not have to follow the actual path which makes up the generator, as long as it stops at every pair of endpoints for the generator lines. We can store every pair of coordinates that are needed in the proper location, regardless of when it was generated, so we have considerable flexibility as to how we are going to create the generator. The von Koch snowflake curve generator is so simple that all we have to do is trace its path with the turtle.

The main part of the program allows the user to enter *level*, which determines how many recursions will be used to generate the figure, and then calls *generate* for each line segment of the initiator. The *generator* function decrements *level* and then determines the coordinates of all points needed to draw the generator in place of the line segment whose beginning and end points passed as parameters to the function. Then, if the level is greater than 0, the function starts a *for* loop, which determines the beginning and end points of each new line segment in the array of points just created by the turtle functions, and then calls *generator* to replace each line segment by a new generator. You should note that the *Xpoints* and *Ypoints* arrays are not global, so that each time *generator* is called, a new pair of coordinate arrays is created. Thus, there can be quite a few of them if *level* is set to a large number.

When *level* is finally decremented to zero, the function actually draws the line segments that are specified by the coordinate arrays at that time and there is no more recursion, so that the program returns to the previous level and continues until all of the *for* loops have been completed.

The Gosper Curve

This variation of the von Koch curve was discovered by W. Gosper. The initiator is a regular hexagon and the generator consists of three segments on a grid of equilateral triangles. This and the next curve are a little peculiar in that the line segment to be replaced does not lie on any of the grid lines. Remembering that the turtle *point* function points the turtle in the direction of the line segment, if you were writing a program to draw this curve, you would have to compute the angle that the first piece of the generator makes with the line segment and turn the turtle in this direction before taking the first step. The program listings have already done that for you in these two curves. Figure 8-4 shows the initiator and the generator laid out on the grid. Applying a little simple geometry shows that if the length from one end of the generator to the other is taken to be 1, the length of each of the three segments is:

```
r = 1/ √ 7                      (Equation 8-2)
```

Since $N = 3$, the fractal dimension of the Gosper curve is:

```
D = log 3 / log (√ 7) = 1.1291 (Equation 8-3)
```

Figure 8-5 shows the resulting curve for levels to 1, 2, 4, and 6. The program to generate this curve is given in Figure 8-6. It is the same as the snowflake program except for the change in the values for the initiator and the modification of the *generate* function.

Figure 8-4: Initiator and Generator for Gosper Curve

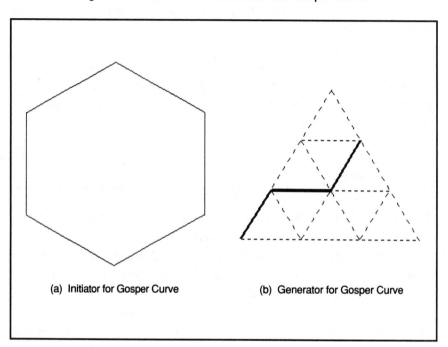

(a) Initiator for Gosper Curve   (b) Generator for Gosper Curve

Figure 8-5: Gosper Curves for Levels 1, 2, 4, and 6

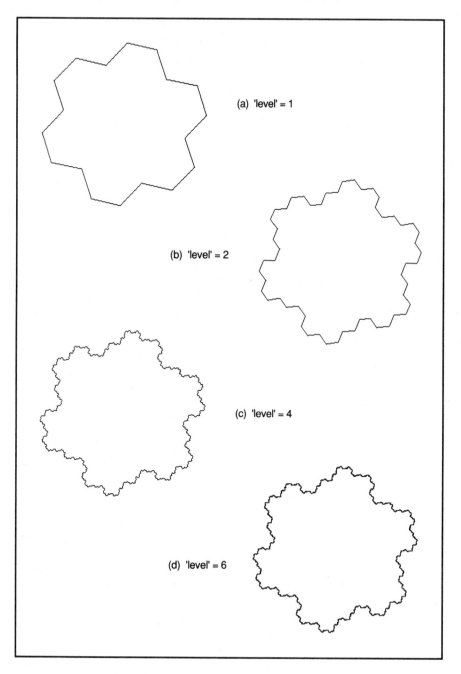

(a) 'level' = 1

(b) 'level' = 2

(c) 'level' = 4

(d) 'level' = 6

Figure 8-6: Program to Generate Gosper Curves

```
                    gosp7 = program to generate gosper curves
```

```c
#include <stdio.h>
#include <math.h>
#include <dos.h>
#include "tools.h"

void generate (float X1, float Y1, float X2, float Y2,
    int level);

int generator_size = 3;
int init_size = 6;
int level;
int initiator_x1[10] = {0,130,130,0,-130,-130},
    initiator_x2[10]={130,130,0,-130,-130,0},
    initiator_y1[10]={150,75,-75,-150,-75,75},
    initiator_y2[10]={75,-75,-150,-75,75,150};
int combination = 0,LINEWIDTH=1, OPERATOR=0,
unsigned long int PATTERN=0xFFFFFFFF;
float turtle_theta;
int i;
float Xpoints[25], Ypoints[25];
float turtle_x,turtle_y,turtle_r;

main()
{

        printf("\nEnter level (1 - 8): ");
        scanf("%d",&level);
        if (level < 1)
            level = 1;
        setMode(16);
        cls(0);
        for (i=0; i<init_size; i++)
            generate(initiator_x1[i], initiator_y1[i],
                initiator_x2[i],initiator_y2[i], level);
        getch();
}
```

```
                          generate() = generates curve
```

```c
void generate (float X1, float Y1, float X2, float Y2,
    int level)
```

```
{
    int j,k,line,set_type;
    float a, b, Xpoints[25], Ypoints[25], temp,temp_r;
    level--;
    turtle_r = sqrt((((X2 - X1)*(X2 - X1) + (Y2 - Y1)*
        (Y2 - Y1))/7.0);
    turtle_x = X1;
    turtle_y = Y1;
    Xpoints[0] = X1;
    Ypoints[0] = Y1;
    Xpoints[3] = X2;
    Ypoints[3] = Y2;
    turtle_theta = point(X1,Y1,X2,Y2);
    turn(19.1);
    step();
    Xpoints[1] = turtle_x;
    Ypoints[1] = turtle_y;
    turn(-60);
    step();
    Xpoints[2] = turtle_x;
    Ypoints[2] = turtle_y;
    if (level == 0)
    {
        for (k=0; k<generator_size; k++)
        {
            drawLine(Xpoints[k],Ypoints[k],
                Xpoints[k+1],Ypoints[k+1],15);
        }
    }
    else
    {
        for (j=0; j<generator_size; j++)
        {
            X1 = Xpoints[j];
            X2 = Xpoints[j+1];
            Y1 = Ypoints[j];
            Y2 = Ypoints[j+1];
            generate (X1,Y1,X2,Y2,level);
        }
    }
}
```

Three-Segment Quadric von Koch Curve

The next few curves are called "quadric" because the initiator is a square. However, there is nothing sacred about the square initiator; it could be any regular polygon or some other weird figure. An example will be given later.

Furthermore, we are going to create our generators on a square grid. For the first of these curves, a three-segment generator will be used; N is the same as for the previous curve, but because of the square grid, the length of a segment is:

```
r = 1 √ 5                        (Equation 8-4)
```

and the fractal dimension is different,

```
D = log 3 / log (√ 5) = 1.3652    (Equation 8-5)
```

Figure 8-7 shows the initiator and generator, and Figure 8-8 shows the curve for various levels. Again, the generic program is used, with appropriate modification to the *generator* function. This function, as modified, is shown in Figure 8-9. Using it to replace the *generator* function of Figure 8-6 will yield the three-segment quadric curve.

Figure 8-7: Initiator and Generator for Three-Segment von Koch Curve

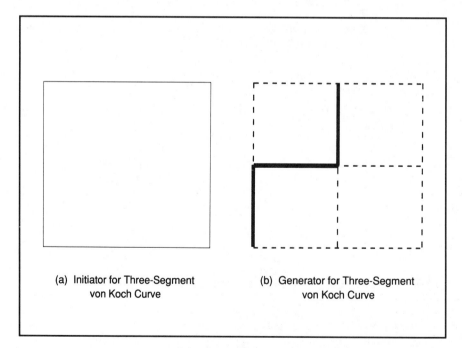

(a) Initiator for Three-Segment
von Koch Curve

(b) Generator for Three-Segment
von Koch Curve

Figure 8-8: Three-Segment von Koch Curves for Levels 1 to 6

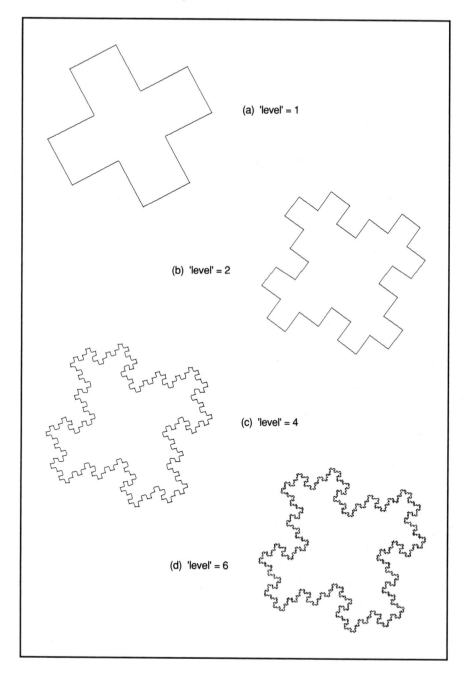

(a) 'level' = 1

(b) 'level' = 2

(c) 'level' = 4

(d) 'level' = 6

Figure 8-9: Generator Function for Three-Segment von Koch Curves

```
                    generate() = Generates curve
```

```
void generate (float X1, float Y1, float X2, float Y2,
    int level)
{
    int j,k,line,set_type;
    float a, b, Xpoints[25], Ypoints[25], temp,temp_r;
    level--;
    turtle_r = sqrt(((X2 - X1)*(X2 - X1) + (Y2 - Y1)*
        (Y2 - Y1))/5.0);
    turtle_x = X1;
    turtle_y = Y1;
    Xpoints[0] = X1;
    Ypoints[0] = Y1;
    Xpoints[3] = X2;
    Ypoints[3] = Y2;
    turtle_theta = point(X1,Y1,X2,Y2);
    turn(26.56);
    step();
    Xpoints[1] = turtle_x;
    Ypoints[1] = turtle_y;
    turn(-90);
    step();
    Xpoints[2] = turtle_x;
    Ypoints[2] = turtle_y;
    if (level == 0)
    {
        for (k=0; k<generator_size; k++)
        {
            drawLine(Xpoints[k],Ypoints[k],
            Xpoints[k+1],Ypoints[k+1],15);
        }
    }
    else
    {
        for (j=0; j<generator_size; j++)
        {
            X1 = Xpoints[j];
            X2 = Xpoints[j+1];
            Y1 = Ypoints[j];
            Y2 = Ypoints[j+1];
            generate (X1,Y1,X2,Y2,level);
        }
    }
}
```

Eight-Segment Quadric von Koch Curve

The next few curves are all going to make use of a square grid and turning angles of 90 degrees. They are a little more regular than the previous curve because the line segment to be replaced falls along the middle horizontal line of the grid. For the first curve to be considered, we will let:

$$r = 1/4 \qquad\qquad \text{(Equation 8-6)}$$

We can now draw various generators, the only limitation being that we want the curve to have no self-overlap and no self-intersection. If we also want the curve to have the highest fractal dimension possible, we need to find the generator for which N is the largest. Mandelbrot states that the highest possible value of N is:

$$N_{max} = 1/2r^2 \qquad\qquad \text{(Equation 8-7)}$$

when r is even and

$$N_{max} = (1 + r^2)/2r^2 \qquad\qquad \text{(Equation 8-8)}$$

when r is odd. Thus, for $r = 1/4$, we find that N_{max} is 8. The fractal dimension of this curve is thus:

$$D = \log 8 \ / \ \log 4 = 1.5 \qquad\qquad \text{(Equation 8-9)}$$

Figure 8-10 shows the initiator and generator for this curve, and Figure 8-11 shows the curve for levels of 1, 2, 4, and 6. The program to generate this curve is the same generic program of Figure 8-6, with the function *generator* replaced by that listed in Figure 8-12, and the parameter *generator_size* changed as follows:

```
int generator_size = 8;
int generator_size = 32;
```

121

Figure 8-10: Initiator and Generator for Eight-Segment von Koch Curve

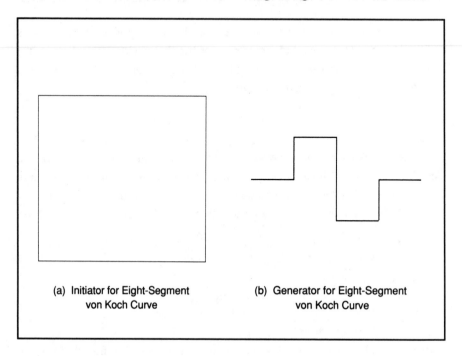

(a) Initiator for Eight-Segment
von Koch Curve

(b) Generator for Eight-Segment
von Koch Curve

Figure 8-11: Eight-Segment von Koch Curves for Levels 1, 2, 4, and 6

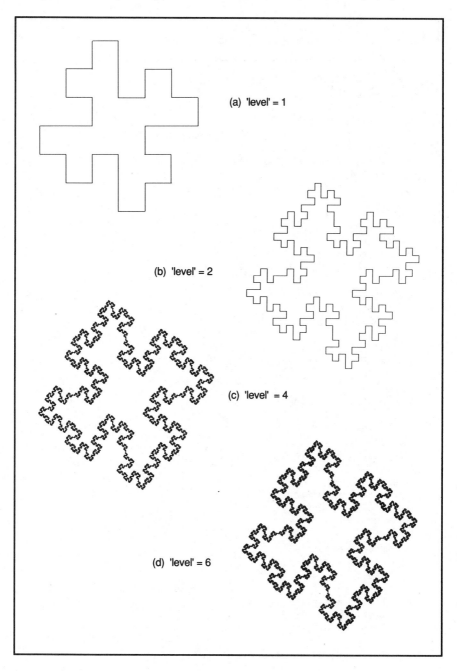

(a) 'level' = 1

(b) 'level' = 2

(c) 'level' = 4

(d) 'level' = 6

Figure 8-12: Generator Function for Eight-Segment von Koch Curves

```
                    generate() = generates curve
```

```
void generate (float X1, float Y1, float X2, float Y2,
    int level)
{
    int j,k,line,set_type;
    float a, b, Xpoints[25], Ypoints[25], temp,temp_r;
    level--;
    turtle_r = sqrt((X2 - X1)*(X2 - X1) + (Y2 - Y1)*(Y2 -
        Y1))/4.0;
    turtle_x = X1;
    turtle_y = Y1;
    Xpoints[0] = X1;
    Ypoints[0] = Y1;
    Xpoints[8] = X2;
    Ypoints[8] = Y2;
    turtle_theta = point(X1,Y1,X2,Y2);
    step();
    Xpoints[1] = turtle_x;
    Ypoints[1] = turtle_y;
    turn(90);
    step();
    Xpoints[2] = turtle_x;
    Ypoints[2] = turtle_y;
    turn(-90);
    step();
    Xpoints[3] = turtle_x;
    Ypoints[3] = turtle_y;
    turn(-90);
    step();
    Xpoints[4] = turtle_x;
    Ypoints[4] = turtle_y;
    step();
    Xpoints[5] = turtle_x;
    Ypoints[5] = turtle_y;
    turn(90);
    step();
    Xpoints[6] = turtle_x;
    Ypoints[6] = turtle_y;
    turn(90);
    step();
    Xpoints[7] = turtle_x;
    Ypoints[7] = turtle_y;
    if (level == 0)
    {
        for (k=0; k<generator_size; k++)
```

```
        {
            drawLine(Xpoints[k],Ypoints[k],
            Xpoints[k+1],Ypoints[k+1],15);
        }
    }
    else
    {
        for (j=0; j<generator_size; j++)
        {
            X1 = Xpoints[j];
            X2 = Xpoints[j+1];
            Y1 = Ypoints[j];
            Y2 = Ypoints[j+1];
            generate (X1,Y1,X2,Y2,level);
        }
    }
}
```

Eighteen-Segment Quadric von Koch Curve

If we let

$$r = 1/6 \hspace{3cm} \text{(Equation 8-10)}$$

we find that Nmax is 18. The fractal dimension of this curve is:

$$D = \log 18 / \log 6 = 1.6131 \hspace{1cm} \text{(Equation 8-11)}$$

Figure 8-13 shows the initiator and generator for this curve and Figure 8-14 shows the curve for levels 1, 2, 3, and 4. The program to generate this curve is the same generic program of Figure 8-6, with the function *generator* replaced by that listed in Figure 8-15, and the parameter *generator_size* changed as follows:

```
int generator_size = 18;
```

Figure 8-13: Initiator and Generator for
Eighteen-Segment von Koch Curve

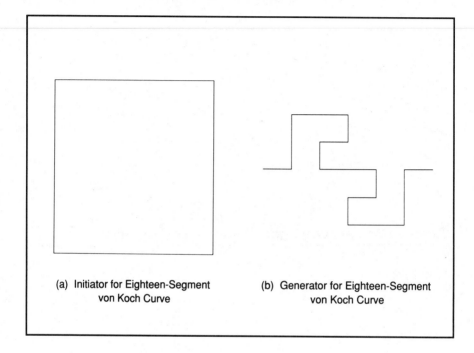

(a) Initiator for Eighteen-Segment
von Koch Curve

(b) Generator for Eighteen-Segment
von Koch Curve

Figure 8-14: Eighteen-Segment von Koch Curves for Levels 1 to 4

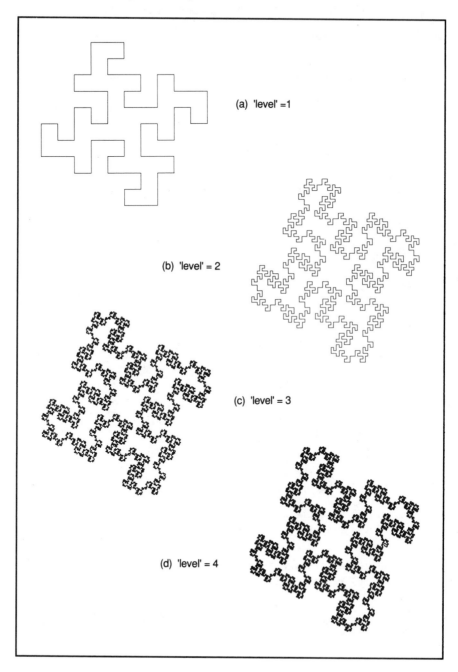

(a) 'level' =1

(b) 'level' = 2

(c) 'level' = 3

(d) 'level' = 4

Figure 8-15: Generator Function for Eighteen-Segment von Koch Curves

```
                    generate() = generates curve
```

```
void generate (float X1, float Y1, float X2, float Y2,
    int level)
{
    int j,k,line,set_type;
    float a, b, Xpoints[25], Ypoints[25], temp,temp_r;

    level--;
    turtle_r = sqrt(((X2 - X1)*(X2 - X1) + (Y2 - Y1)*
        (Y2 - Y1)))/6.0;
    turtle_x = X1;
    turtle_y = Y1;
    Xpoints[0] = X1;
    Ypoints[0] = Y1;
    Xpoints[18] = X2;
    Ypoints[18] = Y2;
    turtle_theta = point(X1,Y1,X2,Y2);
    step();
    Xpoints[1] = turtle_x;
    Ypoints[1] = turtle_y;
    turn(90);
    step();
    Xpoints[2] = turtle_x;
    Ypoints[2] = turtle_y;
    step();
    Xpoints[3] = turtle_x;
    Ypoints[3] = turtle_y;
    turn(-90);
    step();
    Xpoints[4] = turtle_x;
    Ypoints[4] = turtle_y;
    step();
    Xpoints[5] = turtle_x;
    Ypoints[5] = turtle_y;
    turn(-90);
    step();
    Xpoints[6] = turtle_x;
    Ypoints[6] = turtle_y;
    turn(-90);
    step();
    Xpoints[7] = turtle_x;
    Ypoints[7] = turtle_y;
    turn(90);
```

```
step();
Xpoints[8] = turtle_x;
Ypoints[8] = turtle_y;
turn(90);
step();
Xpoints[9] = turtle_x;
Ypoints[9] = turtle_y;
step();
Xpoints[10] = turtle_x;
Ypoints[10] = turtle_y;
turn(-90);
step();
Xpoints[11] = turtle_x;
Ypoints[11] = turtle_y;
turn(-90);
step();
Xpoints[12] = turtle_x;
Ypoints[12] = turtle_y;
turn(90);
step();
Xpoints[13] = turtle_x;
Ypoints[13] = turtle_y;
turn(90);
step();
Xpoints[14] = turtle_x;
Ypoints[14] = turtle_y;
step();
Xpoints[15] = turtle_x;
Ypoints[15] = turtle_y;
turn(90);
step();
Xpoints[16] = turtle_x;
Ypoints[16] = turtle_y;
step();
Xpoints[17] = turtle_x;
Ypoints[17] = turtle_y;
if (level == 0)
{
    for (k=0; k<generator_size; k++)
    {
        drawLine(Xpoints[k],Ypoints[k],
          Xpoints[k+1],Ypoints[k+1],15);
    }
}
else
{
    for (j=0; j<generator_size; j++)
    {
        X1 = Xpoints[j];
        X2 = Xpoints[j+1];
        Y1 = Ypoints[j];
```

```
        Y2 = Ypoints[j+1];
        generate (X1,Y1,X2,Y2,level);
    }
  }
}
```

32-Segment Quadric von Koch Curve

If we let

$$r = 1/8 \qquad \text{(Equation 8-12)}$$

we find that N_{max} is 32. The fractal dimension of this curve is:

$$D = \log 32 \ / \ \log 8 = 1.6667 \qquad \text{(Equation 8-13)}$$

Figure 8-16: Initiator and Generator for 32-Segment von Koch Curve

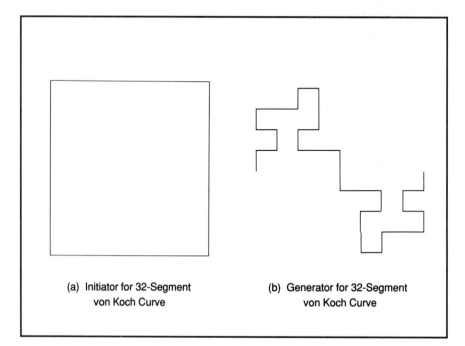

(a) Initiator for 32-Segment
von Koch Curve

(b) Generator for 32-Segment
von Koch Curve

Figure 8-17: 32 Segment von Koch Curves for Levels 1 to 3

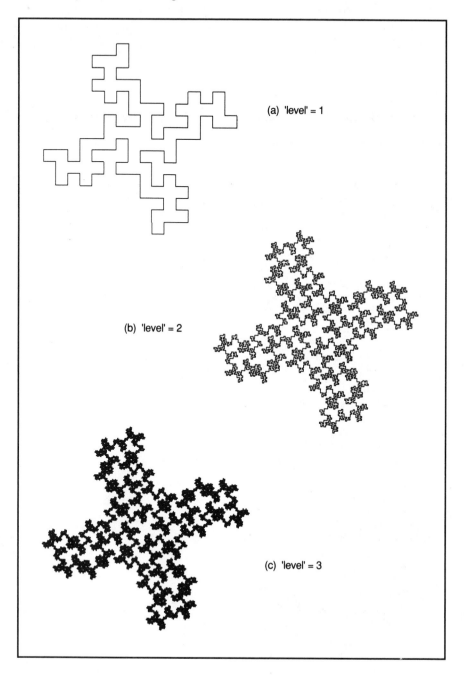

(a) 'level' = 1

(b) 'level' = 2

(c) 'level' = 3

Figure 8-13 shows the initiator and generator for this curve, and Figure 8-14 shows the curve for levels of 1, 2, and 3. The program to generate this curve is the same generic program of Figure 8-6, with the function *generator* replaced by that listed in Figure 8-15, and the parameter *generator_size* changed as follows:

```
int generator_size = 32;
```

Figure 8-18: Generator Function for 32-Segment von Koch Curves

```
                    generate() = generates curve
```

```
void generate (float X1, float Y1, float X2, float Y2,
    int level)
{
    int j,k,line,set_type;
    float a, b, Xpoints[55], Ypoints[55], temp,temp_r;

    level--;
    turtle_r = sqrt((X2 - X1)*(X2 - X1) + (Y2 - Y1)*
        (Y2 - Y1))/8.0;
    turtle_x = X1;
    turtle_y = Y1;
    Xpoints[0] = X1;
    Ypoints[0] = Y1;
    Xpoints[32] = X2;
    Ypoints[32] = Y2;
    turtle_theta = point(X1,Y1,X2,Y2);
    turn(90);
    step();
    Xpoints[1] = turtle_x;
    Ypoints[1] = turtle_y;
    turn(-90);
    step();
    Xpoints[2] = turtle_x;
    Ypoints[2] = turtle_y;
    turn(90);
    step();
    Xpoints[3] = turtle_x;
    Ypoints[3] = turtle_y;
    turn(90);
    step();
    Xpoints[4] = turtle_x;
    Ypoints[4] = turtle_y;
    turn(-90);
    step();
```

```
Xpoints[5] = turtle_x;
Ypoints[5] = turtle_y;
turn(-90);
step();
Xpoints[6] = turtle_x;
Ypoints[6] = turtle_y;
step();
Xpoints[7] = turtle_x;
Ypoints[7] = turtle_y;
turn(90);
step();
Xpoints[8] = turtle_x;
Ypoints[8] = turtle_y;
turn(-90);
step();
Xpoints[9] = turtle_x;
Ypoints[9] = turtle_y;
turn(-90);
step();
Xpoints[10] = turtle_x;
Ypoints[10] = turtle_y;
step();
Xpoints[11] = turtle_x;
Ypoints[11] = turtle_y;
turn(-90);
step();
Xpoints[12] = turtle_x;
Ypoints[12] = turtle_y;
turn(90);
step();
Xpoints[13] = turtle_x;
Ypoints[13] = turtle_y;
turn(90);
step();
Xpoints[14] = turtle_x;
Ypoints[14] = turtle_y;
step();
Xpoints[15] = turtle_x;
Ypoints[15] = turtle_y;
turn(-90);
step();
Xpoints[16] = turtle_x;
Ypoints[16] = turtle_y;
step();
Xpoints[17] = turtle_x;
Ypoints[17] = turtle_y;
turn(90);
step();
Xpoints[18] = turtle_x;
Ypoints[18] = turtle_y;
step();
```

```
Xpoints[19] = turtle_x;
Ypoints[19] = turtle_y;
turn(-90);
step();
Xpoints[20] = turtle_x;
Ypoints[20] = turtle_y;
turn(-90);
step();
Xpoints[21] = turtle_x;
Ypoints[21] = turtle_y;
turn(90);
step();
Xpoints[22] = turtle_x;
Ypoints[22] = turtle_y;
step();
Xpoints[23] = turtle_x;
Ypoints[23] = turtle_y;
turn(90);
step();
Xpoints[24] = turtle_x;
Ypoints[24] = turtle_y;
turn(90);
step();
Xpoints[25] = turtle_x;
Ypoints[25] = turtle_y;
turn(-90);
step();
Xpoints[26] = turtle_x;
Ypoints[26] = turtle_y;
step();
Xpoints[27] = turtle_x;
Ypoints[27] = turtle_y;
turn(90);
step();
Xpoints[28] = turtle_x;
Ypoints[28] = turtle_y;
turn(90);
step();
Xpoints[29] = turtle_x;
Ypoints[29] = turtle_y;
turn(-90);
step();
Xpoints[30] = turtle_x;
Ypoints[30] = turtle_y;
turn(-90);
step();
Xpoints[31] = turtle_x;
Ypoints[31] = turtle_y;
if (level == 0)
{
    for (k=0; k<generator_size; k++)
```

```
        {
            drawLine(Xpoints[k],Ypoints[k],
                Xpoints[k+1],Ypoints[k+1],15);
        }
    }
    else
    {
        for (j=0; j<generator_size; j++)
        {
            X1 = Xpoints[j];
            X2 = Xpoints[j+1];
            Y1 = Ypoints[j];
            Y2 = Ypoints[j+1];
            generate (X1,Y1,X2,Y2,level);
        }
    }
}
```

Fifty-Segment Quadric von Koch Curve

If we let

$$r = 1/10 \qquad\text{(Equation 8-14)}$$

we find that N_{max} is 50. The fractal dimension of this curve is:

$$D = \log 50\ /\ \log 10 = 1.6990 \quad \text{(Equation 8-15)}$$

As the generator contains more and more segments, it becomes less and less obvious how it is obtained. The process is a sort of trial and error one, but at this point it is time to develop some guidelines for generator creation. Figure 8-19 shows the initiator and generator for the fifty-segment curve. The generator grid is also shown. Note that slanting dotted lines have been drawn connecting midpoints of adjacent sides of the grid.

If we are to use the generator to replace line segments that meet at 90-degree angles, we cannot have any part of the generator outside the bounds of the diamond created by these dotted lines. This is sufficient to avoid self-overlapping, but does not prevent self-intersection. To assure against self-intersection, we mentally merge each pair of parallel sides of the diamond. If the generator touches the diamond side at the same point for both sides of a pair, self-intersection will occur. Finally, the easiest way to create the generator is to create it in two parts that are symmetrical (although possibly a mirror image), each beginning at one end of the line segment being replaced and ending at its middle. The constraints are thus:

1. Create a half-generator from one end of the line segment to be replaced to its middle, containing $N_{max}/2$ segments.

2. Do not go outside of the diamond.

3. If the generator intersects a point on one of a pair of parallel diamond sides, it may not intersect a corresponding point of the other of the pair of sides.

This is where the trial and error comes in. You next seek a path that will contain the required number of segments and meet the above constraints. Once you have the half-generator created, you can turn the graph upside down and draw the same half-generator to complete the process. Figure 8-20 shows the fifty-segment curve for levels of 1, 2, and 3. The program to generate this curve is the same generic program of Figure 8-6, with the function *generator* replaced by that listed in Figure 8-21, and the parameter *generator_size* changed as follows:

```
int generator_size = 50;
```

Figure 8-19: Initiator and Generator for Fifty-Segment von Koch Curve

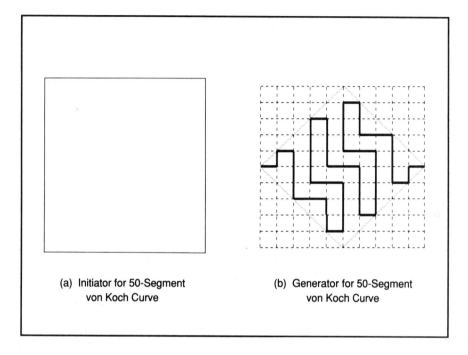

(a) Initiator for 50-Segment
von Koch Curve

(b) Generator for 50-Segment
von Koch Curve

Figure 8-20: Fifty-Segment von Koch Curves for Levels 1 to 3

(a) 'level' = 1

(b) 'level' = 2

(c) 'level' = 3

Figure 8-21: Generator Function for Fifty-Segment von Koch Curves

```
                     generate() = generates curve
```

```
void generate (float X1, float Y1, float X2, float Y2,
    int level)
{
    int j,k,line,set_type;
    float a, b, Xpoints[55], Ypoints[55], temp,temp_r;

    level--;
    turtle_r = sqrt((X2 - X1)*(X2 - X1) + (Y2 - Y1)*
        (Y2 - Y1))/10.0;
    turtle_x = X1;
    turtle_y = Y1;
    Xpoints[0] = X1;
    Ypoints[0] = Y1;
    Xpoints[50] = X2;
    Ypoints[50] = Y2;
    turtle_theta = point(X1,Y1,X2,Y2);
    step();
    Xpoints[1] = turtle_x;
    Ypoints[1] = turtle_y;
    turn(90);
    step();
    Xpoints[2] = turtle_x;
    Ypoints[2] = turtle_y;
    turn(-90);
    step();
    Xpoints[3] = turtle_x;
    Ypoints[3] = turtle_y;
    turn(-90);
    step();
    Xpoints[4] = turtle_x;
    Ypoints[4] = turtle_y;
    step();
    Xpoints[5] = turtle_x;
    Ypoints[5] = turtle_y;
    step();
    Xpoints[6] = turtle_x;
    Ypoints[6] = turtle_y;
    turn(90);
    step();
    Xpoints[7] = turtle_x;
    Ypoints[7] = turtle_y;
    step();
    Xpoints[8] = turtle_x;
    Ypoints[8] = turtle_y;
```

```
turn(-90);
step();
Xpoints[9] = turtle_x;
Ypoints[9] = turtle_y;
step();
Xpoints[10] = turtle_x;
Ypoints[10] = turtle_y;
turn(90);
step();
Xpoints[11] = turtle_x;
Ypoints[11] = turtle_y;
turn(90);
step();
Xpoints[12] = turtle_x;
Ypoints[12] = turtle_y;
step();
Xpoints[13] = turtle_x;
Ypoints[13] = turtle_y;
step();
Xpoints[14] = turtle_x;
Ypoints[14] = turtle_y;
turn(90);
step();
Xpoints[15] = turtle_x;
Ypoints[15] = turtle_y;
step();
Xpoints[16] = turtle_x;
Ypoints[16] = turtle_y;
turn(-90);
step();
Xpoints[17] = turtle_x;
Ypoints[17] = turtle_y;
step();
Xpoints[18] = turtle_x;
Ypoints[18] = turtle_y;
step();
Xpoints[19] = turtle_x;
Ypoints[19] = turtle_y;
step();
Xpoints[20] = turtle_x;
Ypoints[20] = turtle_y;
turn(-90);
step();
Xpoints[21] = turtle_x;
Ypoints[21] = turtle_y;
turn(-90);
step();
Xpoints[22] = turtle_x;
Ypoints[22] = turtle_y;
step();
Xpoints[23] = turtle_x;
```

```
Ypoints[23] = turtle_y;
step();
Xpoints[24] = turtle_x;
Ypoints[24] = turtle_y;
turn(90);
step();
Xpoints[25] = turtle_x;
Ypoints[25] = turtle_y;
step();
Xpoints[26] = turtle_x;
Ypoints[26] = turtle_y;
turn(-90);
step();
Xpoints[27] = turtle_x;
Ypoints[27] = turtle_y;
step();
Xpoints[28] = turtle_x;
Ypoints[28] = turtle_y;
step();
Xpoints[29] = turtle_x;
Ypoints[29] = turtle_y;
turn(90);
step();
Xpoints[30] = turtle_x;
Ypoints[30] = turtle_y;
turn(90);
step();
Xpoints[31] = turtle_x;
Ypoints[31] = turtle_y;
step();
Xpoints[32] = turtle_x;
Ypoints[32] = turtle_y;
step();
Xpoints[33] = turtle_x;
Ypoints[33] = turtle_y;
step();
Xpoints[34] = turtle_x;
Ypoints[34] = turtle_y;
turn(90);
step();
Xpoints[35] = turtle_x;
Ypoints[35] = turtle_y;
step();
Xpoints[36] = turtle_x;
Ypoints[36] = turtle_y;
turn(-90);
step();
Xpoints[37] = turtle_x;
Ypoints[37] = turtle_y;
step();
Xpoints[38] = turtle_x;
```

```
Ypoints[38] = turtle_y;
step();
Xpoints[39] = turtle_x;
Ypoints[39] = turtle_y;
turn(-90);
step();
Xpoints[40] = turtle_x;
Ypoints[40] = turtle_y;
turn(-90);
step();
Xpoints[41] = turtle_x;
Ypoints[41] = turtle_y;
step();
Xpoints[42] = turtle_x;
Ypoints[42] = turtle_y;
turn(90);
step();
Xpoints[43] = turtle_x;
Ypoints[43] = turtle_y;
step();
Xpoints[44] = turtle_x;
Ypoints[44] = turtle_y;
turn(-90);
step();
Xpoints[45] = turtle_x;
Ypoints[45] = turtle_y;
step();
Xpoints[46] = turtle_x;
Ypoints[46] = turtle_y;
step();
Xpoints[47] = turtle_x;
Ypoints[47] = turtle_y;
turn(90);
step();
Xpoints[48] = turtle_x;
Ypoints[48] = turtle_y;
turn(90);
step();
Xpoints[49] = turtle_x;
Ypoints[49] = turtle_y;
if (level == 0)
{
    for (k=0; k<generator_size; k++)
    {
        drawLine(Xpoints[k],Ypoints[k],
        Xpoints[k+1],Ypoints[k+1],15);
    }
}
else
{
    for (j=0; j<generator_size; j++)
```

```
        {
            X1 = Xpoints[j];
            X2 = Xpoints[j+1];
            Y1 = Ypoints[j];
            Y2 = Ypoints[j+1];
            generate (X1,Y1,X2,Y2,level);
        }
    }
}
```

Using Other Initiators

All of the von Koch curves that have been described above using the square initiator can easily be adapted to other regular polygon initiators of five or more sides. (The generators have been set up so as not to be self-overlapping or self-intersecting as long as the sides of the polygon do not intersect at angles of less than 90 degrees. You can experiment with figures other than regular polygons as long as this condition is met.

Figure 8-22 shows the initiator and generator for an eight-segment von Koch curve using a hexagon as the initiator. Figure 8-23 shows the curve for levels 1, 2, 3, and 4. To generate this curve, all you need to do is run the program for the eight-segment von Koch curve, as given above, with the following changes in the initial conditions:

```
int init_size = 6;
int initiator_x1[10] = {-75,75,150,75,-75,-150},
initiator_x2[10]={75,150,75,-75,-150,-75},
initiator_y1[10]={115,115,0,-115,-115,0},
initiator_y2[10]={115,0,-115,-115,0,115};
```

Figure 8-22: Initiator and Generator for Eight-Segment
von Koch Curve with Hexagonal Generator

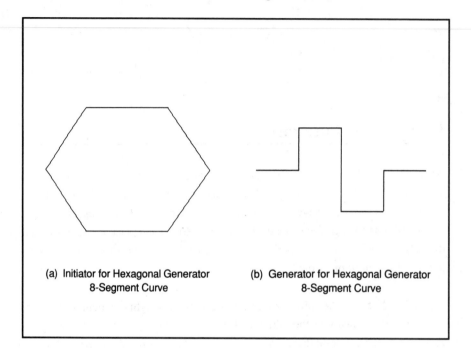

(a) Initiator for Hexagonal Generator
8-Segment Curve

(b) Generator for Hexagonal Generator
8-Segment Curve

Figure 8-23: Hexagonal Eight-Segment von Koch Curves for Levels 1 to 4

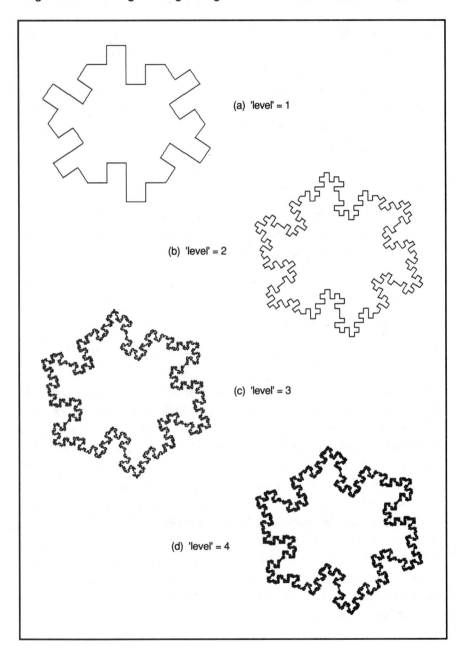

(a) 'level' = 1

(b) 'level' = 2

(c) 'level' = 3

(d) 'level' = 4

Complicated Generators

Take a look at the generator shown in Figure 8-24(a). This generator was discovered by Mandelbrot. It is based upon a grid of equilateral triangles. If the generator consisted of line segments connecting points 0, 1, 2, 3, 4, and 11, it would be rather simple. However, a smaller replica of this simple generator has been inserted between points 4 and 9, and then two regular line segments added to complete the generator. Because two different line segment lengths are used, we must use the expression:

$$\Sigma\ rmD\ =\ 1 \qquad\qquad \text{(Equation 8-16)}$$

to determine the fractal dimension (see Chapter 2). First we need to observe that r for the regular sized segments is 1/3. For the smaller segments, we can use simple trigonometry to ascertain that r is 0.186339. Thus, we have:

$$6(.3333)D\ +\ 5(.186339)D\ =\ 1 \qquad \text{(Equation 8-17)}$$

which gives a fractal dimension of:

$$D\ =\ 1.8575 \qquad\qquad \text{(Equation 8-18)}$$

We can easily handle the change in segment length by simply recalculating the *turtle_r* (length of turtle step) at the appropriate place in the generate program. Now, however, look at Figure 8-24(b), which shows the curve for the second level. In order to make sure the curve is not self-overlapping or self-intersecting, we have to take some considerable liberties with how we use the generator to replace each segment of the previous level. There are four variations of the generator: one is to the right of the original line segment, one is to the left, a third is to the right (but with the generator reversed), and the fourth is to the left with the generator reversed. Unfortunately, these are rather arbitrary and a different set is needed at each level (at least for the first few levels). We have to thank Mandelbrot for discovering the proper variation to use at each position in the first few levels; it gives us a starting place from which we can branch off into our own investigations.

Figure 8-24: Generator and Second Level for Complex Generator Curve

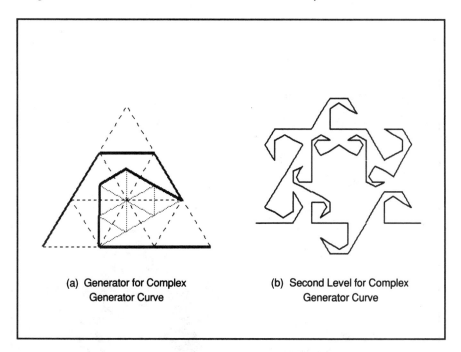

(a) Generator for Complex
Generator Curve

(b) Second Level for Complex
Generator Curve

Our software handles the problem by adding two new parameters, *sign* and *type*. In using the turtle graphics to create our generator, we multiply every angle by *sign*, which starts out the program with a value of 1. As we enter the generator function, we take action based upon the value of *type*. If *type* is 0, nothing is changed. The parameter *sign* retains its original value and the original generator function is produced on the same side as the previous one. If the *type* is 1, *sign* is multiplied by -1, causing all of the turn angles to be reversed so that the generator appears on the opposite side of the line segment from the previous one. If *type* is 2, we make the beginning line segment coordinates the end ones and visa-versa, so that the generator is drawn backwards. We also need to reverse all of the signs for this reverse generator to appear on the same side of the line segment as the previous generator. Finally, for a *type* of 3, we reverse coordinates only so that the generator is both reversed and moved to the opposite side.

Figure 8-25: Complex Generator Curves for Levels 2 to 4

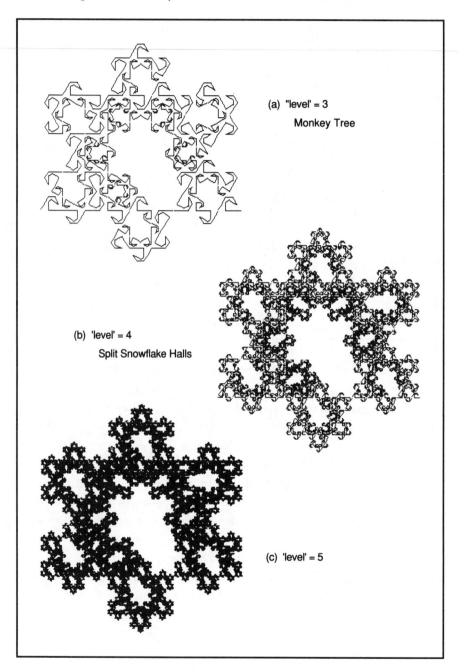

(a) "level' = 3

Monkey Tree

(b) 'level' = 4

Split Snowflake Halls

(c) 'level' = 5

As we enter the recursion process for each level, we have to define what the *type* is to be for every line segment that is to be replaced. This is a somewhat lengthy process, even using C's *switch* statement. Fortunately, in this case we only had to define two levels. The net result is shown in Figure 8-25. Mandelbrot calls the third-level curve a "Monkey's Tree" and the fourth-level curve "Split Snowflake Halls." The fourth-level curve is not quite like Mandelbrot's version, because we did not define the *type* parameter to match his for every line segment.

Figure 8-26 is the listing of the program to generate these curves.

Figure 8-26: Program to Generate Complex Generator Curves

```
          snowhall = program to generate snowflake halls
```

```c
#include <stdio.h>
#include <math.h>
#include <dos.h>
#include "tools.h"

void generate (float X1, float Y1, float X2, float Y2,
    int level,int type,int sign);

int combination = 0,LINEWIDTH=1, OPERATOR=0;
unsigned long int PATTERN=0xFFFFFFFF;
float turtle_theta;
int i;
int generator_size = 12;
int level = 4;
int init_size = 1;
int initiator_x1[10] = {-185},initiator_x2[10]={25},
    initiator_y1[10]={-120},
    initiator_y2[10]={244};
float Xpoints[25], Ypoints[25];
float turtle_x,turtle_y,turtle_r;

main()
{

    int sign=1;
    int set_type=1;

    printf("\nEnter level (1 - 8): ");
    scanf("%d",&level);
    if (level < 1)
```

```
        level = 1;
    setMode(16);
    cls(0);
    for (i=0; i<init_size; i++)
        generate(initiator_x1[i], initiator_y1[i],
            initiator_x2[i], initiator_y2[i],
            level,set_type,sign);
    getch();
}
```

```
 ┌─────────────────────────────────────────────────────────┐
 │                                                         │
 │              generate() = generates curve               │
 │                                                         │
 └─────────────────────────────────────────────────────────┘
```

```
void generate (float X1, float Y1, float X2, float Y2,
    int level, int type, int sign)
{
    int j,k,line,set_type;
    float a, b, Xpoints[25], Ypoints[25], temp,temp_r;


    switch (type)
    {
        case 0: break;

        case 1: sign *= -1;
                break;

        case 2: sign *= -1;
        case 3: temp = X1;
                X1 = X2;
                X2 = temp;
                temp = Y1;
                Y1 = Y2;
                Y2 = temp;
                break;
    }
    level--;
    turtle_r = (sqrt((X2 - X1)*(X2 - X1) + (Y2 - Y1)*
        (Y2 - Y1)))/3.0;
    Xpoints[0] = X1;
    Ypoints[0] = Y1;
    Xpoints[11] = X2;
    Ypoints[11] = Y2;
    turtle_theta = point(X1,Y1,X2,Y2);
    turn(60*sign);
    turtle_x = X1;
    turtle_y = Y1;
    step();
    Xpoints[1] = turtle_x;
    Ypoints[1] = turtle_y;
```

```
step();
Xpoints[2] = turtle_x;
Ypoints[2] = turtle_y;
turn(-60*sign);
step();
Xpoints[3] = turtle_x;
Ypoints[3] = turtle_y;
turn(-60*sign);
step();
Xpoints[4] = turtle_x;
Ypoints[4] = turtle_y;
turn(-120*sign);
step();
turn(60*sign);
step();
Xpoints[9] = turtle_x;
Ypoints[9] = turtle_y;
turn(120*sign);
step();
Xpoints[10] = turtle_x;
Ypoints[10] = turtle_y;
turtle_r = (sqrt((Xpoints[9] - Xpoints[4])*
    (Xpoints[9] - Xpoints[4]) + (Ypoints[9] -
    Ypoints[4])*(Ypoints[9] - Ypoints[4])))/3.0;
turtle_theta = point(Xpoints[4],Ypoints[4],
    Xpoints[9],Ypoints[9]);
turn(-60*sign);
turtle_x = Xpoints[4];
turtle_y = Ypoints[4];
step();
Xpoints[5] = turtle_x;
Ypoints[5] = turtle_y;
step();
Xpoints[6] = turtle_x;
Ypoints[6] = turtle_y;
turn(60*sign);
step();
Xpoints[7] = turtle_x;
Ypoints[7] = turtle_y;
turn(60*sign);
step();
Xpoints[8] = turtle_x;
Ypoints[8] = turtle_y;
if (level == 0)
{
    for (k=0; k<generator_size-1; k++)
    {
        drawLine(Xpoints[k],Ypoints[k],
        Xpoints[k+1],Ypoints[k+1],15);
    }
}
```

```
        else
        {
            for (j=0; j<generator_size-1; j++)
            {
                if (level == 1)
                {
                    switch(j)
                    {
                        case 2:
                        case 8:
                        case 10:
                                set_type = 0;
                                break;
                        case 0:
                        case 5:
                                set_type = 1;
                                break;
                        case 1:
                        case 3:
                        case 4:
                                set_type = 2;
                                break;
                        case 6:
                        case 7:
                        case 9:
                                set_type = 3;
                                break;
                    }
                }
                if (level > 1)
                {
                    switch(j)
                    {
                        case 2:
                        case 8:
                        case 10:
                                set_type = 0;
                                break;
                        case 0:
                                set_type = 1;
                                break;
                        case 1:
                        case 3:
                        case 4:
                                set_type = 2;
                                break;
                        case 5:
                        case 6:
                        case 7:
                        case 9:
                                set_type = 3;
```

```
                    break;
            }
        }
        X1 = Xpoints[j];
        X2 = Xpoints[j+1];
        Y1 = Ypoints[j];
        Y2 = Ypoints[j+1];
        generate (X1,Y1,X2,Y2,level,set_type,sign);
    }
  }
}
```

9

Peano Curves

Chapter 8 described a number of curves which were characterized by self-similarity, no self-intersection, and no self-overlapping. They had fractal dimensions greater than 1 and less than 2. This implies that no matter how many times the recursion process was applied, the curves would never completely fill the plane. In this chapter, we will consider curves whose fractal dimension, D, is 2. They are called Peano curves because the first of the family, which will be described in the next section, was discovered by Giuseppe Peano in 1900. The fractal dimension of 2 has two implications. First, the curves must completely fill the plane. Second, the curves must be self-intersecting—if they fill the plane, there must be an infinity of points at which each curve intersects itself.

The Original Peano Curve

Figure 9-1 shows the generator for the original Peano curve. The initiator is simply a horizontal straight line. Unfortunately, because of all of the self-intersections, it is almost impossible to determine the way in which the Peano curve is drawn, even if arrows are added to the diagram in an attempt to show the flow. As you look at the diagram, first a step is made up, then a step to the left, then another up, then one to the right, then a step down, then one to the right, then one up, then a step to the left, and finally one up. Figure 9-2 shows the Peano curves for levels of 2, 3, and 4. The way in which the generator is drawn can be best understood by looking at the turtle graphics part of the listing for the generator function, which is given in Figure 9-3. The generator consists of nine line segments (N = 9), each of which has a length of 1/3 of the original line (r = 1/3). Thus, the fractal dimension is:

```
D = log 9 / log 3 = 2          (Equation 9-1)
```

The Peano curves are generated by the same generic program shown in Figure 8-6, with the generator function of Figure 9-3 substituted for the original generator function, and the following changes in the initialization conditions:

```
int generator_size = 9;
int init_size = 1;
int initiator_x1[10] = {0},initiator_x2[10]={0},
    initiator_y1[10]={-100}, initiator_y2[10]={100};
```

Figure 9-1: Generator for Original Peano Curve

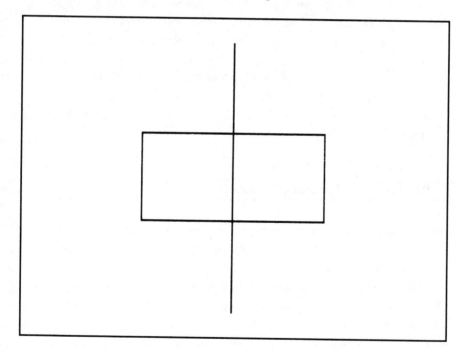

Figure 9-2: Original Peano Curves for Levels 2 to 4

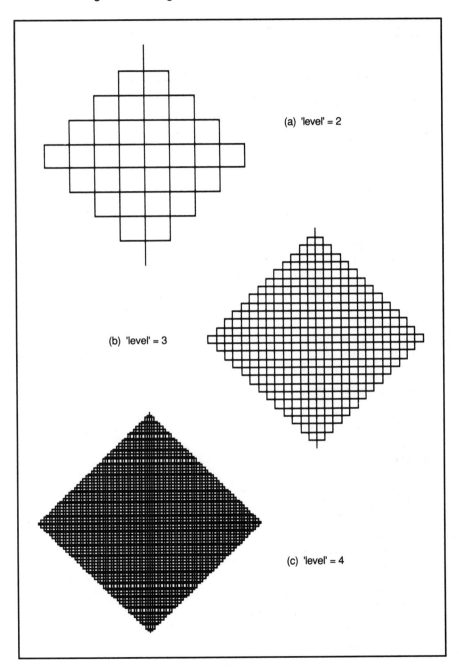

(a) 'level' = 2

(b) 'level' = 3

(c) 'level' = 4

Figure 9-3: Generator Function for Original Peano Curve

```
                    generate() = generates curve
```

```c
void generate (float X1, float Y1, float X2, float Y2,
    int level)
{
    int j,k,line;
    float a, b, Xpoints[25], Ypoints[25];

    level--;
    turtle_r = (sqrt((X2 - X1)*(X2 - X1) + (Y2 - Y1)*
        (Y2 - Y1)))/3.0;
    Xpoints[0] = X1;
    Ypoints[0] = Y1;
    Xpoints[9] = X2;
    Ypoints[9] = Y2;
    turtle_theta = point(X1,Y1,X2,Y2);
    turtle_x = X1;
    turtle_y = Y1;
    step();
    Xpoints[1] = turtle_x;
    Ypoints[1] = turtle_y;
    turn(90);
    step();
    Xpoints[2] = turtle_x;
    Ypoints[2] = turtle_y;
    turn(-90);
    step();
    Xpoints[3] = turtle_x;
    Ypoints[3] = turtle_y;
    turn(-90);
    step();
    Xpoints[4] = turtle_x;
    Ypoints[4] = turtle_y;
    turn(-90);
    step();
    Xpoints[5] = turtle_x;
    Ypoints[5] = turtle_y;
    turn(90);
    step();
    Xpoints[6] = turtle_x;
    Ypoints[6] = turtle_y;
    turn(90);
    step();
    Xpoints[7] = turtle_x;
```

```
Ypoints[7] = turtle_y;
turn(90);
step();
Xpoints[8] = turtle_x;
Ypoints[8] = turtle_y;
if (level > 0)
{
    for (j=0; j<generator_size; j++)
    {
        X1 = Xpoints[j];
        X2 = Xpoints[j+1];
        Y1 = Ypoints[j];
        Y2 = Ypoints[j+1];
        generate (X1,Y1,X2,Y2,level);
    }
}
else
{
    for (k=0; k<generator_size; k++)
    {
        drawLine(Xpoints[k],Ypoints[k],
        Xpoints[k+1],Ypoints[k+1],15);
    }
}
}
```

Modified Peano Curve

Were it not for the self-intersections of the generator for the original Peano curve, it would be a lot easier to trace the curve and see how it is drawn. Thus, a modification of the Peano curve has been developed that rounds off the corners to avoid self-intersection. The resulting generator is shown in Figure 9-4. It must be noted, however, that this modified generator can only be used at the lowest level, just before actual curve drawing. If it is used at higher levels, on recursion the program tries to substitute the generator for each diagonal segment that rounds off a corner, as well as for the regular line segments. Therefore, the generator for the original Peano curve is used at the higher levels. The curve is mathematically interesting because it is not quite a true Peano curve. Because the generator used in the final recursion is a little shorter in length than that of the original Peano curve, the fractal dimension, D, is slightly less than 2. As the number of recursions increases, the fractal dimension changes; as the number of recursions approaches infinity, the fractal dimension approaches 2 as a limit.

Figure 9-4: Generator for Modified Peano Curve

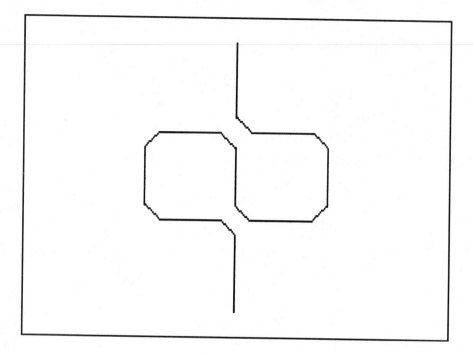

Figure 9-5 shows the resulting modified Peano curves for levels of 2 and 3. To generate these curves, we use the program listed in Figure 9-6. The generator function for all levels above 1 is the same as for the original Peano curve. For level 1, a different generator is used. Instead of defining a turtle step (turtle_r) as 1/3 of the original line segment, it is defined as 1/18. The basic generator is then written to have the turtle traverse the same path as the original Peano curve generator, using the same turn angles, but taking six steps for each step that was taken by the original generator. However, the points that are saved for the coordinate array are different. After saving the first set of coordinates, we next save the location after the fifth step. The next location to be saved is at the end of the first step after the first corner is turned. The remaining locations to be saved are after the fifth step of each line segment and after the first step of the next line segment, except that the fifth step of the very last line segment is not saved. The result, when the lines are drawn, is that a diagonal line connects points 1/6 of the distance on each line segment that would normally meet at the corner.

Figure 9-5: Modified Peano Curves for Levels 2 and 3

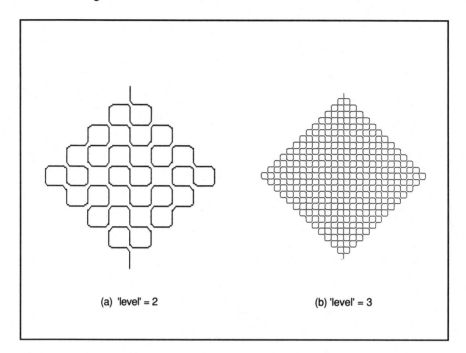

(a) 'level' = 2   (b) 'level' = 3

Figure 9-6: Program to Generate Modified Peano Curves

```
peano2 = program to generate modified peano curve
```

```
#include <stdio.h>
#include <math.h>
#include <dos.h>
#include "tools.h"

void generate (float X1, float Y1, float X2, float Y2,
    int level);
int generator_size = 19;
int level;
int init_size = 1;
int initiator_x1[10] = {0},initiator_x2[10]={0},
    initiator_y1[10]={-200}, initiator_y2[10]={200};
int combination = 0,LINEWIDTH=1, OPERATOR=0;
unsigned long int PATTERN=0xFFFFFFFF;
float turtle_theta;
int i;
```

```c
float Xpoints[25], Ypoints[25],Xptemp,Yptemp;
float turtle_x,turtle_y,turtle_r;

main()
{
    printf("\nEnter level (1 - 8): ");
    scanf("%d",&level);
    if (level < 1)
        level = 1;
    setMode(16);
    cls(0);

    Xptemp = initiator_x1[0];
    Yptemp = initiator_y1[0];
    for (i=0; i<init_size; i++)
        generate(initiator_x1[i], initiator_y1[i],
            initiator_x2[i], initiator_y2[i], level);
    getch();
}
```

```
                    generate() = generates curve
```

```c
void generate (float X1, float Y1, float X2, float Y2,
    int level)
{
    int j,k,line;
    float a, b, Xpoints[25], Ypoints[25];

    level--;
    Xpoints[0] = X1;
    Ypoints[0] = Y1;
    turtle_theta = point(X1,Y1,X2,Y2);
    turtle_x = X1;
    turtle_y = Y1;
    if (level != 0)
    {
        turtle_r = (sqrt((X2 - X1)*(X2 - X1) +
            (Y2 - Y1)*(Y2 - Y1)))/3.0;
        Xpoints[9] = X2;
        Ypoints[9] = Y2;
        step();
        Xpoints[1] = turtle_x;
        Ypoints[1] = turtle_y;
        turn(90);
        step();
        Xpoints[2] = turtle_x;
        Ypoints[2] = turtle_y;
        turn(-90);
```

```
        step();
        Xpoints[3] = turtle_x;
        Ypoints[3] = turtle_y;
        turn(-90);
        step();
        Xpoints[4] = turtle_x;
        Ypoints[4] = turtle_y;
        turn(-90);
        step();
        Xpoints[5] = turtle_x;
        Ypoints[5] = turtle_y;
        turn(90);
        step();
        Xpoints[6] = turtle_x;
        Ypoints[6] = turtle_y;
        turn(90);
        step();
        Xpoints[7] = turtle_x;
        Ypoints[7] = turtle_y;
        turn(90);
        step();
        Xpoints[8] = turtle_x;
        Ypoints[8] = turtle_y;
        for (j=0; j<9; j++)
        {
            X1 = Xpoints[j];
            X2 = Xpoints[j+1];
            Y1 = Ypoints[j];
            Y2 = Ypoints[j+1];
            generate (X1,Y1,X2,Y2,level);
        }
    }
    else
    {
        turtle_r = (sqrt((X2 - X1)*(X2 - X1) +
            (Y2 - Y1)*(Y2 - Y1)))/18.0;
        Xpoints[0] = Xptemp;
        Ypoints[0] = Yptemp;
        Xpoints[19] = X2;
        Ypoints[19] = Y2;
        step();
        Xpoints[1] = turtle_x;
        Ypoints[1] = turtle_y;
        step();
        step();
        step();
        step();
        Xpoints[2] = turtle_x;
        Ypoints[2] = turtle_y;
        step();
        turn(90);
```

```
step();
Xpoints[3] = turtle_x;
Ypoints[3] = turtle_y;
step();
step();
step();
step();
Xpoints[4] = turtle_x;
Ypoints[4] = turtle_y;
step();
turn(-90);
step();
Xpoints[5] = turtle_x;
Ypoints[5] = turtle_y;
step();
step();
step();
step();
Xpoints[6] = turtle_x;
Ypoints[6] = turtle_y;
step();
turn(-90);
step();
Xpoints[7] = turtle_x;
Ypoints[7] = turtle_y;
step();
step();
step();
step();
Xpoints[8] = turtle_x;
Ypoints[8] = turtle_y;
step();
turn(-90);
step();
Xpoints[9] = turtle_x;
Ypoints[9] = turtle_y;
step();
step();
step();
step();
Xpoints[10] = turtle_x;
Ypoints[10] = turtle_y;
step();
turn(90);
step();
Xpoints[11] = turtle_x;
Ypoints[11] = turtle_y;
step();
step();
step();
step();
```

```
Xpoints[12] = turtle_x;
Ypoints[12] = turtle_y;
step();
turn(90);
step();
Xpoints[13] = turtle_x;
Ypoints[13] = turtle_y;
step();
step();
step();
step();
Xpoints[14] = turtle_x;
Ypoints[14] = turtle_y;
step();
turn(90);
step();
Xpoints[15] = turtle_x;
Ypoints[15] = turtle_y;
step();
step();
step();
step();
Xpoints[16] = turtle_x;
Ypoints[16] = turtle_y;
step();
turn(-90);
step();
Xpoints[17] = turtle_x;
Ypoints[17] = turtle_y;
step();
step();
step();
step();
Xpoints[18] = turtle_x;
Ypoints[18] = turtle_y;
Xptemp = Xpoints[18];
Yptemp = Ypoints[18];
for (k=0; k<generator_size-1; k++)
{
    drawLine(Xpoints[k],Ypoints[k],
     Xpoints[k+1],Ypoints[k+1],15);
}
    }
}
```

Cesaro Triangle Curve

Figure 9-7(a) shows the very simple generator that will be used for the next few curves. The initiator in each case will be a horizontal straight line. The generator consists of two sides of a right isoceles triangle. Consequently, N=2 and r = 1/√2. Therefore, the fractal dimension is:

```
D = log 2 / log (√2) = 2     (Equation 9-2)
```

Depending upon the conditions which determine whether this generator is placed to the left or right of each line segment it replaces, many totally different curves can be produced. The first of these to be considered is the Cesaro triangle discovered by Ernest Cesaro in 1905. Figure 9-7(b) shows the first level of this curve. For any level of construction for this curve, the generator is placed to the right of each line segment at the top level, to the left of each line segment of the next lower level, to the right of each line segment of the next lower level, and so on.

Figure 9-7: Generator and First Level for Cesaro Curve

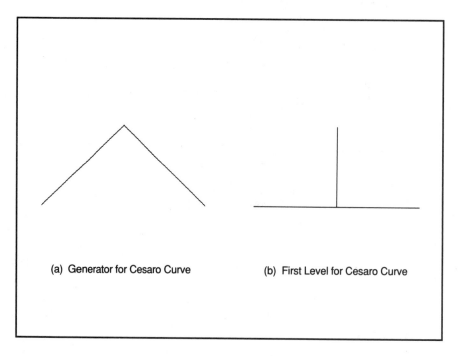

(a) Generator for Cesaro Curve   (b) First Level for Cesaro Curve

Figure 9-8: Cesaro Triangle Curves for Levels 2–12

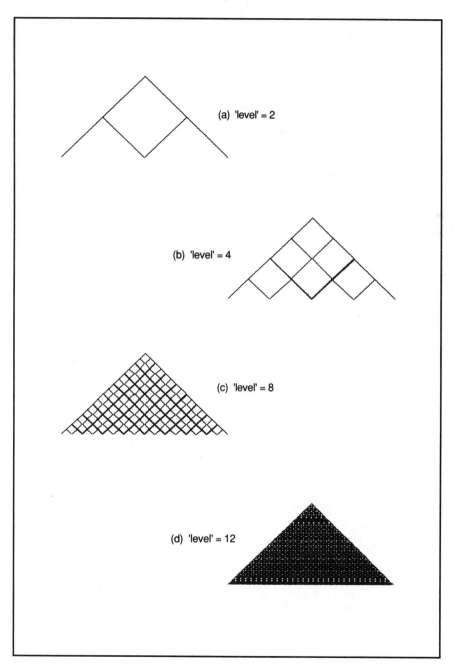

To do this in our program, we multiply the 90-degree turn angle in the generator by one of an array of *sign*. This parameter is set up at the beginning of the program to be +1 for the top level, and alternate in sign for each succeeding lower level. Figure 9-8 shows the resulting Cesaro triangles for levels 2, 4, 8, and 12. The program to generate this curve is listed in Figure 9-9.

Figure 9-9: Program to Generate Cesaro Triangle Curves

```
           cesaro3 = program to generate original cesaro curve
```

```c
#include <stdio.h>
#include <math.h>
#include <dos.h>
#include "tools.h"

void generate (float X1, float Y1, float X2, float Y2,
     int level);

int generator_size = 3;
int level;
int init_size = 1;
int initiator_x1[10] = {-150},initiator_x2[10]={150},
     initiator_y1[10]={0}, initiator_y2[10]={0};
int combination = 0,LINEWIDTH=1, OPERATOR=0;
unsigned long int PATTERN=0xFFFFFFFF;
float turtle_theta;
int i,sign[16],sign1=-1;
float Xpoints[25], Ypoints[25];
float turtle_x,turtle_y,turtle_r;

main()
{
    printf("\nEnter level (1 - 16): ");
    scanf("%d",&level);
    if (level < 1)
        level = 1;
    setMode(16);
    cls(0);
    for (i=level; i>=0; i--)
    {
        sign[i] = sign1;
        sign1 *= -1;
    }
    for (i=0; i<init_size; i++)
        generate(initiator_x1[i], initiator_y1[i],
```

```
              initiator_x2[i], initiator_y2[i], level);
    getch();
}
```

```
┌─────────────────────────────────────────────────────────────┐
│                                                               │
│                  generate() = generates curve                 │
│                                                               │
└─────────────────────────────────────────────────────────────┘
```

```
void generate (float X1, float Y1, float X2, float Y2,
    int level)
{
    int j,k,line;
    float a, b, Xpoints[25], Ypoints[25];

    level--;
    turtle_r = sqrt(((X2 - X1)*(X2 - X1) + (Y2 - Y1)*
        (Y2 - Y1)))/2.0;
    Xpoints[0] = X1;
    Ypoints[0] = Y1;
    Xpoints[2] = X2;
    Ypoints[2] = Y2;
    turtle_theta = point(X1,Y1,X2,Y2);
    turtle_x = X1;
    turtle_y = Y1;
    step();
    Xpoints[3] = turtle_x;
    Ypoints[3] = turtle_y;
    turn(90*sign[level]);
    step();
    Xpoints[1] = turtle_x;
    Ypoints[1] = turtle_y;
    if (level > 0)
    {
        for (j=0; j<generator_size-1; j++)
        {
            X1 = Xpoints[j];
            X2 = Xpoints[j+1];
            Y1 = Ypoints[j];
            Y2 = Ypoints[j+1];
            generate (X1,Y1,X2,Y2,level);
        }
    }
    else
    {
        drawLine(Xpoints[0],Ypoints[0],Xpoints[2],
            Ypoints[2],15);
        drawLine(Xpoints[1],Ypoints[1],Xpoints[3],
            Ypoints[3],15);
    }
}
```

Modified Cesaro Triangle Curve

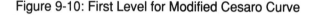

The Cesaro triangle curve described above is a little hard to trace because the line going out at right angles from the center of the original line segment actually retraces itself, but this is not observable in the drawings. A modification of the Cesaro curve is possible by changing the angle of the generator from 90 degrees to 85 degrees for the lowest level before drawing occurs. As with the modified Peano curve, this results in a curve whose fractal dimension is not quite 2, but which approaches 2 as a limit when the number of recursions approaches infinity. Figure 9-10 shows the first level for the modified Cesaro Triangle curve. Figure 9-11 shows the resulting curves for levels 2, 4, 8, and 12. The program to generate this curve is listed in Figure 9-9, with the generator function replaced by that listed in Figure 9-12.

Figure 9-10: First Level for Modified Cesaro Curve

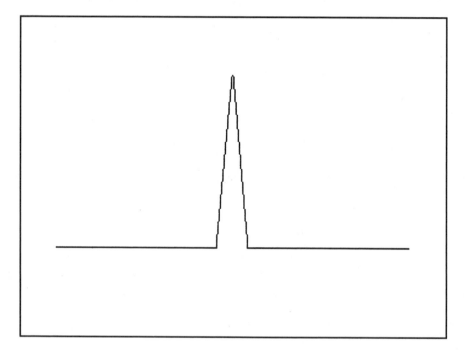

Figure 9-11: Modified Cesaro Triangle Curves for Levels 2–12

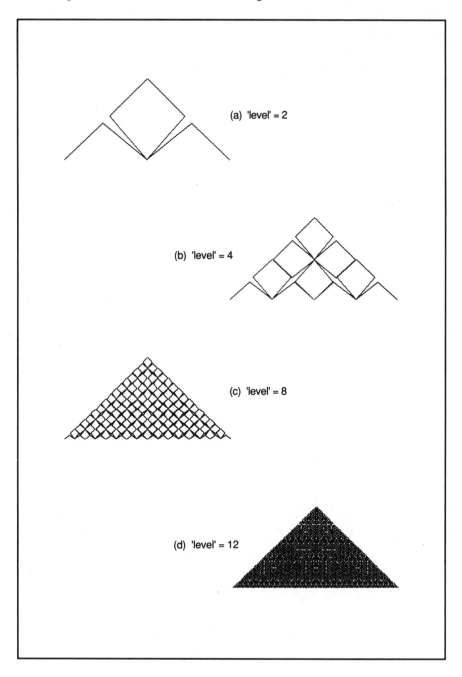

(a) 'level' = 2

(b) 'level' = 4

(c) 'level' = 8

(d) 'level' = 12

We've chosen a slightly different approach here than was used for the modified Peano curve. We generate the three points that are used in the unmodified generator and use them for each step in the recursion process. We also generate two additional points to locate the base of the 85-degree triangle of the two triangles for the first level, and use these points in drawing the actual curve.

Figure 9-12: Generator for Modified Cesaro Curves

```
               generate() = generates curve
```

```c
void generate (float X1, float Y1, float X2, float Y2,
    int level)
{
    int j,k,line;
    float a, b, Xpoints[25], Ypoints[25];

    level--;
    a = sqrt((((X2 - X1)*(X2 - X1) +
        (Y2 - Y1)*(Y2 - Y1)))/2.0;
    b = a * 0.9128442;
    turtle_r = b;
    Xpoints[0] = X1;
    Ypoints[0] = Y1;
    Xpoints[2] = X2;
    Ypoints[2] = Y2;
    turtle_theta = point(X1,Y1,X2,Y2);
    turtle_x = X1;
    turtle_y = Y1;
    step();
    Xpoints[3] = turtle_x;
    Ypoints[3] = turtle_y;
    turn(85*sign[level]);
    turtle_r = a;
    step();
    Xpoints[1] = turtle_x;
    Ypoints[1] = turtle_y;
    turn(-170*sign[level]);
    step();
    Xpoints[4] = turtle_x;
    Ypoints[4] = turtle_y;
    if (level > 0)
    {
        for (j=0; j<generator_size-1; j++)
        {
            X1 = Xpoints[j];
```

```
            X2 = Xpoints[j+1];
            Y1 = Ypoints[j];
            Y2 = Ypoints[j+1];
            generate (X1,Y1,X2,Y2,level);
        }
    }
    else
    {
        drawLine(Xpoints[0],Ypoints[0],Xpoints[3],
            Ypoints[3],15);
        drawLine(Xpoints[2],Ypoints[2],Xpoints[4],
            Ypoints[4],15);
        drawLine(Xpoints[3],Ypoints[3],Xpoints[1],
            Ypoints[1],15);
        drawLine(Xpoints[4],Ypoints[4],Xpoints[1],
            Ypoints[1],15);
    }
}
```

Variation on the Cesaro Curve

Suppose we start with a curve which has the same generator and the same first two levels as the Cesaro curve, but then uses a differing arrangement of placing the generator to the right and left of the original line segment as we go to higher levels. Many different curves can result. One of them is shown for levels 2, 4, 8, and 16 in Figure 9-13. The program that was used to generate these curves is listed in Figure 9-14. This can serve as a basis for your experimentation with various methods of arranging the generator to create a variety of interesting curves.

Figure 9-13: Variation of Cesaro Curves for Levels 2–16

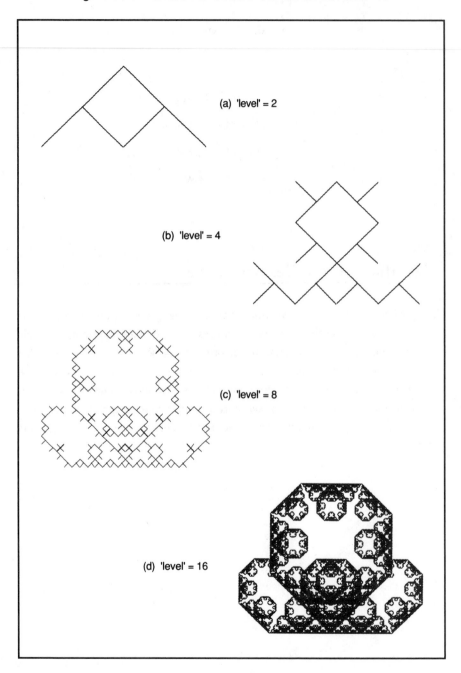

(a) 'level' = 2

(b) 'level' = 4

(c) 'level' = 8

(d) 'level' = 16

Figure 9-14: Program to Generate Variation of Cesaro Curve

```
cesaro1 = program to generate variation on cesaro curve
```

```c
#include <stdio.h>
#include <math.h>
#include <dos.h>
#include "tools.h"

void generate (float X1, float Y1, float X2, float Y2,
    int level,int sign);
int generator_size = 3;
int level;
int init_size = 1;
int initiator_x1[10] = {-150},initiator_x2[10]={150},
    initiator_y1[10]={0}, initiator_y2[10]={0};
int combination = 0,LINEWIDTH=1, OPERATOR=0;
unsigned long int PATTERN=0xFFFFFFFF;
float turtle_theta;
int i,sign=1;
float Xpoints[25], Ypoints[25];
float turtle_x,turtle_y,turtle_r;

main()
{
    printf("\nEnter level (1 - 16): ");
    scanf("%d",&level);
    if (level < 1)
        level = 1;
    setMode(16);
    cls(0);

    for (i=0; i<init_size; i++)
        generate(initiator_x1[i], initiator_y1[i],
            initiator_x2[i],initiator_y2[i], level,sign);
    getch();
}
```

```
generate() = generates curve
```

```c
void generate (float X1, float Y1, float X2, float Y2,
    int level, int sign)
{
    int j,k,line;
    float a, b, Xpoints[25], Ypoints[25];
```

```
level--;
turtle_r = sqrt((((X2 - X1)*(X2 - X1) + (Y2 - Y1)*
    (Y2 - Y1)))/2.0;
Xpoints[0] = X1;
Ypoints[0] = Y1;
Xpoints[2] = X2;
Ypoints[2] = Y2;
turtle_theta = point(X1,Y1,X2,Y2);
turtle_x = X1;
turtle_y = Y1;
step();
Xpoints[3] = turtle_x;
Ypoints[3] = turtle_y;
turn(90*sign);
step();
Xpoints[1] = turtle_x;
Ypoints[1] = turtle_y;
sign = -1;
if (level > 0)
{
    for (j=0; j<generator_size-1; j++)
    {
        X1 = Xpoints[j];
        X2 = Xpoints[j+1];
        Y1 = Ypoints[j];
        Y2 = Ypoints[j+1];
        generate (X1,Y1,X2,Y2,level,sign);
    }
}
else
{
    drawLine(Xpoints[0],Ypoints[0],Xpoints[2],
        Ypoints[2],15);
    drawLine(Xpoints[1],Ypoints[1],Xpoints[3],
        Ypoints[3],15);
}
}

        int init_size = 1;
        int initiator_x1[10] = {-150,150}, initiator_x2[10]=
            {150,-150}, initiator_y1[10]={-50},
            initiator_y2[10]={-50};
```

Polya Triangle Curve

This curve was discovered by George Polya, a professor at Stanford University. The initiator and generator are the same as for the Cesaro curve, but the positioning of the generator is different. Figure 9-15 shows the first and second levels of the curve. As with the Cesaro curve, the position of the first generator alternates from right to left beginning at the top level. For this curve, the position of the generator also alternates with each line segment of a particular level that is replaced. Figure 9-16 shows the resulting curve for levels of 4, 8, and 12. Figure 9-17 lists the program for generating the Polya curve. We use the same technique that was used for the Cesaro curve of having an array of *sign* variables, which are initiated at the beginning of the program. For this curve, we also modify the sign as we pass through the *generate* function. In Chapter 16, we shall discuss the Harter-Heightway dragon curve. Although it is included with the dragons, it is a member of the family of Peano curves discussed in this chapter. It has the same initiator, generator, and first stage as the Polya triangle curve, but then diverges.

Figure 9-15: First Two Levels for Polya Triangle Curve

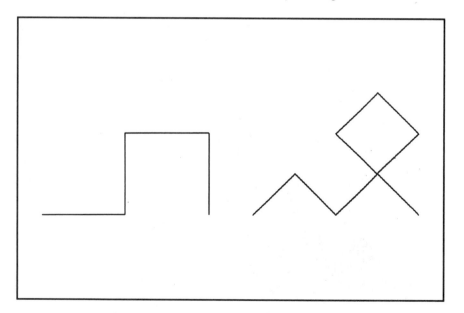

Figure 9-16: Polya Triangle Curves for Levels 4 to 12

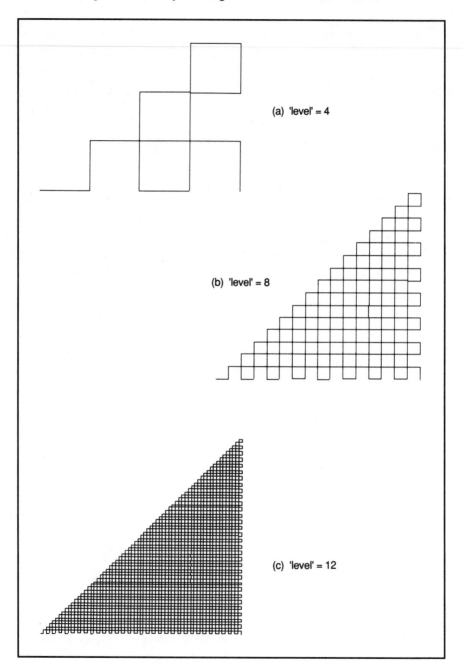

(a) 'level' = 4

(b) 'level' = 8

(c) 'level' = 12

Figure 9-17: Program to Generate Polya Curves

```
                    polya = program to generate polya curve
```

```c
#include <stdio.h>
#include <math.h>
#include <dos.h>
#include "tools.h"

void generate (float X1, float Y1, float X2, float Y2,
    int level);
int combination = 0,LINEWIDTH=1, OPERATOR=0;
unsigned long int PATTERN=0xFFFFFFFF;
float turtle_theta;
int i, sign1 =1;
int generator_size = 3;
int level;
int init_size = 2;
int sign[17];
int initiator_x1[10] = {-150},initiator_x2[10]={150},
    initiator_y1[10]={-75}, initiator_y2[10]={-75};
float Xpoints[25], Ypoints[25];
float turtle_x,turtle_y,turtle_r;

main()
{
    printf("\nEnter level (1 - 16): ");
    scanf("%d",&level);
    if (level < 1)
        level = 1;

    setMode(16);
    cls(0);
    for (i=level; i>0; i--)
    {
        sign[i] = sign1;
        sign1 *= -1;
    }
    for (i=0; i<init_size-1; i++)
    {
        generate(initiator_x1[i], initiator_y1[i],
            initiator_x2[i], initiator_y2[i], level);
    }
    getch();
}
```

179

```
┌─────────────────────────────────────────────────────────────┐
│                                                               │
│                  generate() = generates curve                 │
│                                                               │
└─────────────────────────────────────────────────────────────┘
```

```c
void generate (float X1, float Y1, float X2, float Y2,
    int level)
{
    int j,k,line;
    float a, b, Xpoints[25], Ypoints[25];
    turtle_r = (sqrt((X2 - X1)*(X2 - X1) + (Y2 - Y1)*
        (Y2 - Y1)))/1.41421;
    Xpoints[0] = X1;
    Ypoints[0] = Y1;
    Xpoints[2] = X2;
    Ypoints[2] = Y2;
    turtle_theta = point(X1,Y1,X2,Y2);
    turtle_x = X1;
    turtle_y = Y1;
    turn(sign[level]*(45));
    step();
    Xpoints[1] = turtle_x;
    Ypoints[1] = turtle_y;
    level--;
    if (level > 0)
    {
        for (j=0; j<generator_size-1; j++)
        {
            X1 = Xpoints[j];
            X2 = Xpoints[j+1];
            Y1 = Ypoints[j];
            Y2 = Ypoints[j+1];
            generate (X1,Y1,X2,Y2,level);
            sign[level] *= -1;
        }

    }
    else
    {
        for (k=0; k<generator_size-1; k++)
        {
            drawLine(Xpoints[k],Ypoints[k],
            Xpoints[k+1],Ypoints[k+1],15);
        }
    }
}
```

The Peano-Gosper Curve

Figure 9-18 shows the generator for the Peano-Gosper curve and its associated grid of equilateral triangles. The geometry of the situation can easily be determined from this figure. There are seven line segments (N=7), and the length of each one is:

```
r = 1/√7                        (Equation 9-3)
```

The fractal dimension is

```
D = log 7 / log (√7) = 2    (Equation 9-4)
```

This curve has the interesting characteristic that it just fills the interior of the Gosper curve given in Chapter 6. Figure 9-19 shows the curves for levels 2, 3, and 4. The program for this curve is the generic program of Figure 6-6 with the generator replaced by that shown in Figure 9-20, and the following changes in the initializing conditions:

```
int generator_size = 8;
```

Figure 9-18: Generator for Peano-Gosper Curve

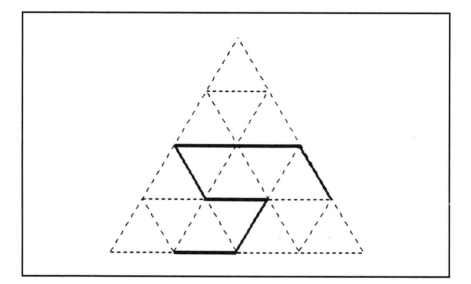

Figure 9-19: Peano-Gosper Curves for Levels 2 to 4

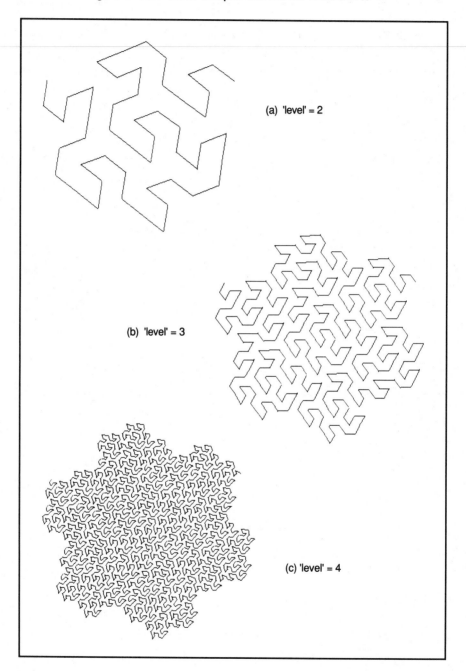

(a) 'level' = 2

(b) 'level' = 3

(c) 'level' = 4

Figure 9-20: Generator for Peano-Gosper Curve

```
                    generate() = generates curve
```

```c
void generate (float X1, float Y1, float X2, float Y2,
    int level, int type)
{
    int j,k,line,set_type;
    float a, b, Xpoints[25], Ypoints[25],sign=1, temp;

    switch (type)
    {
        case 0: break;

        case 1: sign *= -1;
                break;

        case 2: sign *= -1;
        case 3: temp = X1;
                X1 = X2;
                X2 = temp;
                temp = Y1;
                Y1 = Y2;
                Y2 = temp;
                break;
    }
    level--;
    turtle_r = (sqrt((X2 - X1)*(X2 - X1) + (Y2 - Y1)*
        (Y2 - Y1)))/2.6457513;
    Xpoints[0] = X1;
    Ypoints[0] = Y1;
    Xpoints[7] = X2;
    Ypoints[7] = Y2;
    turtle_theta = point(X1,Y1,X2,Y2);
    turn(-19*sign);
    turtle_x = X1;
    turtle_y = Y1;
    step();
    Xpoints[1] = turtle_x;
    Ypoints[1] = turtle_y;
    turn(60*sign);
    step();
    Xpoints[2] = turtle_x;
    Ypoints[2] = turtle_y;
    turn(120*sign);
    step();
    Xpoints[3] = turtle_x;
    Ypoints[3] = turtle_y;
```

```
turn(-60*sign);
step();
Xpoints[4] = turtle_x;
Ypoints[4] = turtle_y;
turn(-120*sign);
step();
Xpoints[5] = turtle_x;
Ypoints[5] = turtle_y;
step();
Xpoints[6] = turtle_x;
Ypoints[6] = turtle_y;
if (level > 0)
{
    for (j=0; j<generator_size-1; j++)
    {
        switch(j)
        {
            case 0:
            case 3:
            case 4:
            case 5:
                    set_type = 0;
                    break;
            case 2:
            case 1:
            case 6:
                    set_type = 3;
                    break;
        }
        X1 = Xpoints[j];
        X2 = Xpoints[j+1];
        Y1 = Ypoints[j];
        Y2 = Ypoints[j+1];
        generate (X1,Y1,X2,Y2,level,set_type);
    }
}
else
{
    for (k=0; k<generator_size-1; k++)
    {
        drawLine(Xpoints[k],Ypoints[k],
        Xpoints[k+1],Ypoints[k+1],15);
    }
}
}
```

We need to make use of a *generate* function which provides for specifying any of the four possible positions of the generator, as we did with several of the von Koch curves.

Peano Seven-Segment Snowflake

Figure 9-21 shows the generator and first stage of a Peano seven-segment snowflake curve, discovered by Mandelbrot. Note the similarity of the generator to that described under the heading "Complicated Generators" in Chapter 6. The only difference is that, where the generator of Chapter 6 used a smaller replica of the curve consisting of the first four line segments and then a line to the end to replace the fifth line segment, this curve does not. The result is that the fractal dimension is different. It is:

$$6(1/3)^D + (\sqrt{3}/3)^D = 1 \qquad \text{(Equation 9-5)}$$

which gives a fractal dimension of:

$$D = 2 \qquad \text{(Equation 9-6)}$$

Like the complicated generator of Chapter 6, there are four choices of generator position and they must be carefully selected for each level and each line segment to assure that the curve is not self-intersecting or self-overlapping. Figure 9-22 shows the curve for levels 2, 3, and 4. The program to generate this curve is given in Figure 9-23.

Figure 9-21: First Two Levels for Peano Seven-Segment Snowflake Curve

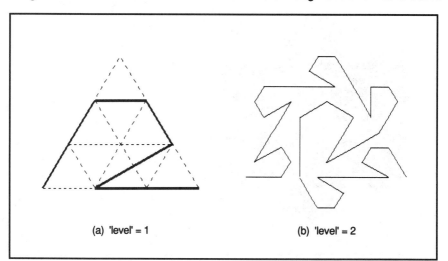

(a) 'level' = 1   (b) 'level' = 2

Figure 9-22: Peano Seven-Segment Snowflake Curves for Levels 2 to 4

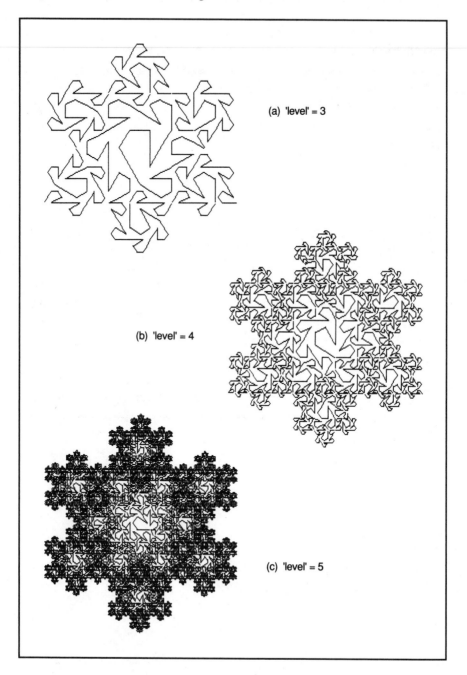

(a) 'level' = 3

(b) 'level' = 4

(c) 'level' = 5

Figure 9-23: Program to Generate Seven-Segment Snowflake

```
        snow7 = generates snowflake with 7 segment generator
```

```c
#include <stdio.h>
#include <math.h>
#include <dos.h>
#include "tools.h"

void generate (float X1, float Y1, float X2, float Y2,
    int level, int type, int sign);

int combination = 0,LINEWIDTH=1, OPERATOR=0;
unsigned long int PATTERN=0xFFFFFFFF;
int color,flag = 0,i,start_level;
int generator_size = 7;
int start_level,level;
int init_size = 1,sign = 1;
int initiator_x1[10] = {-125},initiator_x2[10]={125},
        initiator_y1[10]={0},initiator_y2[10]={0};
float Xpoints[25], Ypoints[25];
float turtle_x,turtle_y,turtle_r,turtle_theta;

main()
{
    printf("\nEnter level (1 - 8): ");
    scanf("%d",&level);
    if (level < 1)
        level = 1;
    start_level = level;
    setMode(16);
    cls(0);

    for (i=0; i<init_size; i++)
    {
        generate(initiator_x1[i], initiator_y1[i],
            initiator_x2[i], initiator_y2[i], level,0,
            sign);
    }
    getch();
}
```

```
                    generate() = generates curve
```

```c
void generate (float X1, float Y1, float X2, float Y2,
```

187

```
        int level, int type, int sign)
{
        int j,k,line,set_type;
        float a, b, Xpoints[25], Ypoints[25], temp,temp_r;

        switch (type)
        {
            case 0: break;

            case 1: sign *= -1;
                    break;

            case 2: sign *= -1;
            case 3: temp = X1;
                    X1 = X2;
                    X2 = temp;
                    temp = Y1;
                    Y1 = Y2;
                    Y2 = temp;
                    break;
        }
        level--;
        turtle_r = (sqrt((X2 - X1)*(X2 - X1) + (Y2 - Y1)*
            (Y2 - Y1)))/3.0;
        Xpoints[0] = X1;
        Ypoints[0] = Y1;
        Xpoints[7] = X2;
        Ypoints[7] = Y2;
        turtle_theta = point(X1,Y1,X2,Y2);
        turtle_x = X1;
        turtle_y = Y1;
        turn(60*sign);
        step();
        Xpoints[1] = turtle_x;
        Ypoints[1] = turtle_y;
        step();
        Xpoints[2] = turtle_x;
        Ypoints[2] = turtle_y;
        turn(-60*sign);
        step();
        Xpoints[3] = turtle_x;
        Ypoints[3] = turtle_y;
        turn(-60*sign);
        step();
        Xpoints[4] = turtle_x;
        Ypoints[4] = turtle_y;
        turn(-60*sign);
        step();
        Xpoints[6] = turtle_x;
        Ypoints[6] = turtle_y;
        turn(-60*sign);
```

```
step();
Xpoints[5] = turtle_x;
Ypoints[5] = turtle_y;
if (level == 0)
{
    for (k=0; k<generator_size; k++)
    {
        drawLine(Xpoints[k],Ypoints[k],
            Xpoints[k+1],Ypoints[k+1],15);
    }
}
else
{
    for (j=0; j<generator_size; j++)
    {
        switch(j)
        {
            case 5:
            case 0:
                    set_type = 1;
                    break;
            case 1:
            case 2:
            case 3:
            case 6:
                    set_type = 2;
                    break;
            case 4:
                    set_type = 3;
                    break;
        }
        X1 = Xpoints[j];
        X2 = Xpoints[j+1];
        Y1 = Ypoints[j];
        Y2 = Ypoints[j+1];
        generate (X1,Y1,X2,Y2,level,set_type,sign);
    }
}
}
```

Peano Thirteen-Segment Snowflake

Figure 9-24 shows the generator and first stage of a Peano thirteen-segment snowflake curve which was also discovered by Mandelbrot. This generator is obtained by replacing the fifth line segment of the generator in Figure 9-21 with a smaller replica of the entire generator of Figure 9-21. To determine the fractal dimension of this curve, we note that Equation 9-5 applied to the curve of the previous section, and that the length of the line segment being replaced was 1. Thus, the fractal dimension is unchanged when this curve is substituted for a line segment, and the fractal dimension of the thirteen-segment snowflake is still 2. More generally, we ought to be able to substitute a generator for any line segment of the original generator and still keep the fractal dimension unchanged.

For this curve also, there are four choices of generator position which must be carefully selected for each level and each line segment to assure that the curve is not self-intersecting or self-overlapping. Figure 9-25 shows the curve for levels of 2, 3, and 4. The program to generate the thirteen-segment curve is listed in Figure 9-26.

Figure 9-24: First Two Levels for Peano Thirteen-Segment
Snowflake Curve

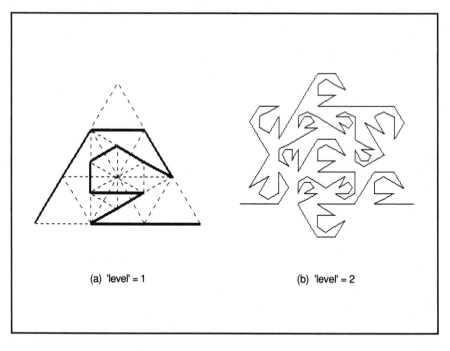

(a) 'level' = 1   (b) 'level' = 2

Figure 9-25: Peano Thirteen-Segment Snowflake Curves for Levels 3 to 5

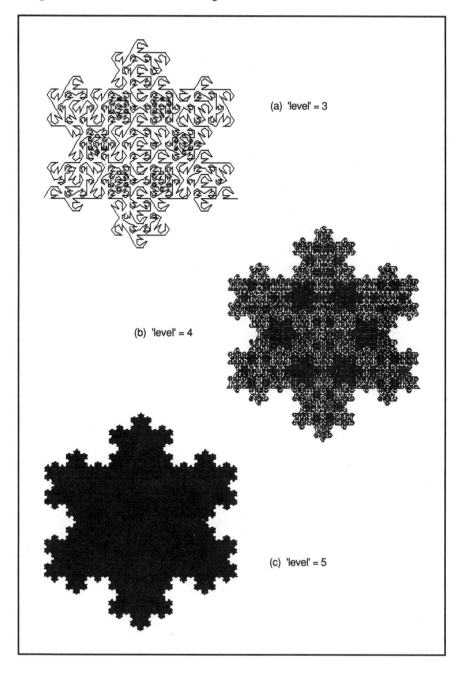

(a) 'level' = 3

(b) 'level' = 4

(c) 'level' = 5

Figure 9-26: Program to Generate Thirteen-Segment Snowflake

```
    snow13 = generates snowflake with 13-segment generator
```

```c
#include <stdio.h>
#include <math.h>
#include <dos.h>
#include "tools.h"

void generate (float X1, float Y1, float X2, float Y2,
    int level, int type, int sign);

int combination = 0,LINEWIDTH=1, OPERATOR=0;
unsigned long int PATTERN=0xFFFFFFFF;
int color,flag = 0,i,start_level;
int generator_size = 13;
int start_level,level;
int init_size = 1,sign = 1;
int initiator_x1[10] = {-125},initiator_x2[10]={125},
    initiator_y1[10]={0},initiator_y2[10]={0};
float Xpoints[25], Ypoints[25];
float turtle_x,turtle_y,turtle_r,
    turtle_theta;

main()
{
    printf("\nEnter level (1 - 8): ");
    scanf("%d",&level);
    if (level < 1)
        level = 1;
    start_level = level;
    setMode(16);
    cls(0);

    for (i=0; i<init_size; i++)
    {
        generate(initiator_x1[i], initiator_y1[i],
            initiator_x2[i], initiator_y2[i], level,0,
            sign);
    }
    getch();
}
```

```
┌─────────────────────────────────────────────────────────────┐
│                                                               │
│               generate() = generates curve                    │
│                                                               │
└─────────────────────────────────────────────────────────────┘
```

```
void generate (float X1, float Y1, float X2, float Y2,
    int level, int type, int sign)
{
    int j,k,line,set_type;
    float a, b, Xpoints[25], Ypoints[25], temp,temp_r;


    switch (type)
    {
        case 0: break;

        case 1: sign *= -1;
                break;

        case 2: sign *= -1;
        case 3: temp = X1;
                X1 = X2;
                X2 = temp;
                temp = Y1;
                Y1 = Y2;
                Y2 = temp;
                break;
    }
    level--;
    turtle_r = (sqrt((X2 - X1)*(X2 - X1) + (Y2 - Y1)*
        (Y2 - Y1)))/3.0;
    Xpoints[0] = X1;
    Ypoints[0] = Y1;
    Xpoints[13] = X2;
    Ypoints[13] = Y2;
    turtle_theta = point(X1,Y1,X2,Y2);
    turtle_x = X1;
    turtle_y = Y1;
    turn(60*sign);
    step();
    Xpoints[1] = turtle_x;
    Ypoints[1] = turtle_y;
    step();
    Xpoints[2] = turtle_x;
    Ypoints[2] = turtle_y;
    turn(-60*sign);
    step();
    Xpoints[3] = turtle_x;
    Ypoints[3] = turtle_y;
    turn(-60*sign);
    step();
    Xpoints[4] = turtle_x;
```

```
Ypoints[4] = turtle_y;
turn(-60*sign);
step();
Xpoints[12] = turtle_x;
Ypoints[12] = turtle_y;
turn(-60*sign);
step();
Xpoints[11] = turtle_x;
Ypoints[11] = turtle_y;
turtle_r = (sqrt((Xpoints[11] - Xpoints[4])*
    (Xpoints[11] - Xpoints[4]) + (Ypoints[11] -
    Ypoints[4])*(Ypoints[11] - Ypoints[4])))/3.0;
turtle_theta = point(Xpoints[4],Ypoints[4],
    Xpoints[11],Ypoints[11]);
turtle_x = Xpoints[4];
turtle_y = Ypoints[4];
turn(-60*sign);
step();
Xpoints[5] = turtle_x;
Ypoints[5] = turtle_y;
step();
Xpoints[6] = turtle_x;
Ypoints[6] = turtle_y;
turn(60*sign);
step();
Xpoints[7] = turtle_x;
Ypoints[7] = turtle_y;
turn(60*sign);
step();
Xpoints[8] = turtle_x;
Ypoints[8] = turtle_y;
turn(60*sign);
step();
Xpoints[10] = turtle_x;
Ypoints[10] = turtle_y;
turn(60*sign);
step();
Xpoints[9] = turtle_x;
Ypoints[9] = turtle_y;
if (level == 0)
{
    for (k=0; k<generator_size; k++)
    {
        drawLine(Xpoints[k],Ypoints[k],
        Xpoints[k+1],Ypoints[k+1],15);
    }
}
else
{
    for (j=0; j<generator_size; j++)
    {
```

```
switch(j)
{
    case 1:
    case 2:
    case 3:
    case 4:
    case 8:
    case 9:
    case 12:
            set_type = 0;
            break;
    case 0:
    case 5:
    case 6:
    case 7:
    case 10:
    case 11:
            set_type = 1;
            break;
}
X1 = Xpoints[j];
X2 = Xpoints[j+1];
Y1 = Ypoints[j];
Y2 = Ypoints[j+1];
generate (X1,Y1,X2,Y2,level,set_type,sign);
    }
  }
}
```

10

The Hilbert Curve

The Hilbert curve is one of the Peano family of curves but it has some subtle differences that make it unique. Figure 10-1 shows the generator and the next level of the Hilbert curve. Since we're used to pretty straightforward application of the generator to the line segments of the initiator or previous level of the curve, it may be quite difficult to visualize what is happening with the Hilbert curve. The parameters that we use are:

$$r = 1/2 \qquad\qquad \text{(Equation 10-1)}$$

and

$$N = 4 \qquad\qquad \text{(Equation 10-2)}$$

In other words, the line segment of the generator is one-half of the line segment to which it is being applied and the generator is applied four times. But to make things more complex, each time that we go to a lower level to run the generator program, we return to the next higher level and draw a line with the same length being used at the lower level. This sounds a little complex. Try tracing it out on Figure 10-1(b). Each time you run the generator program, you have to make sure that it has the proper orientation for the curve to come out correctly.

Starting at the lower right of Figure 10-1(a) we use the generator, then draw a line segment to the left, use the generator again, draw a line segment up, use the generator again, draw a line segment to the right, and then use the generator one final time.

Figure 10-1: Generator and Second Level for Hilbert Curve

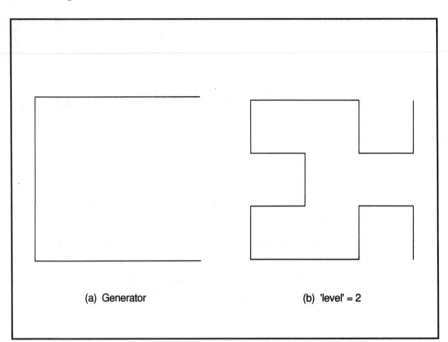

(a) Generator   (b) 'level' = 2

Generating the Hilbert Curve

All of the above becomes quite clear from the program listing of Figure 10-2. This program is quite similar to the generic initiator/generator program of Chapter 8, but since all of our steps are in the $\pm x$ or $\pm y$ directions, we don't use the turtle graphics to keep track of direction but simply step in the proper direction at each operation. You will note that at each level of *generate* except the lowest, we call *generate* recursively a number of times and also draw line segments of the proper length between calls to *generate*. The resulting curves for levels from 3 to 6 are shown in Figure 10-3.

Figure 10-2: Program to Generate Hilbert Curve

hilbert = program to generate Hilbert curves

```
#include <stdio.h>
#include <math.h>
#include <dos.h>
#include "tools.h"

void generate (float r1, float r2);

int level,sign=-1;
int combination = 0,LINEWIDTH=1, OPERATOR=0;
unsigned long int PATTERN=0xFFFFFFFF;
int i;
float x1,x2,y1,y2,r;

main()
{
    float temp;

    printf("Enter level: ");
    scanf ("%d",&level);
    setMode(16);
    cls(0);
    r = 400/(pow(2,level));
    x1 = -200;
    y1 = -200;
    x2 = -200;
    y2 = -200;
    generate(r,0);
    getch();
}
```

```
                    generate() = generates curve
```

```c
void generate (float r1, float r2)
{

    level--;
    if (level > 0)
        generate(r2,r1);
    x2 += r1;
    y2 += r2;
    drawLine(x1,y1,x2,y2,15);
    x1 = x2;
    y1 = y2;
    if (level > 0)
        generate(r1,r2);
    x2 += r2;
    y2 += r1;
    drawLine(x1,y1,x2,y2,15);
    x1 = x2;
    y1 = y2;
    if (level > 0)
        generate(r1,r2);
    x2 -= r1;
    y2 -= r2;
    drawLine(x1,y1,x2,y2,15);
    x1 = x2;
    y1 = y2;
    if (level > 0)
        generate(-r2,-r1);
    level++;
}
```

It is worth noting that there is an entirely different way to generate the Hilbert curve. The program to do this is listed in Figure 10-4. It makes use of four separate functions to do the generate tasks, and, although elegant, tends to obscure what is going on.

Figure 10-3: Hilbert Curve for Levels 3 to 6

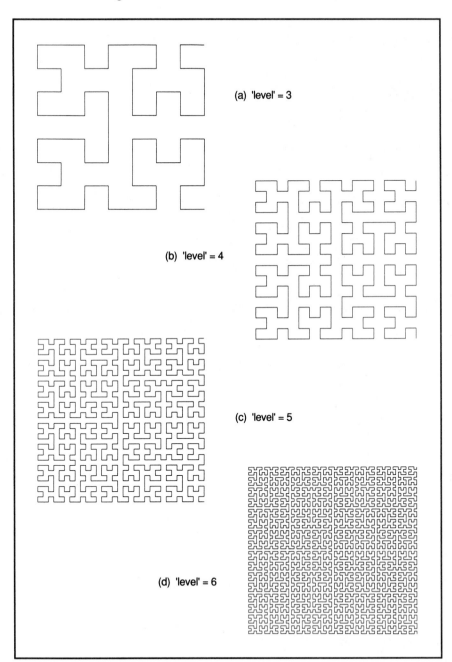

(a) 'level' = 3

(b) 'level' = 4

(c) 'level' = 5

(d) 'level' = 6

Figure 10-4: Alternate Program to Draw Hilbert Curve

```
                hilbert = program to generate Hilbert curves
```

```c
#include <stdio.h>
#include <math.h>
#include <dos.h>
#include "tools.h"

void gen1(int i);
void gen2(int i);
void gen3(int i);
void gen4(int i);

int combination = 0,LINEWIDTH=1, OPERATOR=0;
unsigned long int PATTERN=0xFFFFFFFF;
int xa=0,ya=0, x,y,old_x,old_y, i,j,h=448;
int level;

main()
{
    printf("\nEnter level (1 - 8): ");
    scanf("%d",&level);
    if (level < 1)
        level = 1;
    setMode(16);
    cls(0);

    for (i=1; i<=level; i++)
    {
        h /=2;
        x += h/2;
        y += h/2;
        old_x = x;
        old_y = y;
    }
    gen1(level);
    getch();
}

void gen1(int i)
{
    if(i > 0)
    {
        gen4(i-1);
        x -= h;
        drawLine(old_x,old_y,x,y,15);
        old_x = x;
```

```
        old_y = y;
        gen1(i-1);
        y -= h;
        drawLine(old_x,old_y,x,y,15);
        old_x = x;
        old_y = y;
        gen1(i-1);
        x += h;
        drawLine(old_x,old_y,x,y,15);
        old_x = x;
        old_y = y;
        gen2(i-1);
    }
}

void gen2(int i)
{
    if (i > 0)
    {
        gen3(i-1);
        y += h;
        drawLine(old_x,old_y,x,y,15);
        old_x = x;
        old_y = y;
        gen2(i-1);
        x += h;
        drawLine(old_x,old_y,x,y,15);
        old_x = x;
        old_y = y;
        gen2(i-1);
        y -= h;
        drawLine(old_x,old_y,x,y,15);
        old_x = x;
        old_y = y;
        gen1(i-1);
    }
}

void gen3(int i)
{
    if (i > 0)
    {
        gen2(i-1);
        x += h;
        drawLine(old_x,old_y,x,y,15);
        old_x = x;
        old_y = y;
        gen3(i-1);
        y += h;
        drawLine(old_x,old_y,x,y,15);
        old_x = x;
```

```
        old_y = y;
        gen3(i-1);
        x -= h;
        drawLine(old_x,old_y,x,y,15);
        old_x = x;
        old_y = y;
        gen4(i-1);
    }
}

void gen4(int i)
{
    if (i > 0)
    {
        gen1(i-1);
        y -= h;
        drawLine(old_x,old_y,x,y,15);
        old_x = x;
        old_y = y;
        gen4(i-1);
        x -= h;
        drawLine(old_x,old_y,x,y,15);
        old_x = x;
        old_y = y;
        gen4(i-1);
        y += h;
        drawLine(old_x,old_y,x,y,15);
        old_x = x;
        old_y = y;
        gen3(i-1);
    }
}
```

Fractal Dimension of the Hilbert Curve

If you take a close look at the Hilbert curve, it is evident that after a sufficiently large number of iterations, it will pass through every point in the plane. Going back to the formula for fractal dimension, we have:

$$D = \log(4) / \log(2) = 2 \qquad\qquad \text{(Equation 10-2)}$$

This confirms that the Hilbert curve is a Peano Curve and that it passes through every point on the plane.

Hilbert Curve in Three Dimensions

The Hilbert curve can also be drawn in higher dimensions, but it becomes rather difficult to determine the proper orientations of the generator to assure that every point is covered without duplication. Figure 10-5 shows the second level of a three-dimensional curve. The program to draw these two displays is listed in Figure 10-6. This program breaks down for higher levels, since we haven't found the proper orientations to insert to assure that they would be correct. You're welcome to hunt for these if you want to, but they aren't obvious.

Figure 10-5: Three-Dimensional Hilbert Curve

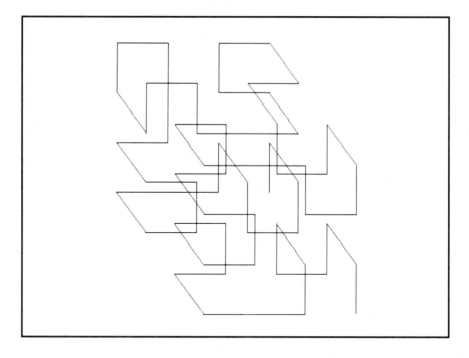

Figure 10-6: Program to Draw Three-Dimensional Hilbert Curve

```
hil3d = program to generate 30 Hilbert curves
```

```c
#include <stdio.h>
#include <math.h>
#include <dos.h>
#include <stdlib.h>
#include "tools.h"
void generate (int a, int b, int c);

int level,max_level;
int combination = 0,LINEWIDTH=1, OPERATOR=0;
unsigned long int PATTERN=0xFFFFFFFF;
int i;
float point[3],x1,x2,y-one,y2,r;
float x_angle = -55, y_angle = 90, z_angle = 0,cx,cy,cz,sx,
    sy,sz;

main()
{
    printf("Enter level: ");
    scanf ("%d",&level);
    max_level = level;
    setMode(16);
    cls(0);
    sx = sin(x_angle*.017453292);
    sy = sin(y_angle*.017453292);
    sz = sin(z_angle*.017453292);
    cx = cos(x_angle*.017453292);
    cy = cos(y_angle*.017453292);
    cz = cos(z_angle*.017453292);

    r = 300/(pow(2,level));
    point[0] = -200;
    point[1] = 50;
    point[2] = 0;
    generate(3,-2,1);
    getch();
}
```

```
generate() = generates curve
```

```c
void generate (int a, int b, int c)
{
```

```
int sign[3] = {1,1,1};

level--;
if (a < 0)
    sign[0] = -1;
a = abs(a)-1;
if (b < 0)
    sign[1] = -1;
b = abs(b)-1;
if (c < 0)
    sign[2] = -1;
c = abs(c)-1;
x1 = point[0]*cx + point[1]*cy + point[2]*cz;
y-one = point[0]*sx + point[1]*sy + point[2]*sz;
if (level > 0)
    generate(-2,1,3);
point[a] += (r*sign[0]);
x2 = point[0]*cx + point[1]*cy + point[2]*cz;
y2 = point[0]*sx + point[1]*sy + point[2]*sz;
drawLine(x1,y1,x2,y2,15);
x1 = point[0]*cx + point[1]*cy + point[2]*cz;
y-one = point[0]*sx + point[1]*sy + point[2]*sz;
if (level > 0)
    generate(3,1,-2);
point[b] += (r*sign[1]);
x2 = point[0]*cx + point[1]*cy + point[2]*cz;
y2 = point[0]*sx + point[1]*sy + point[2]*sz;
drawLine(x1,y1,x2,y2,15);
x1 = point[0]*cx + point[1]*cy + point[2]*cz;
y-one = point[0]*sx + point[1]*sy + point[2]*sz;
if (level > 0)
    generate(3,1,-2);
point[a] -= (r*sign[0]);
x2 = point[0]*cx + point[1]*cy + point[2]*cz;
y2 = point[0]*sx + point[1]*sy + point[2]*sz;
drawLine(x1,y1,x2,y2,15);
x1 = point[0]*cx + point[1]*cy + point[2]*cz;
y-one = point[0]*sx + point[1]*sy + point[2]*sz;
if (level > 0)
    generate(2,-3,1);
point[c] += (r*sign[2]);
x2 = point[0]*cx + point[1]*cy + point[2]*cz;
y2 = point[0]*sx + point[1]*sy + point[2]*sz;
drawLine(x1,y1,x2,y2,15);
x1 = point[0]*cx + point[1]*cy + point[2]*cz;
y-one = point[0]*sx + point[1]*sy + point[2]*sz;
if (level > 0)
    generate(-3,1,2);
point[a] += (r*sign[0]);
x2 = point[0]*cx + point[1]*cy + point[2]*cz;
y2 = point[0]*sx + point[1]*sy + point[2]*sz;
```

```
    drawLine(x1,y1,x2,y2,15);
    x1 = point[0]*cx + point[1]*cy + point[2]*cz;
    y-one = point[0]*sx + point[1]*sy + point[2]*sz;
    if (level > 0)
        generate(-2,3,1);
    point[b] -= (r*sign[1]);
    x2 = point[0]*cx + point[1]*cy + point[2]*cz;
    y2 = point[0]*sx + point[1]*sy + point[2]*sz;
    drawLine(x1,y1,x2,y2,15);
    x1 = point[0]*cx + point[1]*cy + point[2]*cz;
    y-one = point[0]*sx + point[1]*sy + point[2]*sz;
    if (level > 0)
        generate(3,-1,2);
    point[a] -= (r*sign[0]);
    x2 = point[0]*cx + point[1]*cy + point[2]*cz;
    y2 = point[0]*sx + point[1]*sy + point[2]*sz;
    drawLine(x1,y1,x2,y2,15);
    x1 = point[0]*cx + point[1]*cy + point[2]*cz;
    y-one = point[0]*sx + point[1]*sy + point[2]*sz;
    if (level > 0)
        generate(-2,-1,-3);
    level++;
}
```

Using the Hilbert Curve for Display Data Storage

In Chapter 4, we looked at a program for compressing display information and
storing it in a disk file for recovery and redisplay at a later time. The run length
encoding method substantially compressed the data file by requiring only two
bytes to define up to 63 pixels in a color plane if they are all alike. This is not
the optimum run length recording for two reasons. The first is that we are limited to 63 pixels because we only allowed six bits to define the number of pixels
affected. This was done to allow the two most significant bits to be a flag that
indicates that the byte represents a number rather than a data byte. This whole
scheme, in this case, is constrained by the fact that we are trying to work with
bytes; in a word oriented system, we would have more bits available to work
with. The second reason that we don't have optimum compression is that we
record one line at a time from each of the three color planes. Even if there is a
large block of the same color, it is unlikely that the pixel data from one color
plane line will be the same as that from the next.

Now suppose that the color data is represented by a three-dimensional volume in which the x and y dimensions are the same as they were for the display, but the third dimension represents color. We would like to record this as a long string in a single file. One way to do this is to scan through each plane, line by line. But, as pointed out above, when we move from one line to the next, any continuity of color data that might let us use maximum run length compression is lost. What we need is a way of scanning through the three-dimensional space that will give us a one-dimensional result in which points that were close together in the original space will still be close together on the resulting line. Thus a block of a single color on the original display will be lumped together on the resulting line and is suitable for compression to a few bytes.

The Hilbert curve performs exactly this function. It scans an n dimensional surface and reduces it to a one-dimensional line, and it has the characteristic that points that are close together on the n-dimensional surface are close together on the resulting line. Of course, there is some loss of information on the closeness of points because a single dimension cannot possibly have the same degree of spatial associativity that can be achieved with a higher dimension of space. However, this loss is minimal compared with other techniques that might be used for transforming the data. F. H. Preston, A. F. Lehar, and R. J. Stevens of the S. R. D. B. Home Office in England have developed algorithms for using the Hilbert curve to map image data and for compressing the resulting information. They insist on calling the Hilbert curve a *Peano Curve*, which is unfortunate, since, as we have already discovered, there is a whole family of Peano curves, of which the Hilbert curve is only a single specific type. They have published several papers on their results, one of which is referenced in the bibliography of this book.

11

The Sierpinski Curve

The Sierpinski curve is particularly interesting because there are several ways of generating it that seem to start with quite different premises but end up producing essentially the same curve and also because it has practical uses for space-filling required by clustering algorithms used in route optimization.

We are most familiar with the first method of generating the Sierpinski triangle, namely the use of the initiator/generator technique first described in Chapter 8. For this curve, the initiator is a straight line. The generator for the curve and the resulting curve for levels two and three are shown in Figure 11-1. Curves for levels four, six, and eight are shown in Figure 11-2. It's not a very good idea to carry the curve to higher levels than eight, since the triangles begin to fill in too much and detail is lost. The program to generate the Sierpinski triangle is listed in Figure 11-3.

Figure 11-1: Sierpinski Triangles

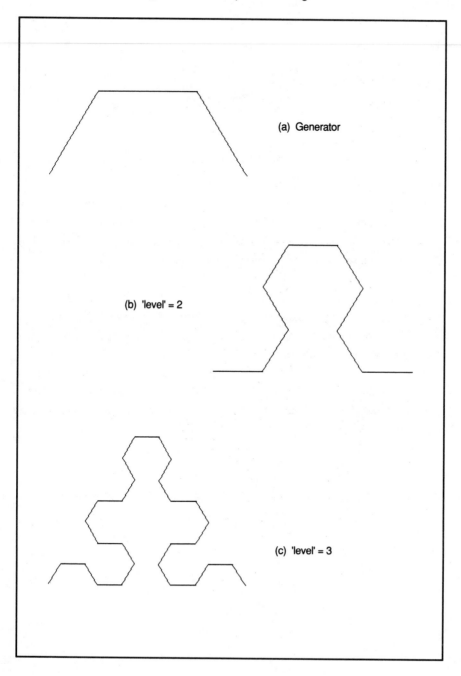

(a) Generator

(b) 'level' = 2

(c) 'level' = 3

Figure 11-2: Higher Levels of Sierpinski Triangles

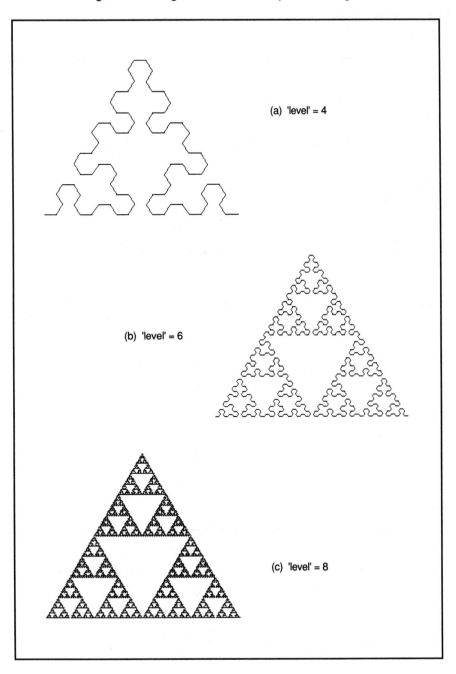

(a) 'level' = 4

(b) 'level' = 6

(c) 'level' = 8

Figure 11-3: Program to Generate Sierpinski Triangles

```
                sierp = program to generate sierpinski curves
```

```c
#include <stdio.h>
#include <math.h>
#include <dos.h>
#include "tools.h"

void generate (float X1, float Y1, float X2, float Y2,
    int level,int sign);
int generator_size = 3;
int init_size = 1;
int level;
int initiator_x1[10] = {-130,130,130,-130}, initiator_x2[10]=
    {130,130,-130,-130}, initiator_y1[10]={0,130,130,-130,
    -130}, initiator_y2[10]={0,130,-130,-130,130};
int combination = 0,LINEWIDTH=1, OPERATOR=0;
unsigned long int PATTERN=0xFFFFFFFF;
int i, sign;
float Xpoints[25], Ypoints[25],x1,x2,y1,y2;
float turtle_x,turtle_y,turtle_r,angle,turtle_theta;

main()
{
    setMode(3);
    printf("\nEnter level (1 - 12): ");
    scanf("%d",&level);
    if (level < 1)
        level = 1;
    setMode(16);
    cls(0);
    for (i=0; i<init_size; i++)
        generate(initiator_x1[i], initiator_y1[i],
            initiator_x2[i],initiator_y2[i], level,1);
    getch();
}
```

```
                        generate() = generates curve
```

```c
void generate (float X1, float Y1, float X2, float Y2,
    int level,int sign)
{
    int j,k,line,int_sign;
    float a, b, Xpoints[25], Ypoints[25], temp,temp_r;
    turtle_r = sqrt((X2 - X1)*(X2 - X1) + (Y2 - Y1)*
```

```
        (Y2 - Y1))/2.0;
    turtle_x = X1;
    turtle_y = Y1;
    Xpoints[0] = X1;
    Ypoints[0] = Y1;
    Xpoints[3] = X2;
    Ypoints[3] = Y2;
    turtle_theta = point(X1,Y1,X2,Y2);
    turn(60*sign);
    step();
    Xpoints[1] = turtle_x;
    Ypoints[1] = turtle_y;
    turn(-60*sign);
    step();
    Xpoints[2] = turtle_x;
    Ypoints[2] = turtle_y;
    level--;
    sign *= -1;
    if (level == 0)
    {
        for (k=0; k<generator_size; k++)
        {
            drawLine(Xpoints[k],Ypoints[k],Xpoints[k+1],
                Ypoints[k+1],15);
        }
    }
    else
    {
        int_sign = sign;
        for (j=0; j<generator_size; j++)
        {
            X1 = Xpoints[j];
            X2 = Xpoints[j+1];
            Y1 = Ypoints[j];
            Y2 = Ypoints[j+1];
            generate (X1,Y1,X2,Y2,level,int_sign);
            int_sign *= -1;
        }
    }
}
```

Sierpinski Gasket

Looking at the triangle of Figure 11-2(c), you'll see that this curve could be produced by starting with one big filled-in triangle and cutting out smaller and smaller ones from it in appropriate places. This is the technique that is used in the program listed in Figure 11-4.

Figure 11-4: Program to Generate Sierpinski Gasket

```
        siergask = program to generate sierpinski triangle gasket
```

```c
#include <stdio.h>
#include <math.h>
#include <dos.h>
#include "tools.h"

void node(int x1, int y01, int x2, int y2, int x3, int y3,
    int x4, int y4, int x5, int y5, int x6, int y6,
    int level,int length);
void sort(int index, int x_coord[], int y_coord[]);
void fillTriangle (int x1, int y01, int x2, int y2,
    int x3, int y3, int color);
void generate (int x1, int y01, int x2, int y2, int x3,
    int y3,int level, int length);
int x1,y01,x2,y2,x3,y3,i,level = 5;
int combination = 0,LINEWIDTH=1, OPERATOR=0;
unsigned long int PATTERN=0xFFFFFFFF;
float turtle_theta;

main()
{
    int x1,x2,x3,y01,y2,y3,length;
    x1 = -256;
    y01 = -220;
    x2 = 256;
    y2 = -220;
    x3 = 0;
    y3 = 223;
    length = 512;
    setMode(16);
    cls(0);
    fillTriangle(x1,y01,x2,y2,x3,y3,15);
    generate(x1,y01,x2,y2,x3,y3,level,length);
    getch();
}
```

```
┌─────────────────────────────────────────────────────────────┐
│                                                               │
│    generate() = splits triangle into four small triangles     │
│                                                               │
└─────────────────────────────────────────────────────────────┘
```

```
void generate (int x1,int y01, int x2, int y2, int x3,
    int y3, int level, int length)
{
    int line_length,x4,y4,x5,y5,x6,y6;
    line_length = length/2;
    x4 = x1 + line_length;
    y4 = y01;
    x5 = x1 + line_length/2;
    y5 = y1 + 1.732*line_length/2;
    x6 = x5 + line_length;
    y6 = y5;
    node (x1,y01,x2,y2,x3,y3,x4,y4,x5,y5,x6,y6,level,
        line_length);
}
```

```
┌─────────────────────────────────────────────────────────────┐
│                                                               │
│       node() = blanks center triangle and calls 'generate'    │
│                    for three surrounding triangles            │
│                                                               │
└─────────────────────────────────────────────────────────────┘
```

```
void node(int x1, int y01, int x2, int y2, int x3, int y3,
    int x4,int y4, int x5, int y5, int x6, int y6,
    int level,int length)
{
    fillTriangle(x4,y4,x5,y5,x6,y6,0);
    if (level == 0)
        return(0);
    generate (x1,y01,x4,y4,x5,y5,level-1,length);
    generate (x4,y4,x2,y2,x6,y6,level-1,length);
    generate (x5,y5,x6,y6,x3,y3,level-1,length);
}
```

We first create and fill a large triangle, using the function *fill_triangle*. Once the triangle is drawn and filled, the program calls the function *generate*, which divides the triangle into four smaller ones. The 'generate' function then calls the function *node*. This function blanks out the center triangle (by using the function *fillTriangle* with the color black) and then calls *generate* (in a recursion process) to operate upon the three peripheral triangles. The procedure continues to whatever level you have entered into the parameter *level*. Note that the technique of removing triangles has a drawback: if you use too high a level, there is insufficient display resolution to preserve the colored portions of the display and the entire original triangle is eventually blanked out. The program to perform this operation is listed in Figure 11-4. The resulting Sierpinski triangle is shown in Figure 11-5. The third method of generating the Sierpinski triangle is through the use of iterated function systems as explained in Chapter 22. A very short and simple code describes the triangle to the IFS and results in a good representation being drawn. For further details, refer to Chapter 22.

Figure 11-5: Sierpinski Gasket

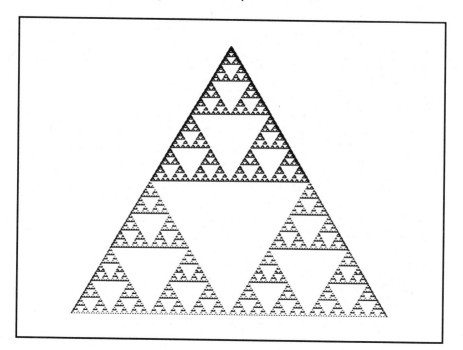

Another Method of Generating the Sierpinski Triangle

There is another method of generating the Sierpinski triangle that makes use of an algorithm similar to that used for generating strange attractors in Chapter 6 and for IFS systems in Chapter 22. The program listing is given in Figure 11-6. It starts out with a point at a random location on the screen, then randomly selects one of three transformations. The first simply creates a new point at half the x and y coordinates of the previous point. The second creates a new point whose *x* coordinate is the previous *x* plus 639 (distance across the display) divided by two, and whose *y* coordinate is half the previous *y* coordinate value. The third transformation creates a new point whose *x* coordinate is the previous *x* plus 320 (half the distance across the display) divided by two, and whose *y* coordinate is the previous *y* coordinate plus 349 (distance down the display) divided by two. The result of plotting 120,000 points is the Sierpinski triangle, as shown in Figure 11-7(a).

Figure 11-6: Another Program to Generate the Sierpinski Triangle

```
            sirchet3 = program to generate Sierpinski
                     triangle with chaos algorithm
```

```
#include <stdio.h>
#include <math.h>
#include <stdlib.h>
#include "tools.h"
float s2,x,y;
int switcher;
long int i;

main()
{
    setMode(16);
    x = 32767/639;
    x = random( )/x;
    y = 32767/349;
    y = random( )y;
    for (i=0; i<120000; i++)
    {
        switcher = 32767/3;
        switcher = rand( )/switcher;
        switch(switcher)
        {
            case 0: x /=2;
                y /=2;
                break;
            case 1: x = (x+639)/2;
                y /=2;
                break;
            case 2: x = (x+320)/2;
                y = (x+349)/2;
        }
        plot(x,y,15);
    }
}
```

Figure 11-7: Sierpinski Triangle and Cousins

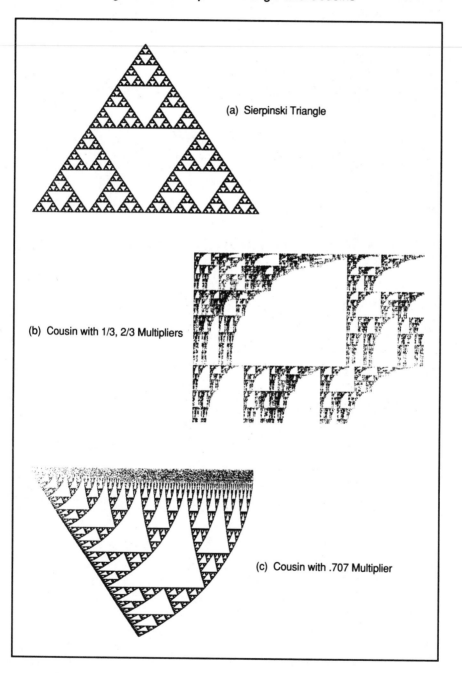

(a) Sierpinski Triangle

(b) Cousin with 1/3, 2/3 Multipliers

(c) Cousin with .707 Multiplier

Figure 11-8: Replacement for *case* Statements to Generate Cousin of the
Sierpinski Triangle with 1/3 and 2/3 Multipliers

```
case 0::x /= 3;
    y /= 3;
    break;
case 1::x = (x + 639)*2/3;
    y /= 3;
    break;
case 2::x = (x + 639)/3;
    y = (y + 349)*2/3;
case 3: x /=3;
    y = (y+349)*2/3;
```

Strange Cousins of the Sierpinski Triangle

I am indebted to my friend Chester Stromswold for pointing out to me the
strange cousins of the Sierpinski triangle that can be generated by slight modifications of the above program. The first variation uses multipliers of 2/3 or 1/3
instead of 1/2 throughout the program. To generate this figure, replace the *case*
statements in Figure 11-6 with the code listed in Figure 11-8. The resulting
figure is shown in Figure 11-7(b). The second variation uses a multiplier of
.7071068 (reciprocal of the square root of two) instead of 1/2 at several critical
places. Figure 11-9 shows the listing for generating this cousin. The resulting
figure is shown in Figure 11-7(c).

Figure 11-9: Program to Generate Cousin of the Sierpinski Triangle
Using .7071068 Multiplier

```
        sirchet2 = program to generate Sierpinski
        triangle   .707 Cousin with chaos algorithm
```

```
#include <stdio.h>
#include <math.h>
#include <stdlib.h>
#include "tools.h"
float  s2, x, y;
int switcher;
```

```
long int i;

main()
{
    setMode(16);
    s2 = sqrt(0.5);
    x = 32767/639;
    x = rand()/x;
    y = 32767/349;
    y = rand()/y;
    for (i=0; i<120000; i++)
    {
        switcher = 322767/3;
        switcher = rand()/switcher;
        switch(switcher)
        {
            case 0: x *=s2;
                y *=s2;
                break;
            case 1: x = sqrt((639.*639. + x*x)/2);
                y *= s2
                break;
            case 2: x = sqrt((320.*320. + x*x)/2.);
                y = sqrt((349.*349 + y*y)/2.);
        }
        plot(x,y,15);
    }
}
```

Sierpinski Box

The same technique described above for the Sierpinski gasket can be applied to create a rectangular figure, which I have called a *Sierpinski box*. The program to create the box is listed in Figure 11-10, and the result is in Figure 11-11. The program is much like that described previously. Filling a rectangle aligned with the rows and columns of the display is a much simpler task than filling a triangle. The function to perform this task is called *fillRect*. Once a large square is created and filled, it is divided into nine smaller squares by a new version of the *generator* function. A new version of the function *node* is then used to blank out the center square and then call *generate* for each of the eight peripheral squares. Again, caution must be used in selecting the value of the parameter *level*. If *level* is too large, lack of display resolution will cause the entire original square to be blanked out.

Figure 11-10: Program to Generate a Sierpinski Box

```
        sierbox = program to generate rectangular Sierpinski box
```

```
#include <stdio.h>
#include <math.h>
#include <dos.h>
#include "tools.h"

void fillRect(int x1, int y1, int x2, int y2,int color);
void node(int x1, int y1, int x2, int y2, int x3, int y3,
    int x4,int y4, int level,int length);
void generate (int x1, int y1, int x2, int y2, int level,
    int length);
int x1,y1,x2,y2,x3,y3;
int level = 3;
int combination = 0,LINEWIDTH=1, OPERATOR=0, ANGLE,
    XCENTER, YCENTER;
unsigned long int PATTERN=0xFFFFFFFF;

main()
{
    int x1,x2,x3,x4,y01,y2,y3,y4,length;
    x1 = -220;
    y01 = -220;
    x2 = 220;
    y2 = 220;
    length = 440;
    setMode(16);
    cls(0);
    fillRect(x1,y01,x2,y2,15);
    generate(x1,y01,x2,y2,level,length);
    getch();
}
```

```
            generate() = Divides box into nine smaller boxes
```

```
void generate(int x1,int y01,int x2,int y2,int level,int length)
{
    int line_length,x3,y3,x4,y4;
    line_length = length/3;
    x3 = x1 + line_length;
    y3 = y01 + line_length;
    x4 = x2 - line_length;
    y4 = y2 - line_length;
    node (x1,y01,x2,y2,x3,y3,x4,y4,level,line_length);
```

```
}
```

```
          node() = blanks middle box and calls 'generate'
                     for  eight surrounding boxes
```

```
void node(int x1, int y01, int x2, int y2, int x3, int y3,
     int x4, int y4, int level,int length)
{
    fillRect(x3,y3,x4,y4,0);
    if (level == 0)
        return(0);
    generate (x1,y01,x3,y3,level-1,length);
    generate (x3,y01,x4,y3,level-1,length);
    generate (x4,y01,x2,y3,level-1,length);
    generate (x1,y3,x3,y4,level-1,length);
    generate (x4,y3,x2,y4,level-1,length);
    generate (x1,y4,x3,y2,level-1,length);
    generate (x3,y4,x4,y2,level-1,length);
    generate (x4,y4,x2,y2,level-1,length);
}
```

```
          fillRect() = fills a rectangle with a specified color
```

```
void fillRect(int x1, int y01, int x2, int y2,int color)
{
    int i,j;
    x1  += 320;
    y01 = 175 - ((y01*93) >> 7);
    x2  += 320;
    y2 = 175 - ((y2*93) >> 7);
    for (i=y2; i<=y01; i++)
    {
        for (j=x1; j<= x2; j++)
            plot(j,i,color);
    }
}
```

Figure 11-11: Sierpinski Box

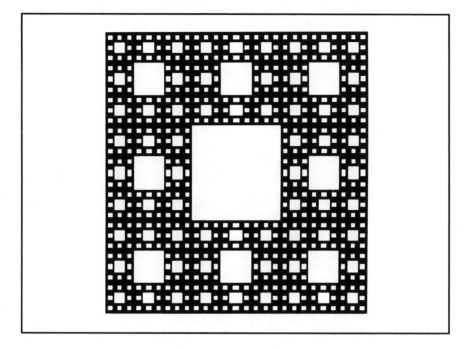

12

Trees

In the past few chapters, we created fractal curves by repeatedly replacing line segments with scaled-down replicas of a generator pattern. The results have been curves that were self-similar—a blown up version of a small section of the curve has a very similar shape to that of a larger portion of the curve. Now, we are going to take a different approach. We will start with a stem; at its end we will branch off in two directions and draw two branches. We will repeatedly perform this process at the end of each new branch. The result is a tree. Since one of the purposes of this exercise is to use these curves to represent trees in nature, we first need to discuss something about real trees.

Real Trees

The rough outline of the tree creation process given above implies that at each node in the tree creating process, we branch off in two directions. The result is a two-dimensional tree, but hopefully it will have some relation to real three-dimensional trees. Before going further, step outside and look at a few real trees. First, note that there are two classes of trees, deciduous (trees whose leaves fall every year) and conifers (evergreens having cones). These two classes of trees are quite different. The conifers tend to have rings of branches at different heights around a central trunk. This does not seem to square at all with the binary branching process, and we will see later that the tree curves that we generate never look like conifers. Secondly, note that deciduous trees, although they are closer in appearance to our model, still are much more complex in their structure. While binary branching is often the rule, there are exceptions—a stem splits into more than two branches, for example. Furthermore, the lengths of stems before branching occurs differ randomly from the norm, as do the diameters of branches.

The reason for making a point of all this is that we are next going to present some data on expressions for modeling trees, but we want to make sure that these are not taken as gospel as representing the way real trees are constructed. In some literature, authors appear to have been overpowered by their ability to express tree structures mathematically, to the point that the model supercedes reality. Remember, the mathematical formulas are a nice way of generating tree curves, but the real tree is much more complex and much more interesting. If you want a real challenge, take the tree program that we will list later and attempt to expand it to cover each of the possible situations for a real tree.

Mathematical Representation of Trees

Everyone seems to be fond of quoting Leonardo da Vinci's observation to the effect that the sum of the cross-sectional areas of all tree branches at a given height is constant. This should not be too surprising; the tree is required to pass nutrients from the roots to the leaves and for a given nutrient requirement one might expect that the "pipe" cross-sectional area required for nutrient transportation would be constant, regardless of height or the number of pipes. When we translate this observation to diameters (or widths when we make our two-dimensional drawings), we have an expression of the form:

$$D_0{}^\alpha = D_1{}^\alpha + D_2{}^\alpha \qquad\qquad \text{(Equation 12-1)}$$

where D_0 is the diameter of the stem, D_1 and D_2 are the diameters of the two branches that the stem splits into, and α is 2 according to da Vinci. There are other forms of tree-like structures. The simple model given above probably applies better to river networks than to trees, since the likelihood that more than two tributaries of a river system would join at the same place is remote. Other trees are found in the human body in the form of the arterial blood transportation system and the bronchi. Investigations have shown that a good approximation for α for the bronchial system is 3 and for the arteries is 2.7.

When we come to construct our program for tree generation, we shall use the expression:

$$B_{n+1} = 2^{-1/\alpha} B_n \qquad \text{(Equation 12-2)}$$

where B_n is the diameter of the lower level branch and B_{n+1} represents the diameter of each of the two branches into which B_n splits. We also need to consider the length of the branches. McMahon studied various typical trees and concluded that a similar recursive formula for length could be written as:

$$L_{n+1} = 2^{-3/(2\alpha)} L_n \qquad \text{(Equation 12-3)}$$

where L_n is the length of the predecessor branch and L_{n+1} is the length of each of the two successor branches after bifurcation.

Tree-Drawing Program

Figure 12-1 lists a program for drawing trees. It permits entering the initial length and width of the stem, the value of α for the left and right sides of the tree, the left and right branching angles, and the level of recursion. You will note that the program is a lot like those we have been using in the previous few chapters. It first computes the right and left width and length factors using equations 12-2 and 12-3. Next it sets up the parameters for the beginning and end of the stem and its width and draws it. The *turtle_theta* parameter is then set up to point in the direction of the stem, and is turned to the left angle. The function *generator* is run recursively until the lowest level is reached, then the *turtle_theta* parameter is reset in the stem direction and turned through the proper angle and the *generate* function is run again. Note that the height and width parameters passed to the *generate* function are scaled down by multiplying by the appropriate scale factors at the time of the function call.

Figure 12-1: Program to Generate Trees

```
                    trees = PROGRAM TO GENERATE TREES
```

```c
#include <stdio.h>
#include <math.h>
#include <dos.h>
#include <stdlib.h>
#include <time.h>
#include "tools.h"

int combination = 0,LINEWIDTH=1, OPERATOR=0;
unsigned long int PATTERN=0xFFFFFFFF;
int i,j;

float height,width,left_alpha,right_alpha,left_angle,
    right_angle,left_width_factor,left_height_factor,
    right_width_factor,right_height_factor;
float x,y,x1,y01;
float turtle_x,turtle_y,turtle_r,turtle_theta;
int level;

void generate(float x, float y, float width, float height,
float angle,int level);

main()
{
    printf("\nEnter stem height: ");
    scanf("%f",&height);
    printf("\nEnter stem width: ");
    scanf("%f",&width);
    printf("\nEnter left alpha: ");
    scanf("%f",&left_alpha);
    printf("\nEnter right alpha: ");
    scanf("%f",&right_alpha);
    printf("\nEnter left branch angle: ");
    scanf("%f",&left_angle);
    printf("\nEnter right branch angle: ");
    scanf("%f",&right_angle);
    printf("\nEnter recursion level: ");
    scanf("%d",&level);
    left_width_factor = pow(2,-1/left_alpha);
    left_height_factor = pow(2,-2/(3*left_alpha));
    right_width_factor = pow(2,-1/right_alpha);
    right_height_factor = pow(2,-2/(3*right_alpha));
    x = 0;
    y = -235;
    LINEWIDTH = width;
```

```
    setMode(16);
    cls(9);
    x1 = 0;
    y01 = y + height;
    drawLine(x,y,x1,y01,15);
    turtle_theta = point(x,y,x1,y01);
    turn(left_angle);
    generate(x1,y01,left_width_factor*width,
        left_height_factor*height,left_angle,level);
    turtle_theta = point(x,y,x1,y1);
    turn(-right_angle);
    generate(x1,y01,right_width_factor*width,
        right_height_factor*height,right_angle,level);
    getch();
}

void generate(float x, float y, float width, float height,
    float angle,int level)
{

    float x1,y01;
    turtle_x = x;
    turtle_y = y;
    turtle_r = height;
    step();
    x1 = turtle_x;
    y01 = turtle_y;
    LINEWIDTH = width;
    level--;
    if (level<3)
    drawLine(x,y,x1,y01,10);
    else drawline(x,y,x1,y01,6);
    if (level > 0)
    {
        turtle_theta = point(x1,y1,x1,y01);
        turn(left_angle);
        generate(turtle_x,turtle_y,left_width_factor*width,
            left_height_factor*height,left_angle,level);
        turtle_theta = point(x,y,x1,y01);
        turn(-right_angle);
        generate(x1,y01,left_width_factor*width,
            left_height_factor*height,right_angle,level);
    }
}
```

The *generate* function begins by setting the turtle coordinates to the x and y coordinates passed to the function (which mark the beginning point for the function's operations. The *turtle_r* (step size) parameter is set to the height that was passed to the function. (The turtle angle was already set properly before the function was called.) The function makes the turtle step, extracts the new coordinates, sets the *LINEWIDTH* parameter to the width passed to the function, decrements *level*, and then draws the line. The colors are set to create a brown trunk and green foliage. If *level* has reached zero, this is the end; otherwise, the function turns the turtle by the left angle, appropriately scales down the length and width, and calls itself to make another left-hand line. When this has been done recursively, the turtle is reaimed to its original position when the function was called, rotated by the right angle, and *generate* is again called with the appropriately scaled parameters to do the right branch.

Note that it is fairly easy to insert parameters into this program that will cause it to attempt to exceed the bounds of the display. The function *drawLine* does not take kindly to having the bounds of the display exceeded. Not only will it attempt to draw lines outside the display, sometimes causing strange things to appear in unusual locations on the display, but also the integer types used in the function can have their capacity exceeded, with strange results. If you want to be absolutely safe, rewrite the *drawLine* function providing safeguards so the display limits cannot be exceeded. However, you can avoid the necessity for this labor by just being very careful which parameters you send to the tree generating program.

Figure 12-2 is a chart of the parameters used to generate the trees that appear in Figures 12-3 through 12-11. Figure 12-3 shows three "stick" trees, each using the same parameters except for different values of α. They will give you an idea of how α affects the tree drawing. Figure 12-4 is set up to look as much like a real bare tree as possible. Figure 12-5 is similar, except that it uses a greater number of iterations to represent leaves. If you ran the program in color, the screen is cleared to light blue (color 9), the stem is drawn brown (color 6), and the lines in the *generate* function are drawn in light green (color 10) for values of *level* less than four and in brown for levels higher than that, giving a fairly realistically colored tree.

Figure 12-6 is a one-sided curve that shows what happens when α is set close to zero. You must have a small value inserted or you will get a *divide by zero* error. Note that all of the displayed curve is generated very quickly and then a lot of time is spent computing nothing that will be displayed. Figure 12-7 makes use of the value of α that is supposed to be representative of the bronchial system. You can decide for yourself whether it is realistic (if you have ever seen a bronchial system) or determine how the parameters should be modified for a better representation.

Figure 12-8 makes use of the value of α that is supposed to represent the arterial system. Figures 12-9 and 12-10 show the interesting curves that are obtained when the branching angle is set to 90 degrees. They don't look much like real trees. Figure 12-11 is the same except that the branching angle is 85 degrees, which gives a cockeyed tilt to the whole picture.

Figure 12-2: Parameters for Tree-Drawing Program

Figure	Height	Width	Left α	Right α	Left Angle	Right Angle	Level
12-3a	100	1	1.1	1.1	25	25	6
12-3b	100	1	1.5	1.5	25	25	6
12-3c	100	1	2.0	2.0	25	25	6
12-4	120	20	2.0	2.2	24	26	6
12-5	80	20	2.0	2.2	20	28	14
12-6	200	35	2.0	0.00001	55	0	18
12-7	75	10	3.0	3.0	33	33	9
12-8	75	10	2.7	2.7	33	33	9
12-9	250	35	1.2	1.2	90	90	10
12-10	250	100	1.0	1.0	90	90	10
12-11	200	35	1.2	1.2	85	85	9

Figure 12-3: Stick Trees with Different α's

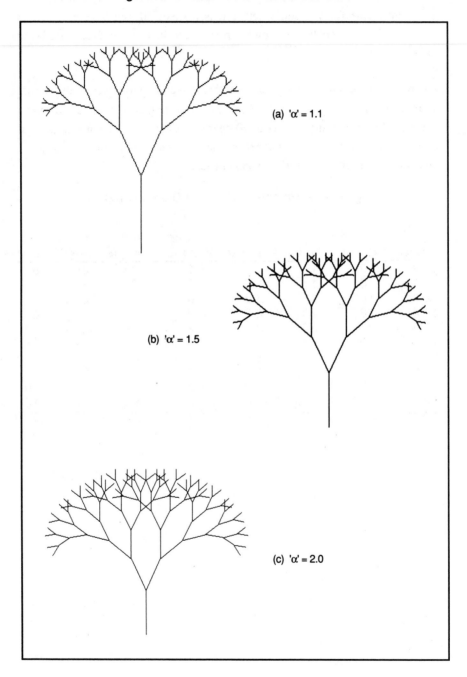

(a) 'α' = 1.1

(b) 'α' = 1.5

(c) 'α' = 2.0

Figure 12-4: Bare Tree

Figure 12-5: Tree with Foliage

Figure 12-6: One-Sided Tree

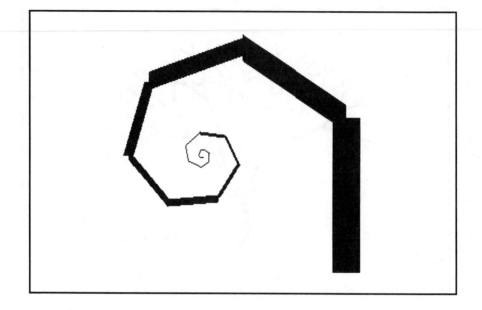

Figure 12-7: Bronchial System Tree

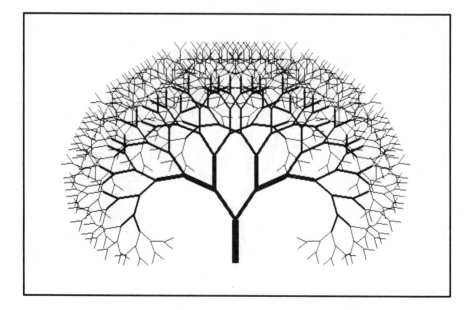

Figure 12-8: Arterial System Tree

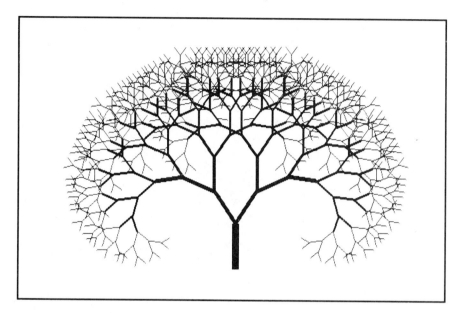

Figure 12-9: Tree with 90-Degree Branch Angles

Figure 12-10: Tree with 90-Degree Branch Angles and Wider Stem

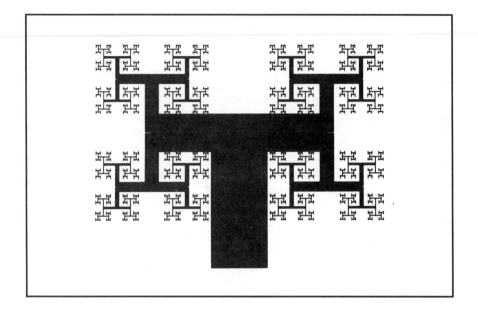

Figure 12-11: Tree with 85-Degree Branch Angles

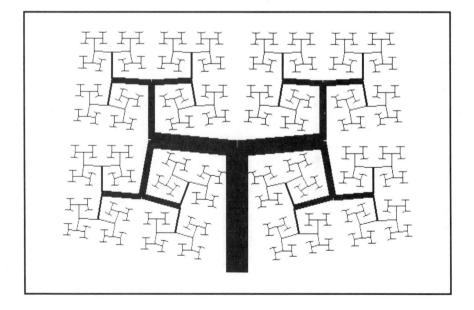

13

Working with Circles

So far, we have done all of our generating of fractals using straight line segments. Since these simple geometric figures have resulted in very complex fractal curves that are of great beauty and interest, we might suspect that we can use circles, which are geometric figures of a greater order of complexity, to generate fractals that are even more interesting. To some extent this is true. The problem is that the geometry required to put together a fractal pattern of circles, determining their radii and their coordinates, is so much more complicated than that used for fractal lines that it has barely been explored. Those who have investigated it are not willing to reveal the secrets of how they compute their fractal curves, although they are more than willing to display their pretty pictures. We'll therefore do the best we can. In this chapter we'll show you how to draw two representative fractals using circles. In the course of this, you will observe that we have to make use of some geometric formulas that rarely occur in geometry books, and when they do, they're not always clearly explained.

With this introduction, you are on your own. The field of circle fractals is a large one with lots of room for discovery, but you may have to do a lot more research into geometry than you thought you might ever want to do.

Apollonian Packing of Circles

This is one of the most basic of fractal curves involving circles. First we draw three circles, each of which is externally tangent to the other two. The result of their joining is a *curvilinear triangle*. Next, we draw the circle that will fit into the curvilinear triangle, being tangent to each of the three given circles. This yields three more, smaller, curvilinear triangles. In a similar manner, we draw a circle in each of these triangles, tangent to the three circles that make up the triangle.

Now, from each curvilinear triangle, three more smaller curvilinear triangles are generated. Continuing the process infinitely yields the ultimate fractal curve, but for practical programming we will stop the process after six or seven iterations; before too long, the circles become so small that they either appear on our screen as dots, or not at all. It can be shown that the resulting curve is fractal and has a Hausdorff-Besicovitch dimension (discovered by Boyd) of approximately 1.3058.

This begs the question of how to perform this repeated circle drawing task. Provided we can figure out how to draw a circle within a curvilinear triangle, knowing the coordinates of the center and the radius of each of the three circles that generate the curvilinear triangle, then we can use a recursive process similar to that we have used for previous fractals to draw repeated circles. It is the former that is the problem, however. Fortunately, by using the principles of analytic geometry, we can determine the x and y coordinates of the new circle, providing we know its radius. The process is tedious but not difficult.

Soddy's Formula

It turns out that there is a formula for the radius of the circle inscribed within the curvilinear triangle, given solely in terms of the radii of the three circles that make up the triangle. It is called *Soddy's formula*. One form of this formula is the expression:

$$2(1/a^2 + 1/b^2 + 1/c^2 + 1/r^2) = (1/a + 1/b + 1/c + 1/r) \qquad \cdot(\text{Eq. } 13\text{-}1)$$

where a, b, and c are the radii of the three given tangent circles and r is the radius of the circle that is to be drawn tangent to the three given circles. The form of the expression that we will work with is:

$$1/r = 1/a + 1/b + 1/c + 2\sqrt{(1/bc + 1/ac + 1/ab)} \qquad (\text{Eq. } 13\text{-}2)$$

Once we know the radius of the circle to be drawn and the radii and center coordinates of the three given circles, we can do some complicated but very straightforward mathematics to determine the *x* and *y* coordinates of the center of the circle to be drawn. We can then draw the circle.

Program for Apollonian Circle Packing

Figure 13-1 lists the program for the Apollonian packing of circles. It first asks for a level to which recursion will continue before the program terminates. Then the three original circles are drawn. If you wish to change the location of these circles, you can either calculate their locations or arrange them by running just the first part of the program several times and changing the circle coordinates until you find the desired location and conditions of tangency by trial and error. Next, the *gen_circle* function is run to draw and fill the new circle in the first (biggest) curvilinear triangle. It starts by using Soddy's formula to determine the radius of the circle to be drawn. Next, it computes the *x* and *y* coordinates of the center for the new circle. Then the circle is filled. The color increments each time a circle that is drawn, so that there will be a distinction between the different circles.

Figure 13-1: Program to Perform Apollonian Packing of Circles

```
                 apollo = apollonian packing of circles
```

```
#include <dos.h>
#include <stdio.h>
#include <stdlib.h>
#include <math.h>
#include "tools.h"

void gen_circle(float xa,float ya,float a,float xb,float yb,
  float b,float xc,float yc,float c, int level);
void node(float xa,float ya,float a,float xb,float yb,
  float b,float xc,float yc,float c, float xs, float ys, float s,
  int level);

int LINEWIDTH = 1, OPERATOR = 0;
int color = 1;
```

```
int level;
unsigned long int PATTERN = 0xFFFFFFFF;
unsigned char PALETTE[16]={0,1,2,3,4,5,20,7,56,57,58,59,60,61,62,63};
float a,b,c,s,xn,yn,cs,bs,xa,xb,xc,ya,yb,yc,xs,ys;

main()
{
    float temp;

    printf("Enter level: ");
    scanf("%d",&level);
    setMode(16);
    a = 625;
    b = 375;
    c = 945;
    xa = -725;
    ya = 235;
    xb = 275;
    yb = 268;
    xc = 180;
    yc = -1048;
    fillOval(xa,ya,a,color++,1.0);
    fillOval(xb,yb,b,color++,1.0);
    fillOval(xc,yc,c,color++,1.0);
    gen_circle(xa,ya,a,xb,yb,b,xc,yc,c,level);
    getch();
}
```

```
          gen_circle() =   function to generate a circle inside
                           a curvilinear triangle
```

```
void gen_circle(float xa,float ya,float a,float xb,float yb,
    float b,float xc,float yc,float c, int level)
{
    float s, temp;

    level--;
    s = 1/a + 1/b + 1/c + 2*(sqrt(1/(b*c) + 1/(c*a) +
        1/(a*b)));
    s = 1/s;
    if (xb == xa)
    {
        temp = (s+a)*(s+a) - (s+c)*(s+c) - xa*xa + xc*xc
            - ya*ya + yc*yc;
        ys = (temp*(xb-xa) - (xc - xa)*((s+a)*(s+a) -
            (s+b)*(s+b) - xa*xa + xb*xb - ya*ya + yb*yb))
            /(2*((yc-ya)*(xb-xa) - (yb-ya)* (xc - xa)));
        xs = (temp - 2*ys*(yc - ya))/(2*(xc - xa));
```

```
    }
    else
    {
        temp = (s+a)*(s+a) - (s+b)*(s+b) - xa*xa + xb*xb
            - ya*ya + yb*yb;
        ys = (temp*(xc-xa) - (xb - xa)*((s+a)*(s+a) -
            (s+c)*(s+c) - xa*xa + xc*xc - ya*ya + yc*yc))
            /(2*((yb-ya)*(xc-xa) - (yc-ya)* (xb - xa)));
        xs = (temp - 2*ys*(yb - ya))/(2*(xb - xa));
    }
    color = (++color)%14 + 1;
    fillOval(xs,ys,s,color,1.0);
    color = (++color)%14 + 1;
    if (level > 0)
        node(xa,ya,a,xb,yb,b,xc,yc,c,xs,ys,s,level);
}
```

```
        node() = function to generate circles in three new
            curvilinear triangles created by 'gen_circle'
```

```
void node(float xa,float ya,float a,float xb,float yb,
    float b,float xc,float yc,float c, float xs, float ys, float s,
    int level)

{
    gen_circle(xa,ya,a,xb,yb,b,xs,ys,s,level);
    gen_circle(xb,yb,b,xc,yc,c,xs,ys,s,level);
    gen_circle(xa,ya,a,xc,yc,c,xs,ys,s,level);
}
```

Note that there are two alternate (and redundant) methods for computing the coordinates of the center of the circle (xs and ys). Unfortunately, if the x coordinates of the centers of two of the three circles making up the curvilinear triangle are the same, using one of these methods will cause a divide by zero, resulting in the program crashing. Consequently, if one pair of x coordinates are equal, the other pair is used. Observe that all three x coordinates cannot be the same; if they were, the three circles would be in a straight line and no curvilinear triangle would be generated. Once the x and y coordinates of the center of the new circle and its radius are known, the *fillOval* function can then be used to fill the new circle. Each time *gen_circle* is called, it reduces the level by one from that transferred by the calling function. When the level is reduced to zero, the function terminates after filling the new circle; otherwise, the function *node* is called to compute and fill circles in each of the three new curvilinear triangles comprising two of the original three circles and the new circle. Plate 3 (in the color section) shows the figure produced by running this program.

Inversion

In producing fractal curves involving circles, there is an interesting mapping technique which can transform a fairly simple pattern of circles into a much more interesting one. The technique also has uses in geometry, where it can often simplify complex relationships so that proofs of theorems become much simpler. The technique is called *inversion*. It makes use of a given circle to map all of the points on a plane onto the plane, except for the point at the very center of the circle. The mapping is done as follows:

1. A line is drawn from the center of the circle (O) to the point to be mapped (P).

2. The new mapped point P' is placed on the line OP so that the product of the distances OP and OP' is equal to the square of the radius of the circle, r^2.

Inversion has several interesting properties. They include:

1. Any circle whose circumference passes through the center of the reference circle, O, maps into a straight line parallel to the tangent through the circle being mapped at O.

2. Any circle which is orthogonal to the circle of inversion inverts into itself.

3. Any other circle maps into a circle.

4. You might suspect that if a circle maps into another circle, the center of the first circle would map into the center of the new circle, but this is not true. If you want to perform an inversion and then plot it on the screen, you cannot successfully use data from the original circle to determine the center and

radius of the mapped circle and then draw it using this information. You must map every point on the circle to its new location and plot it there.

In order to perform the inversions in a real computer program, we make use of the function *inversionOval*, listed in Figure 13-2. This program draws a circle in the same manner as the *drawOval* function in Chapter 5, except that instead of plotting each point of this circle, the function computes the location of the point following inversion and plots a point there instead.

Figure 13-2: Function to Perform Inversion on an Oval

```
          inverseOval() = draws the inverse of an oval with
                          specified center, radius, color, and
                          aspect ratio
```

```
void inverseOval(float x, float y, float b, int color,
    float aspect)
{

    union REGS reg;

    int i, bnew,new_col, new_row;
    float length,new_length;
    long a,a_square, b_square, two_a_square, two_b_square,
        four_a_square, four_b_square,d,row,col;

    b -= LINEWIDTH/2;
    a = b/aspect;

    for (i=1; i<=LINEWIDTH; i++)
    {
        b_square = (long)b*b;
        a_square = (a*a);
        row = b;
        col = 0;
        two_a_square = a_square << 1;
        four_a_square = a_square << 2;
        four_b_square = b_square << 2;
        two_b_square = b_square << 1;
        d = two_a_square * (((long)row  -1)*(row )) + a_square
            + two_b_square*(1-a_square);
        while (a_square*(row ) > b_square * (col))
        {
```

```
length = sqrt((x_o - col - x)*(x_o - col - x) +
    (y_o - row - y)*(y_o - row - y));
new_length = r_sq/length;
new_col = x_o - (x_o - col - x)*new_length/length;
new_row = -y_o + (y_o - row - y)*new_length/length;
plots(new_col,new_row,color);
length = sqrt((x_o + col - x)*(x_o + col - x) +
    (y_o - row - y)*(y_o - row - y));
new_length = r_sq/length;
new_col = x_o - (x_o + col - x)*new_length/length;
new_row = -y_o + (y_o - row - y)*new_length/length;
plots(new_col,new_row,color);
length = sqrt((x_o - col - x)*(x_o - col - x) +
    (y_o + row - y)*(y_o + row - y));
new_length = r_sq/length;
new_col = x_o - (x_o - col - x)*new_length/length;
new_row = -y_o + (y_o + row - y)*new_length/length;
plots(new_col,new_row,color);
length = sqrt((x_o + col - x)*(x_o + col - x) +
    (y_o + row - y)*(y_o + row - y));
new_length = r_sq/length;
new_col = x_o - (x_o + col - x)*new_length/length;
new_row = -y_o + (y_o + row - y)*new_length/length;
plots(new_col,new_row,color);
if (d>= 0)
{
    row--;
    d -= four_a_square*(row);
}
d += two_b_square*(3 + (col<<1));
col++;
}

d = two_b_square * (col + 1)*col + two_a_square*(row *
        (row  -2) +1) + (1-two_a_square)*b_square;
while ((row) + 1)
{
    length = sqrt((x_o - col - x)*(x_o - col - x) +
        (y_o - row - y)*(y_o - row - y));
    new_length = r_sq/length;
    new_col = x_o - (x_o - col - x)*new_length/length;
    new_row = -y_o + (y_o - row - y)*new_length/length;
    plots(new_col,new_row,color);
    length = sqrt((x_o + col - x)*(x_o + col - x) +
        (y_o - row - y)*(y_o - row - y));
    new_length = r_sq/length;
    new_col = x_o - (x_o + col - x)*new_length/length;
    new_row = -y_o + (y_o - row - y)*new_length/length;
    plots(new_col,new_row,color);
    length = sqrt((x_o - col - x)*(x_o - col - x) +
        (y_o + row - y)*(y_o + row - y));
```

```
new_length = r_sq/length;
new_col = x_o - (x_o - col - x)*new_length/length;
new_row = -y_o + (y_o + row - y)*new_length/length;
plots(new_col,new_row,color);
length = sqrt((x_o + col - x)*(x_o + col - x) +
    (y_o + row - y)*(y_o + row - y));
new_length = r_sq/length;
new_col = x_o - (x_o + col - x)*new_length/length;
new_row = -y_o + (y_o + row - y)*new_length/length;
plots(new_col,new_row,color);
if (d<= 0)
{
    col++;
    d += four_b_square*col;
}
row--;
d += two_a_square * (3 - (row<<1));
        }
        b++;
    }
}
```

Pharaoh's Breastplate

Pharaoh's Breastplate is the name given by Mandelbrot to a figure created using inversion. The figure that we are going to generate here is not quite the same as Mandelbrot's, but it does make use of inversion and gives you some idea of how the technique works. Figure 13-3 shows a pattern of circles, before inversion. The two large circles represent the final reference circles. They are mapped by inversion into the upper and lower horizontal lines. The other circles are tangent to each other and to the horizontal lines. They can extend as far to the left and right as you want them to. The number of circles is set by a parameter in a *for* loop. For Figure 13-3, the parameter is set to 3; when we perform the final inversion program, the parameter is set to 20.

A word needs to be said about the number that is inserted into the program for *r_sq*. This is the radius of the reference circle that is used in the inversion mapping. The center of this circle is always at the point of tangency of the two large circles, so that they are mapped into straight lines by the inversion. The radius of the reference circle determines where these two lines are located. All of the other circles that the program generates are referenced to these two lines. When the inversion of these circles takes place, they end up being referenced to the two large circles, so that no matter what value is used for the radius of the reference circle, all of the smaller circles will be referenced to the same place in the final drawing.

Figure 13-3: Pharaoh's Breastplate Circles before Inversion

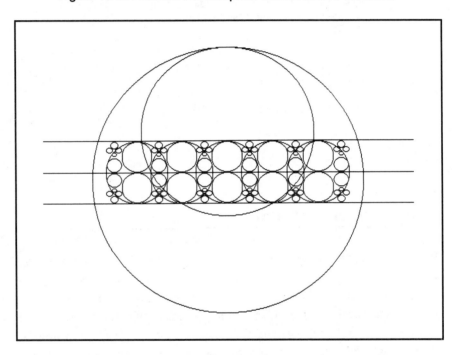

For Figure 13-3, where we are actually showing the uninverted small circles, we chose a value for *r_sq* which would cause the two reference straight lines to appear at a convenient location on the display. There is another consideration, however. The smaller the reference circle radius, the closer together will be the two straight lines which represent the mapping of the two large circles. Consequently, all of the small circles will be smaller, and when we run *inverseOval*, there will be fewer points generated to make up these small circles. If we generate a lot fewer points than we would normally have drawn to produce the inverted circle, the resulting circle will be rather coarse and tend to loose its circular shape. We want to make *r_sq* large, but not so large that we exceed the range of values that the computer can conveniently handle. The value of 400000 used in the *pharaoh* program is a good compromise for this particular program.

In both the program that created Figure 13-3 and the final program, we start by generating the two reference circles and then invert them to create the two parallel lines. (In the final program, the lines are not drawn.) Then we generate all of the necessary circles in reference to the two parallel lines. The mathematics is again complex, but straightforward; if you wish, you can tackle the geometry for determining the radius and center coordinates of each set of circles to see how the results given in the program are obtained. It may be that there are some neat tricks of inversion or recursion that I have missed that will simplify the program, but the approach used here is the simplest one and gets down to a reasonably fine detail of circles. If you want to add more circles, go ahead and compute the necessary radii and center coordinates.

Figure 13-4 is the final program to generate the Pharaoh's breastplate. The resulting picture is shown in Figure 13-5.

Figure 13-4: Program to Generate Pharaoh's Breastplate

```
           pharaoh = program to generate pharaoh's breastplate
```

```
#include <stdio.h>
#include <math.h>
#include "tools.h"
#include <stdlib.h>
#include <dos.h>

void inverseOval(float x, float y, float b, int color,
    float aspect);
void gen_circle(float x,float y,float radius);

unsigned long int PATTERN = 0xFFFFFFFF;
int i,j,LINEWIDTH = 1,OPERATOR=0;
double a_line,b_line,x_o,y_o,radius,r_sq,height;

main()
{

    float xbig,ybig,rbig,xtan,ytan,rtan;
```

```
setMode(16);
cls(0);
r_sq = 400000;
xbig = 0;
ybig = 0;
rbig = 220;
rtan = 140;
xtan = 0;
ytan = ybig + rbig - rtan;
y_o = ybig - rbig;
x_o = xbig;
drawOval(xbig, ybig,rbig,15,1.0);
drawOval(xtan,ytan,rtan,15,1.0);
a_line = r_sq/(2*rbig);
b_line = r_sq/(2*rtan);
height = (b_line - a_line);
radius = height/2;
height = radius*sqrt(2.0);
for (i=0; i<20; i++)
{
    gen_circle(x_o + height*i,y_o + a_line + radius,
        radius);
    gen_circle(x_o + height*i,y_o + a_line + radius/2,
        radius/2);
    gen_circle(x_o + height*i,y_o + b_line - radius/2,
        radius/2);
    gen_circle(x_o + height*i + height/2,y_o + a_line +
        3*radius/4,radius/4);
    gen_circle(x_o + height*i + height/2,y_o + b_line -
        3*radius/4,radius/4);
    gen_circle(x_o + height*i + height/2,y_o + a_line +
        radius/8, radius/8);
    gen_circle(x_o + height*i + height/2,y_o + b_line -
        radius/8, radius/8);
    gen_circle(x_o + height*i + height/2,y_o + a_line +
        5*radius/12,radius/12);
    gen_circle(x_o + height*i + height/2,y_o + b_line -
        5*radius/12,radius/12);
    gen_circle(x_o + height*i + 0.4*height,y_o + a_line +
        0.3*radius,radius/10);
    gen_circle(x_o + height*i + 0.6*height,y_o + a_line +
        0.3*radius,radius/10);
    gen_circle(x_o + height*i + 0.4*height,y_o + b_line -
        0.3*radius,radius/10);
    gen_circle(x_o + height*i + 0.6*height,y_o + b_line -
        0.3*radius,radius/10);
}
getch();
}
```

```
                gen_circle() = performs two inversions
```

```
void gen_circle(float x,float y,float radius)
{
    inverseOval(x,y,radius,15,1.0);
    inverseOval(-x,y,radius,15,1.0);
}
```

Figure 13-5: Pharaoh's Breastplate

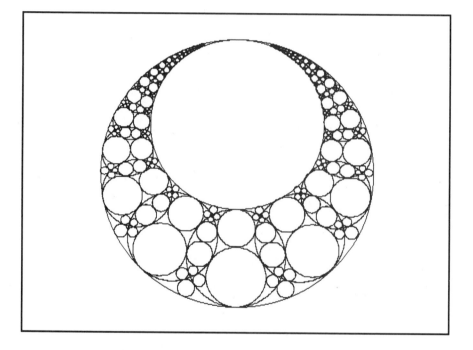

14

The Mandelbrot Set

The Mandelbrot set is probably the most well-known of the fractal curves. In almost every magazine, you will come across an article on the Mandelbrot set and some examples of the pictures of its displays. Almost every bulletin board has a Mandelbrot set program. Originally, the Mandelbrot set was discovered by Benoit Mandelbrot when he was investigating the behavior of the iterated function:

$$z_{n+1} = z_n^2 + c \qquad\qquad \text{(Equation 14-1)}$$

where both z and c are complex numbers. First, to get a feel for the function, consider the very simple situation where z_0 is a real number and c is zero. If z_0 is 1, the value of z remains at 1, no matter how many iterations are performed. If z_0 is less than 1, the function z_n will approach zero as n approaches infinity. If z_0 is greater than one, z_n will approach infinity.

The speed at which z_n approaches zero for numbers less than one or approaches infinity for numbers greater than one depends upon the original value of the function z_0. The smaller this value, the faster the function will approach zero for starting values less than one. The larger the value, the faster the function will approach infinity for starting values greater than one.

This over-simplified example is fairly easy to understand. When z_0 becomes a complex number and/or c becomes a complex number instead of zero, the situation becomes much more complex. In fact, for years mathematicians steered away from the complexities of this kind of expression, assuming that it eventually reached limiting values in some fairly regular fashion. It was only when computers were applied extensively to the problem that it was discovered that the behavior of the expressions was quite chaotic and that the result of performing many iterations of the expression for various values yielded fractal curves.

In plotting the function in some meaningful way, we want to show what happens to the expression for some range of reasonable initial conditions. To do this, we shall perform a sufficient number of iterations to determine the behavior of the iterated function. One attractor for the Mandelbrot set is infinity. It can be shown that if the magnitude of the function ever exceeds two, it will eventually be attracted to infinity.

For practical purposes, we find that for most cases, if the magnitude of the function does not exceed two within 512 iterations, it probably never will. We will color such points black. The rest of the colors that we have available will be used to indicate the speed with which the function is approaching infinity, based upon the number of iterations that are required for the magnitude to become greater than two.

What we have done is to cycle through the sixteen colors available to us on the EGA, incrementing the color value once for each iteration. Thus, there is a color change each time the number of iterations required to blow up increases by one. However, what you do with the colors is pretty much up to your own imagination. You can cycle as has been done here or with groups of iterations assigned to different color values, and you can assign colors any way you wish. The result is often not only artistic, but reveals a different meaning about how the function behaves as the parameters are changed.

Once we know what we are going to do with the colors, we have to decide what the x and y coordinates of our mapping of the function will represent. There are two basic ways to go here. One is to let z_0 be equal to zero and let the x and y coordinates of the display represent the real and imaginary parts of c as they change over some selected range of values. This gives rise to the well-known Mandelbrot set.

The other approach is to select a value for *c* and let the x and y axis be equal to the real and imaginary parts of z_0 as it changes over a selected range of values. This gives rise to the Julia sets, which will be described in Chapter 15. Interestingly enough, the Mandelbrot set forms a sort of map of the Julia sets; if you select a point on the Mandelbrot set and enlarge the area around it sufficiently, you get a pattern that is very similar to the Julia set for that same point. Thus, you can use the Mandelbrot set to determine which Julia sets you would like to plot.

Simplified Mandelbrot Set Program

Figure 14-1 lists a plain vanilla program for generating the Mandelbrot set. The heart of the algorithm consists of two *for* loops and one *while* loop. The *for* loops make sure that each pixel in the vertical and horizontal directions is assigned a color value by the algorithm.

Figure 14-1: Program to Generate Mandelbrot Set

```
         mandel = program to map the Mandelbrot set
```

```
#include <stdio.h>
#include <math.h>
#include <dos.h>
#include <process.h>
#include "tools.h"

const int maxcol = 640;
const int maxrow = 350;
const int max_colors = 16;

int max_iterations = 512;
int max_size = 4;
int LINEWIDTH=1, OPERATOR=0x00, ANGLE, XCENTER, YCENTER;
unsigned long int PATTERN=0xFFFFFFFF;
float Q[350];
float XMax,YMax,XMin,YMin;

main()
{
    float P,deltaP, deltaQ, X, Y, Xsquare, Ysquare;
```

```
int i,color, row, col,error,response,repeat=0x30;

XMax = 1.2;
XMin = -2.0;
YMax = 1.2;
YMin = -1.2;
setMode(16);
cls(7);
deltaP = (XMax - XMin)/(maxcol);
deltaQ = (YMax - YMin)/(maxrow);
Q[0] = YMax;
for (row=1; row<=maxrow; row++)
Q[row] = Q[row-1] - deltaQ;
P = XMin;
for (col=0; col<maxcol; col++)
{
    if (kbhit() != 0)
        exit(0);
    for (row=0; row<=maxrow; row++)
    {
        X = Y = Xsquare = Ysquare = 0.0;
        color = 1;
        while ((color<max_iterations) && ((Xsquare +
            Ysquare) < max_size))
        {
            Xsquare = X*X;
            Ysquare = Y*Y;
            Y *= X;
            Y += Y + Q[row];
            X = Xsquare - Ysquare + P;
            color ++;
        }
        plot(col, row, (color % max_colors));
    }
    P += deltaP;
}
getch();
}
```

The *while* loop performs the successive iterations of the equations until the magnitude of the square of the function is larger than 4 or until the number of iterations reaches 512, whichever occurs first. In squaring the complex function z, and adding the complex number c, the real part is:

$$x_n = x_{n-1}^2 - y_{n-1}^2 + p \qquad \text{(Equation 14-2)}$$

and the imaginary part is:

$$y_n = 2x_{n-1}y_{n-1} + q \qquad \text{(Equation 14-3)}$$

In determining how to optimize the performance of our algorithm, we need to be aware of the fact that the *while* loop can be iterated as many as 1.147×10^8 times, the *for* loop for rows is iterated 224,000 times, and the *for* loop for columns is called only 640 times. Thus, it is important to minimize the time spent in calculations in the *while* loop, and fairly important to minimize the time spent in the *for* loop for rows. The time spent in the *for* loop for columns is relatively insignificant. We have minimized time spent in the *while* loop by using the square of the magnitude $(x^2 + y^2)$ for the comparison, so that we don't have to perform any square roots. In addition, in computing y, we have avoided multiplying by two by substituting an addition, which is a much faster process.

In the row *for* loop, we have avoided computing the value of q at each pass through the loop. This would require a total of 224,000 calculations of q during passes through the loop, although there are only 350 distinct values of q used. Consequently, we calculate these 350 values first and put them in an array and then select the proper one for each pass through the loop. The program includes a test of the keyboard with provision to exit when a key is struck, in case the user doesn't want to complete a picture.

This test, however, is done within the outermost *for* loop. This means that, if a key is struck, the program will complete the column that it is working on before exiting. This delays the exit a little, but prevents the key check from slowing up the program while a picture is being drawn. Plate 4 is a picture of the entire Mandelbrot set as drawn by this program. The lettered locations indicate points for P and Q for Julia sets.

Improved Mandelbrot Set Program

The program described above produces the Mandelbrot set, but it doesn't have any bells and whistles to make our job easier. An improved program would have the following characteristics:

1. It should be capable of saving a partial picture at any time we want to interrupt it and then picking up from where it left off to complete the picture at some future time.

2. It should be capable to save a completed picture and redisplay it on the screen in just a few seconds.

3. It should be capable of selecting a small section of a picture and blowing it up to a full screen display.

4. It should be capable of modifying the EGA palette to display any desired colors.

The program listed in Figure 14-2 will meet all of the requirements for the improved program. The program begins by asking for a screen number between 00 and 99. Whatever number is entered becomes part of a file name of the form *mandel##.pcx*, where ## is the screen number entered. The *restore_screen* function described in Chapter 4 is then run to display this file on the screen. If the file is not found, or if it is not a proper *.pcx* file, the function displays a diagnostic message and returns a zero to the calling program.

Figure 14-2: Improved Mandelbrot Set Program

```
        cmandel = advanced program to map the Mandelbrot set
```

```c
#include <stdio.h>
#include <math.h>
#include <dos.h>
#include <process.h>
#include "tools.h"
```

```
const int maxcol = 639;
const int maxrow = 349;
const int max_colors = 16;
int CURSOR_X=0,CURSOR_Y=0,col,row;
int max_iterations = 512;
int max_size = 4;
int LINEWIDTH=1, OPERATOR=0x00, ANGLE, XCENTER, YCENTER;
unsigned long int PATTERN=0xFFFFFFFF;
unsigned char PALETTE[16]={0,1,2,3,4,5,20,7,56,57,58,59,60,
    61,62,63};
int colors[16]={0,1,2,3,4,5,20,7,56,57,58,59,60,61,62,63};
double Q[350];
float TXMax,TXMin,TYMax,TYMin;
union LIMIT XMax,YMax,XMin,YMin,Pval,Qval;

char file_name[13] = {"mandel00.pcx"};


main()
{
    double P,deltaP, deltaQ, X, Y, Xsquare, Ysquare;
    int i,color, row, col,error,response,repeat=0x30,
        start_col;

    printf("\nEnter background and 15 other colors separated"
        " by commas: ");
        scanf("%d,%d,%d,%d,%d,%d,%d,%d,%d,%d,%d,%d,%d,%d,"
            "%d,%d",&colors[0],&colors[1],&colors[2],
            &colors[3],&colors[4],&colors[5],&colors[6],
            &colors[7],&colors[8],&colors[9],&colors[10],
            &colors[11],&colors[12],&colors[13],&colors[14],
            &colors[15]);
    printf("Enter screen number (00 -  99): ");
    file_name[6] = getche();
    file_name[7] = getche();
    getch();
    error = restore_screen(file_name);
    for (i=0; i<16; i++)
        setEGApalette(i,colors[i]);
    if (error == 0)
    {
        printf("\nEnter 0 to generate first Mandelbrot "
            "screen");
        printf("\nEnter 1 to exit: ");
        response = getche();
        if (response != 0x30)
            exit(0);
        else
        {
            XMax.f = 1.2;
            XMin.f = -2.0;
```

```
            YMax.f = 1.2;
            YMin.f = -1.2;
            start_col = 0;
            setMode(16);
            cls(7);
        }
    }
    else
    {
        if (error < 639)
        {
            start_col = 8 * (error/8);
            remove(file_name);
        }
        else
        {
            start_col = 0;
            move_cursor(0,15,0,0);
            move_cursor(1,15,CURSOR_X,CURSOR_Y);
            cls(7);
            XMax.f = TXMax;
            XMin.f = TXMin;
            YMax.f = TYMax;
            YMin.f = TYMin;
        }

    }

    while (repeat == 0x30)
    {
        deltaP = (XMax.f - XMin.f)/(maxcol);
        deltaQ = (YMax.f - YMin.f)/(maxrow);
        Q[0] = YMax.f;
        for (row=1; row<=maxrow; row++)
        Q[row] = Q[row-1] - deltaQ;
        P = XMin.f + start_col * deltaP;
        for (col=start_col; col<maxcol; col++)
        {
            if (kbhit() != 0)
            {
                save_screen(0,0,col,349,file_name);
                exit(0);
            }
            for (row=0; row<=maxrow; row++)
            {
                X = Y = Xsquare = Ysquare = 0.0;
                color = 1;
                while ((color<max_iterations) && ((Xsquare +
                Ysquare) < max_size))
                {
                    Xsquare = X*X;
```

```
                    Ysquare = Y*Y;
                    Y = 2*X*Y + Q[row];
                    X = Xsquare - Ysquare + P;
                    color ++;
                }
                plot(col, row, (color % max_colors));
            }
            P += deltaP;

        }
        save_screen(0,0,639,349,file_name);
        getch();
        gotoxy(10,24);
        printf("Enter '0' to run another plot, '1' to "
            "quit: ");
        repeat = getche();
        if (repeat == 0x30)
        {
            move_cursor(0,15,0,0);
            move_cursor(1,15,CURSOR_X,CURSOR_Y);
            XMax.f = TXMax;
            XMin.f = TXMin;
            YMax.f = TYMax;
            YMin.f = TYMin;
            start_col = 0;
            setMode(16);
            cls(7);
        }
    }
}
```

The program then gives the user the choice of running the original Mandelbrot set program or exiting. If the first choice is selected, the proper limits for the display are set up, the starting column is designated as zero and the program then generates a Mandelbrot set. If the file is successfully displayed, but the ending column value (returned by the *restore_screen* function) is less than that for a full screen, it implies that only a partial Mandelbrot set was generated and saved.

In this case, the display limits are extracted from the file information by the *restore_screen* function and placed in the global limit variables *XMax, XMin, YMax,* and *YMin.* The starting column is set to the beginning of the first byte preceding the end column limit, the display file is then erased, and the program proceeds to complete the display and then save it to the same file name previously used by the partial display. If the end column limit is 639, indicating that the display is complete, the program assumes that the user wants to generate a new Mandelbrot set from only a portion of this display.

The *move_cursor* function is then called twice. The first time, it is a type 0, which means that the cursor is drawn as the upper left corner of a rectangle. As the cursor moves across the Mandelbrot display, the values of *XMin* and *YMax* for the current cursor position are displayed at the bottom of the display. When the appropriate point for the corner is reached, the *Ent* key is hit, whereupon the *move_cursor* function is run again as type 1, which displays the lower right corner of a rectangle.

The coordinates selected for the top left corner remain displayed on the screen, and the coordinates for the current cursor position for *XMax* and *YMin* are also displayed and change as the cursor is moved about the display. The *move_cursor* function is set up so that the lower right corner can never be set above or to the left of the top left corner. When the proper position for this corner is set, hitting the *Ent* key again causes the program to begin to generate a new Mandelbrot set, with the bounds selected by the cursor.

The algorithm for generating the Mandelbrot set is just the same as that used in the program shown in Figure 14-1. However, when the program is interrupted by a keystroke, instead of exiting immediately, the program first saves the partially completed display in a disk file using the *save_screen* function described in Chapter 4.

This function always creates a new file name for the screen being saved unless the screen is one that was partially completed previously, in which case the same file name is used. The screen is then saved to the designated file, with the ending column limit variable set to the column number that was most recently completed by the Mandelbrot generating part of the program.

Figure 14-3: Parameters for Mandelbrot Set Color Plates

Plate #	XMin	XMax	YMin	YMax
4	-2.0	1.2	-1.2	1.2
5	-0.702973	-0.642879	0.374785	0.395415
—	-0.691594	-0.690089	0.386608	0.387494
6	-0.691060	-0.690906	0.387103	0.387228
7	-0.793114	-0.723005	0.037822	0.140974
—	-0.749337	-0.744948	0.109349	0.115851
8	-0.745465	-0.745387	0.112896	0.113034
9	-0.745464	-0.745388	0.112967	0.113030

If the program is not interrupted by a keystroke, it runs until the Mandelbrot set display is completed and then performs the same kind of process just described to save the completed display to a new disk file. The program then displays at the bottom of the screen "Enter '0' to run another plot, '1' to quit: ". If you type a 1, the program will terminate; if you type in a 0, the program will run the *move_cursor* function twice to permit you to select a sub-section of the display you just finished to be drawn as a full-sized Mandelbrot set. The program keeps looping, generating a Mandelbrot set, saving it, and allowing you to select the bounds for the next one, until a one is entered at the command described above, causing the loop to terminate and the program to run to completion. Expansions of the Mandelbrot set are shown in Plates 5 through 9. Figure 14-3 shows the bounds used for the various color pictures.

Precision Considerations

You will observe that the values of X, *deltaX*, etc. used in the program in Figure 14-2 are classified as *double*. The precision of numbers available in C determines how far we can expand the Mandelbrot set before the calculations begin to break down so that the pictures are so distorted they're worthless. If you don't plan to expand the Mandelbrot set any further than shown in the color plates, you can change the double type in the program to *float* and maybe achieve a faster running program, although some versions of C are just as fast for doubles as for floats. The use of the doubles, as shown, permits you to go one level further with the expansion. If you wish to go further yet, you will need to make the boundary values (*XMax*, *XMin*, *YMax*, and *YMin*) into doubles. This involves some complications, since you will have to create a new *union* statement to allow each of these variables to be either a double or a string of characters. You will then have to rearrange the header contents of the *.pcx* files and change the *save_screen* and *restore_screen* functions accordingly. This is not recommended except for advanced C programmers.

Using Other Color Combinations

The program listed in Figure 14-2 provides a good utilitarian display of the characteristics of the Mandelbrot set. As we get into highly expanded sections of this set, we come upon displays of exceptional beauty, which can be enhanced by the way in which we use our color capabilities. The first thing that we have to decide is what shades (out of 64) will be used for the sixteen palettes of the EGA, or what shades (out of 256K) will be used for the color registers assigned to the sixteen palette registers of the VGA in mode 12H. Figure 14-4 lists a program that displays the default shades of the sixteen EGA palettes and permits changing each one to any of the 64 available colors.

The palette number is given above each color block, and as a palette is changed, the selected color number appears below the color block. When you have chosen the desired shades, you can exit this program, but first copy down the palette and color numbers for use in your program. If you want to, you can assign the same color to two or three adjacent palettes, which will reduce the amount of detail in your display, but may enhance the beauty of the picture and/or emphasize certain details that you wish to stress. Plate 9 makes use of these techniques.

Figure 14-4: Program to Display and Change EGA Palette Colors

```
                palette = program to select colors for palette
```

```
#include <stdio.h>
#include <math.h>
#include <dos.h>
#include "tools.h"

void fillRect(int x1, int y1, int x2, int y2, int color);

#define convert(x,y) {x=(x+319); y=(175-((93*y) >> 7));}

int LINEWIDTH=1, OPERATOR=0, ANGLE, XCENTER, YCENTER;
unsigned long int PATTERN=0xFFFFFFFF;
unsigned int PALETTE[16]={0,1,2,3,4,5,20,7,56,57,58,59,60,61,
    62,63};

main()
{
    int i,j,k=0;

    setMode(16);
    gotoxy(4,6);
    printf("0   1   2   3   4   5   6   7   8   9  10"
        "  11  12  13  14  15");
    for (i=0; i<16; i++0
        fillRect((32*i-303),100,(32*(i+1)-303),0,i);
    while (k<150)
    {
        gotoxy(20,22);
        printf("                                   ");
        gotoxy(20,23);
        printf("                                   ");
        gotoxy(20,22);
        printf("Enter palette number: ");
        scanf("%d",&j);
        gotoxy(20,23);
        printf("Enter color number: ");
        scanf("%d",&k);
        if (k > 150)
        break;
        setEGApalette(j,k);
        gotoxy(3+4*j,15);
        printf("%2d",k);
    }
}
```

---

fillRect() = fills a rectangle whose top left and
            bottom right corners are specified
            with a specific color

```
void fillRect(int x1, int y1, int x2, int y2, int color)
{
    int i,first,last,begin,end,start_mask,end_mask,mask,dummy,
        page, xs,xe;
    long int y1L, y2L,j;
    #define seq_out(index,val)    {outp(0x3C4,index);\
                                   outp(0x3C5,val);}
    #define graph_out(index,val)  {outp(0x3CE,index);\
                                   outp(0x3CF,val);}
    unsigned int offset;
    char far * mem_address;

    convert(x1,y1);
    convert(x2,y2);

    y1L = y1*80L;
    y2L = y2*80L;
    begin = x1/8;
    end = x2/8;
    first = x1 - begin*8;
    last = x2 - end*8 + 1;
    start_mask = 0xFF >> first;
    end_mask = 0xFF << (8-last);
    for (j=y1L; j<=y2L; j+=80)
    {
        offset = j + begin;
        mem_address = (char far *) 0xA0000000L + offset;
        graph_out(8,start_mask);
        seq_out(2,0x0F);
        dummy = *mem_address;
        *mem_address = 0;
        seq_out(2,color);
        *mem_address = start_mask;
        for (i=begin+1; i<end; i++)
        {
            offset = j + i;
            mem_address = (char far *) 0xA0000000L + offset;
            graph_out(8,0xFF);
            seq_out(2,0x0F);
            dummy = *mem_address;
            *mem_address = 0;
            seq_out(2,color);
            *mem_address = 0xFF;
```

```
        }
        offset = j + end;
        mem_address = (char far *) 0xA0000000L + offset;
        graph_out(8,end_mask);
        seq_out(2,0x0F);
        dummy = *mem_address;
        *mem_address = 0;
        seq_out(2,color);
        *mem_address = end_mask;
        seq_out(2,0x0F);
        graph_out(3,0);
        graph_out(8,0xFF);
    }
}
```

Other Mandelbrot-Like Sets

Although the Mandelbrot set has received all of the publicity, it is the mapping of only a single iterated function, namely that of Equation 14-1. It is not as widely known that for every iterated function there is a set similar to the Mandelbrot set. We'll look at dragon curves in Chapter 16 and phoenix curves in Chapter 17. These curves are so-named because plotting them with the same mapping as used for Julia curves in the next chapter gives pictures that are similar to the shape of dragons and phoenixes. Each of these sets has a Mandelbrot-like map. Figure 14-5 is a program to generate the Mandelbrot-like set for dragon curves. The resulting map is shown in Plate 10. Figure 14-6 is a program to generate the Mandelbrot-like set for phoenix curves. The resulting map is shown in Plate 11.

Figure 14-5: Program to Generate Mandelbrot-Like Set for Dragon Curves

```
        csdragon = advanced program to map the dragon set
```

```
#include <stdio.h>
#include <math.h>
#include <dos.h>
#include <process.h>
#include "tools.h"

const int maxcol = 640;
```

```c
const int maxrow = 350;
const int max_colors = 16;
int CURSOR_X=320,CURSOR_Y=175,col,row;
int max_iterations = 256;
int max_size = 4;
int LINEWIDTH=1, OPERATOR=0x00, ANGLE, XCENTER, YCENTER;
unsigned long int PATTERN=0xFFFFFFFF;
unsigned char PALETTE[16]={0,1,2,3,4,5,20,7,56,57,58,59,
    60,61,62,63};
float Q[350];
float TXMax,TXMin,TYMax,TYMin;
union LIMIT XMax,YMax,XMin,YMin;

char file_name[13] = {"drgset00.pcx"};

FILE *f1;

main()
{
    float P,deltaP, deltaQ, X, Y, Xsquare, Ysquare,
        Xtemp,Ytemp;
    int i,color, row, col,error,response,repeat=0x30,
        start_col;

    printf("Enter screen number (00 -  99): ");
    file_name[6] = getche();
    file_name[7] = getche();
    getch();
    error = restore_screen(file_name);
    if (error == 0)
    {
        printf("\nEnter 0 to generate first Dragon "
            "Set screen");
        printf("\nEnter 1 to exit: ");
        response = getche();
        if (response != 0x30)
            exit(0);
        else
        {
            XMax.f = 4.2;
            XMin.f = -2.2;
            YMax.f = 1.5;
            YMin.f = -1.5;
            setMode(16);
            cls(7);
            start_col = 0;
        }
    }
    else
    {
```

07

```
    if (error < 639)
    {
        start_col = 8 * (error/8);
        remove(file_name);
    }
    else
    {
        start_col = 0;
        move_cursor(0,15,0,0);
        move_cursor(1,15,CURSOR_X,CURSOR_Y);
        setMode(16);
        cls(7);
        XMax.f = TXMax;
        XMin.f = TXMin;
        YMax.f = TYMax;
        YMin.f = TYMin;
    }
}
while (repeat == 0x30)
{
    deltaP = (XMax.f - XMin.f)/(maxcol);
    deltaQ = (YMax.f - YMin.f)/(maxrow);
    Q[0] = YMax.f;
    for (row=1; row<=maxrow; row++)
    Q[row] = Q[row-1] - deltaQ;
    P = XMin.f + start_col * deltaP;
    for (col=start_col; col<maxcol; col++)
    {
        if (kbhit() != 0)
        {
            save_screen(0,0,col,349,file_name);
             exit(0);
        }
        for (row=0; row<=maxrow; row++)
        {
            X = 0.50;
            Y = 0.0;
            color = 0;
            while (((X*X + Y*Y) < max_size) &&
                (color<max_iterations))
            {
                Xtemp = (Y - X)*(Y + X) + X;
                Ytemp = X * Y;
                Ytemp = Ytemp + Ytemp - Y;
                X = P * Xtemp + Q[row] * Ytemp;
                Y = Q[row] * Xtemp - P * Ytemp;
                color++;
            }
            plot(col, row, (color % max_colors));
        }
        P += deltaP;
```

```
            }
        save_screen(0,0,639,349,file_name);
        getch();
        gotoxy(10,24);
        printf("Enter '0' to run another plot, '1' to"
            " quit: ");
        repeat = getche();
        if (repeat == 0x30)
        {
            move_cursor(0,15,0,0);
            move_cursor(1,15,CURSOR_X,CURSOR_Y);
            XMax.f = TXMax;
            XMin.f = TXMin;
            YMax.f = TYMax;
            YMin.f = TYMin;
            start_col = 0;
            setMode(16);
            cls(7);
        }
    }
}
```

Figure 14-6: Program to Generate Mandelbrot-Like
Set for Phoenix Curves

```
    csphenix = advanced program to map the set for phoenix
```

```
#include <stdio.h>
#include <math.h>
#include <dos.h>
#include <process.h>
#include "tools.h"

const int maxcol = 640;
const int maxrow = 350;
const int max_colors = 16;
int CURSOR_X=0,CURSOR_Y=0,col,row;
int max_iterations = 32;
int max_size = 4;
int LINEWIDTH=1, OPERATOR=0x00, ANGLE, XCENTER, YCENTER;
unsigned long int PATTERN=0xFFFFFFFF;
unsigned char PALETTE[16]={0,1,2,3,4,5,20,7,56,57,58,59,60,61,62,63};
float Q[350];
float TXMax,TXMin,TYMax,TYMin;
union LIMIT XMax,YMax,XMin,YMin;
```

```
char file_name[13] = {"phenst00.pcx"};

FILE *f1;

main()
{
    float P,deltaP, deltaQ, X, Y, Xsquare, Xisquare,Xtemp,
        Xitemp,Xi,Yi;
    int i,color, row, col,error,response,repeat=0x30,start_col;

    printf("Enter screen number (00 -  99): ");
    file_name[6] = getche();
    file_name[7] = getche();
    getch();
    error = restore_screen(file_name);
    if (error == 0)
    {
        printf("\nEnter 0 to generate first Phoenix Set "
            "screen");
        printf("\nEnter 1 to exit: ");
        response = getche();
        if (response != 0x30)
            exit(0);
        else
        {
            XMax.f = 1.5;
            XMin.f = -2.1;
            YMax.f = 2.0;
            YMin.f = -2.0;
            start_col = 0;
            setMode(16);
            cls(7);
        }
    }
    else
    {
        if (error < 639)
        {
            start_col = 8 * (error/8);
            remove(file_name);
        }
        else
        {
            start_col = 0;
            move_cursor(0,15,0,0);
            move_cursor(1,15,CURSOR_X,CURSOR_Y);
            setMode(16);
            cls(7);
            XMax.f = TXMax;
            XMin.f = TXMin;
            YMax.f = TYMax;
```

```
            YMin.f = TYMin;
        }
    }
    while (repeat == 0x30)
    {
        deltaP = (XMax.f - XMin.f)/(maxcol);
        deltaQ = (YMax.f - YMin.f)/(maxrow);
        Q[0] = YMax.f;
        for (row=1; row<=maxrow; row++)
            Q[row] = Q[row-1] - deltaQ;
        P = XMin.f + start_col * deltaP;
        for (col=start_col; col<maxcol; col++)
        {
            if (kbhit() != 0)
            {
                save_screen(0,0,col,349,file_name);
                exit(0);
            }
            for (row=0; row<=maxrow; row++)
            {
                Y = 0;
                Yi = 0;
                X = 0;
                Xi = 0;
                color = 0;
                Xsquare = Xisquare = 0;
                while ((color<max_iterations) &&
                    ((Xsquare + Xisquare) < max_size))
                {
                    Xsquare = X*X;
                    Xisquare = Xi*Xi;
                    Xtemp = Xsquare - Xisquare + P + Q[row]*Y;
                    Xitemp = 2*X*Xi + Q[row]*Yi;
                    Y = X;
                    Yi = Xi;
                    X = Xtemp;
                    Xi = Xitemp;
                    color++;
                }
                plot(col, row, color%max_colors);
            }
            P += deltaP;
        }
        save_screen(0,0,639,349,file_name);
        getch();
        gotoxy(10,24);
        printf("Enter '0' to run another plot, '1' to quit: ");
        repeat = getche();
        if (repeat == 0x30)
        {
            move_cursor(0,15,0,0);
```

```
        move_cursor(1,15,CURSOR_X,CURSOR_Y);
        XMax.f = TXMax;
        XMin.f = TXMin;
        YMax.f = TYMax;
        YMin.f = TYMin;
        start_col = 0;
        setMode(16);
        cls(7);
    }
  }
}
```

15

Julia Sets

Chapter 14 discussed the Mandelbrot set, which is produced by plotting the values of the iterated equation:

$$z_{n+1} = z_n^2 + c \qquad \text{(Equation 15-1)}$$

with the x display coordinate corresponding to the real part of c over a selected range and the y display coordinate corresponding to the imaginary part of c over a selected range. For each calculation, the beginning value of z is taken as 0.

It was pointed out that there is another way in which the equation which produces the Julia sets can be mapped onto the display which produces the Julia sets. For this other technique, a particular value is selected for c. The equation is then processed for various values of z_0 over a selected range. The x coordinate of the display corresponds to the real part of z_0, and the y coordinate corresponds to the imaginary part of z_0.

It was also mentioned that the Mandelbrot set forms a sort of map of all of the possible Julia sets. Plate 4 shows the Mandelbrot set, with arrows identifying the location corresponding to the particular value of c for each of the fourteen Julia sets, eight of which are displayed in plates 12–19 in the color section. The first thing to note is where interesting Julia sets occur on the Mandelbrot map. The most interesting patterns occur for values of c that are very close to the boundary of the Mandelbrot set and usually also near a cusp. It is also interesting, but not very useful, to note that if a particular portion of the Mandelbrot set is expanded to a large enough scale, the resulting pattern is very much like the

Julia set for the value of c at the center of the expansion. You can verify this by selecting a value for drawing a particular Julia set, and then expanding the Mandelbrot set around the same point, using the program in Chapter 14.

Drawing Julia Sets

Figure 15-1 is a program for plotting Julia sets. When the program begins, you are asked to enter the maximum number of iterations that will be performed by the iteration loop. You are then asked for a background color and six display colors. Next, you are given a choice of quitting, finishing, or expanding a Julia set, or creating a new set. If you decide to quit, the program terminates. If you decide to create a new set, you are asked to enter two digits to form a screen number.

The program then displays the Mandelbrot set having the file name *mandelxx.pcx*, where *xx* are the two digits that you have just entered. If such a file doesn't exist, or is not a legitimate *.pcx* file, the program prints a diagnostic message and terminates. If a Mandelbrot set display does appear, you are given the opportunity to move a cursor arrow to select the P (real part of c) and Q (imaginary part of c) values for a Julia set. As the cursor arrow moves about the screen, the values of P and Q are displayed at the bottom of the screen. The cursor moves one pixel each time one of the arrow keys is hit, or 10 pixels at a time if the shift and arrow keys are hit simultaneously.

If you chose to complete or expand a Julia set, you are asked to enter two numbers for the Julia set screen number. The program then attempts to display a file having the file name *julia0xx.pcx,* where *xx* are the two numbers that you just entered. Again, if the file does not exist, or is not a legitimate *.pcx* file, the program terminates. Otherwise, the file is displayed.

If the file is an incomplete display, the program picks up where it left off and continues work on completing the display. If the file is complete, the program displays a cursor in the upper-left corner, and permits you to select *XMin* and *YMax* values for your expanded display with the cursor arrows. When the cursor is correctly positioned, hitting Ent displays the cursor in the lower-right corner and allows you to select the desired values of *XMax* and *YMin*.

The program then begins to run a set of nested loops very similar to those described for the Mandelbrot set program, except that *P* and *Q* are held constant and the initial values of *X* and *Y* are varied as the program generates a result for each pixel. A color is plotted to the appropriate pixel after the equation has "blown up" (by exceeding the magnitude of 2) or the specified maximum number of iterations has occurred. The color will be either the background color, if the maximum number of iterations did not occur, or a display color representing the value of the end result if the program looped through the maximum number of iterations without blowing up.

Number of Iterations

As this program is used at points very near the border of the Mandelbrot set, a situation occurs where the precision of the computer is inadequate to prevent the value of the iterated equation from "drifting off," and finally "blowing up" if enough iterations take place (even though it would not blow up if the computer were absolutely accurate). Thus, if you enter a very large number of iterations, the program will not only be inordinately slow, but the result will be a completely blank screen, painted in the background color.

As you begin to reduce the number of iterations, you will start getting a display which has a great amount of detail, but also a large number of lost points. The number of iterations required to present a display which is a good compromise between adequate detail and reasonably complete representation of the pattern varies depending upon the exact values which you have selected for *P* and *Q*. That is why the program has been set up to allow you to enter the number of iterations. A good number to begin with is 64 iterations. Then, if the display is sparse, with a large number of isolated points, you can decrease the number of iterations. Whereas if the display has large blobs of the same color and appears to lack detail, you can increase the number of iterations.

Figure 15-1: Program to Generate Julia Sets

```
            cjulia = advanced program to map the Julia sets
```

```c
#include <conio.h>
#include <stdio.h>
#include <math.h>
#include <dos.h>
#include <process.h>
#include "tools.h"
#include <ctype.h>

const int maxcol = 639;
const int maxrow = 349;
const int max_colors = 16;
int CURSOR_X=0,CURSOR_Y=0,col,row;
int max_iterations;  /* = 96;  32 for dust    64 normal  */
int max_size = 4;
int LINEWIDTH=1, OPERATOR=0x00:
unsigned long int PATTERN=0xFFFFFFFF;
unsigned char PALETTE[16]={0,1,2,3,4,5,20,7,56,57,58,59,60,61,
    62,63};
int colors[7]={0,1,2,3,4,5,20,7};
float P,Q;
float TXMax,TXMin,TYMax,TYMin;
union LIMIT XMax,YMax,XMin,YMin,Pval,Qval;

char file_name[13] = {"mandel00.pcx"};
char file_name2[13] = {"julia000.pcx"};

FILE *f1,*f2;

main()
{
    float deltaX, deltaY, X, Y, Xsquare, Ysquare;
    int i,color, row, col,error,response,repeat=0x30,start_col;

    clrscr();
    printf("Enter '0' to quit, '1' to expand "
        "or finish julia, '2' for new plot: ");
    do
        repeat = getch();
    while ((repeat != 0x30) && (repeat != 0x31) &&
        (repeat != 0x32));

    while (repeat != 0x30)
    {
        printf("\nEnter number of iterations: ");
```

```
scanf("%d",&max_iterations);
printf("\nEnter background and six other colors "
    "separated by commas: ");
scanf("%d,%d,%d,%d,%d,%d,%d",&colors,&colors[1],
    &colors[2],&colors[3],&colors[4],&colors[5],
    &colors[6]);
if (repeat == 0x32)
{
    printf("\nEnter mandelbrot set number (00 - 99): ");
    file_name[6] = getche();
    file_name[7] = getche();
    if ((isdigit(file_name[6])) && (isdigit(file_name
        [7])))
        error = restore_screen(file_name);
    else
        exit(0);
    start_col = 0;
    move_cursor(2,15,0,0);
    XMax.f = 1.8;
    XMin.f = -1.8;
    YMax.f = 1.2;
    YMin.f = -1.2;
    P = Pval.f;
    Q = Qval.f;
    cls(7);
}
else
{
    printf("\nEnter julia screen number (00 - 99): ");
    file_name2[6] = getche();
    file_name2[7] = getche();
    if ((isdigit(file_name2[6])) &&
        (isdigit(file_name2[7])))
        error = restore_screen(file_name2);
    else
        exit(0);
    if (error == 0)
        exit(0);
    else
    {
        if (error < 639)
        {
            start_col = 8 * (error/8);
            remove(file_name2);
            P = Pval.f;
            Q = Qval.f;
        }
        else
        {
            move_cursor(0,15,0,0);
            move_cursor(1,15,CURSOR_X,CURSOR_Y);
```

```
                    XMax.f = TXMax;
                    XMin.f = TXMin;
                    YMax.f = TYMax;
                    YMin.f = TYMin;
                    P = Pval.f;
                    Q = Qval.f;
                    start_col = 0;
                    cls(7);
                }
            }
    }
    if (colors[0] <64)
    {
        setEGApalette(0,colors[0]);
        setEGApalette(1,colors[1]);
        setEGApalette(2,colors[2]);
        setEGApalette(3,colors[3]);
        setEGApalette(4,colors[4]);
        setEGApalette(5,colors[5]);
        setEGApalette(6,colors[6]);
    }
    deltaX = (XMax.f - XMin.f)/(maxcol);
    deltaY = (YMax.f - YMin.f)/(maxrow);
    for (col=start_col; col<=maxcol; col++)
    {
        if (kbhit() != 0)
        {
            Pval.f = P;
            Qval.f = Q;
            save_screen(0,0,col,349,file_name2);
            exit(0);
        }
        for (row=0; row<=maxrow; row++)
        {
            X = XMin.f + col * deltaX;
            Y = YMax.f - row * deltaY;
            Xsquare = 0;
            Ysquare = 0;
            color = 0;
            while ((color<max_iterations) &&
                ((Xsquare + Ysquare) < max_size))
            {
                Xsquare = X*X;
                Ysquare = Y*Y;
                Y = 2*X*Y + Q;
                X = Xsquare - Ysquare + P;
                color++;
            }
            gotoxy(24,24);
            if (color >= max_iterations)
                color = ((int)((Xsquare + Ysquare) *6.0))%6
```

```
                        + 1;
                else
                    color = 0;
                plot(col, row, color);
            }
        }
        Pval.f  = P;
        Qval.f = Q;
        save_screen(0,0,639,349,file_name2);
        getch();
        gotoxy(1,24);
        printf("File Name: %s    Enter '0' = quit, '1' = expand "
            " plot, '2' = new plot: ",file_name2);
        repeat = getche();
    }
    getch();
}
```

Selecting Colors

You will notice that the use of colors is quite different in the Julia set program from what it was in the program for generating Mandelbrot sets. In the Mandelbrot set program, all of the values for which the iterated expression did not blow up and head for infinity after the maximum number of iterations, are colored black. The rest of the points are colored depending upon how many iterations took place before the expression exceeded the magnitude of 2. The colors are recycled so that for each increment in the number of iterations, a different color is used than was used to represent the previous number.

For the Julia sets, we color everything that blows up with the background color, and then cycle through six different colors to represent the values taken on by the expression after the maximum number of iterations. If you want to use the same scheme that was used for the Mandelbrot program, you will get displays that look somewhat similar to blow ups of the Mandelbrot set. Or you can keep the coloring technique used by the program, and use the default colors by entering the first color number as greater than 64, and then hitting Ent.

The second approach is to enter the proper color numbers when you are prompted by the program. If you're not sure what colors you want to use, you can use the *palette* program described in Chapter 14 to select a set of colors that go well together. Then enter them into the Julia set program at the prompt.

When a Julia set is drawn, the resulting color combinations are sometimes different from what you planned when you were modifying the color palette at the beginning of the program. It is for this reason, that we included the program *colors* in Chapter 5. If you don't like the colors of a display screen, you can run the *colors* program.

Colors first asks you for a file name, and then displays that file on the screen if it is a legitimate *.pcx* file. You can then enter a palette number from 0 to 15, followed by a return. Hitting the left and right cursor arrows then moves that palette color backward or forward through the 64 colors available for the EGA. When you find a color you like, hit Ent and you will be ready to enter another palette number. When you are done changing colors, enter a palette number greater than 15, and the program will save the newly colored display in a file called *colorsxx.pcx*, where *xx* is a number between 0 and 99.

The colors program displays the palette number and color number at the bottom of the screen as you are changing colors and palettes. Before the screen is rewritten to the new file, it is read again from the original file so that the palette and color information disappears and is not written to the new file. Do not be dismayed that the redrawn screen is in the original color combination; the new colors that you have selected have been saved and will be transferred to the new disk file.

Julia Set Displays

Figure 15-2 shows the parameters used in representative Julia set displays. Some of these are shown in Plates 12 through 19. The location of these Julia displays on the Mandelbrot set is shown in Plate 4.

Figure 15-2: Parameters for Julia Set Pictures

Location	Plate #	Iterations	P	Q	Colors
A	12	128	0.238498	0.519198	56,62,62,46,35,18,52
B	13	96	-0.743036	0.113467	0,16,34,2,18,22,23
C	—	64	-0.192175	0.656734	0,1,17,43,31,63,11
D	14	32	0.108294	-0.670487	0,46,38,62,54,55,63
E	—	64	-0.392488	-0.587966	39,1,13,21,47,54,62
F	—	256	-0.392488	-0.587966	63,1,2,3,4,5,20
G	15	32	0.138341	0.649857	1,32,12,4,36,37,38
H	16	24	0.278560	-0.003483	25,32,36,54,38,62,63
I	—	48	-1.258842	0.065330	4,54,51,1,47,44,20
J	—	48	-1.028482	-0.264756	48,51,2,38,4,16,20
K	—	64	0.268545	-0.003483	32,55,36,25,4,5,20
L	17	64	0.268545	-0.003483	32,55,36,25,4,5,20
M	—	24	0.268545	-0.003483	32,55,36,25,4,5,20
N	18	256	0.318623	0.044699	1,62,25,8,62,62,7
O	19	48	0.318623	0.429799	1,38,46,54,62,55,63

A few comments need to be made on these displays. E and F are pictures generated using the same values of P and Q, but with different color schemes and a different number of iterations. They give a clear comparison of how detail increases, but parts of the display disappear when the number of iterations increases. K, L, and M also have identical values of P and Q. L was produced by continuing the program after K was generated, and using the cursor to select a new area for enlargement. The new limits are: $XMin$ = -0.673239, $XMax$ = -0.171831, $YMin$ = 0.171928, and $YMax$ = 0.402292. The picture in M uses only twenty-four iterations. This is obviously too few in this case, so that too much detail is lost. The picture does provide some interesting patterns, however.

Binary Decomposition

We have been drawing Julia sets which show a background color if the iteration of the Julia equation blows up to infinity, and which show one of a set of six other colors to indicate the value of the magnitude of z when the equation does not blow up. The program is designed to anticipate the range of values that might be encountered, and split this into six groups of equal width, one for each color.

After we have performed the iterations for each value of the Julia set, there is another piece of information available that we have thus far ignored—the direction of the vector heading for infinity when we are in regions where the function blows up to infinity.

You will remember that at each iteration we obtain a complex number. Furthermore, the test for the function blowing up is that the magnitude of this complex number achieves a value greater than 2. Now, if we consider the real and imaginary parts of the number when that magnitude is achieved, they can be considered to represent a vector in the complex plane which has a direction from the origin as well as a magnitude. We determine what the direction angle is, and then color the corresponding point on the Julia picture black if that angle is between 0 and 180 degrees, and white if the angle is between 180 and 360 degrees. (All points that don't blow up have an angle too, namely that of the root which they settle down to, but that information isn't too interesting so we just color it black.)

Figure 15-3 is a simplified Julia program to do binary decomposition. You could modify the more detailed Julia program given in Figure 15-1 to do the same thing, or you can use the binary decomposition technique with some of the other curves that will be discussed in future chapters. Figure 15-4 shows the result of binary decomposition for two Julia sets. The first makes use of a value of 0 for c. If you were to put this value into the Julia set program of Figure 15-1, the result would be rather uninteresting—producing only a circle.

You can see that much more detail occurs when binary decomposition is performed. The second part of the figure shows binary decomposition of a more typical Julia set. The program of Figure 15-3 includes values of P and Q for both pictures. As it is currently set up, you will get the second picture; if you comment out the second set of P and Q values, you will get the first picture.

Figure 15-3: Program for Binary Decomposition of Julia Sets

```
bindecom = program for binary decomposition
```

```c
#include <stdio.h>
#include <stdlib.h>;
#include <math.h>
#include <dos.h>
#include <process.h>
#include "tools.h"


void plot(int x, int y, int color);
void setMode(int mode);

const int maxcol = 639;
const int maxrow = 349;
const int max_colors = 16;


char strings[80];
int col,row,i;
int max_iterations = 64;
int max_size = 4;
int LINEWIDTH=1, OPERATOR=0;
unsigned long int PATTERN=0xFFFFFFFF;
float P,Q,Xmax= 2.0, Xmin=-2.0, Ymax=1.50, Ymin=-1.50,theta;

main()
{
    float deltaX, deltaY, X, Y, Xsquare, Ysquare,Ytemp,temp1,
        temp2;
    int color, row, col;

    setMode(16);
    cls(7);
    P = 0;
    Q = 0;
    P = .318623;
    Q = .0429799;
    deltaX = (Xmax - Xmin)/(maxcol);
    deltaY = (Ymax - Ymin)/(maxrow);
    for (col=0; col<=maxcol; col++)
    {
        if (kbhit() != 0) break;
        for (row=0; row<=maxrow; row++)
        {
            X = Xmin + col * deltaX;
```

```
            Y = Ymax - row * deltaY;
            Xsquare = 0;
            Ysquare = 0;
            i = 0;
            while ((i<max_iterations) && ((Xsquare +
                Ysquare) < max_size))
            {
                Xsquare = X*X;
                Ysquare = Y*Y;
                Ytemp = 2*X*Y;
                X = Xsquare - Ysquare + P;
                Y = Ytemp + Q;
                i++;
            }
            if (X == 0)
                color = 15;
            else
            {
                theta = acos(fabs(X)/(sqrt(X*X + Y*Y)));
                if ((X<0) && (Y>=0))
                    theta += 1.5707963;
                if ((X<0) && (Y<0))
                    theta += 3.14159625;
                if ((X>0) && (Y<0))
                    theta += 4.7123889;
                if ((theta>=0) && (theta<=3.14159625))
                    color = 15;
                else
                    color = 0;
            }
            plot(col, row, color);
        }
    }
    getch();
}
```

Figure 15-4: Binary Decomposition of Julia Sets

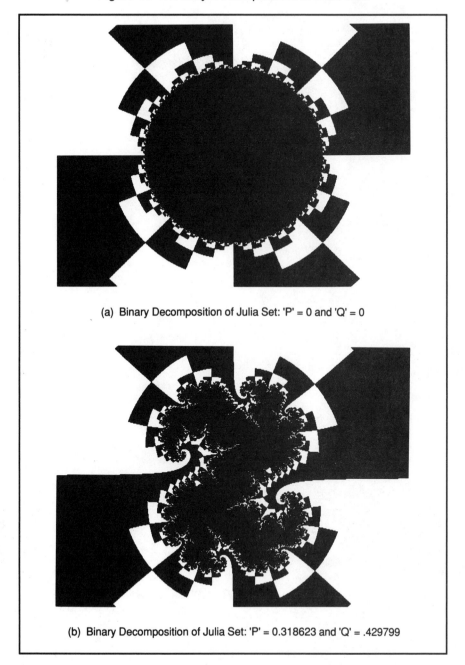

(a) Binary Decomposition of Julia Set: 'P' = 0 and 'Q' = 0

(b) Binary Decomposition of Julia Set: 'P' = 0.318623 and 'Q' = .429799

16

Dragon Curves

The term "dragon curves" covers a lot of territory. Most of these curves were so-named because they looked somewhat like the traditional conception of a mythical dragon. There are several families of curves, however, each with its own distinct mathematical origin. Some of these dragon curves are variations of other curves that we have already dealt with and should really have been included with them. Nevertheless, we have chosen to put all the dragons together in this chapter.

If you have seen some of the traditional Chinese embroidered dragons, you can note the resemblances as you look at the dragon curves in the later pages of this chapter. Some of the prettiest and most dragon-like curves are the "self-squared" dragons first discovered by Mandelbrot. To complicate matters, all of the curves that are produced from variations of the self-squared dragon equation are called "dragons" even though some of them do not look anything like dragons, which makes the whole classification very confusing.

Harter-Heightway Dragon

The Harter-Heightway dragon is one of the family of curves created with the initiator/generator technique described in Chapter 6. The first three levels of this curve are shown in Figure 16-1. It can be seen that the first two levels look just like the Polya triangle sweep discussed in Chapter 8. Two additional rules cause this curve to diverge from the Polya triangle so that the dragon curve is generated:

Figure 16-1: First Three Levels of Harter-Heightway Dragon

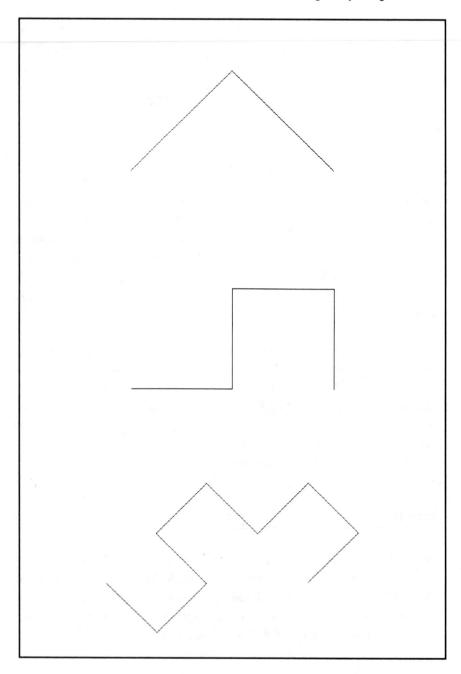

1. The generator alternates between the right and left of the line segment it is replacing.

2. The first position at each level is always to the right. We use the generic *curvegen* program described in Chapter 6 to generate the dragon curve. However, we must add to the generator function a *sign* variable, which causes the alternation around the line segment being replaced.

Twin Dragon

It is interesting to see what happens when the same initiator is used, but traversed in the opposite direction. The dragon that is generated fits exactly against the dragon described above. The program of Figure 16-2 is already set up to generate the twin dragon, in that it changes color at the end of the *for* loop, and that the proper values for the initiator are given to provide the backward traversing of the original initiator line.

For the single dragon, *int_level* was set to 1, so that only one pass is made through the *for* loop and the second set of initiator values is not used. By simply changing the *int_level* to 2, you can generate the twin dragons in contrasting colors. The twin dragon curve is shown in Plate 20 of the color section. The exact fit between the two dragons appears in the plate, but to fully appreciate how they mesh together, one needs to run the program and watch as the borders of the second dragon are drawn.

Figure 16-2 is the program that is used to generate both the Harter-Heightway dragon and the twin dragon. The various levels of detail may be produced by changing the parameter *level*. Figure 16-3 shows the dragon figure produced by setting *level* to 16.

Figure 16-2: Program to Generate Harter-Heightway
and Twin Dragons

```
twindrag = program to generate a twin dragon
```

```c
#include <stdio.h>
#include <math.h>
#include <dos.h>
#include "tools.h"

void generate (float X1, float Y1, float X2, float Y2,
    int level, int sign);

union LIMIT XMax,XMin,YMax,YMin,Pval,Qval;
int combination = 0,LINEWIDTH=1, OPERATOR=0;
unsigned long int PATTERN=0xFFFFFFFF;
float turtle_theta;
/*int i,flag[24],color = 10;*/
int i,flag[24],color = 15;
int generator_size = 3;
int level;
int init_size = 1;
int initiator_x1[10] = {-150,150},initiator_x2[10]={150,-150},
    initiator_y1[10]={-25,-25}, initiator_y2[10]={-25,-25};
float Xpoints[25], Ypoints[25];
float turtle_x,turtle_y,turtle_r;
unsigned char PALETTE[16]={0,1,2,3,4,5,20,7,56,57,58,59,60,
    61,62,63};

main()
{

    int sign = 1;

    printf("\nEnter level (1 - 16): ");
    scanf("%d",&level);
    if (level < 1)
        level = 1;
    setMode(16);
    cls(0);

    for (i=0; i<init_size; i++)
    {
        generate(initiator_x1[i], initiator_y1[i],
            initiator_x2[i], initiator_y2[i], level, sign);
        color = 13;
    }
```

```
    getch();
}
```

```
┌─────────────────────────────────────────────────────────────┐
│                                                               │
│                 generate() = generates curve                  │
│                                                               │
└─────────────────────────────────────────────────────────────┘
```

```
void generate (float X1, float Y1, float X2, float Y2,
    int level, int sign)
{
    int j,k,line,sign2=-1;
    float a, b, Xpoints[25], Ypoints[25];
    turtle_r = (sqrt((X2 - X1)*(X2 - X1) + (Y2 - Y1)*
        (Y2 - Y1)))/1.41421;
    Xpoints[0] = X1;
    Ypoints[0] = Y1;
    Xpoints[2] = X2;
    Ypoints[2] = Y2;
    turtle_theta = point(X1,Y1,X2,Y2);
    turtle_x = X1;
    turtle_y = Y1;
    turn(sign*(45));
    step();
    Xpoints[1] = turtle_x;
    Ypoints[1] = turtle_y;
    level--;
    if (level > 0)
    {
        for (j=0; j<generator_size-1; j++)
        {
            X1 = Xpoints[j];
            X2 = Xpoints[j+1];
            Y1 = Ypoints[j];
            Y2 = Ypoints[j+1];
            generate (X1,Y1,X2,Y2,level,sign2);
            sign2 *= -1;
        }
    }
    else
    {
        for (k=0; k<generator_size-1; k++)
        {
            drawLine(Xpoints[k],Ypoints[k],
            Xpoints[k+1],Ypoints[k+1],color);
        }
    }
}
```

Figure 16-3: Harter-Heightway Dragon

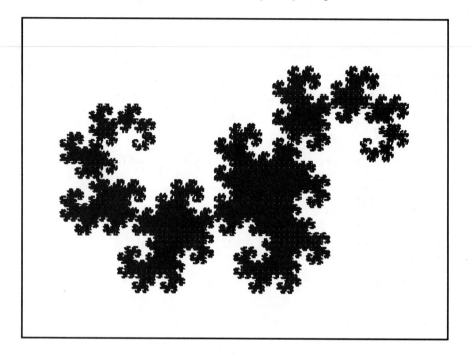

Julia Dragon

The Julia sets were described in detail in Chapter 15. Depending upon the parameters selected, many different shapes may be created. Some of them, deliberately omitted in Chapter 15, are very dragon-like. One such dragon uses 64 iterations, with palettes 0 to 6 set to the colors 42, 32, 36, 54, 38, 62, and 63, and the parameters of P = 0.383725 and Q = 0.147851.

Self-Squared Dragons

The figures that Mandelbrot calls "self-squared dragons" result from iterations of
the expression:

$$z_{n-1} = cz_n(1-z_n) \hspace{3cm} \text{(Equation 16-1)}$$

where both z and c are complex numbers, the number c being represented in our
program by $c = p + iq$. You will note that if both c and z are real, the equation is
the same as that for the population growth curve that we discussed in Chapter 7.
As far as I know, no one has looked into the relationship between the bifurcation
diagrams and the corresponding dragon curves in detail. This might be a good
project for a home computer enthusiast.

Figure 16-4 is the detailed program for generating the self-squared dragon curves.
Note that the program is very similar to the program for generating the Julia sets,
except for the code that actually performs the iterations of the equation. The
program starts (unless you opt to display a dragon curve) with the diagram
corresponding to the Mandelbrot set for dragons.

This curve appears in Plate 10. Figure 16-5 lists the parameters for some typical
dragon curves. These pictures are plates 21 and 22. As in the case of the Julia
sets, increasing the number of iterations increases the detail of the display, but
insufficient computer accuracy causes parts of the display to be lost as the iterated
values drift away from the attractor. Typically, if we continue to increase the
number of iterations, the figure will become fragmented, and finally disappear
altogether.

Figure 16-4: Program to Generate Self-Squared Dragons

```
            cdragon = advanced program to map the dragon curves
```

```c
#include <ctype.h>
#include <conio.h>
#include <stdio.h>
#include <math.h>
#include <dos.h>
#include <process.h>
#include "tools.h"

const int maxcol = 639;
const int maxrow = 349;
const int max_colors = 16;
int CURSOR_X=0,CURSOR_Y=0,col,row;
int max_iterations;
int max_size = 4;
int LINEWIDTH=1, OPERATOR=0x00, ANGLE;
unsigned long int PATTERN=0xFFFFFFFF;
unsigned char PALETTE[16]={0,1,2,3,4,5,20,7,56,57,58,59,60,
    61,62,63};
int colors[8] = {0,1,2,3,4,5,20,7};
float P,Q;
float TXMax,TXMin,TYMax,TYMin;
union LIMIT XMax,YMax,XMin,YMin,Pval,Qval;

char file_name[13] = {"drgset00.pcx"};
char file_name2[13] = {"dragon00.pcx"};

FILE *f1,*f2;

main()
{
    float deltaX, deltaY, X, Y, Xsquare, Ysquare,Ytemp,
        temp_sq,temp_xy;
    int i,color, row, col,error,response,repeat=0x32,start_col;

    setMode(3);
    printf("Enter '0' to quit, '1' to expand "
        "or finish dragon, '2' for new plot: ");
    do
        repeat = getch();
```

```
while ((repeat != 0x30) && (repeat != 0x31) &&
    (repeat != 0x32));

while (repeat != 0x30)
{
    printf("\nEnter number of iterations: ");
    scanf("%d",&max_iterations);
    printf("\nEnter background and six other colors "
        "separated by commas: ");
    scanf("%d,%d,%d,%d,%d,%d,%d",&colors,&colors[1],
        &colors[2],&colors[3],&colors[4],&colors[5],
        &colors[6]);
    if (repeat == 0x32)
    {
        printf("\nEnter dragon map number "
            "(00 - 99): ");
        file_name[6] = getche();
        file_name[7] = getche();
        if ((isdigit(file_name[6])) && (isdigit(file_name
            [7])))
            error = restore_screen(file_name);
        else
            exit(0);
        start_col = 0;
        move_cursor(2,15,0,0);
        XMax.f = 1.4;
        XMin.f = -.4;
        YMax.f = .8;
        YMin.f = -.8;
        P = Pval.f;
        Q = Qval.f;
        cls(7);
    }
    else
    {
        printf("\nEnter dragon screen number "
            "(00 - 99): ");
        file_name2[6] = getche();
        file_name2[7] = getche();
        if ((isdigit(file_name2[6])) &&
            (isdigit(file_name2[7])))
            error = restore_screen(file_name2);
        else
            exit(0);
        if (error == 0)
            exit(0);
        else
        {
```

```
        if (error < 639)
        {
            start_col = 8 * (error/8);
            remove(file_name2);
            P = Pval.f;
            Q = Qval.f;
        }
        else
        {
            move_cursor(0,15,0,0);
            move_cursor(1,15,CURSOR_X,CURSOR_Y);
            XMax.f = TXMax;
            XMin.f = TXMin;
            YMax.f = TYMax;
            YMin.f = TYMin;
            P = Pval.f;
            Q = Qval.f;

            start_col = 0;
            cls(7);
        }
    }
}
if (colors[0] <64)
{
    setEGApalette(0,colors[0]);
    setEGApalette(1,colors[1]);
    setEGApalette(2,colors[2]);
    setEGApalette(3,colors[3]);
    setEGApalette(4,colors[4]);
    setEGApalette(5,colors[5]);
    setEGApalette(6,colors[6]);
}
deltaX = (XMax.f - XMin.f)/(maxcol);
deltaY = (YMax.f - YMin.f)/(maxrow);
for (col=start_col; col<=maxcol; col++)
{
    if (kbhit() != 0)
            Pval.f = P;
            Qval.f = Q;
            save_screen(0,0,col,349,file_name2);
            fclose(f2);
            f2 = fopen (file_name2,"wb");
            Pval.f = P;
            Qval.f = Q;
            save_screen(0,0,col,349,
                file_name2);
```

```
                        exit(0);
                }
        for (row=0; row<=maxrow; row++)
        {
            X = XMin.f + col * deltaX;
            Y = YMax.f - row * deltaY;
            Xsquare = 0;
            Ysquare = 0;
            color = 0;
            while ((color<max_iterations) &&
                ((Xsquare + Ysquare) < max_size))
            {
                Xsquare = X*X;
                Ysquare = Y*Y;
                temp_sq = Ysquare - Xsquare;
                temp_xy = X*Y;
                temp_xy += temp_xy;
                Ytemp = Q*(temp_sq + X)-
                    P*(temp_xy - Y);
                X = P*(temp_sq + X)
                    + Q*(temp_xy - Y);
                Y = Ytemp;
                color++;
            }
            if (color >= max_iterations)
            {
                color = ((int)((Xsquare + Ysquare)
                    *6.0))%6 + 1;
            }
            else
                color = 0;
            plot(col, row, color);
        }
    }
            Pval.f = P;
            Qval.f = Q;
            save_screen(0,0,639,349,file_name2);
    getch();
    gotoxy(1,24);
    printf("File Name: %s    Enter '0' = quit, '1' = "
        "expand plot, '2' = new plot: ",file_name2);
    repeat = getche();
    }
    getch();
}
```

Figure: 16-5: Parameters for Dragons

Plate	Iterations	P	Q	Colors
21	256	1.646009	0.967049	0,1,52,62,38,44,20
—	64	1.646009	0.967049	0,1,2,3,4,5,20
—	64	2.447261	-0.924069	0,62,43,1,9,55,20
—	64	1.325508	0.786533	8,1,2,3,4,5,20
—	64	1.415414	0.856803	0,63,62,52,4,5,20
—	32	1.415414	0.856803	57,24,2,18,10,62,63
—	128	1.255399	0.691977	0,57,58,59,60,61,63
—	64	2.797809	-0.657593	8,1,2,3,4,5,20
—	64	3.018153	-0.098854	5,16,2,38,10,62,36
22	64	2.998122	0.004298	43,1,2,3,4,5,46,7,57
				57,58,59,60,61,62,63
				(See text)

San Marcos Dragon

Plate 43 shows what Mandelbrot calls the "San Marcos Dragon," because it reminded him of the San Marcos Square in Venice, with its reflection from a wet pavement. To enhance this fantasy, I've used a special color scheme in which everything where y is greater than or equal to zero is colored in brighter shades, and everything for y less than zero (the reflection) is colored in darker shades.

Figure 16-6 lists the code that must be inserted in the dragon program of Figure 16-4 to perform the proper coloring. This code is inserted in place of the lines that define color just prior to the *plot* statement. Since the *cdragon* program is only set to allow you to use six colors, you will need to modify the statements at the beginning of the program to permit all sixteen colors to be entered and to be used in *setEGApalette* statements. Alternately, you can keep to the default colors, and use the colors program to modify the colors of the finished display.

Figure 16-6: Code for Coloring San Marcos Dragon

```
if (color >= max_iterations)
    color = (int)((Xsquare + Ysquare)*100)%6+1;
else
    color = 0;
if (row < 175)
    color += 8;
```

Dragon Outlines

Before we leave the subject of dragons, it is worth looking at another technique for representing at least the outlines of dragon curves. This involves running the dragon equation backward. Instead of using Equation 16-1, we solve the equation for z_n in terms of z_{n+1}.

We then take a representative point and iterate it many times (in this case 12,000 times), plotting the location of the point at each iteration. (Each iteration requires taking a square root, which could give either a positive or negative result. To achieve good results from our display, the program is set up to randomly select either the positive or negative square root at each iteration.)

The result of all this is that the point tends to be attracted to the outline of the dragon curve. (The first few points are a little wild before the curve settles down, so we don't plot the first ten points.) This technique doesn't provide the full beauty and detail of the full-fledged dragon curve program, but it is much faster, and is therefore useful in discovering the shape of a dragon before you take the time to make a detailed plot.

This also serves as an introduction to techniques that will be gone into in much greater detail in the chapter on iterated function systems (Chapter 22). (We have already encountered this method at work in generating the strange attractors in Chapter 6.) Figure 16-7 lists the program to generate dragon outlines. Two typical results of running this program are shown in Figure 16-8 (page 304).

Figure 16-7: Program to Generate Dragon Outlines

```
                dragout = program to generate dragon outlines
```

```
#include <stdio.h>
#include <math.h>
#include <dos.h>
#include "tools.h"

int i, OPERATOR = 0x00,row,col;
int x_center = 320, y_center = 175;
float x = .50001, y = 0,P,Q,magnitude,scale,temp,temp_x,temp_y;

main()
{
    printf("Enter P and Q (real and imaginary parameters) "
        "separated by comma): ");
    scanf("%f,%f",&P,&Q);
    magnitude = P*P + Q*Q;
    P = 4*P/magnitude;
    Q = -4*Q/magnitude;
    printf("\nEnter Scale: ");
    scanf("%f",&scale);
    scale = x_center*scale;
    setMode(16);
    cls(0);
    for (i=0; i<12000; i++)
    {
        temp_x = x*P - y*Q;
        y = x*Q + y*P;
        temp_y = y;
        x = 1 - temp_x;
```

```
            magnitude = sqrt(x*x + y*y);
            y = sqrt((-x + magnitude)/2);
            x = sqrt((x + magnitude) /2);
            if (temp_y < 0)
                x = -x;
            if (rand() < 16163)
            {
                x = -x;
                y = -y;
            }
            x = (1 - x)/2;
            y = y/2;


            col = scale*(x-.5) + x_center;
            row = y_center - scale*y;
            if ((i > 10) && (col >= 0) && (col < 640) && (row >= 0)
                && (row < 350))
                plot (col,row,15);
        }
    getch();
}
```

Figure 16-8: Dragon Outlines

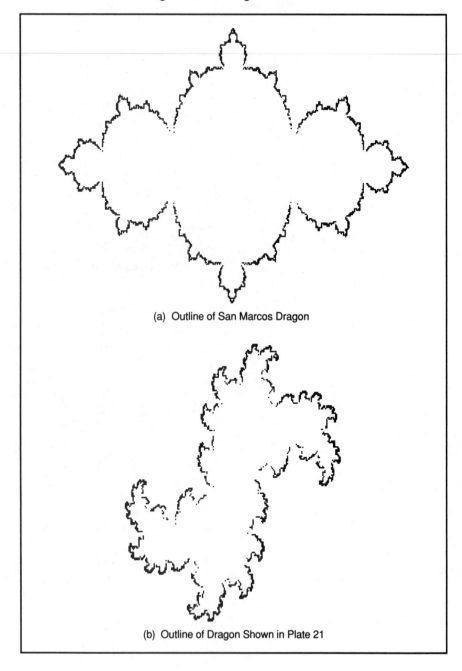

(a) Outline of San Marcos Dragon

(b) Outline of Dragon Shown in Plate 21

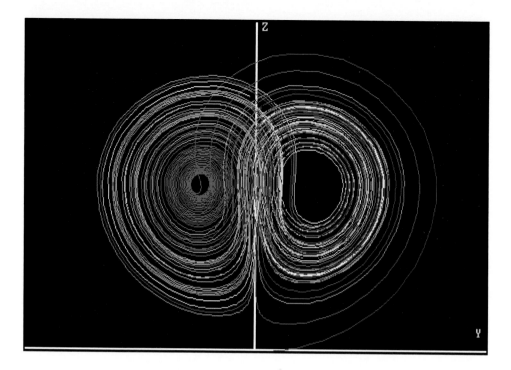

Plate 1: Lorenz Attractor Projected on YZ Plane

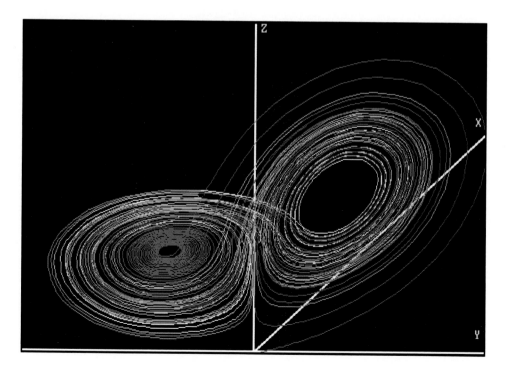

Plate 2: Three-Dimensional View of Lorenz Attractor

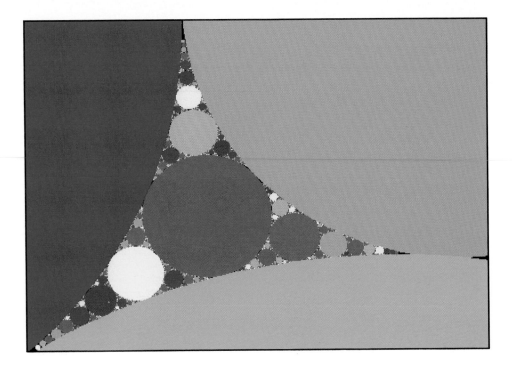

Plate 3: Apollonian Packing of Circles

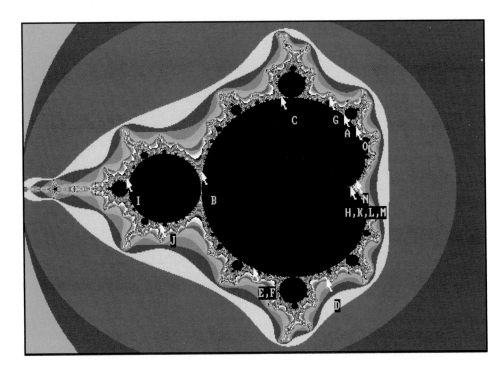

Plate 4: Mandelbrot Set Showing Locations for Julia Sets

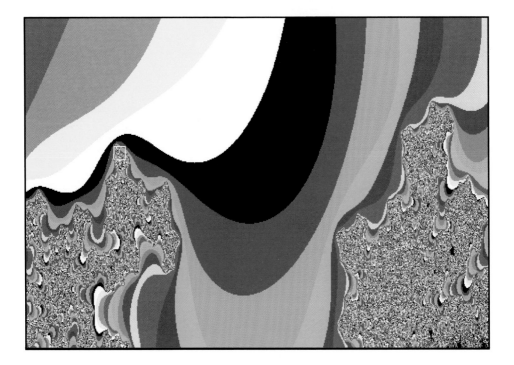

Plate 5: Expansion of an Area in Plate 4

Plate 6: Expansion of an Area in Plate 5

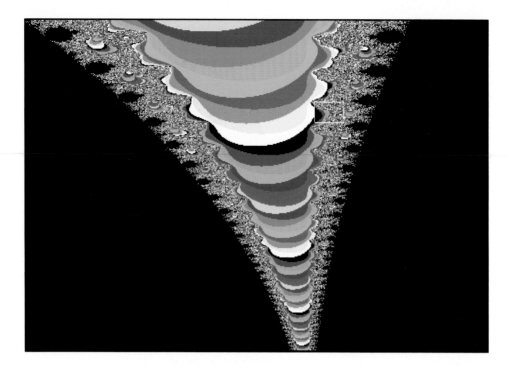

Plate 7: Expansion of an Area in Plate 4

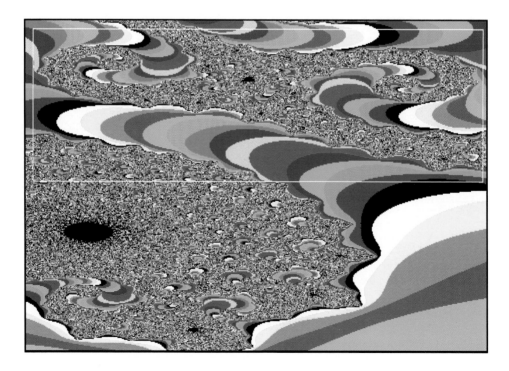

Plate 8: Expansion of an Area in Plate 7

Plate 9: Expansion of Marked Area in Plate 8 with Color Changes

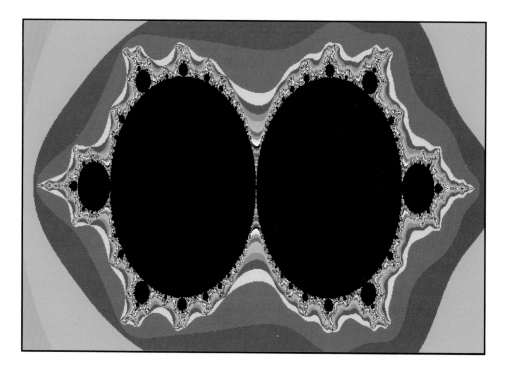

Plate 10: Mandelbrot-Like Set for Dragon Curves

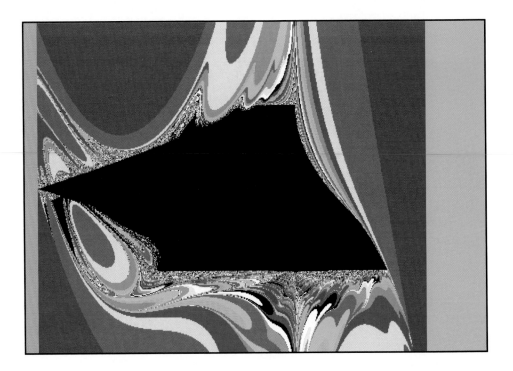

Plate 11: Mandelbrot-Like Set for Phoenix Curves

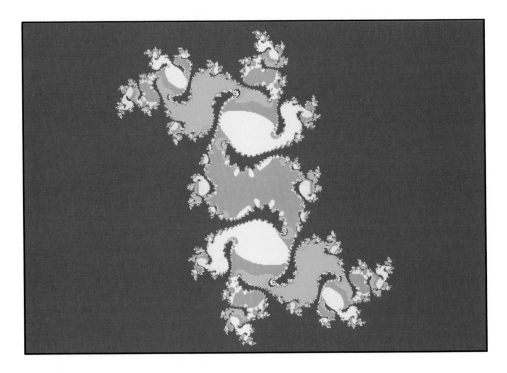

Plate 12: Julia Set from Location A of Mandelbrot Set

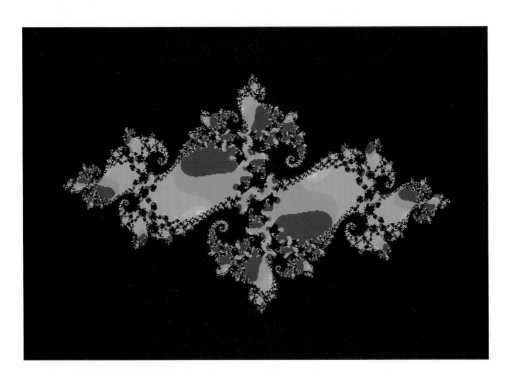

Plate 13: Julia Set from Location B of Mandelbrot Set

Plate 14: Julia Set from Location D of Mandelbrot Set

Plate 15: Julia Set from Location G of Mandelbrot Set

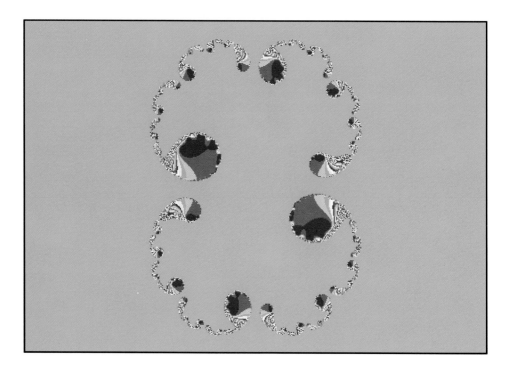

Plate 16: Julia Set from Location H of Mandelbrot Set

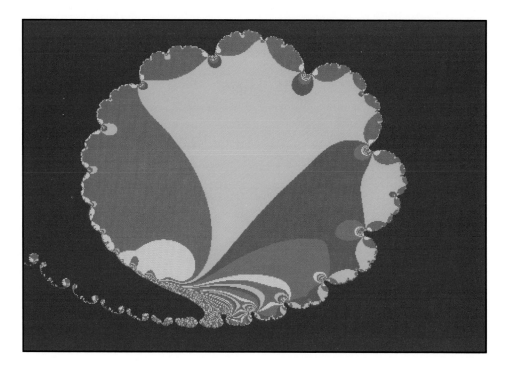

Plate 17: Julia Set from Location L of Mandelbrot Set

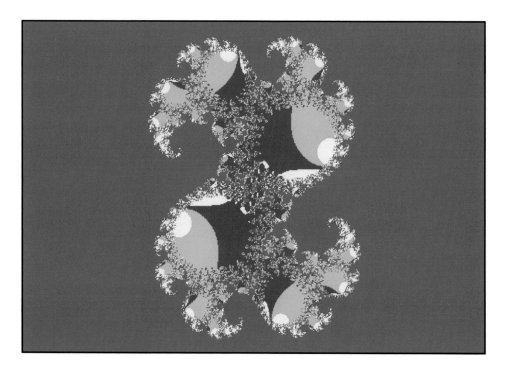

Plate 18: Julia Set from Location N of Mandelbrot Set

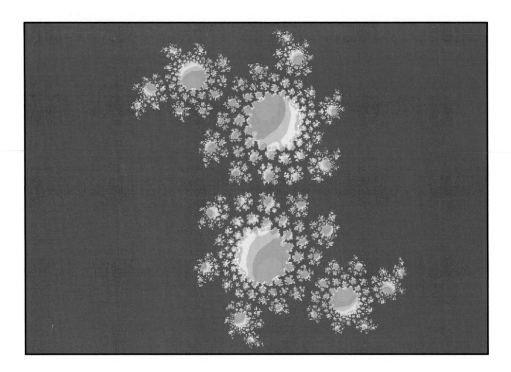

Plate 19: Julia Set from Location O of Mandelbrot Set

Plate 20: Twin Dragon Curve

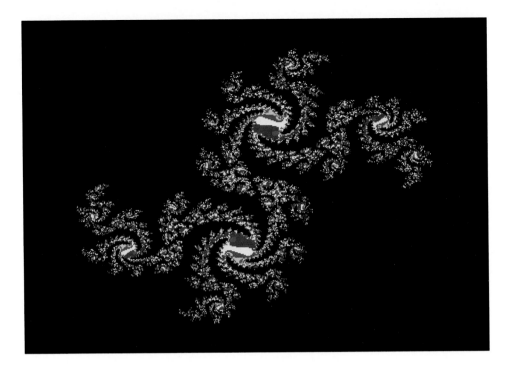

Plate 21: Self-Squared Dragon

Plate 22: San Marcos Dragon

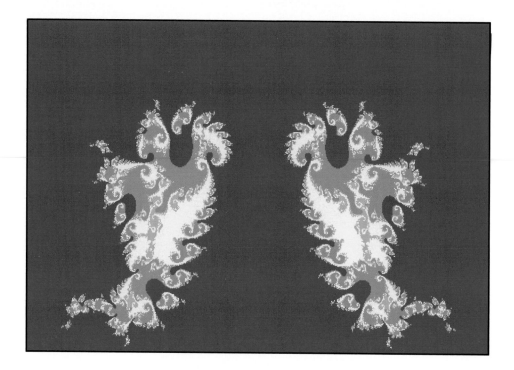

Plate 23: Original Phoenix Curve

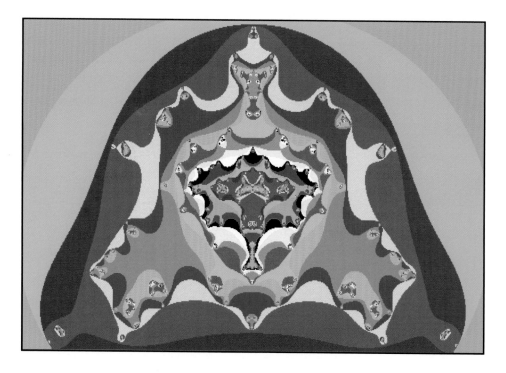

Plate 24: Phoenix Curve

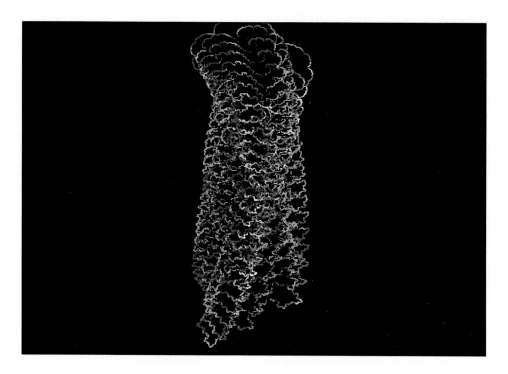

Plate 25: Three-Dimensional Dragon

Plate 26: Three-Dimensional Dragon

Plate 27: Solution of $z^3 - 1 = 0$ by Newton's Method

Plate 28: Solution of $z^3 - 2z - 5 = 0$ by Newton's Method

Plate 29: Oak Creek Canyon

Plate 30: Pike's Peak at Sunrise

Plate 31: Earth Viewed from the Moon

Plate 32: Three-Dimensional Ferns

17

Phoenix Curves

The phoenix curve was discovered by Shigehiro Ushiki at Kyoto University. The equations for the phoenix curve are:

$$x_{n+1} = x_n^2 + p + qy_n \qquad \text{(Equation 17-1)}$$

$$y_{n+1} = x_n \qquad \text{(Equation 17-2)}$$

where both x and y are complex. Plate 23 shows the original phoenix curve. To generate this curve, the values selected for p and q are:

$$p = 0.56667 \qquad \text{(Equation 17-3)}$$

$$q = -0.5 \qquad \text{(Equation 17-4)}$$

and 128 iterations are performed. The graph is of x in the complex plane, but in order to make the phoenixes stand up correctly, the axes are inverted from normal usage, with the x axis representing the imaginary part of x and the y axis representing the real part of x. Figure 17-1 lists the program to generate phoenix curves. It is quite similar to the programs we used to generate the Julia and dragon curves, but there are some significant differences.

The first difference is the method of coloring the display. This is a good point to reiterate the methods that we have been using to color our displays. The methods used for Mandelbrot sets, Julia sets, dragon curves, and the original phoenix curve are summarized in Figure 17-2. The program in Figure 17-1 includes the methods for Mandelbrot sets, Julia sets, and the original phoenix curve; you can comment out whichever ones you don't want.

Figure 17-1: Program to Generate Phoenix Curves

```
cphoenix = advanced program to map the phoenix curves
```

```c
#include <ctype.h>
#include <conio.h>
#include <stdio.h>
#include <math.h>
#include <dos.h>
#include <process.h>
#include "tools.h"

const int maxcol = 640;
const int maxrow = 350;
const int max_colors = 16;
int CURSOR_X=0,CURSOR_Y=0,col,row;
int max_iterations;
int max_size = 4;
int LINEWIDTH=1, OPERATOR=0x00, ANGLE, XCENTER, YCENTER;
unsigned long int PATTERN=0xFFFFFFFF;
unsigned char PALETTE[16]={0,1,2,3,4,5,20,7,56,57,58,59,60,
    61,62,63};
int colors[7]={88};
float P,Q;
float TXMax,TXMin,TYMax,TYMin;
union LIMIT XMax,YMax,XMin,YMin,Pval,Qval;

char file_name[13] = {"phenst00.pcx"};
char file_name2[13] = {"phenix00.pcx"};

FILE *f1,*f2;

main()
{

    float deltaX, deltaXi, X, Y, Xsquare, Ysquare,Ytemp,
        temp_sq, temp_xy,Xi,Xisquare,Yi,Xtemp,Xitemp;
    int i,color, row, col,error,response,repeat=0x32,start_col;

    clrscr();
    printf("Enter '0' to quit, '1' to expand "
        "or finish phoenix  '2' for new plot: ");
    do
        repeat = getch();
    while ((repeat != 0x30) && (repeat != 0x31) &&
        (repeat != 0x32));

    while (repeat != 0x30)
```

```
{
    printf("\nEnter number of iterations: ");
    scanf("%d",&max_iterations);
    printf("\nEnter background and three other colors separated"
        " by commas: ");
    scanf("%d,%d,%d,%d",&colors,&colors[1],&colors[2],
        &colors[3]);
    if (repeat == 0x32)
    {
        printf("\nEnter phoenix map number "
            "(00 - 99): ");
        file_name[6] = getche();
        file_name[7] = getche();
        getch();
        if ((isdigit(file_name[6])) && (isdigit(file_name
            [7])))
        error = restore_screen(file_name);
        else
            exit(0);
        start_col = 0;
        move_cursor(2,15,0,0);
        XMax.f = 1.5;
        XMin.f = -1.5;
        YMax.f = 1.2;
        YMin.f = -.7;
        P = Pval.f;
        Q = Qval.f;
        printf("\nP: %f   Q: %f",P,Q);
        getch();
        cls(7);
    }
    else
    {
        printf("\nEnter phoenix screen number "
            "(00 - 99): ");
        file_name2[6] = getche();
        file_name2[7] = getche();
        if ((isdigit(file_name2[6])) &&
            (isdigit(file_name2[7])))
            error = restore_screen(file_name2);
        else
            exit(0);
        if (error == 0)
            exit(0);
        else
        {
            if (error < 639)
            {
                start_col = 8 * (error/8);
                remove(file_name2);
                P = Pval.f;
```

```
                        Q = Qval.f;
            }
                else
                {
                    move_cursor(0,15,0,0);
                    move_cursor(1,15,CURSOR_X,CURSOR_Y);
                    XMax.f = TXMax;
                    XMin.f = TXMin;
                    YMax.f = TYMax;
                    YMin.f = TYMin;
                    P = Pval.f;
                    Q = Qval.f;
                    start_col = 0;
                    cls(7);
                }
            }
        }
        if (colors[0] <64)
        {
            setEGApalette(0,colors[0]);
            setEGApalette(1,colors[1]);
            setEGApalette(2,colors[2]);
            setEGApalette(3,colors[3]);
        }
        else
        {
            setEGApalette(0,1);
            setEGApalette(1,57);
            setEGApalette(2,2);
            setEGApalette(3,62);
        }
          deltaX = (YMax.f - YMin.f)/(maxrow - 1);
          deltaXi = (XMax.f - XMin.f)/(maxcol - 1);
        for (col=start_col; col<=maxcol; col++)
        {
            if (kbhit() != 0)
            {
                Pval.f = P;
                Qval.f = Q;
                save_screen(0,0,col,349,file_name2);
                exit(0);
            }
            for (row=0; row<=maxrow; row++)
            {
                Y = 0;
                Yi = 0;
                X = YMax.f - row * deltaX;
                Xi = XMin.f + col * deltaXi;
                color = 0;
                Xsquare = Xisquare = 0;
                while ((color<max_iterations) && ((Xsquare +
```

```
                        Xisquare) < max_size))
                {
                    Xsquare = X*X;
                    Xisquare = Xi*Xi;
                    Xtemp = Xsquare - Xisquare + P + Q*Y;
                    Xitemp = 2*X*Xi + Q*Yi;
                    Y = X;
                    Yi = Xi;
                    X = Xtemp;
                    Xi = Xitemp;
                    color++;
                }
/*      COLOR TECHNIQUE FOR ORIGINAL PHOENIX CURVE      */

/*              if (color >= max_iterations)
                {
                    color = 3;
                }
                else
                    if (color >= 64)
                        color = 2;
                    else
                        if (color >= 32)
                            color = 1;
                        else
                            color = 0;
*/
/*      COLOR TECHNIQUE FOR MANDELBROT SETS      */

/*              if (color >= max_iterations)
                    color = 0;
                else
                    color = color % 16;
*/

/*      COLOR TECHNIQUE FOR JULIA SETS      */

                if (color >= max_iterations)
                    color = ((int)((Xsquare + Ysquare)
                        *6.0))%6 + 1;
                else
                        color = 0;
                    plot(col, row, color);
            }
        }
        Pval.f = P;
        Qval.f = Q;
        save_screen(0,0,639,349,file_name2);
        getch();
        gotoxy(1,25);
        printf("File Name: %s      Enter '0' = quit, '1' = "
```

```
            "expand plot, '2' = new plot: ",file_name2);
        repeat = getche();
    }
    getch();
}
```

Figure 17-2: Coloring Techniques

Type of Figure	Background Color	Other Colors
Mandelbrot Set	All points that do not blow up during all iterations.	Cycle through 15 other colors for number of iterations required for blow-up.
Julia Set	All points that blow up to infinity during iterations.	Cycle through 6 other colors for ranges of values of magnitude of result after iterations are complete.
Original Phoenix Curve	All points that do not blow up during all iterations.	Three colors: first for blow-up in 1 to 32 iterations; second for blow-up in 33 to 64 iterations; third for blow-up in more than 64 iterations.

Maps of the Phoenix Curves

In Chapter 14 we showed a set that was the equivalent of the Mandelbrot set for phoenix curves. In previous chapters we used the Mandelbrot set as a map to permit us to select likely locations for interesting Julia sets, and we have used the equivalent of the Mandelbrot set for dragon curves to perform a similar function in selecting likely dragon curves. The use of the set that acts as a map of the phoenix curves is much less straightforward. First, consider that we have used the parameters $XMin$, $YMin$, $XMax$, and $YMax$ to save the minimum and maximum values corresponding to the start of the x and y axes and the end of the x and y axes, respectively, and that we have saved these values in the screen files. For the Mandelbrot and Julia sets, and for their equivalents for the dragon curves, the *XMin* and *XMax* values corresponded either to the real part of a parameter of the equation or to the real part of the initial value of the function being iterated. Similarly, the values of *YMin* and *YMax* represented the values of the imaginary part. For the phoenix equivalent of the Mandelbrot set, there are two parameters and we always take them as being real numbers. (There is no reason why this has to be true; one could make both parameters complex numbers, resulting in a function that is a lot more complicated, but might possibly result in some astounding new and previously undiscovered curves.) At any rate, the set is plotted with P on the x axis and Q on the y axis, but there is no correspondence between the real and imaginary parts of any parameter and the x and y axes for this curve.

When we come to the program that generates the phoenix curves themselves, the plotting is such that the real part of the variable x is plotted on the y axis and the imaginary part of x is plotted on the x axis. This requires that the program do a little juggling when it retrieves the *XMin* values and the P and Q parameters for a screen file, in order to put them into the proper parameters for the program to properly generate the phoenix curve.

The correspondence between the Mandelbrot-like set for phoenix curves and the phoenix curves themselves is much less meaningful than it was for Julia sets and dragon curves. Since phoenix curves are differently arranged and plot different parameters than the curve that is supposed to function as a map, it is less likely that cusps on the map will result in interesting phoenix curves. In fact, the parameters used to generate the original phoenix curve of Plate 23 do not appear to be at any interesting point on the map display. The values are also quite critical for the most interesting displays, although you can produce a curve similar to the original phoenix curve by coming as close to the values give in Equations 17-3 and 17-4 as you can get with the cursor, using the program. Plate 24 shows a phoenix curve that was generated using parameters selected from the map display.

Since the map display did not prove too useful in obtaining optimum parameters, it is likely that there are other curves in this family that are as interesting as the original phoenix curve, but their parameters have not been discovered yet. The parameters for some interesting phoenix curves are shown in Figure 17-3. Plate 24 was generated using the color technique of the Mandelbrot set. Whichever color technique is selected makes quite a difference in the appearance of the resulting picture.

Figure 17-3: Parameters of Phoenix Curves

Plate #	p	q
23	0.56667	-0.50000
—	0.288732	0.510029
24	0.356338	-1.209169
—	-0.550704	-1.255014

18

Three-Dimensional Dragons

Some of the most interesting fractal curves have been generated by Alan Norton at IBM's Thomas J. Watson Research Center. Norton specializes in expressing the dragon equation in three-dimensional form, using quaternions. His three-dimensional dragon pictures are not only beautiful, but provide an eerie sense of familiarity, no doubt because fractals are the language of natural things. Norton uses IBM's computer resources to plot a million or more points in three dimensions to generate a three-dimensional dragon curve. He then runs a ray-tracing program which determines the illumination of every point, and the positioning of it on a two-dimensional display. Needless to say, this is beyond the capability of our personal computers.

Nevertheless, we don't want to give up on three-dimensional dragons. The program given below will make use of the dragon outline program given in Chapter 16 to draw cross-sections of the three-dimensional dragon outline. Using *P* as the third dimension, it will calculate repeated dragon outlines and project them from three-dimensional to two-dimensional space. The results are less complete than Norton's, but give the appearance of three-dimensional displays.

Method of Projection

Suppose we have a program that generates all of the coordinate information needed to create an object in three-dimensional space. Our problem is that we somehow want to display this information on the two-dimensional display screen. The three-dimensional space is defined by the coordinate system (x, y, z) centered at (0, 0, 0). The display screen is defined by the coordinate system (vx, vy) with its origin at (0, 0).

First, we place the three-dimensional space so that its origin coincides with the origin of the display screen. Now, each of the axes of the three-dimensional co-ordinate system makes an angle with the display plane. We shall call the angle between the x axis and the display plane α, the angle between the y axis and the display plane ß, and the angle between the z axis and the display plane Γ. Pro-jection of the three-dimensional space onto the display plane now becomes very simple. There is only one line that can be drawn perpendicular to the display plane which intersects any particular point (x, y, z) in the three-dimensional space. The point where this line intersects the display plane is the projection of the three-dimensional point onto the display plane. The equations for making this projection are:

```
vx = x cos α + y cos ß + z cos Γ                (Equation 18-1)

vy = x sin α + y sin ß + z sin Γ                (Equation 18-2)
```

While you can use any angles that you desire for α, ß, and Γ, some orientations are not very interesting. You have to be particularly careful not to orient the three-dimensional figure so that the two-dimensional projection of it is just a flat on view of one side, with all information about the third dimension lost. The most common angles that are used are those used for isometric drawing, where α and ß are 30 degrees and Γ is 90 degrees; and the orientation used in many geom-etry books, where α and ß are 0, and Γ is 135 degrees.

Programming the Three-Dimensional Dragon

Figure 18-1 is a listing of a program to generate three-dimensional dragons. You will recognize the heart of this program as the program from Chapter 16 which draws the outline of dragons. We use the same two dimensions as in Chapter 16 for two of the three dimensions of our dragon, and the parameter P (the real part of the multiplier) as the third dimension. The program allows you to enter the projection angles, the scale, the parameter Q (the imaginary part of the multi-

plier), and an *x* and *y* offset. We reiterate the outline drawing program over a
range of values of *P*, but for each point that is calculated we use the projection
equations given in the section above to determine where to plot the point on the
display screen, instead of plotting it directly. The result is a three-dimensional
dragon image.

Figure 18-1: Program to Draw Three-Dimensional Dragons

```
                    3ddrag = program to generate 3-D dragon outlines
```

```
#include <stdlib.h>
#include <stdio.h>
#include <math.h>
#include <dos.h>
#include "tools.h"

void projection(float x3, float y3, float z3);
float (degrees_to_radians(float degrees);;

union LIMIT XMin,YMin,XMax,YMax,Pval,Qval;
int i, j, OPERATOR = 0x00,row,col,color1;
int x_center = 320, y_center = 175;
float x = .50001, y = 0,z,P,Q,k,sx,cx,sy,cy,sz,cz,
    magnitude,scale,temp,temp_x,temp_y,step_size=.4,ymax,ymin;
float rad_per_degree=0.0174533,alpha,beta,gamma;
float QVal,x_offset, y_offset,upper_limit = 3, lower_limit = -3;
int color;
unsigned char PALETTE[16]={0,1,2,3,4,5,20,7,56,57,58,59,60,61,
    62,63};

main()
{
    printf("\nEnter alpha: ");
    scanf("%f",&alpha);
    printf("\nEnter beta: ");
    scanf("%f",&beta);
    printf("\nEnter gamma: ");
    scanf("%f",&gamma);
    printf("\nEnter scale: ");
    scanf("%f",&scale);
    scale = x_center * scale;
    printf("\nEnter X offset: ");
    scanf("%f",&x_offset);
    printf("\nEnter Y offset: ");
    scanf("%f",&y_offset);
```

```
printf("\nEnter Q parameter: ");
scanf("%f",&QVal);
if (QVal == 0)
{
    step_size = 0.1;
    upper_limit = 1.0;
    lower_limit = -1.0;
}
setMode(16);
cls(0);
alpha = degrees_to_radians(alpha);
sx = sin(alpha);
cx = cos(alpha);
beta = degrees_to_radians(beta);
sy = sin(beta);
cy = cos(beta);
gamma = degrees_to_radians(gamma);
sz = sin(gamma);
cz = cos(gamma);
color = 1;
for (k= upper_limit; k>=lower_limit; k-=step_size)
{
    if ((k<1.0) && (k>-1.0))
        step_size = 0.1;
    x=.50001;
    y = 0;
    if (QVal == 0)
    {
        magnitude = 1;
        Q = 4*sqrt(1-k*k);
    }
    else
    {
        magnitude = k*k + QVal*QVal;
        Q = -4*QVal/magnitude;
    }
    P = 4*k/magnitude;
    for (i=0; i<12000; i++)
    {
        temp_x = x*P - y*Q;
        y = x*Q + y*P;
        temp_y = y;
        x = 1 - temp_x;
        magnitude = sqrt(x*x + y*y);
        y = sqrt((-x + magnitude)/2);
        x = sqrt((x + magnitude) /2);
        if (temp_y < 0)
            x = -x;
        if (rand() < 16163)
        {
            x = -x;
```

```
            y = -y;
        }
        x = (1 - x)/2;
        y = y/2;
        z =  P/2;
        if (i>10)
            projection (x, y, z);
    }
}
save_screen(0,0,639,349,"3ddrag00.pcx");
getch();
}
```

```
    projection() = projects three dimensions on two dimensions
```

```
void projection(float x3, float y3, float z3)
{
    float temp_x, temp_y;
    int col, row, color;

    temp_x = x3*cx + y3*cy + z3*cz;
    temp_y = x3*sx + y3*sy + z3*sz;

    col = scale * (temp_x-.5) + x_center + x_offset;
    row =  y_center - scale*temp_y + y_offset;
    color = (int)abs(y3*7)%7 + 1;
    if (y3>0)
        color+=8;
    if ((col>=0) && (col<640) &&(row>=0) && (row<350))
        plot (col,row,color);
}
```

```
        degrees_to_radians() = converts degrees to radians
```

```
float (degrees_to_radians(float degrees);
{
    float angle;

    while (degrees >= 360)
        degrees -= 360;
    while (degrees < 0)
        degrees += 360;
    angle = rad_per_degree*degrees;
    return angle;
}
```

The weakness of this technique for drawing three-dimensional figures is that it does not provide cues for separating out hidden surfaces and eliminating them, and it has no way to determine the illumination that should be associated with each point. The first is not a major objection. We see the dragon as a sort of semi-transparent entity in which we see the hidden parts of the figure through the parts that are in front. This gives us a better understanding of the geometry involved, and is not a great hardship since semi-transparent dragons are certainly within the realm of possibility. As for the lighting problem, the program makes a crude attempt to alleviate this by using dark colors to paint points of rearward surfaces, and light colors to paint the forward ones.

The program provides for two computation options. If you enter a value of 0 for Q, the program computes values over a range of -1 to +1 for the P value . As the program steps through various values of P, it holds the magnitude of $P + iQ$ constant at 1, so that values are taken around a unit circle. Plate 26 is an example of this mode of the program in action. The angles that were used are $\alpha = 30$ degrees, $\beta = -30$ degrees, and $\Gamma = 90$ degrees. The scale factor was 0.20, the x displacement was 0, and the y displacement was +10. Needless to say, the value entered for Q was 0.

The other mode of operation occurs when a value of Q other than 0 is entered. The program then holds the value of Q constant and steps through a range of values of P from -3.0 to +3.0. Plate 25 is an example of this mode of operation. For this picture, the angles were $\alpha = 15$ degrees, $\beta = -15$ degrees, and $\Gamma = 90$ degrees. The scale factor was 0.3 and the value entered for Q was 0.967049. No offsets were used.

These examples give you some good starting points for your own investigations. Be warned, however, that it easy to select unfortunate combinations of values which result in nothing being displayed at all because all points are beyond the display limits. The best thing to do is use a very small scale factor (0.1 or less) for your first attempt. This will show you what the display looks like and give you some idea of the scale factor and offsets required for a well-centered final display.

19

Newton's Method

Newton's method is an iterated numerical approximation technique developed by Sir Isaac Newton to obtain the solutions of equations that do not have a closed form solution. The method works as follows:

1. Suppose we have the generalized equation:

```
f(z) = 0                        (Equation 19-1)
```

where z may be a complex number.

2. Make a guess as to a root of this equation. Call the guess z_0.

3. Compute the expression:

```
z_{n+1} = z_n - (f(z_n))/(f'(z_n))       (Equation 19-2)
```

where f' is the derivative of f, and we start with z_0 on the right side of the equation to obtain z_1 on the left side.

4. Now repeat this process as many times as you desire. Each new value for z will be a closer approximation to the root of the equation.

Observe that this iteration process is very similar to that which we have used in previous chapters to obtain the Julia, dragon, and phoenix curves. Thus, we have opened the door for plotting curves for a very wide family of equations, and for obtaining graphical results which have a mathematical meaning.

Programs for Plotting Newton's Method Curves

We shall provide programs for plotting the curves of two Newton's method equation solutions. From there on, you're on your own as to setting up similar programs for any equations you can dream up. Figure 19-1 is the listing of a program to obtain the Newton's method solution of the equation:

$$z^3 - 1 = 0 \qquad\qquad \text{(Equation 19-3)}$$

Figure 19-2 is the listing of a program to obtain the Newton's method solution of the equation:

$$z^3 - 2z - 5 = 0 \qquad\qquad \text{(Equation 19-4)}$$

Figure 19-1: Program to Solve $z^3 - 1 = 0$

```
        cnewton3 = map of Newton's method for solving Z³ =  1
```

```
#include <stdio.h>
#include <math.h>
#include <dos.h>
#include <process.h>
#include "tools.h"

const int maxcol = 639;
const int maxrow = 349;
const int max_colors = 16;


char strings[80];
int col,row,i;
int max_iterations = 64;
int max_size = 4;
int LINEWIDTH=1, OPERATOR=0, ANGLE, XCENTER, YCENTER;
int CURSOR_X=0,CURSOR_Y=0;
unsigned long int PATTERN=0xFFFFFFFF;
float  Xmax = 3.5, Xmin=-3.5, Ymax=2.50, Ymin=-2.50;

main()
{
    double deltaX, deltaY, X, Y, Xsquare,Xold,Yold,
        Ysquare,Ytemp,temp1,temp2,denom,theta;
    int color, row, col;
```

```
setMode(16);
cls(7);
deltaX = (Xmax - Xmin)/(maxcol);
deltaY = (Ymax - Ymin)/(maxrow);
for (col=0; col<=maxcol; col++)
{
    if (kbhit() != 0)
        break;
    for (row=0; row<=maxrow; row++)
    {
        X = Xmin + col * deltaX;
        Y = Ymax - row * deltaY;
        Xsquare = 0;
        Ysquare = 0;
        Xold = 42;
        Yold = 42;
        for (i=0; i<max_iterations; i++)
        {
            Xsquare = X*X;
            Ysquare = Y*Y;
            denom = 3*((Xsquare - Ysquare)*(Xsquare -
                Ysquare) + 4*Xsquare*Ysquare);
            if (denom == 0)
                denom = .00000001;
            X = .6666667*X + (Xsquare - Ysquare)/denom;
            Y = .6666667*Y - 2*X*Y/denom;
            if ((Xold == X) && (Yold == Y))
                break;
            Xold = X;
            Yold = Y;
        }
        if (X>0)
            color = i%5;
        else
        {
            if ((X<-.3) && (Y>0))
                color = (i%5) + 5;
            else
                color = (i%6) + 10;
        }
        plot(col, row, color);
    }
}
getch();
}
```

Figure 19-2: Program to Solve $z^3 - 2z - 5 = 0$

```
cnewton = map of Newton's method for solving Z³-2z - 5 = 0
```

```c
#include <stdio.h>
#include <math.h>
#include <dos.h>
#include <process.h>
#include "tools.h"

const int maxcol = 639;
const int maxrow = 349;
const int max_colors = 16;

char strings[80];
int col,row,i;
int max_iterations = 64;
int max_size = 4;
int LINEWIDTH=1, OPERATOR=0, ANGLE, XCENTER, YCENTER;
int CURSOR_X=0,CURSOR_Y=0;
unsigned long int PATTERN=0xFFFFFFFF;
float  Xmax = 3.5, Xmin=-3.5, Ymax=2.50, Ymin=-2.50;

main()
{
    double deltaX, deltaY, X, Y, Xsquare,
        Ysquare,Ytemp,temp1,temp2,temp3,denom,numer,theta;
    int color, row, col;
    float Xold,Yold,Xnew,Ynew;

    setMode(16);
    cls(7);
    deltaX = (Xmax - Xmin)/(maxcol);
    deltaY = (Ymax - Ymin)/(maxrow);
    for (col=0; col<=maxcol; col++)
    {
        if (kbhit() != 0)
            break;
        for (row=0; row<=maxrow; row++)
        {
            X = Xmin + col * deltaX;
            Y = Ymax - row * deltaY;
            Xsquare = 0;
            Ysquare = 0;
            Xold = 42;
            Yold = 42;
            for (i=0; i<max_iterations; i++)
            {
```

```
            Xsquare = X*X;
            Ysquare = Y*Y;
            denom = (3*Xsquare - 3*Ysquare - 2);
            denom = denom*denom + 36*Xsquare*Ysquare;
            if (denom == 0)
                denom = .00000001;
            temp1 = X*Xsquare - 3*X*Ysquare - 2*X -5;
            temp2 = 3*Xsquare - 3*Ysquare - 2;
            temp3 = 3*Xsquare*Y - Ysquare*Y - 2*Y;
            X = X - (temp1 * temp2 - 6*X*Y*temp3)/denom;
            Y = Y - (temp1 * (-6*X*Y) + temp3 * temp2)
                /denom;
            Xnew = X;
            Ynew = Y;
            if ((Xold == Xnew) && (Yold == Ynew))
                break;
            Xold = X;
            Yold = Y;
        }
        if (X>0)
            color = i%5;
        else
        {
            if ((X<-.3) && (Y>0))
                color = (i%5) + 5;
            else
                color = (i%6) + 10;
        }
        plot(col, row, color);
        }
    }
    getch();
}
```

Mathematical Meaning of the Curves

Plate 27 shows the resulting curve from running the program of Figure 19-1. If you will look at the program listing, you will see that the colors are grouped in sets of 5, 5, and 6, respectively. Since Newton's method always settles on one of the roots of the equation, we don't need to worry about the expression blowing up to infinity. What we have done, is provide three groups of colors, one for each of the three roots of the equation to which the solution may be attracted.

You need some a prior knowledge of where the roots are located in order to do this. One way to get this information is to run the program for a little while and print out the resulting root. However, this is not necessary for the equation $z^3 - 1 = 0$, which can be directly solved since one root is obviously 1. Dividing the equation by $z - 1$ leaves a quadratic equation which can be solved by the quadratic formula to obtain roots of $-.5 \pm .8666i$. Knowing that the ultimate value of z will always be one of these three values, we can devise some "if" tests to determine which color group to use. Later, we used *colors* to change the sixteen default colors, so that the group that is attracted toward the root 1 is shades of blue, the group for $-.5+.866i$ is shades of green, and the group for $-.5-.8666i$ is shades of red.

Plate 28 shows the resulting curve from running the program of Figure 19-2. The roots of this equation are different from the roots given above, but once they were determined, it was observed that the same tests used for the first program could differentiate between the three sets of roots.

Note that for either program, the different shades of a basic color represent the number of iterations that were required for the program to converge to a root. The test for the first program is simply that the same x and y values occurred on the current iteration as occurred for the previous one. For the second program, convergence is somewhat slower, so that making two successive values match to double precision required more iterations than were practical to keep running time short, so the values were converted to single precision before the test was made.

Now it is time to consider what these curves mean. Any point on the figure represents a complex number which can be used as a starting point for the Newton's method process. It was once assumed that you started by making a "good guess" as to the value of a root, and that Newton's method would then converge to the nearest root. The two figures show very plainly that this is not true. There are lots of color mixtures and isolated islands of one color within another, which demonstrate that it is quite possible to pick an initial value that converges to a root quite far away from the initial value.

Note particularly in Plate 28, the mixed color areas on the left side of the figure. In these areas, a very tiny change in the initial value selected will result in convergence to a totally different root. Another thing that is of interest is the path which the variable takes on its way to convergence. We have not attempted to plot this, but it appears to be very interesting. Note that if we take one of the initial tiny points of green, for example, on the left side of Plate 28, it must land on a green point at every step in the convergence process. If it landed on another color, the succeeding iterations would be just the same as if we had begun at that point, so convergence would be to a different root, which is a contradiction of terms.

20

Brownian Motion

Up until now, we have been looking at fractals that are deterministically defined by relatively simple iterated equations. It is tempting to think that by using these techniques, we can mathematically describe (and consequently realistically represent) any natural phenomena. But no matter how much rich and apparently irregular detail appears in fractal curves, they are never exactly like natural phenomena, which is filled with random irregularities. Your body may have been generated by the regular fractal patterns defined by your genetic structure, but the scar on your arm that you got when you cut yourself when you were twelve years old is a random departure from the fractal pattern that cannot be covered by the mathematical expressions. Nature is full of these random departures from regularity, and to properly represent them, we need to look at introducing some randomness into our fractal techniques.

The first detailed investigation of such randomness in nature was conducted by Robert Brown in 1828. Brown was looking at the movement of pollen particles. This movement had irregularites for which there was no mathematical explanation. Similar movements have since been observed in the dispersion of minute particles through a fluid and in the mixture of different colored gases. Investigations of this random movement, called the *Brownian motion* (after its discoverer), have suggested that it occurs in particles so small that collisions on a molecular level are not regular from all directions, so that the unsymmetric application of kinetic molecular forces causes the particles to be propelled in random direction and with random velocities over time.

This chapter will introduce techniques for generating representations of Brownian motion. The resulting curves are not too interesting in themselves, but the tools used here are powerful in generating natural scenes through fractal means. Unfortunately, in the next chapter, where we provide some scene drawing techniques, we have not been able to make too much use of the randomized methods. They do appear in one program—a scene of earth viewed from the moon—but they don't make a significant difference at the level of computation required to be compatible with the limitations of personal computers. They do play a significant part in creating some of the breathtaking scenes that have been produced on mainframe computers; consequently, this introduction to the subject is included so that you can achieve some familiarity with the subject and so that you will have the tools for your own experimentation.

One-Dimensional Brownian Motion

The simplest form of Brownian motion occurs when time is divided into units and plotted along the x axis and the length traveled by a particle in that time interval is plotted on the y axis. For this case, the y values have been shown to have a gaussian distribution. Figure 20-1 lists a program to plot the simple Brownian motion.

Figure 20-1: Program to Generate Brownian Fractals

```
          brownian() = program to generate Brownian fractals
```

```c
#include <stdio.h>
#include <math.h>
#include <dos.h>
#include "tools.h"

float gauss(unsigned seed);
void subdivide (int f1, int f2, float std);

float Fh[257],ratio;
char combination= 0x00;
unsigned long int PATTERN=0xFFFFFFFF;
unsigned int seed=3245;
int LINEWIDTH = 1;
```

```
main()
{
    float scale=1000,h=.87,std;
    int i;

    while (seed != 0)
    {
        setMode(3);
        printf("Enter seed (0 to quit): ");
        scanf("%d",&seed);
        Fh[0] = gauss(seed) * scale;
        Fh[256] = gauss(0) * scale;
        ratio = pow(2,-h);
        std = scale*ratio;
        subdivide(0,256,std);
        setMode(16);
        for (i=0; i<256; i++)
            drawLine(2*i-260,Fh[i],2*(i+1)-260,Fh[i+1],15);
        drawLine(-260,0,252,0,14);
        getch();
    }
}
```

```
        subdivide() = function to subdivide line and compute
                      amplitude at each point
```

```
void subdivide (int f1, int f2, float std)
{
    int fmid;
    float stdmid;

    fmid = (f1 + f2)/2;
    if (( fmid != f1) && (fmid != f2))
    {
        Fh[fmid] = (Fh[f1] + Fh[f2])/2.0 + gauss(0) * std;
        stdmid = std*ratio;
        subdivide(f1,fmid,stdmid);
        subdivide(fmid,f2,stdmid);
    }
}
```

```
┌─────────────────────────────────────────────────────────────┐
│          gauss() = function to return a gaussian variable     │
└─────────────────────────────────────────────────────────────┘
```

```
float gauss(unsigned seed)
{
    int k;
    float value,exponent,gauss;

    if (seed != 0)
        srand(seed);
    k = rand() - 16383;
    value = k/5461.0;
    exponent = -(value*value)/2.;
    gauss = .15915494*exp(exponent);
    k = rand();

    if (k > 16383)
        gauss *= -1;
    return(gauss);
}
```

The program begins with determining a random value of the Brownian function at the beginning and end of the plot. This determines the *y* value of the function at the endpoints. If you want to take some sort of random curve, defined by line segments, and replace the line segments with Brownian curves, you need to set the beginning and end points for each line segment to match the beginning and end coordinates of the line to assure continuity of the function from one line segment to the next. Alternately, you can use random settings for the beginning and end points of the first line segment, then use the value that you obtained for the end point of that segment as the beginning point for the next line segment and find a random end point for that line segment, and so forth.

Before proceeding further, let's look at the function *gauss,* which returns a random number that has a gaussian distribution. This function begins by looking at a *seed* parameter. If this parameter is some number other than zero, the function reseeds the random number generator; if the seed is zero, the random number generator proceeds to generate random numbers without being restarted. The random number generator returns integers between 0 and 32767. The first thing we do is get a random number and subtract 16383 from it so that we have a random number between -16383 and +16384. Next, we find a floating point number between -3.0 and +3.0 by dividing the number that we obtained in the above step by

5461. This gives us a point at which to read off a value from the gaussian distribution. This value (v), for a given number n, is:

$$v = (1/2\pi)(exp)n^2/2 \qquad\qquad \text{(Equation 20-1)}$$

Note that the gaussian distribution always results in a positive number. Since we want to return a number that has equal chances of being positive or negative, we next select another random number and use it to determine the sign of the number that is returned by the function.

The heart of this program is a function called *subdivide*. On the first pass, this function divides the line connecting the beginning and end points at the center, and then uses *gauss* to obtain a random value of the gaussian distribution, which is multiplied by a scale factor and stored in an array as the *y* coordinate of the brownian function at that point. It then calls itself recursively twice to perform the same procedure with each half of the line, reducing the scale factor for these new iterations by a specified ratio. This recursive process continues until the computed midpoint is the same as one of the ends of the line. Since the line co-ordinates are integer values, this means that the array of points has been filled so the function terminates.

The main program, after determining the beginning and end points, establishes the scale factor and reduction ratio that will be used, then calls *subdivide* to fill the array of points, and then utilizes a *for* loop to draw a line between each pair of adjacent points. Before each iteration of this process, you are given the opportunity to enter a seed for the random number generator. Each different seed results in a unique Brownian curve. If you enter the seed *0*, the curve for a zero seed will be plotted, but the program will terminate upon the next entry of a character on the keyboard. Figure 20-2 shows several representations of Brownian motion obtained from this program.

Figure 20-2: Typical One-Dimensional Brownian Motion

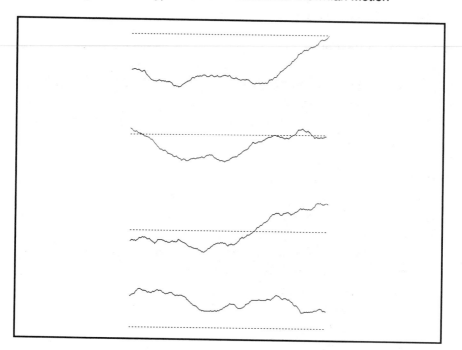

Two-Dimensional Brownian Motion

The above program was confined to describing particle motion in a single dimension. If we now expand to consider the motion of a Brownian particle on a plane, we have two methods of graphing our result. The first technique makes use of a three-dimensional graph and shows particle position in two dimensions plotted against time. The second method uses a two-dimensional graph and simply plots the path of the particle without reference to the time involved. We shall use this second technique.

Figure 20-3 lists a program to produce a graph of Brownian motion using this technique. It is essentially the same as the program listed in Figure 20-1 except that we have increased the number of points to be computed, changed the scale, and provided for calculating of two dimensions for each point and saving these values in two arrays. The program then draws a line between each two adjacent sets of *x* and *y* coordinates. Figure 20-4 shows several resulting Brownian motion curves obtained using this program.

Figure 20-3: Program to Generate Two-Dimensional Brownian Fractals

```
brown2d = program to generate two-dimensional Brownian fractals
```

```c
#include <stdio.h>
#include <math.h>
#include <dos.h>
#include <tools.h>

float gauss(unsigned seed);
void plot(int x, int y, int color);
void subdivide (int f1, int f2, float std);
void setMode(int mode);

float Fh[2049],Fw[2049],ratio;
char combination= 0x00;
unsigned long int PATTERN=0xFFFFFFFF;
unsigned int seed=3245;
int LINEWIDTH = 1;

main()
{
    float scale=2000,h=.87,std;
    int i;

    while (seed != 0)
    {
        setMode(3);
        printf("Enter seed (0 to quit): ");
        scanf("%d",&seed);
        Fh[0] = 0;
        Fh[2048] = gauss(seed) * scale;
        Fw[0] = 0;
        Fw[2048] = gauss(0) * scale;
        ratio = pow(2,-h);
        std = scale*ratio;
        subdivide(0,2048,std);
        setMode(16);
        for (i=0; i<2048; i++)
            drawLine(Fw[i],Fh[i],Fw[i+1],Fh[i+1],15);
        PATTERN = 0x0F0F0F0F;
        drawLine(-260,0,252,0,15);
        drawLine(0,-220,0,220,15);
        PATTERN = 0xFFFFFFFF;
```

```
        getch();
    }
}

void subdivide (int f1, int f2, float std)
{
    int fmid;
    float stdmid;

    fmid = (f1 + f2)/2;
    if (( fmid != f1) && (fmid != f2))
    {
        Fh[fmid] = (Fh[f1] + Fh[f2])/2.0 + gauss(0) * std;
        Fw[fmid] = (Fw[f1] + Fw[f2])/2.0 + gauss(0) * std;
        stdmid = std*ratio;
        subdivide(f1,fmid,stdmid);
        subdivide(fmid,f2,stdmid);
    }
}

float gauss(unsigned seed)
{
    int k;
    float value,exponent,gauss;

    if (seed != 0)
        srand(seed);
    k = rand() - 16383;
    value = k/5461.0;
    exponent = -(value*value)/2.;
    gauss = .15915494*exp(exponent);
    k = rand();

    if (k > 16383)
        gauss *= -1;
    return(gauss);
}
```

Figure 20-4: Typical Two-Dimensional Brownian Motion

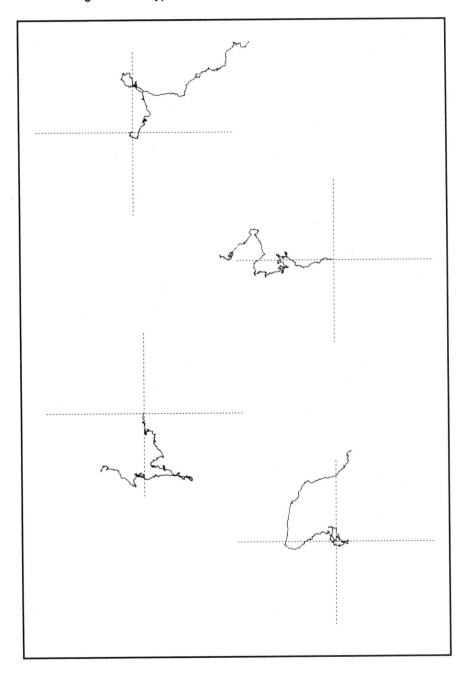

21

Fractal Landscapes

Some of the most interesting pictures created through the use of fractals are of extremely realistic landscape scenes. In Mandelbrot's book, *The Fractal Geometry of Nature*, are scenes of rugged mountains and of a planet rising above a desolate landscape created by Richard Voss at the Thomas J. Watkins Research Laboratory, which have become almost classics in the art of fractal scene generation. We still look at these pictures in breathless amazement at their degree of realism. Other scenes including mountains, lakes, and oceans have been created by Gary Mastin, Peter Watterberg, and John Mareda at Sandia National Laboratories. The creators of these scenes seem to be quite reluctant to reveal the details of the computer code that they use to produce them, so we can only guess as to the exact details of how they were created.

In general, the technique seems to be that of transforming Gaussian noise to the frequency domain, passing it through a 1/f filter, and then transforming the result back to the time domain. Using the result to generate three-dimensional shapes and then illuminating the shapes from a fictious light source, using a ray-tracing program, appears to be the method to produce delightful landscapes. We take note, however, that a number of adjustments need to be made to the raw data before a life-like scene appears. Since we don't have the code, we don't know exactly how much "tweaking" was done before these expressions of mathematics began to approach art.

The technique above can require an hour or more of processing time on a VAX computer; obviously it is not well-suited to the capabilities of our PCs. In fact, attempts to adapt fractal scene generation to motion pictures encounters prohibitive costs in computer time (even for the movies, which are not noted for economizing), so more efficient techniques were developed. Fournier, Fussell, and Carpenter developed the midpoint displacement method as an efficient and inexpensive method of generating fractal landscapes. Mandelbrot points out that this technique is not as mathematically sound as the one he was using and consequently the landscapes are not as realistic, but for all practical purpose they are perfectly acceptable. Moreover, it is our good fortune that an adaptation of this technique can produce interesting scenes on a personal computer.

Midpoint Displacement Technique

Figure 21-1(a) shows the first step in the midpoint displacement process. We start with a triangle, then go to the midpoint of each side of the triangle and displace it along the line and at right angles to the line. The amount of each displacement is determined by applying a Gaussian random multiplier to a proportion of the line length. Next we connect each displaced midpoint to the two nearest apexes of the triangle. We then connect together each pair of displaced midpoints. Finally, we throw away the original sides of the triangle.

In the figure, we show the original triangle sides as wide lines and the new lines as thin lines. For clarity, we didn't throw away the original triangle lines in the figure; you can do that in your imagination. The result of this process is that we have replaced the original triangle with four new triangles. We then apply the same process to each of the four new triangles, generating four more triangles from each so that we then have sixteen triangles. This step is shown in Figure 21-1(c), although the sixteen new triangles are a little hard to pick out.

What happens when we have two triangles that have a common side? (Even if we start with a single triangle, this situation arises after the first set of displacements is performed.) If we are creating scenes on a large scale using a mainframe computer, there is no problem in saving the coordinates of each new side as it is generated, so that once we have performed the midpoint displacement for a side, that same midpoint displacement is used for each triangle in which the side occurs.

Figure 21-1: Midpoint Displacement of Triangle Sides

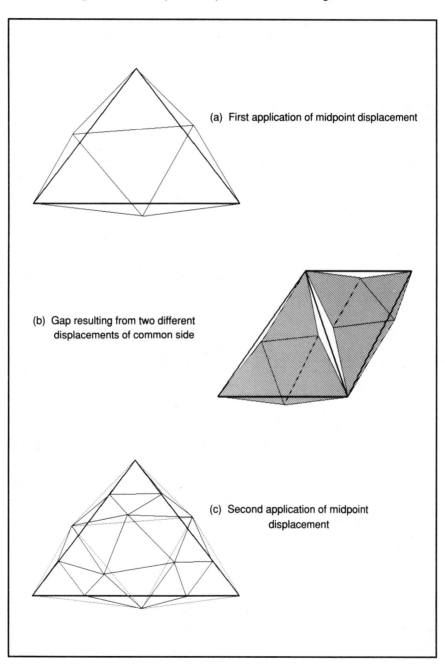

(a) First application of midpoint displacement

(b) Gap resulting from two different displacements of common side

(c) Second application of midpoint displacement

For our smaller home computers, we prefer recursive techniques that are most efficient when we calculate the coordinates of one new triangle at the smallest level, fill it with some color, and then forget about it completely. Figure 21-1(b) shows what might happen when we do this.

In this particular case, the displacement of the common side for the first triangle is toward the inside of the first triangle, and the displacement for the same side in the second triangle is toward the inside of the second triangle. If we assume that this is at the lowest level, and fill the resulting triangles with color, it is evident that there is a gap that is not filled, and will leave an objectionable unfilled space in the resulting picture.

There are two ways of approaching this problem. Michael Batty, at the University of Wales Institute of Science and Technology, has been applying this technique to BASIC programs for use with small computers. At each level of the recursion process except the lowest one, he creates a smaller triangle than the original and paints it with a color. Hopefully this triangle is small enough so that it will not mask the desired irregularity of surfaces that is created by the midpoint displacement process, yet large enough so that it will color in those regions where gaps might occur at the next downward level of the process. This technique will be used in the program to generate the Earth Viewed from the Moon picture that is described below.

Another interesting approach is to use the coordinates of the undisplaced midpoint of the line that we are working on to generate a unique number. This number is used as a seed for the random number generator of the computer, which then generates the random numbers for displacement along and perpendicular to the line. When the same line occurs in another triangle, since its undisplaced midpoint still has the same coordinates, the seed that is generated for the random number generator will be the same and the displacement will be the same, so that there is no possibility of a gap occurring.

Immediately the question arises, "Are these really random displacements?" The answer is, "Of course not!" But, then, what are they? They are certainly more random than displacements that might be generated by any arbitrary technique, but the are also much less random than if they were generated by truly random numbers that were created without the generator being reset for each line. Interestingly enough, the resulting boundaries for this process are much rougher than those achieved by Batty's process, so that using the same basic generator data for the two processes does not result in pictures that are equally pleasing or realistic looking.

Oak Creek Canyon

Figure 21-2 lists a program for generating a western scene that is supposed to be reminescent of Oak Creek Canyon near Sedona, Arizona. Before going into the program in detail, we need to consider what percentage of the picture realism is contributed by fractals and what part is artistic endeavor by the programmer. To help get a handle on this, take a look at Figure 21-3, which is a line drawing showing the triangles specified by data input to the program. This is the artist's contribution to the basic format of the picture. In addition, the parameters that are used with the function *midpoint* to specify the displacement of the midpoint of each line of each triangle have a lot to do with how rugged the landscape looks and its overall shape. Now look at the final picture as shown in Plate 29 to see the result of combining artistic feeling with fractal scene generation.

Figure 21-2: Program to Generate Desert Scene

```
     sedona = program to generate Oak Creek Canyon landscape
```

```
#include <stdio.h>
#include <math.h>
#include <dos.h>
#include <stdlib.h>
#include "tools.h"

void cactus (int x1, int y-one, int scale, int level, int color1,
    int color2);
void gen_quad (int x1, int y-one, int x2, int y2, int x3,
    int y3, int x4, int y4, int level, int color1, int color2);
void generate(int x1, int y-one, int x2, int y2, int x3, int y3,
    int level, int color1,int color2);
void midpoint();
void node(int x1, int y-one, int x2, int y2, int x3, int y3,
```

```
        int x4, int y4, int x5, int y5, int x6, int y6, int level,
        int color1, int color2);
void plot_triangle(int x1, int y-one, int x2, int y2, int x3,
        int y3, int color1,int color2);
float random_no (float limit_start, float limit_end);

union LIMIT XMax,XMin,YMax,YMin;
int combination = 0,LINEWIDTH=1, OPERATOR=0;
unsigned long int PATTERN=0xFFFFFFFF;
int i,j;
int y_max = 280;
int level[26] = {3,3,3,3,3,3,4,4,4,4,4,4,4,4,4,4,4,4,4,4,4,
    4,4,4,4,4};
int x1[26] = {-330,-90,-90,120,120,120,  -160,-120,-120,-80,
    -80,-50,-50,-50, 80,104,104,128,128,152,152,200,
    -470,-350,-220,-200};
int y-one[26] = {-110,-110,-110,-110,-110,-110, -10,-10,-10,-10,
    -10,-10,-10,-10, 50,50,50,50,50,50,50,50,
    -300,-280,-280,-280};
int x2[26] = {-160,-160,0,0,80,200,  -160,-160,-120,-120,-80,
    -80,-50,0, 100,100,104,104,128,128,152,152,
    -250,-60,80,230};
int y2[26] = {0,0,0,0,50,50,  220,220,190,190,230,230,100,180,
    180,180,200,205,215,215,160,160,  -110,-140,-130,-120};
int x3[26] = {-90,0,120,80,200,340,  -120,-120,-80,-80,-50,
    -50,0,0,104,104,128,128,152,152,200,200,
    300,300,340,580};
int y3[26] = {-110,0,-110,50,50,-110,  -10,220,-10,200,-10,
    235,180,-10, 50,200,50,210,50,220,50,140,
    -300,-300,-300,-300};
int xz,yz,xp,yp;
int color_value=2;
unsigned char PALETTE[16]={0,1,2,3,4,5,20,7,56,57,58,59,60,
    61,62,63};
float x,y;
main()
{
    setMode(16);
    cls(9);
    for (i=0; i<22; i++)
        generate(x1[i],y-one[i],x2[i],y2[i],x3[i],y3[i],level[i],
            4,12);
    y_max = -100;
    gen_quad(-330,-260,-330,-100,330,-100,330,-260,4,6,14);
    y_max = 0;
    cactus(-110,-130,3,4,2,10);
    cactus(-200,-120,2,4,2,10);
    cactus(0,-160,4,4,2,10);
    cactus(210,-200,6,4,2,10);
    getch();
}
```

```
┌─────────────────────────────────────────────────────────────────┐
│                                                                   │
│         node() = runs 'generate' for four new triangles           │
│                                                                   │
└─────────────────────────────────────────────────────────────────┘
```

```
void node(int x1, int y-one, int x2, int y2, int x3, int y3,
    int x4,int y4, int x5, int y5, int x6, int y6, int level,
    int color1, int color2)
{
    if (level == 0)
        return(0);
    generate (x1,y-one,x4,y4,x6,y6,level-1,color1,color2);
    generate (x6,y6,x5,y5,x3,y3,level-1,color1,color2);
    generate (x4,y4,x2,y2,x5,y5,level-1,color1,color2);
    generate (x4,y4,x5,y5,x6,y6,level-1,color1,color2);
}
```

```
┌─────────────────────────────────────────────────────────────────┐
│                                                                   │
│         generate() = makes four new triangles from original       │
│                             triangle                              │
│                                                                   │
└─────────────────────────────────────────────────────────────────┘
```

```
void generate(int x1, int y-one, int x2, int y2, int x3, int y3,
    int level, int color1, int color2)
{
    int x4,x5,x6,y4,y5,y6,ax,bx,cx,ay,by,cy;

    x = x2 - x1;
    y = y2 - y-one;
    midpoint();
    x4 = x1 + xz -xp;
    y4 = y-one + yz - yp;
    ax = -xp;
    ay = -yp;
    x = x3-x1;
    y = y3-y-one;
    midpoint();
    x6 = x1 + xz;
    y6 = y-one + yz;
    cx = xp;
    cy = yp;
    x = x3-x2;
    y = y3-y2;
    midpoint();
    x5 = x2 + xz;
    y5 = y2 + yz;
    bx = -xp;
    by = -yp;

    if (level == 0)
```

```
    {
        plot_triangle(x1,y-one,x4,y4,x6,y6,color1,color2);
        plot_triangle(x6,y6,x5,y5,x3,y3,color1,color2);
        plot_triangle(x4,y4,x5,y5,x6,y6,color1,color2);
        plot_triangle(x4,y4,x2,y2,x5,y5,color1,color2);
    }
    else
    {
        plot_triangle(x1,y-one,x4+ax,y4+ay,x6+cx,y6+cy,color1,
            color2);
        plot_triangle(x6+cx,y6+cy,x5+bx,y5+by,x3,y3,color1,
            color2);
        plot_triangle(x4+ax,y4+ay,x5+bx,y5+by,x6+cx,y6+cy,
            color1, color2);
        plot_triangle(x4+ax,y4+ay,x2,y2,x5+bx,y5+by,color1,
            color2);
        node(x1,y-one,x2,y2,x3,y3,x4,y4,x5,y5,x6,y6,level,color1,
            color2);
    }
}
```

```
        plot_triangle() = determines which color to use and
                          then calls 'fill_triangle'
```

```
void plot_triangle(int x1, int y-one, int x2, int y2, int x3,
    int y3,int color1, int color2)
{
    int ytt,color;
    float zt;

    if (y-one > y2)
        ytt = y-one;
    else
        ytt = y2;
    if (ytt < y3)
        ytt = y3;
    zt = (y_max+240)*(1-(float)(ytt+240)/(y_max+240)*
        (float)(ytt+240)/(y_max+240));
    if (random(y_max+241) <= zt)
        color = color1;
    else
        color = color2;
    if (ytt + 240 < (.35 * (y_max + 240)))
        color = color1;
    if (ytt+240 > (.92 * (y_max+240)))
        color = color2;
    fillTriangle(x1,y-one,x2,y2,x3,y3,color);
}
```

```
┌─────────────────────────────────────────────────────────────┐
│         midpoint() = determines displaced midpoint for a side │
└─────────────────────────────────────────────────────────────┘
```

```
void midpoint()
{
    float r,w;
    int sign1,sign2;

    r = 0.5 + random_no(0,.16666);
    w = random_no(.03,.07);
    xz = r*x - w*y;
    yz = r*y + w*x;
    xp = 0.05*y;    .
    yp = -0.05*x;
}
```

```
┌─────────────────────────────────────────────────────────────┐
│         random_no() = determines random number (positive or   │
│                       negative) between two limits            │
└─────────────────────────────────────────────────────────────┘
```

```
float random_no (float limit_start,
    float limit_end)
{
    float result;

    limit_end -= limit_start;
    limit_end = 16383.0/limit_end;
    result = (rand() - 16383)/limit_end;
    if (result >= 0)
        result += limit_start;
    else
        result -= limit_start;
    return(result);
}
```

```
┌─────────────────────────────────────────────────────────────┐
│         gen_quad() = runs 'generate' for a quadralateral      │
│                      with no gap between two triangles        │
└─────────────────────────────────────────────────────────────┘
```

```
void gen_quad (int x1, int y-one, int x2, int y2, int x3, int y3,
    int x4, int y4, int level, int color1, int color2)
{
    generate(x1,y-one,x2,y2,x3,y3,level,color1,color2);
    generate(x1,y-one,x4,y4,x3,y3,level,color1,color2);
}
```

```
                    cactus() = generates cactus shape
```

```c
void cactus (int x1, int y-one, int scale, int level, int color1,
    int color2)
{
    gen_quad(x1,y-one,x1,y-one+21*scale,x1+1.6*scale,y-one+22*scale,x1+
        1.6*scale,y-one,level,color1,color2);
    gen_quad(x1+1.4*scale,y-one,x1+1.4*scale,y-one+22*scale,x1+
        3*scale, y-one+21*scale,x1+3*scale,y-one,level,color1,
        color2);
    gen_quad(x1,y-one+9*scale,x1+7*scale,y-one+9*scale,x1+7*scale,
        y-one+12*scale, x1,y-one+12*scale,0,color1,color2);
    gen_quad(x1,y-one+9*scale,x1+6*scale,y-one+9*scale,x1+7*scale,
        y-one+12*scale, x1,y-one+12*scale,level,color1,color2);
    gen_quad(x1+7*scale,y-one+9*scale,x1+7*scale,y-one+16*scale,
        x1+8.5*scale,y-one+17*scale,x1+8.5*scale,y-one+9*scale,
        level,color1,color2);
    gen_quad(x1+8.4*scale,y-one+9*scale,x1+8.4*scale,y-one+16*scale,
        x1+10*scale,y-one+17*scale,x1+10*scale,y-one+10*scale,
        level,color1,color2);
    gen_quad(x1,y-one+7*scale,x1-6*scale,y-one+7*scale,x1-6*scale,
        y-one+10*scale, x1,y-one+10*scale,0,color1,color2);
    gen_quad(x1,y-one+7*scale,x1-6*scale,y-one+7*scale,x1-6*scale,
        y-one+10*scale, x1,y-one+10*scale,level,color1,color2);
    gen_quad(x1-7*scale,y-one+8*scale,x1-7*scale,y-one+12*scale,
        x1-5.4*scale, y-one+13*scale,x1-5.4*scale,y-one+7*scale,
        level,color1,color2);
    gen_quad(x1-5.6*scale,y-one+7*scale,x1-5.6*scale,y-one+13*scale,
        x1-4*scale, y-one+12*scale,x1-4*scale,y-one+7*scale,level,
        color1,color2);

}
```

The program to paint this scene uses Michael Batty's technique of filling reduced triangles at intermediate stages to avoid objectionable gaps. First, let's look at the function *generate*. This function determines the length in *x* and *y* for each line making up the input triangle, and then calls *midpoint* to determine the *x* and *y* displacements of the midpoint for that line. The coordinates of the displaced midpoint are stored and the displacements needed to define a reduced triangle to be filled at levels above the lowest level are stored in *ax*, *ay*, *bx*, *by*, *cx*, and *cy*.

Figure 21-3: Input Data for Oak Creek Canyon Scene

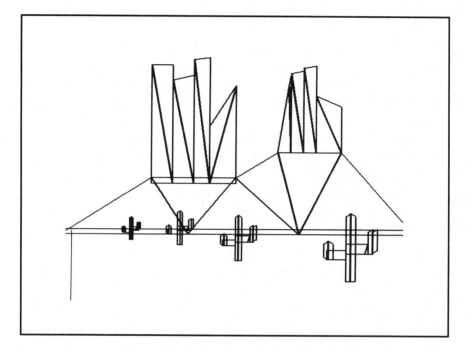

If we are at the lowest level (level 0), the function next calls *plot_triangle* to determine the fill color and fill each of the four new triangles. If the lowest level has not been reached, the function calls *plot_triangle* to fill each of four reduced triangles, and then calls *node*, which recursively calls *generate* to generate four new triangles for each of the four triangles that was just generated.

Take a quick look at the function *node* and you will see that it returns if the level is 0 and otherwise calls *generate* for each of the four triangles created by the current run of *generate*. Note that the way the program is set up, it should not ever be possible to enter *node* with the level set to 0. However, just in case, the first *if* statement provides added assurance that the program can never get into an endless loop.

For convenience, there is also a function *gen_quad*, which merely runs *generate* for two triangles that make up a quadralateral. Since many of the shapes in this scene are of a quadralateral nature, this function makes it easier to define them in the data.

Next we'll look at the function *midpoint* in a little more detail, but first, look at *random_no*, which midpoint uses in determining the random displacement. The inputs to this function are the lower and upper limits of a random number to be generated. These limits have a special meaning in this case, however. Both limits are assumed to be entered as positive numbers. The returned random number will be either a negative number that lies between the negative values of the two numbers entered or a positive number that lies between the two positive values of the limits. First, the function takes the difference between the two limits. It then divides 16,383 by this difference to obtain a limit to be applied to the integer random number routine.

The *rand* function is then called. This function returns a random number between 0 and 32,767. From the returned number, 16,283 is subtracted, giving a number between -16383 and 16,384. This number is divided by the limit determined above to give a number that is between the maximum negative and maximum positive values of the difference between the two input limits. If the resulting number is negative, the starting limit is subtracted; if it is positive, the starting limit is added, giving a result that is between the negative values of the two limts or between their positive values. This number is returned by the function.

The function *midpoint* begins by selecting a random number that represents the displacement of the midpoint along the line whose *x* distance is stored in *x* and whose *y* distance is stored in *y*. This distance is half the line length plus or minus a random value between zero and one-sixth times the line length. Next, the displacement at right angles to the line is computed. It is the line length times a random number between 0.03 and 0.07 or between -0.03 and -0.07. Batty determines the direction of the line and then applies trigonometric conversions to the displacements along and at right angles to the line to determine the displacements in the *x* and *y* directions. However, this is not really necessary, since if you work out the trigonometry involved, you will find that the sines and cosines of angles cancel out and the result is those expressions given in the function for *xz* and *yz*. The function also computes *xp* and *yp*, which represent the reductions in size that are applied to create the reduced triangles that are color-filled at levels higher than zero.

Now lets take a look at the function *plot_triangle*. Its inputs are the coordinates of the three apexes of a triangle and two color values for the triangle. It also makes use of the global variable *y_max* which is an altitude value that controls the color selection. The function begins by selecting the *y* value of the highest apex of the triangle to use as the test criteria. It then creates a test variable, *zt*, according to the formula:

$$zt = \frac{(y\ max)(1\ -\ ytt)}{(y\_max)(ytt/y\_max)} \qquad \text{(Equation 21-1)}$$

where *y_max* is the control altitude and *ytt* is the altitude of the highest apex of the triangle. Note, however, that both y's are in terms of system coordinates which can take on any value between -240 and +240, so that in the function 240 is added to every y value to make it a positive altitude. Once the value of *zt* is determined, the function selects a random number between zero and *y_max* and compares it with the test value *zt*. If the random number is less than or equal to *zt*, the first color is selected; otherwise the second color is selected. Finally, if the altitude of *ytt* is below a selected limit, the color selection is overridden and the first color is selected. If the altitude of *ytt* is above a selected limit, the color selection is overridden and the second color selected. The function then runs *fillTriangle* to fill the triangle with the selected color and then returns.

The *plot_triangle* function is where you can do a lot of experimentation to modify your scenes and provide them with additional color variations that are more complex than the ones used in the scenes depicted in this book. There is no reason why you need to be restriced to two colors; you can have several variations for different altitude levels. You don't need to have altitude as the criteria for color selection; you can select any criteria that you desire. You can also vary the controlling altitude and/or the overriding limits.

Finally, there is the function *cactus*. This function has as inputs an *x* and *y* coordinate, a scale factor, a level, and two colors. It includes the necessary *gen_quad* function calls to create a picture of a cactus located at the *x* and *y* coordinates, in a size determined by *scale* and with the specified level and colors.

With these preliminaries out of the way, we are ready to look at the main program. It begins by running a *for* loop which calls *generate* twenty-two times to create the red rock cliffs. It then runs *gen_quad* once to paint the yellow and brown desert floor. It then runs *cactus* four times to create four cactii at different locations and of different sizes.

Pike's Peak at Sunrise

Figure 21-4 lists a program for generating a scene of Pike's Peak near Colorado Springs, Colorado at sunrise. Figure 21-5 is a line drawing showing the triangles specified by data input, which are the artist's contribution to the program. The final picture appears in Plate 30.

Figure 21-4: Program to Generate Pike's Peak Scene

```
        pikespk = program to generate Pike's Peak landscape
```

```c
#include <stdio.h>
#include <math.h>
#include <dos.h>
#include <stdlib.h>
#include <time.h>
#include "tools.h"

void generate(int x1, int y-one, int x2, int y2, int x3, int y3,
    int level,int color1, int color2);
void midpoint();
void node(int x1, int y-one, int x2, int y2, int x3, int y3,
    int x4,int y4, int x5, int y5, int x6, int y6, int level,
    int color1, int color2);
void plot_triangle(int x1, int y-one, int x2, int y2, int x3,
    int y3,int color1,int color2);
float random_no (float limit_start, float limit_end);

int combination = 0,LINEWIDTH=1, OPERATOR=0;
unsigned long int PATTERN=0xFFFFFFFF;
unsigned char PALETTE[16]={0,1,2,3,4,5,20,7,56,57,58,59,60,
```

```
    61,62,63};
int interim;
int i,j;
int y_max = 180;
int level[12] = {6,6,5,5,5,5,4,4,4,4};
int x1[12] = {-220,-780,-480,-100,-770,-550,-220,-200};
int y-one[12] = {-240,-200,0,-260,-300,-280,-280,-280};
int x2[12] = {120,40,-240,240,-250,-60,80,230};
int y2[12] = {100,130,60,40,-110,-140,-130,-120};
int x3[12] = {500,420,0,500,600,400,340,580};
int y3[12] = {-40,-120,-60,-180,-300,-300,-300,-300};
int colors[16] = {0,1,2,11,10,10,34,31,47,58,18,2,6,27,62,63};
float xz,yz,xp,yp;
int color_value=2;
float x,y;

main()
{
    randomize();
    setMode(16);
    for (i=0; i<16; i++)
        setEGApalette(i,colors[i]);
    cls(13);
    i=0;
    for (i=0; i<4; i++)
    {
        if (i==1)
            y_max = 160;
        else
            y_max = 180;
        generate(x1[i],y-one[i],x2[i],y2[i],x3[i],y3[i],level[i],
            i+3,i+7);
    }
    fillTriangle(-320,-200,-320,-110,319,-110,1);
    fillTriangle(319,-110,319,-200,-320,-200,1);
    y_max = -100;
    for (i=4; i<8; i++)
        generate(x1[i],y-one[i],x2[i],y2[i],x3[i],y3[i],level[i],
            11,12);
    getch();
}

void midpoint()
{
    float r,w;
    unsigned int seed;
    unsigned long int seed_gen;

    seed_gen = 350*(y+240) + x + 320;
    seed = seed_gen%32760 + 2;
    srand(seed);
```

```
    r = 0.5 + random_no(0,.16666);
    w = random_no(.015,.035);
    xz = r*x - (w+.05)*y;
    yz = r*y + (w + .05)*x;
}
```

```
        generate() = finds coordinates of four triangles
                     making up a larger triangle
```

```
void generate(int x1, int y-one, int x2, int y2, int x3, int y3,
    int level,int color1, int color2)
{
    int x4,x5,x6,y4,y5,y6,ax,bx,cx,ay,by,cy;

    x = (x2-x1);
    y = (y2-y-one);
    midpoint(x,y);
    x4 = x1 + xz;
    y4 = y-one + yz;
    x = x1-x3;
    y = y-one-y3;
    midpoint(x,y);
    x6 = x3 + xz;
    y6 = y3 + yz;
    x = (x3-x2);
    y = (y3-y2);
    midpoint(x,y);
    x5 = x2 + xz;
    y5 = y2 + yz;
    if (level == 0)
    {
        plot_triangle(x1,y-one,x6,y6,x4,y4,color1,color2);
        plot_triangle(x2,y2,x4,y4,x5,y5,color1,color2);
        plot_triangle(x3,y3,x5,y5,x6,y6,color1,color2);
        plot_triangle(x4,y4,x5,y5,x6,y6,color1,color2);
    }
    else
        node(x1,y-one,x2,y2,x3,y3,x4,y4,x5,y5,x6,y6,level,color1,
            color2); }
```

```
                random_no() = gets a floating point random number
                              between two limits
```

```
float random_no (float limit_start, float limit_end)
{
    float result;

    limit_end -= limit_start;
    limit_end = 16383.0/limit_end;
    result = (rand() - 16383)/limit_end;
    if (result >= 0)
        result += limit_start;
    else
        result -= limit_start;
    return(result);
}
```

```
                node() = runs 'generate' for four triangles
```

```
void node(int x1, int y-one, int x2, int y2, int x3, int y3,
    int x4, int y4, int x5, int y5, int x6, int y6, int level,
    int color1, int color2)
{
    if (level == 0)
        return;
    generate (x1,y-one,x6,y6,x4,y4,level-1,color1,color2);
    generate (x2,y2,x4,y4,x5,y5,level-1,color1,color2);
    generate (x3,y3,x5,y5,x6,y6,level-1,color1,color2);
    generate (x4,y4,x5,y5,x6,y6,level-1,color1,color2);
}
```

```
    plot_triangle() = determines colors to use to fill a triangle.
```

```
void plot_triangle(int x1, int y-one, int x2, int y2, int x3,
    int y3, int color1, int color2)
{
    int ytt,color;
    float zt;

    if (y-one > y2)
        ytt = y-one;
```

```
else
    ytt = y2;
if (ytt < y3)
    ytt = y3;
zt = (y_max+240)*(1-(float)(ytt+240)/(y_max+240)*
    (float)(ytt+240)/(y_max+240));
if (random(y_max+241) <= zt)
    color = color1;
else
    color = color2;
if (ytt + 240 < (.25 * (y_max + 240)))
    color = color1;
if (ytt+240 > (.98 * (y_max+240)))
    color = color2;
fillTriangle(x1,y-one,x2,y2,x3,y3,color);
}
```

Figure 21-5: Input Data for Pike's Peak Scene

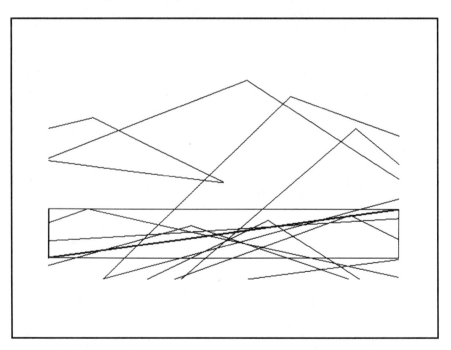

The program to paint this scene uses the technique of reseeding the random number generator for each line, prior to computing the midpoint displacement. First, let's look at the function *generate*. It begins very much like *generate* for the last program, except that the variables for defining the reduced triangle at higher levels are no longer needed. In addition, the program calls *plot_triangle* for the four new triangles only at the lowest (zero) level; at higher levels, it calls *node* to do the recursion, without any triangle filling. The *node* function is exactly the same as that used with the previous program.

The *midpoint* function is very similar to the one used in the previous program. However, it begins by generating a seed to be used with the *random_no* function. The seed makes use of the *x* and *y* distance of the line being operated upon. Both *x* and *y* values have biases added to assure that they will always be positive. The *y* value is then multiplied by 350 and added to the *x* value to produce a unique number.

Next, this number is taken modulo 32760 so that it will not exceed the seed value permitted for the random number generator. The random number generator is then reset with this seed. The remainder of the function is the same as that used in the previous program except that the limits of displacement perpendicular to the line are different, and a small bias is added to the *y* displacement and subtracted from the *x* displacement. The function *random_no* is the same used with the previous function.

The *plot_triangle* function is the same as that used by the previous program except that the limits for overriding the random color selection have been changed.

Earth Viewed from the Moon

Figure 21-6 lists a program for generating a scene of the earth viewed from the moon. Figure 21-7 is a line drawing showing the triangles specified by data input , which are the artist's contribution to the program. The final picture appears in Plate 31.

Figure 21-6: Program to Generate Earth Viewed from the Moon

```
        planet = program to generate planet from moon
```

```c
#include <stdio.h>
#include <math.h>
#include <dos.h>
#include <stdlib.h>
#include <time.h>
#include "tools.h"

#define convert(x,y) {x = (x + 319); y = (175-((93*y) >> 7));}

void ranFillOval(int x, int y, int b, int color, float aspect);
void generate(int x1, int y-one, int x2, int y2, int x3, int y3,
    int level, int color1,int color2);
void gen_quad (int x1, int y-one, int x2, int y2, int x3, int y3,
    int x4, int y4, int level, int color1, int color2);
void midpoint();
void node(int x1, int y-one, int x2, int y2, int x3, int y3,
    int x4, int y4, int x5, int y5, int x6, int y6, int level,
    int color1, int color2);
void plot_triangle(int x1, int y-one, int x2, int y2, int x3,
    int y3, int color1,int color2,int type);
void plot(int x, int y, int color);
void sort(int index, int x_coord[], int y_coord[]);

int combination = 0,LINEWIDTH=1, OPERATOR=0;
unsigned long int PATTERN=0xFFFFFFFF;
unsigned char PALETTE[16]={0,1,2,3,4,5,20,7,56,57,58,59,60,
    61,62,63};
int i,j;
int y_max = 280;
int level[26] = {3,3,3,3,3,3,4,4,4,4,4,4,4,4,4,4,4,4,4,4,4,
    4,4,4,4,4};
int x1[27] = {-100,-200,200,12,-280,20, -470,-350,-220,-200};
int y-one[27] = {-30,-110,-110,140,-210,-210, -300,-280,-280,
    -280};
int x2[27] = {-210,-160,-160,0,0,80, -250,-60,80,230};
int y2[27] = {210,0,0,0,0,50, -110,-140,-130,-120,0};
int x3[27] = {0,-90,0,120,80,200, 300,300,340,580};
int y3[27] = {-80,-110,0,-110,50,50, -300,-300,-300,-300};
int xz,yz,xp,yp,type,row,col;
int xa[35] = {-82,-80,-90,-70,-50,-30,-25,25,40,42,20,35,40,50,
    60,60,-28, 70,100,70,108,81,60,45,48,96,45,38,-8,0,-20,
    -28};
int xb[35] = {-70,-70,-80,-50,-30,25,-25,40,65,65,40,38,40,
    60,60,70,-28,100,127,129,92,70,56,48,54,100,38,46,12,14,
```

```
        14,8};
int  xc[35] = {-70,-70,-80,-50,-50,20,30,40,40,58,40,37,50,50,
        70,75,20,100,129,120,83,70,45,60,60,54,106,65,12,40,14,-8};
int  xd[35] = {-90,-80,-90,-70,-30,20,20,25,50,50,20,40,50,60,
        70,75,20,70,100,108,81,108,45,56,96,45,100,106,8,44,0,-30};
int  ya[35] = {52,52,76,80,76,38,10,80,90,55,50,3,60,60,52,55,
        80,115,120,109,76,80,-130,-124,-90,-70,-60,-50,0,-10,10,
        90};
int  yb[35] = {52,52,76,80,80,30,30,80,70,70,40,5,8,52,38,38,20,
        120,116,104,58,95,-124,-90,-65,-60,-50,-25,0,-10,10,80};
int  yc[35] = {60,80,80,55,56,38,10,90,80,70,3,-5,60,20,38,40,
        20,106,104,76,60,110,-124,-100,-100,-65,-50,-25,-18,-30,-
        18,75};
int  yd[35] = {60,80,77,55,38,30,30,90,60,60,3,-4,20,27,38,40,
        74,109,106,76,80,76,-124,-124,-70,-60,-60,-50,-18,-30,-18,
        85};
int  color_value=2;
int  level1 = 4;
float x,y;
long int x_center, y_center, radius;

main()
{

    setMode(16);
    cls(0);

    setEGApalette(0,8);
    setEGApalette(1,57);
    setEGApalette(3,20);
    setEGApalette(6,60);
    x_center = -100;
    y_center = 0;
    radius = 150;
    for (i=0; i<2000; i++)
    {
        row = rand()/93;
        col = rand()/51;
        plot(col,row,15);
    }
    fillOval(-100,0,152,1,1.0);
    type = 1;
    for (i=0; i<32; i++)
    {
        gen_quad(xa[i]+x_center,ya[i]+y_center,xb[i]+x_center,
            yb[i]+y_center,xc[i]+x_center,yc[i]+y_center,
            xd[i]+x_center,yd[i]+y_center,level1,2,3);
    }
    ranFillOval(-100,0,152,0,1.0);
    type = 0;
    y_max = -60;
```

```
    for (i=6; i<10; i++)
    {
        generate(x1[i],y-one[i],x2[i],y2[i],x3[i],y3[i],level[i],
            14,6);
    }
    fillOval(-180,-200,10,6,.35);
    fillOval(0,-160,10,6,.35);
    fillOval(40,-220,16,6,.3);
    fillOval(100,-170,6,6,.35);
    fillOval(200,-190,12,6,.35);
    fillOval(-220,-130,8,6,.35);
    fillOval(280,-150,8,6,.35);
    getch();
}
```

```
        fillTriangle() = fills a triangle in specified color
```

```
void fillTriangle (int x1, int y-one, int x2, int y2, int x3,
    int y3, int color)
{

    #define sign(x) ((x) > 0 ? 1:  ((x) == 0 ? 0:  (-1)))

    int dx, dy, dxabs, dyabs, i, index=0, j, k, px, py, sdx,
    sdy, x, y, xpoint[4], ypoint[4], toggle, old_sdy,sy0;
    long int check,xa,ya;
    int *x_coord, *y_coord;

    x_coord = (int *) malloc(4000 * sizeof(int));
    y_coord = (int *) malloc(4000 * sizeof(int));
    xpoint[0] = x1 + 319;
    ypoint[0] = 175 - ((y-one*93L) >> 7);
    xpoint[1] = x2 + 319;
    ypoint[1] = 175 - ((y2*93L) >> 7);
    xpoint[2] = x3 + 319;
    ypoint[2] = 175 - ((y3*93L) >> 7);
    xpoint[3] = xpoint[0];
    ypoint[3] = ypoint[0];
    i = 3;
    px = xpoint[0];
    py = ypoint[0];
    if (ypoint[1] == ypoint[0])
    {
        x_coord[index] = px;
        y_coord[index++] = py;
    }
    for (j=0; j<i; j++)
    {
```

```
dx = xpoint[j+1] - xpoint[j];
dy = ypoint[j+1] - ypoint[j];
sdx = sign(dx);
sdy = sign(dy);
if (j==0)
{
    old_sdy = sdy;
    sy0 = sdy;
}
dxabs = abs(dx);
dyabs = abs(dy);
x = 0;
y = 0;
if (dxabs >= dyabs)
{
    for (k=0; k<dxabs; k++)
    {
        y += dyabs;
        if (y>=dxabs)
        {
            y -= dxabs;
            py += sdy;
            if (old_sdy != sdy)
            {
                old_sdy = sdy;
                index--;
            }
            x_coord[index] = px+sdx;
            y_coord[index++] = py;
        }
        px += sdx;
    }
}
else
{
    for (k=0; k<dyabs; k++)
    {
        x += dxabs;
        if (x>=dyabs)
        {
            x -= dyabs;
            px += sdx;
        }
        py += sdy;
        if (old_sdy != sdy)
        {
            old_sdy = sdy;
            if (sdy != 0)
                index--;
        }
```

```
                    x_coord[index] = px;
                    y_coord[index++] = py;
                }
            }
        }
    index--;
    if (sy0 + sdy== 0)
        index--;
    sort(index,x_coord,y_coord);
    toggle = 0;
            if (x_coord[0] < 0)
                x_coord[0] = 0;
            if (x_coord[0] > 639)
                x_coord[0] = 639;
    for (i=0; i<index; i++)
    {
        if (x_coord[i+1] < 0)
            x_coord[i+1] = 0;
        if (x_coord[i+1] > 639)
            x_coord[i+1] = 639;
        if ((y_coord[i] == y_coord[i+1]) && (toggle == 0) &&
            (y_coord[i] >= 0) && (y_coord[i] < 350))
        {
            for (j=x_coord[i]; j<=x_coord[i+1]; j++)
            {
                xa = j - 319;
                ya = (175 - y_coord[i])*128L/93;
                if (((xa-x_center)*(xa-x_center) + (ya
                    - y_center)*(ya - y_center))
                    < (radius*radius) || (type == 0))
                    plot(j,y_coord[i],color);
            }
            toggle = 1;
        }
        else
            toggle = 0;
    }

    free(x_coord);
    free(y_coord);
}
```

```
         sort() = sorts coordinate pairs for drawing and
                      filling polygons
```

```
void sort(int index, int x_coord[], int y_coord[])
{
    int d=4,i,j,k,temp;
```

```
    while (d<=index)
        d*=2;
    d-=1;
    while (d>1)
    {
        d/=2;
            for (j=0; j<=(index-d); j++)
        {
            for (i=j; i>=0; i-=d)
            {
                if ((y_coord[i+d] < y_coord[i]) ||
                    ((y_coord[i+d] == y_coord[i]) &&
                    (x_coord[i+d] <= x_coord[i])))
                {
                    temp = y_coord[i];
                    y_coord[i] = y_coord[i+d];
                    y_coord[i+d] = temp;
                    temp = x_coord[i];
                    x_coord[i] = x_coord[i+d];
                    x_coord[i+d] = temp;
                }
            }
        }
    }
}

void node(int x1, int y-one, int x2, int y2, int x3, int y3,
    int x4,int y4, int x5, int y5, int x6, int y6, int level,
    int color1, int color2)
{
    if (level == 0)
        return(0);
    generate (x1,y-one,x4,y4,x6,y6,level-1,color1,color2);
    generate (x6,y6,x5,y5,x3,y3,level-1,color1,color2);
    generate (x4,y4,x2,y2,x5,y5,level-1,color1,color2);
    generate (x4,y4,x5,y5,x6,y6,level-1,color1,color2);
}

void generate(int x1, int y-one, int x2, int y2, int x3, int y3,
    int level, int color1, int color2)
{
    int x4,x5,x6,y4,y5,y6,ax,bx,cx,ay,by,cy;

    x = x2 - x1;
    y = y2 - y-one;
    midpoint(x,y);
    x4 = x1 + xz -xp;
    y4 = y-one + yz - yp;
    ax = -xp;
    ay = -yp;
```

```
    x = x3-x1;
    y = y3-y-one;
    midpoint(x,y);
    x6 = x1 + xz;
    y6 = y-one + yz;
    cx = xp;
    cy = yp;
    x = x3-x2;
    y = y3-y2;
    midpoint(x,y);
    x5 = x2 + xz;
    y5 = y2 + yz;
    bx = -xp;
    by = -yp;

    if (level == 0)
    {
        plot_triangle(x1,y-one,x4,y4,x6,y6,color1,color2,0);
        plot_triangle(x6,y6,x5,y5,x3,y3,color1,color2,0);
        plot_triangle(x4,y4,x5,y5,x6,y6,color1,color2,0);
        plot_triangle(x4,y4,x2,y2,x5,y5,color1,color2,0);
    }
    else
    {
        plot_triangle(x1,y-one,x4+ax,y4+ay,x6+cx,y6+cy,color1,
            color2,0);
        plot_triangle(x6+cx,y6+cy,x5+bx,y5+by,x3,y3,color1,
            color2,0);
        plot_triangle(x4+ax,y4+ay,x5+bx,y5+by,x6+cx,y6+cy,
            color1, color2,0);
        plot_triangle(x4+ax,y4+ay,x2,y2,x5+bx,y5+by,color1,
            color2,0);
        node(x1,y-one,x2,y2,x3,y3,x4,y4,x5,y5,x6,y6,level,color1,
            color2);
    }
}


void plot_triangle(int x1, int y-one, int x2, int y2, int x3,
    int y3,int color1, int color2,int type)
{
    int ytt,color;
    float zt;

    if (y-one > y2)
        ytt = y-one;
    else
        ytt = y2;
    if (ytt < y3)
        ytt = y3;
    zt = (y_max+240)*(1-(float)(ytt+240)/(y_max+240)*
```

```
            (float)(ytt+240)/(y_max+240));
    if (type == 0)
    {
        if (random(y_max+241)<= zt)
            color = color1;
        else
            color = color2;
        if (ytt + 240 < (.35 * (y_max + 240)))
            color = color1;
        if (ytt+240 > (.92 * (y_max+240)))
            color = color2;
    }
    else
    {
        if (rand() <= 24000)
            color = color1;
        else
            color = color2;
    }
    fillTriangle(x1,y-one,x2,y2,x3,y3,color);
}

void midpoint()
{
    float r,w;
    int sign1,sign2;

    if (rand() > 16383)
        sign1 = 1;
    else
        sign1 = -1;
    if (rand() > 16383)
        sign2 = 1;
    else
        sign2 = -1;
    r = 0.5 + sign1*(float)rand()/196602.0;
    w =  ((float)(rand()/819175.0) + 0.03)*sign2;
    r = 0.5 + gauss()/6;
    w =  gauss()/25 + .03;
    xz = r*x - w*y;
    yz = r*y + w*x;
    xp = 0.05*y;
    yp = -0.05*x;
}

float gauss(void)
{
    int k;
    float value,exponent,gauss;

    k = rand() - 16383;
```

```
    value = k/5461.0;
    exponent = -(value*value)/2.;
    gauss = .15915494*exp(exponent);
    k = rand();

    if (k > 16383)
        gauss *= -1;
    return(gauss);
}
```

```
    ranFillOval() = draws an oval centered at (x,y) with
                    radius in y direction of 'b' with
                    aspect ratio 'aspect' and fills it
                    randomly with color 'color'
```

```c
void ranFillOval(int x, int y, int b, int color, float aspect)
{
    union REGS reg;

    #define seq_out(index,val)   {outp(0x3C4,index);\
                    outp(0x3C5,val);}
    #define graph_out(index,val)  {outp(0x3CE,index);\
                    outp(0x3CF,val);}

    unsigned int offset;
    char far * mem_address;
    float a,aspect_square;
    int col,row,dummy,mask,end_x,end_y,kx;
    long a_square,b_square,b_test;

    a = b/aspect;
    a_square = a*a;
    b = (93*b) >> 7;
    b_square = b*b;
    convert (x,y);
    end_x = x+a;
    end_y = y+b;
    for (col=x-a; col<=end_x; col++)
    {
        b_test = b_square - (b_square*(col-x)*(col-x))/
            a_square;
        mask = 0x80 >> ((col) % 8);
        graph_out(8,mask);
        seq_out(2,0x0F);
        for (row=y-b; row<=end_y; row++)
        {
            kx = rand()/(32767/(1.3*radius));
            if (((row-y)*(row-y) <= b_test) && (kx < (col-x+
```

```
        20)))
    {
        offset = (long)row*80L + ((long)(col)/8L);
        mem_address = (char far *) 0xA0000000L +
            offset;
        dummy = *mem_address;
        *mem_address = 0;
        seq_out(2,color);
        *mem_address = 0xFF;
        seq_out(2,0x0F);
    }
    }
    }
    graph_out(3,0);
    graph_out(8,0xFF);
}
```

Figure 21-7: Input Data for Moon Scene

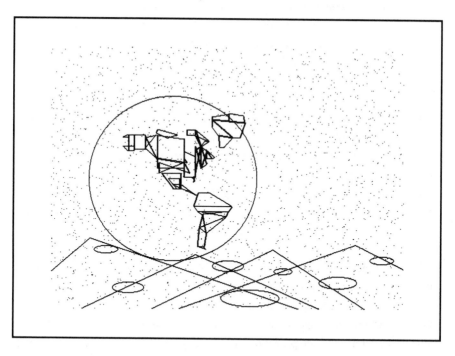

The program to paint this scene uses Michael Batty's technique of avoiding gaps by filling in reduced size triangles at higher levels. There are a few significant differences in this program from the two programs described previously. The *node* and *generate* functions, however, are exactly the same as those used in the program to create Oak Creek Canyon. Note that the data for the planetary surface is referenced to an arbitrary zero reference point and that the actual call of *generate* modifies this reference to be the center of the planetary circle.

The *midpoint* function is similar to the one used in the previous program, but it uses different limits and calls a gaussian random function instead of a straight random number. The gaussian function is *gauss*. It does not require any inputs, but instead, internally, uses a random number to choose a point on the positive half of a gaussian distribution and then gets another random number to determine whether this result should be positive or negative.

The *plot_triangle* function is the same as that used by the previous program except that the limits for overriding the random color selection have been changed and a new type parameter has been added. For a type *0* selection, the same technique for selecting colors based on altitude is used, but this technique is not appropriate for the planetary surface, where altitude is not involved, so for painting this surface, a color selection based strictly upon a random number selection is used.

This program also makes use of two new functions. The *fillTriangle* function is just the same as that used in the *tools* library except that it makes use of global variables that define the center and radius of a circle. If any point plotted by the new version of *fillTriangle* falls outside of the designated circle, it is not plotted. This permits the planetary surface to be defined without having to precisely determine that it will fit inside the planetary circle; the *fillTriangle* function automatically cuts off anything that wants to extend outside.

The second new function is *ranFillOval*. This is the same as the *fillOval* function in the library, except that it is set up so that when each point within the oval is determined, a random decision is made as to whether or not to plot this point. The probabilities are such that almost no points are plotted on the left side of the circle, and the probability of plotting points increases as one proceeds to the right of the circle. After the planet is painted, this function is run with the same planetary circle defined and the background color as the designated color. It then blanks out some of the planetary circle to give the appearance of shading to indicate curvature of the sphere.

The main program first sets the color palette and then randomly plots 2000 white points to represent stars in the night sky. It fills in a circle for the planet, then executes a *for* loop to paint the planetary surface on the circle. It then makes use of *ranFillOval* to provide the shading to give the circle the appearance of a sphere. Next, another *for* loop is run to generate the moon's surface. Finally, several ovals are drawn on the moon's surface to represent meteor craters.

22

Iterated Function Systems

Michael Barnsley at the Georgia Institute of Technology calls it the "Chaos Game" or more formally "Iterated Function Systems". A point is moved about the screen, randomly being translated, rotated, and scaled by one of several affine transformations. Ultimately, an image of the attractors is produced. We have already seen this technique at work in Chapter 6 where it generated the image of some strange attractors; in Chapter 16, where it produced the outlines of dragon curves; and in Chapter 18, where it generated three-dimensional dragons. Barnsley uses the technique to generate scenes in which a minimum of input data and a simple conversion program produce tremendous amounts of detail, representative of compression ratios of up to 10,000 compared to the original pixel data needed to create a similar scene.

Affine Transformations

The primary tool used in generating scenes with iterated function systems (IFS) is the affine transformation. As used here, this is a rotation, translation, and scaling of the coordinates of a point on the display screen (x,y) to a new position represented by (xn,yn). The transformation is performed as follows:

$$\begin{bmatrix} xn \\ yn \end{bmatrix} = w\begin{bmatrix} x \\ y \end{bmatrix} = \begin{bmatrix} a & b \\ c & d \end{bmatrix}\begin{bmatrix} x \\ y \end{bmatrix} + \begin{bmatrix} e \\ f \end{bmatrix} \qquad \text{(Equation 22-1)}$$

$$= \begin{bmatrix} ax + by + e \\ cx + dy + f \end{bmatrix}$$

The parameters a, b, c, and d perform a rotation, and their magnitudes result in the scaling. (For the whole system to work properly, the scaling must always result in a shrinkage of the distances between points; otherwise repeated iterations will result in the function blowing up to infinity, which is something your computer won't like. The parameters e and f cause a linear translation of the point being operated upon. Given that you apply this transformation to a geometric figure, the figure will be translated to a new location and there rotated and shrunk to a new, smaller size.

The Deterministic Algorithm

Before we begin playing the "chaos game," we should note that there is a deterministic version of the method. When we use this method, we take each point on our display screen and apply to it each of the affine transformations that make up our IFS for a particular desired figure. The new points are then plotted, and then the same process is applied again as many times as necessary to obtain a final result. Figure 22-1 lists the parameters required to generate a Sierpinski triangle and a fern leaf using the deterministic algorithm. (You probably thought that by the time we were through with Chapter 11 you had seen every possible way to generate a Sierpinski triangle, yet two more methods are given in this chapter.) Figure 22-2 lists the program to generate figures using the deterministic algorithm.

At this point, we need to be aware of two significant problems with the deterministic program. First, we have to have a lot of memory available. Just to specify all of the points on our current screen requires 224K of memory locations and a like number of locations are required for storing the transformed points as we generate them.

Figure 22-1: Parameters for Deterministic Generation of Sierpinski Triangle and Fern Leaf

Figure	a	b	c	d	e	f
Sierpinski Triangle	0.5	0	0	0.5	75	0
	0.5	0	0	0.5	0	150
	0.5	0	0	0.5	150	150
Fern Leaf	0	0	0	0.16	0	0
	0.85	0.04	-0.04	0.85	0	40
	0.2	-0.26	0.23	0.22	0	40
	-0.15	0.28	0.26	0.24	0	10

Figure 22-2: Program to Generate Figures Using Deterministic Algorithm

```
ifsdet = program to generate figures using deterministic algorithm
```

```c
#include <stdio.h>
#include <math.h>
#include <dos.h>

void cls(int color);
void plot(int x, int y, int color, int page);
int readPixel(int x, int y, int page);
void setMode(int mode);
void setPage(int page);

float a[8] = {.5 ,.5, .5}, b[8] = {0,0,0}, c[8] = {0,0,0},
    d[8] = {.5,.5,.5} ,e[8] = {75,0,150},f[8] = {0,150,150};
/*
float a[8] = {0,.85, .2,-.15}, b[8] = {0,.04,-.26,.28},
    c[8] = {0,-.04,.23,.26}, d[8] = {.16,.85,.22,.24}
    ,e[8] = {0,0,0,0}, f[8] = {0,40,40,10};
*/
int i, j, k,m,iter,color,dis_page = 1, back_page = 0,temp,
    index;
int OPERATOR = 0x00;
char ch;

main ()
```

```
{
    setMode(16);
    for (i=0; i<300; i++)
    {
        plot (i+100,0,15,0);
        plot (i+100,299,15,0);
        plot (399,i,15,0);
        plot (100,i,15,0);
    }
    while ((ch = getch()) != 0x0D)
    {
        setPage(dis_page);
        cls(0);
        for (i=0; i<300; i++)
        {
            for (j=0; j<300; j++)
            {
                color = readPixel(i+100,j,back_page);
                if (color != 0)
                {
                    iter = 0;
                    while (a[iter] != NULL)
                    {
                        k = a[iter]*i + b[iter]*j +
                        e[iter];
                        m = c[iter]*i + d[iter]*j +
                        f[iter++];
                        if ((k<540) && (m<350)  &&
                        (k>=-100) && (m>=0))
                            plot(k+100,m,15,
                                dis_page);
                    }
                }
            }
        }
        temp = dis_page;
        dis_page = back_page;
        back_page = temp;
    }
}
```

```
┌─────────────────────────────────────────────────────────┐
│                                                         │
│              setMode() = sets video mode                │
│                                                         │
└─────────────────────────────────────────────────────────┘
```

```
void setMode(int mode)

{
```

```
    union REGS reg;
    reg.h.ah = 0;
    reg.h.al = mode;
    int86 (0x10,&reg,&reg);
}
```

```
                setPage() = sets the active display page
```

```
void setPage(int page)
{

    union REGS reg;

    reg.h.ah = 5;
    reg.h.al = page;
    int86 (0x10,&reg,&reg);
}
```

```
        plot() = plots a point on the screen at designated
                 system coordinates using selected color
```

```
void plot(int x, int y, int color, int page)
{

    #define seq_out(index,val)   {outp(0x3C4,index);\
                    outp(0x3C5,val);}
    #define graph_out(index,val) {outp(0x3CE,index);\
                    outp(0x3CF,val);}

    unsigned int offset;
    int dummy,mask;
    char far * mem_address;

    offset = (long)y * 80L + ((long)x / 8L);
    if (page == 1)
        mem_address = (char far *) 0xA8000000L + offset;
    else
        mem_address = (char far *) 0xA0000000L + offset;
    mask = 0x80 >> (x % 8);
    graph_out(8,mask);
```

```
    seq_out(2,0x0F);
    dummy = *mem_address;
    *mem_address = 0;
    seq_out(2,color);
    *mem_address = 0xFF;
    seq_out(2,0x0F);
    graph_out(3,0);
    graph_out(8,0xFF);

}
```

```
                        cls() = clears the screen
```

```
void cls(int color)
{
    union REGS reg;

    reg.x.ax = 0x0600;
    reg.x.cx = 0;
    reg.x.dx = 0x184F;
    reg.h.bh = color;
    int86(0x10,&reg,&reg);
}
```

```
                readPixel = read a pixel from the screen
```

```
int readPixel(int x, int y, int page)
{

    union REGS reg;

    reg.h.ah = 0x0D;
    reg.h.bh = page;
    reg.x.cx = x;
    reg.x.dx = y;
    int86 (0x10,&reg,&reg);
    return (reg.h.al);
}
```

Figure 22-3: Generation of Sierpinski Triangle by Deterministic Algorithm

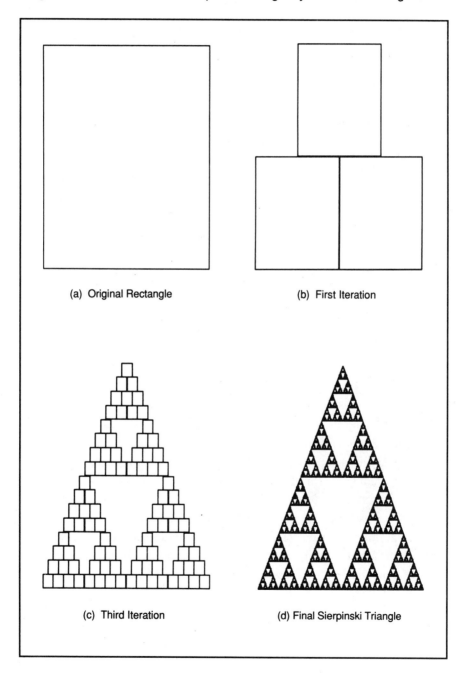

(a) Original Rectangle

(b) First Iteration

(c) Third Iteration

(d) Final Sierpinski Triangle

That is why a deterministic program in Barnsley's book, *Fractals Everywhere*, limits the resulting picture to a tiny size of 100 x 100 pixels. We get around the problem by making use of the two screens that are available for graphics with the EGA when it has its full memory complement. This makes the program a little slow, but still practical. That is why this program includes special versions of some of the functions that are normally part of the tools library.

The special versions include a parameter that specifies which of the two pages is to be operated upon. We begin by writing our starting figure (a rectangle) out to screen 0. Then, we use two *for* loops to read each pixel from the screen in turn. If the pixel is not black (the background color) we apply each affine transformation to the point and plot all the new points generated on screen 1. When the loops are complete, we give the user an opportunity to exit by hitting *Ent* or to make another run by hitting any other key. If the user elects to continue, the loops are gone through again, this time reading from screen 1 and storing the transformed points on screen 0. The program, as listed, will produce the Sierpinski triangle. Figure 22-3 shows the original rectangle, the first iteration of the program, and two iterations further along. After about eight iterations, no further change in the program can be observed on the screen.

Generating a Deterministic Fern

You may have noted in the deterministic program listing that one set of data for the affine transformations was commented out. If you remove the /* and */ that enclose this data, and comment out the other set of data instead, the program will generate a fern leaf. This, however, brings up another problem with the use of the deterministic algorithm. If you aren't careful about the range over which you examine points for transformation, you may get some very weird results. Our Sierpinski triangle worked very well when we transformed over a range of 0 to 200 in both *x* and *y* directions. Now look what happens when we use this same range for the fern leaf. The result is shown in Figure 22-4(a).

Figure 22-4: Generation of Fern Leaf by Deterministic Algorithm

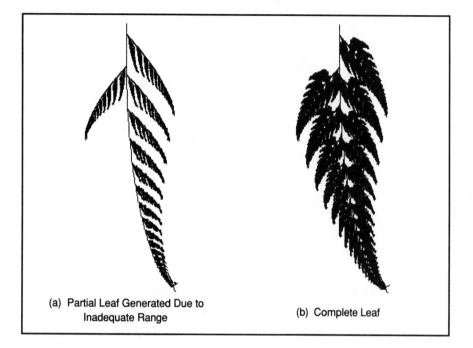

(a) Partial Leaf Generated Due to
    Inadequate Range

(b) Complete Leaf

Somehow, we have generated only one side of each leaflet and have only managed to put one half-leaflet on the left side of the stem. Now change the *for* loop for the x coordinate to have a range from -100 to +200. You will now get the whole leaf, as shown in Figure 22-4(b). Another drawback of the deterministic algorithm—illustrated when we try to draw the fern—is the slowness of the process for certain figures. In order to get the pictures in Figure 22-4, we had to go through 32 iterations of the program, and even more wouldn't be out of place. This is quite a lot compared to the few iterations required to produce a good representation of the Sierpinski triangle. There is no simple way to determine in advance how many iterations of the deterministic program are needed to produce a good picture.

Using the Chaos Algorithm

Figure 22-5 is a table of parameters for several figures that can be generated using the Chaos algorithm. The program for drawing these pictures is listed in Figure 22-6. The program is fairly straightforward. However, the determination of the probabilities needs to be noted. The program works by selecting one of the affine transformations at random with some probability that approximately represents the percentage of the picture that will be painted by that transformation. One might expect that summing the probabilities with which one selects each affine transformation, the result would be one (namely, we always have to select one of the transformations). That is true, but to speed up the operation of the program, we have adapted the probability numbers to match the random number routine included in most C language libraries. This function returns an integer between 0 and 32,767. Thus, the fractional probabilities for each transformation have been scaled up by multiplying them by 32,767.

Figure 22-5: Parameters for Generation of Pictures
Using Chaos Algorithm

Figure	a	b	c	d	e	f	p
Sierpinski	0.5	0	0	0.5	0	0	10813
Triangle	0.5	0	0	0.5	1.0	0	21626
	0.5	0	0	0.5	0.5	0.5	32767
Fern Leaf	0	0	0	0.16	0	0	328
	0.2	-0.26	0.23	0.22	0	0.2	2621
	-0.15	0.28	0.26	0.24	0	0.2	4915
	0.85	0.04	-0.04	0.85	0	0.2	32767
Tree	0	0	0	0.5	0	0	1638
	0.1	0	0	0.1	0	0.2	6553
	0.42	-0.42	0.42	0.42	0	0.2	19660
	-0.42	0.42	-0.42	0.42	0	0.2	32767
Cantor	0.333	0	0	0.333	0	0	10813
Tree	0.333	0	0	0.333	1	0	21626
	0.667	0	0	0.667	0.5	0.5	32767

Note that this program has a background color, a foreground color, x and y scale factors, and x and y offsets included for each picture. The background color is determined by the number from 0 to 15 that is passed to the *cls* function. The foreground color is a number from 0 to 15 passed to the *image_draw* function.

The *xscale* and *yscale* numbers determine the size of the picture; you can modify them as you desire to enlarge or reduce the picture. The *xoffset* and *yoffset* parameters have been selected so that the pictures are nicely centered; you can modify these if you want to reposition the picture on the display.

Figure 22-6: Program to Generate Pictures Using Chaos Algorithm

```
        image = program to generate iterated function systems
```

```c
#include <stdio.h>
#include <math.h>
#include <dos.h>

/* USER WRITTEN INCLUDES */
#include "tools.h"

/* GLOBALS */


int LINEWIDTH,OPERATOR,XCENTER,YCENTER,ANGLE;
unsigned long int PATTERN;

void image_draw(int color);
void plots(int x, int y, int color);

int adapt,mode;
int j, k, xscale,yscale,xoffset,yoffset,pr,p[4],pk[4];
long unsigned int i;
float a[4],b[4],c[4],d[4],e[4],f[4],x,y,newx;

main()
{
    setMode(16);
    a[0] =0; a[1] = .2; a[2] = -.15; a[3] = .85;
    b[0] = 0; b[1] = -.26; b[2] = .28; b[3] = .04;
    c[0] = 0; c[1] = .23; c[2] =.26; c[3] = -.04;
    d[0] = .16; d[1] = .22; d[2] = .24; d[3] = .85;
    e[0] = 0; e[1] = 0; e[2] = 0; e[3] = 0;
    f[0] = 0; f[1] = .2; f[2] = .2; f[3] = .2;
    p[0] = 328; p[1] = 2621; p[2] = 4915; p[3] = 32767;
    xscale = 300;
    yscale = 300;
    xoffset = -50;
    yoffset = -180;
    cls (1);
    image_draw(10);
```

```
    getch();

    a[0] = 0; a[1] = .1; a[2] = .42; a[3] = .42;
    b[0] = 0; b[1] = 0; b[2] = -.42; b[3] = .42;
    c[0] = 0; c[1] = 0; c[2] = .42; c[3] = -.42;
    d[0] = .5; d[1] = .1; d[2] = .42; d[3] = .42;
    e[0] = 0; e[1] = 0; e[2] = 0; e[3] = 0;
    f[0] = 0; f[1] = .2; f[2] = .2; f[3] = .2;
    p[0] = 1638; p[1] = 6553; p[2] = 19660; p[3] = 32767;
    xscale = 750;
    yscale = 750;
    xoffset = 0;
    yoffset = -160;
    cls(9);
    image_draw(13);
    getch();

    a[0] = .5; a[1] = .5; a[2] = .5; a[3] = 0;
    b[0] = 0; b[1] = 0; b[2] = 0; b[3] = 0;
    c[0] = 0; c[1] = 0; c[2] = 0; c[3] = 0;
    d[0] = .5; d[1] = .5; d[2] = .5; d[3] = 0;
    e[0] = 0; e[1] = 1.; e[2] = .5; e[3] = 0;
    f[0] = 0; f[1] = 0; f[2] = .5; f[3] = 0;
    p[0] = 10813; p[1] = 21626; p[2] = 32767; p[3] = 32767;
    xscale = 200;
    yscale = 200;
    xoffset = -200;
    yoffset = -160;
    cls(7);
    image_draw(12);
    getch();

    cls(2);
    a[0] = .333; a[1] = .333; a[2] = .667; a[3] = 0;
    b[0] = 0; b[1] = 0; b[2] = 0; b[3] = 0;
    c[0] = 0; c[1] = 0; c[2] = 0; c[3] = 0;
    d[0] = .333; d[1] = .333; d[2] = .667; d[3] = 0;
    e[0] = 0; e[1] = 1.; e[2] = .5; e[3] = 0;
    f[0] = 0; f[1] = 0; f[2] = .5; f[3] = 0;
    p[0] = 10813; p[1] = 21626; p[2] = 32767; p[3] = 32767;
    xscale = 120;
    yscale = 140;
    xoffset = -100;
    yoffset = -160;
    image_draw(14);
    getch();

}

void image_draw(int color)
{
```

```
    int px,py;

    x = 0;
    y = 0;
    for (i=1; i<=10000; i++)
    {
        j = rand();
        k = (j < p[0]) ? 0 : ((j < p[1]) ? 1 : ((j < p[2])
            ? 2 : 3));
        newx = (a[k]* x + b[k] * y + e[k]);
        y = (c[k] * x + d[k] * y + f[k]);
        x = newx;
                px = x*xscale + xoffset;
                py = (y*yscale + yoffset);
        if ((px>=-320) && (px<320)  && (py>=-240) && (py<240))
            plots (px,py,color);
    }
}

void plots(int x, int y, int color)
{

    #define convert(x,y)    {x = (x + 319);
                            y = (175 - ((93*y) >> 7));}

    convert(x,y);
    plot(x,y,color);
}
```

Another thing that you might be interested in doing is to expand the display so that only a portion of the picture appears as an enlarged display. You can do this by changing the scale parameters. The resulting pictures are shown in Figure 22-7.

Figure 22-7: Pictures Generated by Chaos Algorithm

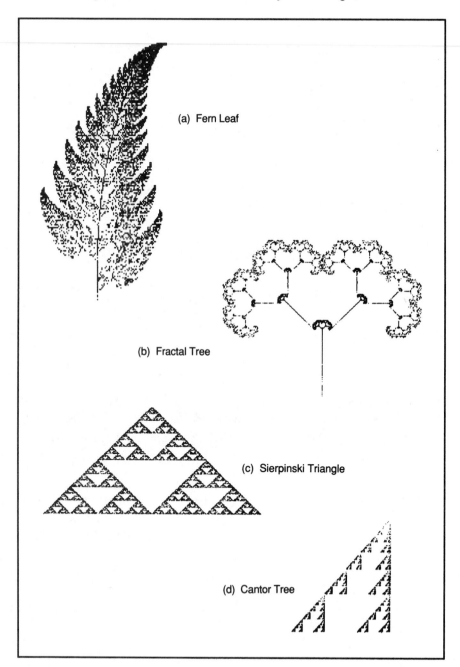

(a) Fern Leaf

(b) Fractal Tree

(c) Sierpinski Triangle

(d) Cantor Tree

The Collage Theorem

Now that you have used the program to generate some pictures with the Chaos algorithm, you may be getting anxious to create some original pictures of your own. I regret to tell you that this is a difficult process that will require some original programming on your part. The theoretical proof that this can be done at all appears in Barnsley's book, where he proves what he calls the *Collage theorem*. The proof won't help you too much, however, unless you are a mathematician who is expert in set theory.

Basically, what the theorem says is that if you can take some picture, or portion of a picture, and by performing affine transformations end up with smaller (possibly distorted) versions of the original picture which can be placed so that they fill in the original picture without very much overlap, without running very far outside the original picture boundaries and without leaving much of any blank space, then by using these same affine transformations in the Chaos algorithm you can produce a good representation of the original picture. Barnsley has a number of examples.

Now, how do you go about using this theorem. Barnsley doesn't supply any examples that give much clue as to how it is done. (That's not surprising, since he has just formed a company that will do the job for you if you have a quarter of a million dollars.) You might begin by adding to your computer the capablity to display frames captured from a video camera, or you might start with an artist's picture drawn, for example, with PC Paintbrush. Then, you need a program that will perform an affine transformation on the picture or a portion of the picture. It needs to show the result of the transformation and give you the capability to change the transformation parameters until you have the transformed version superimposed just as you want it on part of the original picture. You do this several more times, until you have the whole picture covered. Your program then needs to give you the parameters of each of your final affine transformations. You should then be able to insert these in the chaos algorithm program given above, although you may have to modify it to permit it to handle colors in a more sophisticated manner. If this sounds like a very large undertaking, it is. Maybe it will appear in my next book on advanced fractal programming.

The Chaos Algorithm in Three Dimensions

It is possible to make three-dimensional pictures using affine transformations having the form:

$$
\begin{bmatrix} xn \\ yn \\ zn \end{bmatrix} = w \begin{bmatrix} x \\ y \\ z \end{bmatrix} = \begin{bmatrix} a & b & c \\ d & e & f \\ g & h & m \end{bmatrix} \begin{bmatrix} x \\ y \\ y \end{bmatrix} + \begin{bmatrix} n \\ q \\ r \end{bmatrix} \qquad \text{Equation 22-2}
$$

$$
= \begin{bmatrix} ax + by + cz & + n \\ dx + ey + fz & + q \\ gx + hy + mz & + r \end{bmatrix}
$$

We don't have the capability to display the resulting picture in three dimensions, so we use the same projection technique that was used for the three-dimensional dragons in Chapter 18. Figure 22-8 shows the parameters for a three-dimensional fern leaf. The program in Figure 22-9 is a listing of a program to generate the three-dimensional fern leaf four times, using a different shade of green or yellow and different projection angles for each pass through the loop. The program was set up with the projection angles built in, because it takes considerable experimentation to get the right selection of angles to give a pleasing display. The resulting display is shown in Plate 31.

Figure 22-8: Parameters for Three-Dimensional Fern Leaf

a	b	c	d	e	f	g	h	m	n	q	r	p
0	0	0	0.5	.18	0	0	0	0	0	0	0	328
.83	0	0	0.5	.86	.1	0	-.12	.84	0	1.62	0	27879
.22	-.23	0	.24	.22	0	0	0	.32	0	.82	0	30173
-.22	.23	0	.24	.22	0	0	0	.32	0	.82	0	32767

You can have a lot of fun experimenting with this program, by changing offsets and scale factors for each pass through the loop, by modifying the angles, and by increasing the number of passes through the loop to add additional fern leaves.

Figure 22-9: Program to Generate Three-Dimensional Pictures Using Chaos Algorithm

```
        image3d = program to generate three-dimensional
                  iterated function systems
```

```
#include <stdio.h>
#include <math.h>
#include <dos.h>
#include "tools.h"

int LINEWIDTH,OPERATOR,XCENTER,YCENTER,ANGLE;
unsigned long int PATTERN;
unsigned char PALETTE[16]={0,1,2,3,4,5,20,7,56,57,58,59,60,61,
    62,63};

void image_draw(void);
void plots(int x, int y, int color);
float degrees_to_radians(float degrees);

int adapt,mode;
int j, k, index, xscale,yscale,xoffset,yoffset,pr,p[4],pk[4];
int hues[8] = {2,10,11,14};
long unsigned int i;
float a[4],b[4],c[4],d[4],e[4],f[4],g[4],h[4],m[4],n[4],q[4],
    r[4], ca,cb,cg,sa,sb,sg,x,y,z,newx,newy,alpha[4] = {30,45,
    15,95}, beta[4] = {115,105,70,40},gamma[4]={25,70,20,-30};
float rad_per_degree=0.0174533;
main()
{
    setMode(16);
    setEGApalette(0,8);
    setEGApalette(2,2);
    setEGApalette(10,58);
    setEGApalette(11,62);
    setEGApalette(14,26);
    a[0] =0; a[1] = .83; a[2] = .22; a[3] = -.22;
    b[0] = 0; b[1] = 0; b[2] = -.23; b[3] = .23;
    c[0] = 0; c[1] = 0; c[2] = 0; c[3] = 0;
    d[0] = 0; d[1] = 0; d[2] = .24; d[3] = .24;
    e[0] = .18; e[1] = .86; e[2] = .22; e[3] = .22;
    f[0] = 0; f[1] = .1; f[2] = 0; f[3] = 0;
```

```
        g[0] = 0; g[1] = 0; g[2] = 0; g[3] = 0;
        h[0] = 0; h[1] = -.12; h[2] = 0; h[3] = 0;
        m[0] = 0; m[1] = .84; m[2] = .32; m[3] = .32;
        n[0] = 0; n[1] = 0; n[2] = 0; n[3] = 0;
        q[0] = 0; q[1] = 1.62; q[2] = .82; q[3] = .82;
        r[0] = 0; r[1] = 0; r[2] = 0; r[3] = 0;
        p[0] = 328; p[1] = 27879 ; p[2] = 30173; p[3] = 32767;
        xscale = 40;
        yscale = 50;
        xoffset = 60;
        yoffset = -180;
        cls (0);
        for (index=0; index<4; index++)
        {
            ca = cos(alpha[index]*0.0174533);
            cb = cos(beta[index]*0.0174533);
            cg = cos(gamma[index]*0.0174533);
            sa = sin(alpha[index]*0.0174533);
            sb = sin(beta[index]*0.0174533);
            sg = sin(gamma[index]*0.0174533);
            image_draw();
        }
        getch();
}

void image_draw(void)
{

    int px,py;
    float vx,vy;

    x = 0;
    y = 0;
    z = 0;
    for (i=1; i<=10000; i++)
    {
        j = rand();
        k = (j < p[0]) ? 0 : ((j < p[1]) ? 1 : ((j < p[2])
            ? 2 : 3));
        newx = (a[k]* x + b[k] * y + c[k] * z + n[k]);
        newy = (d[k] * x + e[k] * y + f[k] * z + q[k]);
        z = g[k] * x + h[k] * y + m[k] * z + r[k];
        x = newx;
        y = newy;
        vx = x*ca + y*cb + z*cg;
        px = vx*xscale + xoffset;
        vy = x*sa + y*sb + z*sg;
        py = (vy*yscale + yoffset);
        if ((px>=-320) && (px<320)  && (py>=-240) && (py<240))
            plots (px,py,hues[index]);
    }
```

```
}

void plots(int x, int y, int color)
{

    #define convert(x,y)    {x = (x + 319);
                             y = (175 - ((93*y) >> 7));}

    convert(x,y);
    plot(x,y,color);
}

float degrees_to_radians(float degrees)
{
    float angle;

    while (degrees >= 360)
        degrees -= 360;
    while (degrees < 0)
        degrees += 360;
    angle = rad_per_degree*degrees;
    return angle;
}
```

Appendix A
Tools Library

Publics by module:

```
CLS         size = 49
            _cls

DISPLAY     size = 61
            _display

DRAWLINE    size = 512
            _drawLine

DRAWOVAL    size = 767
            _drawOval

FILLOVAL    size = 940
            _fillOval

FILLTRI     size = 917
            _fillTriangle

MOVCURS2    size = 1846
            _move_cursor                        _plot_point

PLOT        size = 116
            _plot

PLOTS       size = 53
            _plots

POINT       size = 209
            _point
```

```
READPIX     size = 51
            _readPixel

READSCR     size = 65
            _read_screen

RESTORE     size = 814
            _restore_screen

SAVESCRN    size = 858
            _save_screen

SETEGA      size = 58
            _setEGApalette

SETMODE     size = 38
            _setMode

STEP        size = 109
            _step

TURN        size = 24
            _turn
```

```
                    cls() = clears the sreen
```

```
#include "tools.h"

void cls(int color)
{
    #include <dos.h>
    union REGS reg;

    reg.x.ax = 0x0600;
    reg.x.cx = 0;
    reg.x.dx = 0x184F;
    reg.h.bh = color;
    int86(0x10,&reg,&reg);
}
```

```
                display() = displays byte on screen
```

```c
#include "tools.h"

void display(unsigned long int address, int color_plane,
    unsigned char ch)
{
    #include <dos.h>

    #define seq_out(index,val)  {outp(0x3C4,index);\
                    outp(0x3C5,val);}
    char far * mem_address;
    char dummy;

    mem_address = (char far *) 0xA0000000L + address;
    dummy = *mem_address;
    seq_out(2,(0x01 << color_plane));
    *mem_address = ch;
}
```

```
            drawLine() = draws a line from one set of coordinates
                    to another in a designated color
```

```c
#include "tools.h"

void drawLine(int x1, int y1, int x2, int y2, int color)
{
    #include <dos.h>

    extern int LINEWIDTH;
    extern unsigned long int PATTERN;
    union REGS reg;

    #define sign(x) ((x) > 0 ? 1:  ((x) == 0 ? 0:  (-1)))

    int dx, dy, dxabs, dyabs, i, j, px, py, sdx, sdy, x, y;
    unsigned long int mask=0x80000000;

    x1  += 320;
    y1 = 175 - ((y1*93) >> 7);
    x2  += 320;
    y2 = 175 - ((y2*93) >> 7);
    dx = x2 - x1;
```

```
        dy = y2 - y1;
        sdx = sign(dx);
        sdy = sign(dy);
        dxabs = abs(dx);
        dyabs = abs(dy);
        x = 0;
        y = 0;
        px = x1;
        py = y1;
        if (dxabs >= dyabs)
        {
            for (i=0; i<dxabs; i++)
            {
                mask = mask ? mask : 0x80000000;
                y += dyabs;
                if (y>=dxabs)
                {
                    y -= dxabs;
                    py += sdy;
                }
                px += sdx;
                if (PATTERN & mask)
                    {
                    for (j=-LINEWIDTH/2; j<=LINEWIDTH/2; j++)
                        plot(px,py+j,color);
                }
                mask >>= 1;
            }
        }
        else
        {
            for (i=0; i<dyabs; i++)
            {
                mask = mask ? mask : 0x80000000;
                x += dxabs;
                if (x>=dyabs)
                {
                    x -= dyabs;
                    px += sdx;
                    }
                py += sdy;
                if (PATTERN & mask)
                {
                    for (j=-LINEWIDTH/2; j<=LINEWIDTH/2; j++)
                        plot(px+j,py,color);
                }
                    mask >>= 1;
            }
        }
}
```

```
        drawOval() = draws an oval centered at (x,y) with
                     radius in y direction of 'b' with
                     aspect ratio 'aspect' in color 'color'
```

```c
#include "tools.h"
#include <stdlib.h>
#include <math.h>

void drawOval(int x, int y, int b, int color, float aspect)
{
    #include <dos.h>

    extern int LINEWIDTH;

    union REGS reg;

    int col, i, row, bnew;
    long a,a_square, b_square, two_a_square, two_b_square,
        four_a_square, four_b_square,d;

    b  -= LINEWIDTH/2;
    a = b/aspect;
    b = (b*93) >> 7;
    x  += 320;
    y = 175 - ((y*93) >> 7);

    for (i=1; i<=LINEWIDTH; i++)
    {
        b_square = (long)b*b;
        a_square = (a*a);
        row = b;
        col = 0;
        two_a_square = a_square << 1;
        four_a_square = a_square << 2;
        four_b_square = b_square << 2;
        two_b_square = b_square << 1;
        d = two_a_square * (((long)row  -1)*(row )) + a_square +
            two_b_square*(1-a_square);
        while (a_square*(row ) > b_square * (col))
        {
            plot(col+x,row+y,color);
            plot(col+x,y-row, color);
            plot(x-col,row+y,color);
            plot(x-col,y-row,color);
            if (d>= 0)
            {
                row--;
                d -= four_a_square*(row);
```

```
        }
        d += two_b_square*(3 + (col << 1));
        col++;
    }

    d = two_b_square * (col + 1)*col + two_a_square*(row *
            (row  -2) +1) + (1-two_a_square)*b_square;
    while ((row) + 1)
    {
        plot(col+x,row+y,color);
        plot(col+x,y-row, color);
        plot(x-col,row+y,color);
        plot(x-col,y-row,color);
        if (d<= 0)
        {
            col++;
            d += four_b_square*col;
        }
        row--;
        d += two_a_square * (3 - (row <<1));
    }
    b++;
    }
}
```

```
    fillOval() = draws an oval centered at (x,y) with
                 radius in y direction of 'b' with
                 aspect ratio 'aspect' and fills it
                 with color 'color'
```

```
#include "tools.h"
#include <stdlib.h>

void fillOval(float x_cen, float y_cen, float radius,
    int color, float aspect)
{
    #include <dos.h>

    union REGS reg;

    #define seq_out(index,val)  {outp(0x3C4,index);\
                   outp(0x3C5,val);}
    #define graph_out(index,val)  {outp(0x3CE,index);\
                   outp(0x3CF,val);}

    unsigned int offset;
    char far * mem_address;
```

```
    float a,b,aspect_square;
    long x,y,col,row,dummy,mask,start_x, start_y,end_x,end_y;
    float a_square,b_square,b_test;

    a = radius/aspect;
    a_square = a*a;
    b = .729*radius;
    b_square = b*b;
    x = x_cen + 319;
    y = 175 - (.729*y_cen);
    start_x = max(0,x-a);
    end_x = min (639,x+a);
    start_y = max(0,y-b);
    end_y = min(349,y+b);

    for (col=start_x; col<=end_x; col++)
    {
        b_test = b_square - (b_square*(col-x)*(col-x))/a_square;
        mask = 0x80 >> ((col) % 8);
        graph_out(8,mask);
        seq_out(2,0x0F);
        for (row=start_y; row<=end_y; row++)
            if ((row-y)*(row-y) <= b_test)
            {
                offset = row*80L + ((col)/8L);
                mem_address = (char far *) 0xA0000000L +
                    offset;
                dummy = *mem_address;
                *mem_address = 0;
                seq_out(2,color);
                *mem_address = 0xFF;
                seq_out(2,0x0F);
            }
    }
    graph_out(3,0);
    graph_out(8,0xFF);
}
```

```
        fillTriangle() = fills a triangle in specified color
```

```
void fillTriangle (int x1, int y1, int x2, int y2, int x3,
    int y3, int color)
{

    #define sign(x) ((x) > 0 ? 1:  ((x) == 0 ? 0:  (-1)))
```

```
int dx, dy, dxabs, dyabs, i, j, k, px, py, sdx, sdy, x, y,
    xpoint[4], ypoint[4], xa[350],xb[350], start,end;
long int check;
int x_coord[350], y_coord[350];

for (i=0; i<350; i++)
{
    xa[i] = 640;
    xb[i] = 0;
}
xpoint[0] = x1 + 320;
ypoint[0] = 175 - ((y1*93L) >> 7);
xpoint[1] = x2 + 320;
ypoint[1] = 175 - ((y2*93L) >> 7);
xpoint[2] = x3 + 320;
ypoint[2] = 175 - ((y3*93L) >> 7);
xpoint[3] = xpoint[0];
ypoint[3] = ypoint[0];
px = xpoint[0];
py = ypoint[0];
for (j=0; j<3; j++)
{
    dx = xpoint[j+1] - xpoint[j];
    dy = ypoint[j+1] - ypoint[j];
    sdx = sign(dx);
    sdy = sign(dy);
    dxabs = abs(dx);
    dyabs = abs(dy);
    x = 0;
    y = 0;
    if (dxabs >= dyabs)
    {
        for (k=0; k<dxabs; k++)
        {
            y += dyabs;
            px += sdx;
            if (y>=dxabs)
            {
                y -= dxabs;
                py += sdy;
            }
            if ((py>=0) && (py<=349))
            {
                if (px < xa[py])
                    xa[py] = px;
                if (px > xb[py])
                    xb[py] = px;
            }
        }
    }
    else
```

```
        {
            for (k=0; k<dyabs; k++)
            {
                py += sdy;
                x += dxabs;
                if (x>=dyabs)
                {
                    x -= dyabs;
                    px += sdx;
                }
                if ((py>=0) && (py<=349))
                {
                    if (px < xa[py])
                        xa[py] = px;
                    if (px > xb[py])
                        xb[py] = px;
                }
            }
        }
    }
    if (ypoint[0] < ypoint[1])
    {
        start = ypoint[0];
        end = ypoint[1];
    }
    else
    {
        start = ypoint[1];
        end = ypoint[0];
    }
    for (i=0; i<350; i++)
    {
        if (xa[i] < 0)
            xa[i] = 0;
        if (xb[i] > 639)
            xb[i] = 639;
    }
    if (ypoint[2] < start)
        start = ypoint[2];
    if (ypoint[2] > end)
        end = ypoint[2];
    if (start < 0)
        start = 0;
    if (end > 349)
        end = 349;
    for (i=start; i<=end; i++)
    {
        for (j=xa[i]; j<=xb[i]; j++)
            plot(j,i,color);
    }
```

```
}
```

```
          _____
         |                                                |
         |      move_cursor() = moves cursor and saves position      |
         |                                                |
         |_____|
```

```c
#include <stdio.h>
#include "tools.h"

void move_cursor(int type,int color,int min_col, int min_row)
{
    #include <dos.h>

    extern int CURSOR_X,CURSOR_Y;
    extern union LIMIT XMax,YMax,XMin,YMin,Pval,Qval;
    extern float TXMax,TXMin,TYMax,TYMin;
    union REGS reg;

    unsigned int mask;
    int i,j,image,image_store[256],index,ch,temp,limit[7];
    char far *base;

    limit[0] = 11;
    limit[1] = 9;
    limit[2] = 10;
    limit[3] = 10;
    limit[4] = 12;
    limit[5] = 14;
    limit[6] = 14;
    do
    {
        index = 0;
        switch(type)
        {
            case 0:
                for (i=0; i<16; i++)
                    image_store[index++] = plot_point
                        (CURSOR_X+i,CURSOR_Y,
                        color);
                for (i=1; i<16; i++)
                    image_store[index++] = plot_point
                        (CURSOR_X,CURSOR_Y+i,
                        color);
                break;
            case 1:
                for (i=0; i<16; i++)
                    image_store[index++] = plot_point
                        (CURSOR_X+15,CURSOR_Y+i,
```

```
                color);
        for (i=0; i<15; i++)
            image_store[index++] = plot_point
                (CURSOR_X+i,CURSOR_Y+15,
                color);
        break;
    case 2:
        for (j=0; j<7; j++)
        {
            for(i=j; i<limit[j]; i++)
            {
                if((i==8) && (j ==5))
                    i=10;
                if((i==8) && (j ==6))
                    i=12;
                image_store[index++] = plot_point
                    (CURSOR_X+j,CURSOR_Y+i,
                    color);
            }
        }
        image_store[index++] = plot_point(CURSOR_X+7,
            CURSOR_Y+7,color);
}
ch = getch();
if (ch != 0x0D)
{
    if (ch == 0)
        ch = getch() + 256;
    index = 0;
    switch(type)
    {
        case 0:
            for (i=0; i<16; i++)
                plot_point(CURSOR_X+i,CURSOR_Y,
                    image_store[index++]);
            for (i=1; i<16; i++)
                plot_point(CURSOR_X,CURSOR_Y+i,
                    image_store[index++]);
            break;
        case 1:
            for (i=0; i<16; i++)
                plot_point(CURSOR_X+15,CURSOR_Y+i,
                    image_store[index++]);
            for (i=0; i<15; i++)
                plot_point(CURSOR_X+i,CURSOR_Y+15,
                    image_store[index++]);
            break;
        case 2:
            for (j=0; j<7; j++)
            {
                for(i=j; i<limit[j]; i++)
```

415

```
                {
                    if((i==8) && (j ==5))
                        i=10;
                    if((i==8) && (j ==6))
                        i=12;
                    plot(CURSOR_X+j,
                        CURSOR_Y+i,
                        image_store[index++]);
                }
            }
            plot(CURSOR_X+7,CURSOR_Y+7,
                image_store[index++]);
        }
    reg.h.ah = 2;
    int86(0x16,&reg,&reg);
    if ((reg.h.al & 0x03) != 0)
    {
        switch(ch)
        {
            case 56:
                if (CURSOR_Y > min_row)
                    CURSOR_Y -= 10;
                break;
            case 52:
                if (CURSOR_X > min_col)
                    CURSOR_X -= 10;
                break;
            case 54:
                if (CURSOR_X < 629)
                    CURSOR_X += 10;
                break;
            case 50:
                if (CURSOR_Y < 329)
                    CURSOR_Y += 10;
        }
    }
    else
    {
        switch(ch)
        {
            case 333:
                if (CURSOR_X < 639)
                    CURSOR_X++;
                break;
            case 331:
                if (CURSOR_X > min_col)
                    CURSOR_X--;
                break;
            case 328:
                if (CURSOR_Y > min_row)
                    CURSOR_Y--;
```

```
                    break;
                case 336:
                    if (CURSOR_Y < 335)
                        CURSOR_Y++;
                    break;
            }
        }
        switch(type)
        {
            case 0:

                TXMin = XMin.f + (XMax.f - XMin.f)/
                    639*(CURSOR_X);
                TYMax = YMax.f - (YMax.f - YMin.f)/
                    349*CURSOR_Y;
                gotoxy(5,24);
                printf("XMin= %f   YMax= %f",TXMin,TYMax);
                break;
            case 1:
                TXMax = XMin.f + (XMax.f - XMin.f)/
                    639*(CURSOR_X + 16);
                TYMin = YMax.f - (YMax.f - YMin.f)/
                    349*(CURSOR_Y + 16);
                gotoxy(41,24);
                printf("  XMax= %f   YMin= %f",TXMax,TYMin);
                break;

            case 2:
                Pval.f = XMin.f + (XMax.f - XMin.f)/639*
                    CURSOR_X;
                Qval.f = YMax.f - (YMax.f - YMin.f)/
                    349*CURSOR_Y;
                gotoxy(5,24);
                printf("  P= %f   Q= %f     ",Pval.f,Qval.f);
            }
        }
    }
    while (ch != 0x0D);
}
```

```
        plot_point() = plots a point at (x,y) in color
                       for EGA or VGA, using Turbo C port
                       output functions and returns
                       original point color
```

```
int plot_point(int x, int y, int color)
{
```

417

```
#define seq_out(index,val)  {outp(0x3C4,index);\
                outp(0x3C5,val);}
#define graph_out(index,val)  {outp(0x3CE,index);\
                outp(0x3CF,val);}
#define EGAaddress 0xA0000000L

int index,old_color=0;
unsigned char mask, dummy,exist_color;
char far *mem_address;

mem_address = (char far *) (EGAaddress +
    ((long)y * 80L + ((long)x / 8L)));
mask = 0x80 >> (x % 8);
for (index = 0; index<4; index++)
{
    graph_out(4,index);
    graph_out(5,0);
    exist_color = *mem_address & mask;
    if (exist_color != 0)
        old_color |=(0x01<<index);
}
graph_out(8,mask);
seq_out(2,0x0F);
dummy = *mem_address;
*mem_address = 0;
seq_out(2,color);
*mem_address = 0xFF;
seq_out(2,0x0F);
graph_out(3,0);
graph_out(8,0xFF);
return(old_color);
}
```

```
        plot() = plots a point at (x,y) in color for EGA,
                using assembly language at critical points.
```

```
#include "tools.h"

void plot(int x, int y, int color)
{
    #include <dos.h>

    unsigned int offset;
    int mask;
    offset = (long)y * 80L + ((long)x / 8L);
    mask = 0x80 >> (x % 8);
    _ES = 0xA000;
```

```
    _BX = offset;
    _CX = color;
    _AX = mask;
    asm MOV    AH,AL
    asm MOV    AL,08
    asm MOV    DX,03CEH
    asm OUT    DX,AX
    asm MOV    AX, 0FF02H
    asm MOV    DL, 0C4H
    asm OUT    DX,AX
    asm OR ES:[BX],CH
    asm MOV    BYTE PTR ES: [BX],00H
    asm MOV    AH,CL
    asm OUT    DX,AX
    asm MOV    BYTE PTR ES: [BX],0FFH
    asm MOV    AH,0FFH
    asm OUT    DX,AX
    asm MOV    DL,0CEH
    asm MOV    AX,0003
    asm OUT    DX,AX
    asm MOV    AX,0FF08H
    asm OUT    DX,AX
}
```

```
        plots() = plots a point on the screen at designated
                  system coordinates using selected color
```

```
void plots(int x, int y, int color)
{

    #define convert(x,y) {x = (x + 319);   y = (175 -
        ((93*y)/128));}

    convert(x,y);
    plot(x,y,color);
}
```

```
        point() = sets the beginning angle for turtle
                  in tenths of a degree
```

```c
#include <math.h>
#include "tools.h"

float point(float x1, float y_one, float x2, float y2)
{

    float theta;
    if ((x2 - x1) == 0)
        if (y2 > y_one)
            theta = 90;
        else
            theta = 270;
    else
        theta = atan((y2-y_one)/(x2-x1))*57.295779;
    if (x1>x2)
        theta += 180;
    return(theta);
}
```

```
             readPixel = reads a pixel from the screen
```

```c
#include "tools.h"

int readPixel(int x, int y)
{
    #include <dos.h>

    union REGS reg;

    reg.h.ah = 0x0D;
    reg.x.cx = x;
    reg.x.dx = y;
    int86 (0x10,&reg,&reg);
    return (reg.h.al);
}
```

420

```
┌─────────────────────────────────────────────────────────────────┐
│                                                                   │
│           read_screen() = reads a byte from screen                │
│                                                                   │
└─────────────────────────────────────────────────────────────────┘
```

```c
#include "tools.h"

unsigned char read_screen(unsigned long int address,
    int color_plane)
{

    #include <dos.h>
    #define graph_out(index,val)  {outp(0x3CE,index);\
                    outp(0x3CF,val);}
    char far * mem_address;
    unsigned char pixel_data;

    mem_address = (char far *) 0xA0000000L + address;
    graph_out(4,color_plane);
    graph_out(5,0);
    pixel_data = *mem_address;
    return (pixel_data);
}
```

```
┌─────────────────────────────────────────────────────────────────┐
│                                                                   │
│           restore_screen() = paint screen from disk data          │
│                                                                   │
└─────────────────────────────────────────────────────────────────┘
```

```c
#include <stdio.h>
#include "tools.h"
#include <stdlib.h>

extern union LIMIT XMax, XMin, YMax, YMin, Pval, Qval;

int restore_screen(char file_name[])
{
    #include <dos.h>
    #define graph_out(index,val)  {outp(0x3CE,index);\
                    outp(0x3CF,val);}
    FILE *fsave;
    unsigned char ch,ch1,red,green,blue,color,
        line_length,end;
    int line_end,i,j,k,m,pass,x1,y1,x2,y2;
    if ((fsave = fopen(file_name,"rb")) == NULL)
    {
        printf("\nCan't find %s.\n",file_name);
    return(0);
```

```
        }
        else
        {
            ch = fgetc(fsave);
            if (ch != 0x0A)
            {
                printf("\n%s is not a valid ZSoft file.\n",
                file_name);
                fclose(fsave);
            return(0);
            }
        }
        setMode(16);
        cls(0);

        for (i=1; i<4; i++)
            ch = fgetc(fsave);
        x1 = getw(fsave);
        y1 = getw(fsave);
        x2 = getw(fsave);
        y2 = getw(fsave);
        for (i=12; i<16; i++)
            ch = fgetc(fsave);
        for (i=0; i<16; i++)
        {
            red = fgetc(fsave)/85;
            green = fgetc(fsave)/85;
            blue = fgetc(fsave)/85;
            color = ((red & 0x01) << 5) | ((red & 0x02)
                << 1) | ((green & 0x01) << 4) | (green
                & 0x02) | ((blue & 0x01) << 3) | ((blue &
                0x02) >> 1);
            setEGApalette(i,color);
        }

        for (i=64; i<70; i++)
            ch = fgetc(fsave);
        for (i=0; i<4; i++)
            XMax.c[i] = fgetc(fsave);
        for (i=0; i<4; i++)
            XMin.c[i] = fgetc(fsave);
        for (i=0; i<4; i++)
            YMax.c[i] = fgetc(fsave);
        for (i=0; i<4; i++)
            YMin.c[i] = fgetc(fsave);
        for (i=0; i<4; i++)
            Pval.c[i] = fgetc(fsave);
        for (i=0; i<4; i++)
            Qval.c[i] = fgetc(fsave);
        for (i=94; i<128; i++)
            ch = fgetc(fsave);
```

```
graph_out(8,0xFF);
graph_out(3,0x10);
for (k=y1; k<y2; k++)
{
    i = k*80 + (x1/8);
    line_end = k* 80 + (x2/8)+1;
    j = 0;
    while (j < 4)
    {
        ch1 = fgetc(fsave);
        if ((ch1 & 0xC0) != 0xC0)
        {
            display(i, j, ch1);
            i++;
            if (i >= line_end)
            {
                j++;
                i = k*80 + (x1/8);
            }
        }
        else
        {
            ch1 &= 0x3F;
            pass = ch1;
            ch = fgetc(fsave);
            for (m=0; m<pass; m++)
            {
                display(i, j, ch);
                i++;
                if (i >= line_end)
                {
                    j++;
                    i = k*80 + (x1/8);
                }
            }
        }
    }
}
graph_out(3,0);
graph_out(8,0xFF);
fclose(fsave);
return(x2);
}
```

```
┌─────────────────────────────────────────────────────────────┐
│                                                             │
│          save_screen() = save screen to disk file           │
│                                                             │
└─────────────────────────────────────────────────────────────┘
```

```c
#include "tools.h"
#include <stdio.h>

void save_screen(int x1, int y1, int x2, int y2,
    char file_name[])
{

    extern union LIMIT XMax,XMin,YMax,YMin,Pval,Qval;
    extern unsigned char PALETTE[16];
    int i,j,k,add1,add2,number,num_out, line_length, end,
        start_line, end_line;
    unsigned char ch,ch1,old_ch,red,green,blue;
    FILE *fsave;

    sound (256);
    while (file_name[6] < 0x3A)
    {
        if ((fsave = fopen (file_name,"rb")) != NULL)
        {
            file_name[7]++;
            if (file_name[7] >= 0x3A)
            {
                file_name[7] = 0x30;
                file_name[6]++;
            }
            fclose(fsave);
        }
        else
        {
            fclose(fsave);
            fsave = fopen(file_name,"wb");
            fputc(0x0A,fsave);
            fputc(0x05,fsave);
            fputc(0x01,fsave);
            fputc(0x04,fsave);
            putw(x1,fsave);
            putw(y1,fsave);
            putw(x2,fsave);
            putw(y2,fsave);
            putw(640,fsave);
            putw(350,fsave);
            ch = 0x00;
            for (i=0; i<16; i++)
            {
                red = (((PALETTE[i] & 0x20) >> 5) |
                    ((PALETTE[i] & 0x04) >> 1)) * 85;
```

```
    green = (((PALETTE[i] & 0x10) >> 4) |
        (PALETTE[i] & 0x02)) * 85;
    blue = (((PALETTE[i] & 0x08) >> 3) |
        ((PALETTE[i] & 0x01) << 1)) * 85;
    fputc(red,fsave);
    fputc(green,fsave);
    fputc(blue,fsave);
}
fputc(0x00,fsave);
fputc(0x04,fsave);
start_line = x1/8;
end_line = x2/8 + 1;
line_length = end_line - start_line;
end = start_line + line_length * 4 + 1;
putw(line_length,fsave);
putw(1,fsave);
for (i=0; i<4; i++)
    fputc(XMax.c[i],fsave);
for (i=0; i<4; i++)
    fputc(XMin.c[i],fsave);
for (i=0; i<4; i++)
    fputc(YMax.c[i],fsave);
for (i=0; i<4; i++)
    fputc(YMin.c[i],fsave);
for (i=0; i<4; i++)
    fputc(Pval.c[i],fsave);
for (i=0; i<4; i++)
    fputc(Qval.c[i],fsave);
for (i=94; i<128; i++)
    fputc(' ',fsave);
for (k=y1; k<y2; k++)
{
    add1 = 80*k;
    number = 1;
    j = 0;
    add2 = (start_line);
    old_ch = read_screen(add1 + add2++,0);
    for (i=add2; i<end; i++)
    {
        if (i == end - 1)
            ch = old_ch - 1;
        else
        {
            if ((add2) == end_line)
            {
                j++;
                add2 = (start_line);
            }
            ch = read_screen(add1 + add2,
                j);
        }
```

```
                    if ((ch == old_ch) && number < 63)
                        number++;
                    else
                    {
                        num_out = ((unsigned char)
                            number | 0xC0);
                        if ((number != 1) ||
                            ((old_ch & 0xC0) ==
                            0xC0))
                            fputc(num_out,fsave);
                        fputc(old_ch,fsave);
                        old_ch = ch;
                        number = 1;
                    }
                    add2++;
                }
            }
        fclose(fsave);
        break;
        }
    }
    nosound();
}
```

```
┌──────────────────────────────────────────────────────────┐
│                                                            │
│    setEGApalette() = sets the color for an EGA palette number │
│                                                            │
└──────────────────────────────────────────────────────────┘
```

```
#include "tools.h"

extern unsigned char PALETTE[16];

void setEGApalette(int palette, int color)
{
    #include <dos.h>

    union REGS reg;

    PALETTE[palette] = color;
    reg.h.ah = 0x10;
    reg.h.al = 0;
    reg.h.bh = color;
    reg.h.bl = palette;
    int86(0x10,&reg,&reg);
}
```

```
┌──────────────────────────────────────────────────────────┐
│                                                          │
│              setMode() = sets video mode                 │
│                                                          │
└──────────────────────────────────────────────────────────┘
```

```c
#include "tools.h"

void setMode(int mode)
{
    #include <dos.h>

    union REGS reg;

    reg.h.ah = 0;
    reg.h.al = mode;
    int86 (0x10,&reg,&reg);
}
```

```
┌──────────────────────────────────────────────────────────┐
│                                                          │
│     step() = advances turtle by step r in current direction │
│                                                          │
└──────────────────────────────────────────────────────────┘
```

```c
#include "tools.h"

void step (void)
{
    #include <math.h>
    extern float turtle_x;
    extern float turtle_y;
    extern float turtle_r;
    extern float turtle_theta;

    turtle_x += turtle_r*cos(turtle_theta*.017453292);
    turtle_y += turtle_r*sin(turtle_theta*.017453292);
}
```

```
┌──────────────────────────────────────────────────────────┐
│                                                          │
│         turn() = changes turtle pointing direction.       │
│               Angle is in tenths of a degree              │
│                                                          │
└──────────────────────────────────────────────────────────┘
```

```c
#include "tools.h"

void turn(float angle)
```

```
{
    extern float turtle_theta;

    turtle_theta += angle;
}
```

Appendix B

Programs for Hercules Graphics Adapter

I strongly urge you to get an EGA or VGA card and monitor if you are going to get at all serious about fractals. Some of the programs in this book cannot even be run without such a card; others can be run, but their beauty or meaning is severely degraded on a monochrome display. On the other hand, if you have purchased this book and are not going to get a high resolution color monitor capability, you need to do something to recoup your investment, right? So here are the functions needed for a *tools* library that is compatible with the Hercules graphics adapter and the revised versions of those programs that are worth a try at running in monochrome. Since this book was primarily designed for color, you aren't going to find quite as much support for monochrome. If you bought the disk that comes with the book, you will find when you dearchive the Hercules software that a compiled library for Turbo C has been supplied, but not one for Microsoft C. If the Turboc C library does not work with Microsoft C, you will have to compile each of the *tools* functions and then combine them into a library with the Microsoft *LIB* program.

You will also note that the functions *save_screen* and *restore_screen*, which are used to save a graphics screen to a disk file and then read it back to the screen, are not supplied in a Hercules compatible version. If you plan to save and restore screens, you will have to write your own software using the versions that are given for the EGA/VGA as a guide. The display programs that use these functions have been modified for the Hercules so that screens are neither saved or restored.

Tools Library for Hercules Graphics Adapter

Publics by module

```
CHARACT   size = 2726
          _char_table              _write_big_char
          _write_big_str           _write_horz_char
          _write_horz_str          _write_vert_char
          _write_vert_str          _write_vid_char
          _write_vid_str

CLS       size = 111
          _cls

DISPLAY   size = 93
          _display

DRAWLINE  size = 538
          _drawLine

DRAWOVAL  size = 934
          _drawOval

FILLOVAL  size = 652
          _fillOval

FILLTRI   size = 944
          _fillTriangle

GETPAGE   size = 34
          _getPage

MOVCURS2  size = 1518
          _move_cursor                         _plot_point

PLOT      size = 131
          _plot

PLOTS     size = 71
          _plots

POINT     size = 209
          _point

SETMODE   size = 277
```

```
        _graph_reg_data                    _setMode
        _text_reg_data

STEP    size = 109
        _step

TURN    size = 24
        _turn



/*

            CHARACTER WRITING FUNCTIONS
            write horizontal and vertical
            and vertical characters and strings.

*/

#include "tools.h"
#include "chars.h"

void write_horz_char(int x, int y, int ch, int color)
{
    int offset,i,j;
    unsigned char char_test;

        x = ((x + 319)*18) >> 4;
    y = 174 - ((93*y) >> 7);
    offset = (ch - 32) * 14;
    for (i=0; i<14; i++)
    {
        for (j=0; j<8; j++)
        {
            char_test = 0x80 >> j;
                if ((char_table[offset+i] & char_test) != 0)
            {
                if (color == 1)
                    plot(x+j,y+i,1);
                else
                    plot(x+j,y+i,0);
            }
            else
            {
                if (color == 1)
                    plot(x+j,y+i,0);
                else
                    plot(x+j,y+i,1);
            }
        }
    }
```

```
            if (color == 1)
                plot(x+j,y+i,0);
            else
                plot(x+j,y+i,1);
    }
}

void write_vert_char(int x, int y, int ch, int color)
{
    int offset,i,j;
    unsigned char char_test;

    x = ((x + 319)*18) >> 4;
    y = 174 - ((93*y) >> 7);
    offset = (ch - 32) * 14;
    for (i=0; i<14; i++)
    {
        for (j=0; j<8; j++)
        {
            char_test = 0x80 >> j;
                if ((char_table[offset+i] & char_test) != 0)
            {
                if (color == 1)
                    plot(x+i,y-j,1);
                else
                    plot(x+i,y-j,0);
            }
            else
            {
                if (color == 1)
                    plot(x+i,y-j,0);
                else
                    plot(x+i,y-j,1);
            }
        }
    }
}

void write_horz_str(int x, int y, char *string, int color)
{
    int p=0;

    while (string[p])
    {
        write_horz_char(x,y,string[p++],color);
        x += 8;
        if (x>312)
        {
            x=-319;
            y += 20;
        }
```

```
    }
}

void write_vert_str(int x, int y, char *string, int color)
{
    int p=0;

    while (string[p])
    {
        write_vert_char(x,y,string[p++],color);
        y += 12;
        if (y>228)
        {
            y=-239;
            x += 14;
        }
    }
}

/*

                cls() = Clears the Screen

*/

#include "tools.h"

void cls(void)
{
    #include <dos.h>

    union REGS reg;

    char far *address;
        unsigned char ch;
        unsigned int i;

        outp(0x3B8,2);
        ch = inp(0x3B8);
        if (ch == 0x8A)
            for (i=0; i<0x7FFF; i++)
                {
                    address = (char far *) 0xB8000000L + i;
            *address = 0;
                    outp(0x3B8,0x8A);
                }
        else
                for (i=0; i<0x7FFF; i++)
                {
                    address = (char far *) 0xB0000000L + i;
            *address = 0;
```

```
                        outp(0X3B8,0x0A);
            }
}
/*

            display() = displays byte on screen

*/

#include "tools.h"

void display(unsigned long int address, int color_plane,
    unsigned char ch)
{
    #include <dos.h>

    char far * mem_address;
    unsigned char regis;
        outp(0x3B8,2);
    regis = inp(0x3B8);
    if (regis == 0x8A)
    {
        mem_address = (char far *) 0xB8000000L + address;
        *mem_address = ch;
        outp(0x3B8,0x8A);
    }
        else
    {
        mem_address = (char far *) 0xB0000000L + address;
        *mem_address = ch;
        outp(0X3B8,0x0A);
    }
}

/*

    drawLine() = draws a line from one set of coordinates
                to another in a designated color

*/

#include "tools.h"

extern unsigned long int PATTERN;
extern int LINEWIDTH;

void drawLine(int x1, int y1, int x2, int y2, int color)
{
    #define sign(x) ((x) > 0 ? 1:  ((x) == 0 ? 0:  (-1)))
```

```
int dx, dy, dxabs, dyabs, i, j, px, py, sdx, sdy, x, y;
unsigned long int mask=0x80000000;

    x1 = ((x1 + 319)*18) >> 4;
y1 = 174 - ((93*y1) >> 7);
    x2 = ((x2 + 319)*18) >> 4;
y2 = 174 - ((93*y2) >> 7);

dx = x2 - x1;
dy = y2 - y1;
sdx = sign(dx);
sdy = sign(dy);
dxabs = abs(dx);
dyabs = abs(dy);
x = 0;
y = 0;
px = x1;
py = y1;
if (dxabs >= dyabs)
{
    for (i=0; i<dxabs; i++)
    {
        mask = mask ? mask : 0x80000000;
        y += dyabs;
        if (y>=dxabs)
        {
            y -= dxabs;
            py += sdy;
        }
        px += sdx;
        if (PATTERN & mask)
            {
            for (j=-LINEWIDTH/2; j<=LINEWIDTH/2; j++)
                plot(px,py+j,color);
        }
        mask >>= 1;
    }
}
else
{
    for (i=0; i<dyabs; i++)
    {
        mask = mask ? mask : 0x80000000;
        x += dxabs;
        if (x>=dyabs)
        {
            x -= dyabs;
            px += sdx;
            }
        py += sdy;
        if (PATTERN & mask)
```

```
            {
                for (j=-LINEWIDTH/2; j<=LINEWIDTH/2; j++)
                    plot(px+j,py,color);
            }
                mask >>= 1;
        }
    }
}

/*

    drawOval() = draws an oval with specified center,
                 radius, color and aspect ratio.

*/

#include "tools.h"

extern int LINEWIDTH;

void drawOval(int x, int y, int b, int color, float aspect)
{
    int i;
        float a_temp;
    long a_square, b_square, two_a_square, two_b_square,
        four_a_square, four_b_square, d, a, row, col;

    x = ((x + 319)*18) >> 4;
    y = 174 - ((93*y) >> 7);
    a_temp = b/aspect;
    a = (((int)(a_temp * 18)) >> 4) - LINEWIDTH/2;
    b = ((93*b) >> 7) - LINEWIDTH/2;

    for (i=1; i<=LINEWIDTH; i++)
    {
        b_square = b*b;
        a_square = a*a;
        row = b;
        col = 0;
        two_a_square = a_square << 1;
        four_a_square = a_square << 2;
        four_b_square = b_square << 2;
        two_b_square = b_square << 1;
        d = two_a_square * ((row  -1)*(row )) + a_square +
            two_b_square*(1-a_square);
        while (a_square*(row ) > b_square * (col))
        {
            plot(col+x,row+y,color);
            plot(col+x,y-row, color);
            plot(x-col,row+y,color);
            plot(x-col,y-row,color);
```

```
            if (d>= 0)
            {
                row--;
                d -= four_a_square*(row);
            }
            d += two_b_square*(3 + (col << 1));
            col++;
        }

        d = two_b_square * (col + 1)*col + two_a_square*(row *
                    (row  -2) +1) + (1-two_a_square)*b_square;
        while ((row) + 1)
        {
            plot(col+x,row+y,color);
                plot(col+x,y-row, color);
            plot(x-col,row+y,color);
            plot(x-col,y-row,color);
            if (d<= 0)
            {
                col++;
                d += four_b_square*col;
            }
            row--;
            d += two_a_square * (3 - (row <<1));
        }
        b++;
        a++;
    }
}

/*

    fillOval() = draws an oval centered at (x,y) with
                radius in y direction of 'b' with
                aspect ratio 'aspect' and fills it
                with color 'color'.

*/

#include <stdio.h>
#include <stdlib.h>
#include <math.h>
#include "tools.h"

void fillOval(float x_cen, float y_cen, float radius,
    int color, float aspect)
{
    #include <dos.h>

    union REGS reg;
```

```
#define seq_out(index,val)  {outp(0x3C4,index);\
                   outp(0x3C5,val);}
#define graph_out(index,val)  {outp(0x3CE,index);\
                   outp(0x3CF,val);}
```

```
unsigned int offset;
char far * mem_address;
float a,b,aspect_square;
int x,y,col,row,dummy,mask,start_x, start_y,end_x,end_y;
float a_square,b_square,b_test;

a = radius/aspect;
a_square = a*a;
b = .729*radius;
b_square = b*b;
x = x_cen + 319;
y = 175 - (.729*y_cen);
start_x = max(0,x-a);
end_x = min (639,x+a);
start_y = max(0,y-b);
end_y = min(349,y+b);

for (col=start_x; col<=end_x; col++)
{
    b_test = b_square - (b_square*(col-x)*(col-x))/
        a_square;
    for (row=start_y; row<=end_y; row++)
        if ((long)(row-y)*(row-y) <= b_test)
        {
            plot (col,row,color);
        }
}
}

/*

    fillTriangle() = fills a triangle in specified color

*/


void fillTriangle (int x1, int y01, int x2, int y2, int x3,
    int y3, int color)
{

    #define sign(x) ((x) > 0 ? 1:  ((x) == 0 ? 0:  (-1)))

    int dx, dy, dxabs, dyabs, i, j, k, px, py, sdx, sdy, x, y,
        xpoint[4], ypoint[4], xa[350],xb[350],
        start,end;
    long int check;
```

```
int x_coord[350], y_coord[350];

for (i=0; i<350; i++)
{
    xa[i] = 640;
    xb[i] = 0;
}
xpoint[0] = ((x1 + 319)*18) >> 4;
ypoint[0] = 174 - ((y01*93L) >> 7);
xpoint[1] = ((x2 + 319)*18) >> 4;
ypoint[1] = 174 - ((y2*93L) >> 7);
xpoint[2] = ((x3 + 319)*18) >> 4;
ypoint[2] = 174 - ((y3*93L) >> 7);
xpoint[3] = xpoint[0];
ypoint[3] = ypoint[0];
px = xpoint[0];
py = ypoint[0];
for (j=0; j<3; j++)
{
    dx = xpoint[j+1] - xpoint[j];
    dy = ypoint[j+1] - ypoint[j];
    sdx = sign(dx);
    sdy = sign(dy);
    dxabs = abs(dx);
    dyabs = abs(dy);
    x = 0;
    y = 0;
    if (dxabs >= dyabs)
    {
        for (k=0; k<dxabs; k++)
        {
            y += dyabs;
            px += sdx;
            if (y>=dxabs)
            {
                y -= dxabs;
                py += sdy;
            }
            if ((py>=0) && (py<=349))
            {
                if (px < xa[py])
                    xa[py] = px;
                if (px > xb[py])
                    xb[py] = px;
            }
        }
    }
    else
    {
        for (k=0; k<dyabs; k++)
        {
```

```
                py += sdy;
                x += dxabs;
                if (x>=dyabs)
                {
                    x -= dyabs;
                    px += sdx;
                }
                if ((py>=0) && (py<=349))
                {
                    if (px < xa[py])
                        xa[py] = px;
                    if (px > xb[py])
                        xb[py] = px;
                }
            }
        }
    }
if (ypoint[0] < ypoint[1])
{
    start = ypoint[0];
    end = ypoint[1];
}
else
{
    start = ypoint[1];
    end = ypoint[0];
}
for (i=0; i<350; i++)
{
    if (xa[i] < 0)
        xa[i] = 0;
    if (xb[i] > 639)
        xb[i] = 639;
}
if (ypoint[2] < start)
    start = ypoint[2];
if (ypoint[2] > end)
    end = ypoint[2];
if (start < 0)
    start = 0;
if (end > 349)
    end = 349;
for (i=start; i<=end; i++)
{
    for (j=xa[i]; j<=xb[i]; j++)
        plot(j,i,color);
}

}
```

```
/*

              getPage() = Returns Active Page Number

*/

#include "tools.h"

int getPage(void)
{
    #include <dos.h>

    unsigned char ch;

        ch = inp(0x3B8);
        if (ch == 0x8A)
            return 1;
        else
                return(0);
 }



/*

        move_cursor() = moves cursor and saves position

*/

#include <stdio.h>
#include "tools.h"

void move_cursor(int type,int color,int min_col, int min_row)
{
    #include <dos.h>

    extern int CURSOR_X,CURSOR_Y;
    extern union LIMIT XMax,YMax,XMin,YMin,Pval,Qval;
    extern float TXMax,TXMin,TYMax,TYMin;
    union REGS reg;

    unsigned int mask;
    int i,j,image,image_store[256],index,ch,temp,limit[7];
    char far *base;

    limit[0] = 11;
    limit[1] = 9;
    limit[2] = 10;
    limit[3] = 10;
    limit[4] = 12;
    limit[5] = 14;
```

```
limit[6] = 14;
do
{
    index = 0;
    switch(type)
        {
        case 0:
            for (i=0; i<16; i++)
                image_store[index++] = plot_point
                    (CURSOR_X+i,CURSOR_Y,
                    color);
            for (i=1; i<16; i++)
                image_store[index++] = plot_point
                    (CURSOR_X,CURSOR_Y+i,
                    color);
            break;
        case 1:
            for (i=0; i<16; i++)
                image_store[index++] = plot_point
                    (CURSOR_X+15,CURSOR_Y+i,
                    color);
            for (i=0; i<15; i++)
                image_store[index++] = plot_point
                    (CURSOR_X+i,CURSOR_Y+15,
                    color);
            break;
        case 2:
            for (j=0; j<7; j++)
            {
                for(i=j; i<limit[j]; i++)
                {
                    if((i==8) && (j ==5))
                        i=10;
                    if((i==8) && (j ==6))
                        i=12;
                    image_store[index++] = plot_point
                        (CURSOR_X+j,CURSOR_Y+i,
                        color);
                }
            }
            image_store[index++] = plot_point(CURSOR_X+7,
                CURSOR_Y+7,color);
        }
    ch = getch();
    if (ch != 0x0D)
    {
        if (ch == 0)
            ch = getch() + 256;
        index = 0;
        switch(type)
        {
```

```
        case 0:
            for (i=0; i<16; i++)
                plot_point(CURSOR_X+i,CURSOR_Y,
                    image_store[index++]);
            for (i=1; i<16; i++)
                plot_point(CURSOR_X,CURSOR_Y+i,
                    image_store[index++]);
            break;
        case 1:
            for (i=0; i<16; i++)
                plot_point(CURSOR_X+15,CURSOR_Y+i,
                    image_store[index++]);
            for (i=0; i<15; i++)
                plot_point(CURSOR_X+i,CURSOR_Y+15,
                    image_store[index++]);
            break;
        case 2:
            for (j=0; j<7; j++)
            {
                for(i=j; i<limit[j]; i++)
                {
                    if((i==8) && (j ==5))
                        i=10;
                    if((i==8) && (j ==6))
                        i=12;
                    plot(CURSOR_X+j,
                        CURSOR_Y+i,
                        image_store[index++]);
                }
            }
            plot(CURSOR_X+7,CURSOR_Y+7,
                image_store[index++]);
        }
reg.h.ah = 2;
int86(0x16,&reg,&reg);
if ((reg.h.al & 0x03) != 0)
{
    switch(ch)
    {
        case 56:
            if (CURSOR_Y > min_row)
                CURSOR_Y -= 10;
            break;
        case 52:
            if (CURSOR_X > min_col)
                CURSOR_X -= 10;
            break;
        case 54:
            if (CURSOR_X < 629)
                CURSOR_X += 10;
            break;
```

```
                    case 50:
                        if (CURSOR_Y < 329)
                            CURSOR_Y += 10;
                }
            }
            else
            {
                switch(ch)
                {
                    case 333:
                        if (CURSOR_X < 639)
                            CURSOR_X++;
                        break;
                    case 331:
                        if (CURSOR_X > min_col)
                            CURSOR_X--;
                        break;
                    case 328:
                        if (CURSOR_Y > min_row)
                            CURSOR_Y--;
                        break;
                    case 336:
                        if (CURSOR_Y < 335)
                            CURSOR_Y++;
                        break;
                }
            }
            switch(type)
            {
                case 0:

                    TXMin = XMin.f + (XMax.f - XMin.f)/
                        639*(CURSOR_X);
                    TYMax = YMax.f - (YMax.f - YMin.f)/
                        349*CURSOR_Y;
                    break;
                case 1:
                    TXMax = XMin.f + (XMax.f - XMin.f)/
                        639*(CURSOR_X + 16);
                    TYMin = YMax.f - (YMax.f - YMin.f)/
                        349*(CURSOR_Y + 16);
                    break;

                case 2:
                    Pval.f = XMin.f + (XMax.f - XMin.f)/639*
                        CURSOR_X;
                    Qval.f = YMax.f - (YMax.f - YMin.f)/
                        349*CURSOR_Y;
            }
        }
    }
```

```c
    while (ch != 0x0D);
}


/*

    plot_point() = Plots a point at (x,y) in color
                   for Enhanced Graphics Adapter, using
                   Turbo C port output functions and
                   returns original point color
/*


int plot_point(int x, int y, int color)
{

    int index,page,offset;
    unsigned char mask, dummy,exist_color;
    char far *address;

    page = getPage();
    offset = 0x2000 * (y%4) + 0x8000 * page + 90 * (y/4) + x/8;
    mask = 0x80 >> (x%8);
    address = (char far *)0xB0000000L + offset;
    if ((*address & mask) != 0)
    {
        exist_color = 1;
            *address &= ~mask;
    }
    else
    {
            *address |= mask;
        exist_color = 0;
    }
    return(exist_color);
}

/*

    plot() = plots a point to the screen at designated
             location in screen coordinates in selected
             color.

*/

#include "tools.h"

void plot(int x, int y, int color)
{
    unsigned int offset;
    int page;
```

```
        char mask;
        char far *address;

        page = getPage();
        offset = 0x2000 * (y%4) + 0x8000 * page + 90 * (y/4) + x/8;
        mask = 0x80 >> (x%8);
        address = (char far *)0xB0000000L + offset;
        if (color == 1)
            *address |= mask;
        else
            *address &= ~mask;
}

/*

        plots() = plots a point to the screen at designated
                  location in system coordinates

*/

#include "tools.h"

void plots(int x, int y, int color)
{
        unsigned int offset;
        int page;
        char mask;
        char far *address;

        x = ((x + 319)*18) >> 4;
        y = 174 - ((93*y) >> 7);
            page = getPage();
        plot(x,y,color);
}



/*

        point() = sets the beginning angle for turtle
                  in tenths of a degree

/*

#include <math.h>
#include "tools.h"

float point(float x1, float y_one, float x2, float y2)
{

        float theta;
```

```
    if ((x2 - x1) == 0)
        if (y2 > y_one)
            theta = 90;
        else
            theta = 270;
    else
        theta = atan((y2-y_one)/(x2-x1))*57.295779;
    if (x1>x2)
        theta += 180;
    return(theta);
}



/*

        setMode() = Sets Video Mode (Text or Graphics

*/

#include "tools.h"

char graph_reg_data[12] = {0x35,0x2D,0x2E,
        0x07,0x5B,0x02,0x57,0x57,0x02,0x03,0x00,
        0x00},text_reg_data[12] = {0x61,0x50,0x52,
        0x0F,0x19,0x06,0x19,0x19,0x02,0x0D,0x0B,0x0C};

void setMode(int mode)
{
    #include <dos.h>

    char far *address;
    unsigned int i;

    if (mode == 0)
    {
        outp (0x3BF,0);
        outp (0x3B8,0);
        for (i=0; i<12; i++)
        {
            outp (0x3B4,i);
            outp (0x3B5,text_reg_data[i]);
        }
        for (i=0; i<=0x7FFF; i+=2)
        {
            address = (char far *)0xB0000000L + i;
            *address = 00;
            *(address + 1) = 0x07;
        }
        outp (0x3B8,0x28);
    }
    else
```

```
    {
        outp (0x3BF,3);
        outp (0x3B8,2);
        for (i=0; i<12; i++)
        {
            outp (0x3B4,i);
            outp (0x3B5,graph_reg_data[i]);
        }
        for (i=0; i<=0x7FFF; i++)
        {
            address = (char far *)0xB0000000L + i;
            *address = 0x00;
            address = (char far *)0xB8000000L + i;
            *address = 0x00;
        }
        outp (0x3B8,0x0A);
    }
    address = (char far *)0x00000449L;
    *address = mode;
}



/*

   step() = advances turtle by step r in current direction

*/

#include "tools.h"

void step (void)
{
    #include <math.h>
    extern float turtle_x;
    extern float turtle_y;
    extern float turtle_r;
    extern float turtle_theta;

    turtle_x += turtle_r*cos(turtle_theta*.017453292);
    turtle_y += turtle_r*sin(turtle_theta*.017453292);
}


/*

        turn() = changes turtle pointing direction
                 angle is in tenths of a degree

*/

#include "tools.h"
```

```
void turn(float angle)
{
    extern float turtle_theta;

    turtle_theta += angle;
}
```

Fractal Programs for Hercules Graphics Adapter

```
/*

        3ddrag = PROGRAM TO GENERATE 3D DRAGON OUTLINES

*/

#include <stdlib.h>
#include <stdio.h>
#include <math.h>
#include <dos.h>
#include "tools.h"

void projection(float x3, float y3, float z3);
float degrees_to_radians(float degrees);;

union LIMIT XMin,YMin,XMax,YMax,Pval,Qval;
int i, j, OPERATOR = 0x00,row,col,color1;
int x_center = 320, y_center = 175;
float x = .50001, y = 0,z,P,Q,k,sx,cx,sy,cy,sz,cz,
    magnitude,scale,temp,temp_x,temp_y,step_size=.4,ymax,ymin;
float rad_per_degree=0.0174533,alpha,beta,gamma;
float QVal,x_offset, y_offset,upper_limit = 3, lower_limit = -3;
int color;
unsigned char PALETTE[16]={0,1,2,3,4,5,20,7,56,57,58,59,60,61,
    62,63};

main()
{
    printf("\nEnter alpha: ");
    scanf("%f",&alpha);
    printf("\nEnter beta: ");
    scanf("%f",&beta);
    printf("\nEnter gamma: ");
    scanf("%f",&gamma);
    printf("\nEnter scale: ");
    scanf("%f",&scale);
    scale = x_center * scale;
    printf("\nEnter X offset: ");
    scanf("%f",&x_offset);
    printf("\nEnter Y offset: ");
```

```
    scanf("%f",&y_offset);
    printf("\nEnter Q parameter: ");
    scanf("%f",&QVal);
    if (QVal == 0)
    {
        step_size = 0.1;
        upper_limit = 1.0;
        lower_limit = -1.0;
    }
    setMode(1);
    cls();
    alpha = degrees_to_radians(alpha);
    sx = sin(alpha);
    cx = cos(alpha);
    beta = degrees_to_radians(beta);
    sy = sin(beta);
    cy = cos(beta);
    gamma = degrees_to_radians(gamma);
    sz = sin(gamma);
    cz = cos(gamma);
    color = 1;
    for (k= upper_limit; k>=lower_limit; k-=step_size)
    {
        if ((k<1.0) && (k>-1.0))
            step_size = 0.1;
        x=.50001;
        y = 0;
        if (QVal == 0)
        {
            magnitude = 1;
            Q = 4*sqrt(1-k*k);
        }
        else
        {
            magnitude = k*k + QVal*QVal;
            Q = -4*QVal/magnitude;
        }
        P = 4*k/magnitude;
        for (i=0; i<12000; i++)
        {
            temp_x = x*P - y*Q;
            y = x*Q + y*P;
            temp_y = y;
            x = 1 - temp_x;
            magnitude = sqrt(x*x + y*y);
            y = sqrt((-x + magnitude)/2);
            x = sqrt((x + magnitude) /2);
            if (temp_y < 0)
                x = -x;
            if (rand() < 16163)
            {
```

```
            x = -x;
            y = -y;
        }
        x = (1 - x)/2;
        y = y/2;
        z =  P/2;
        if (i>10)
            projection (x, y, z);
    }
}
getch();
setMode(0);
}

void projection(float x3, float y3, float z3)
{
    float temp_x, temp_y;
    int col, row, color;

    temp_x = x3*cx + y3*cy + z3*cz;
    temp_y = x3*sx + y3*sy + z3*sz;

    col = scale * (temp_x-.5) + x_center + x_offset;
    row =  y_center - scale*temp_y + y_offset;
    if ((col>=0) && (col<720) &&(row>=0) && (row<348))
        plot (col,row,1);
}

float degrees_to_radians(float degrees)
{
    float angle;

    while (degrees >= 360)
        degrees -= 360;
    while (degrees < 0)
        degrees += 360;
    angle = rad_per_degree*degrees;
    return angle;
}

/*

            apollo = APOLLONIAN PACKING OF CIRCLES

*/

#include <dos.h>
#include <stdio.h>
#include <stdlib.h>
#include <math.h>
#include "tools.h"
```

```
void gen_circle(float xa,float ya,float a,float xb,float yb,
    float b,float xc,float yc,float c, int level);
void node(float xa,float ya,float a,float xb,float yb,
    float b,float xc,float yc,float c, float xs, float ys, float s,
    int level);


int LINEWIDTH = 1, OPERATOR = 0;
int color = 1;
int level;
unsigned long int PATTERN = 0xFFFFFFFF;
unsigned char PALETTE[16]={0,1,2,3,4,5,20,7,56,57,58,59,60,61,
    62,63};
float a,b,c,s,cs,bs,xa,xb,xc,ya,yb,yc,xs,ys;

main()
{
    float temp;

    printf("Enter level: ");
    scanf("%d",&level);
    setMode(1);
    a = 625;
    b = 375;
    c = 945;
    xa = -725;
    ya = 235;
    xb = 275;
    yb = 268;
    xc = 180;
    yc = -1048;
    fillOval(xa,ya,a,1,1.0);
    fillOval(xb,yb,b,1,1.0);
    fillOval(xc,yc,c,1,1.0);
    gen_circle(xa,ya,a,xb,yb,b,xc,yc,c,level);
    getch();
    setMode(0);
}

void gen_circle(float xa,float ya,float a,float xb,float yb,
    float b,float xc,float yc,float c, int level)
{
    float s, temp;

    level--;
    s = 1/a + 1/b + 1/c + 2*(sqrt(1/(b*c) + 1/(c*a) + 1/(a*b)));
    s = 1/s;
    temp = (s+a)*(s+a) - (s+b)*(s+b) - xa*xa + xb*xb - ya*ya +
        yb*yb;
    ys = (temp*(xc-xa) - (xb - xa)*((s+a)*(s+a) - (s+c)*(s+c)
```

```
            - xa*xa + xc*xc - ya*ya + yc*yc))/(2*((yb-ya)*(xc-xa)
            - (yc-ya)* (xb - xa)));
    xs = (temp - 2*ys*(yb - ya))/(2*(xb - xa));
    fillOval(xs,ys,s,1,1.0);
    if (level > 0)
        node(xa,ya,a,xb,yb,b,xc,yc,c,xs,ys,s,level);
}

void node(float xa,float ya,float a,float xb,float yb,
    float b,float xc,float yc,float c, float xs, float ys,
    float s, int level)
{
    gen_circle(xa,ya,a,xb,yb,b,xs,ys,s,level);
    gen_circle(xb,yb,b,xc,yc,c,xs,ys,s,level);
    gen_circle(xa,ya,a,xc,yc,c,xs,ys,s,level);
}

/*

        bifurc = GENERATES BIFURCATION DIAGRAMSLES

*/

#include <conio.h>
#include <stdio.h>
#include <dos.h>
#include <math.h>
#include "tools.h"

char ch;
int LINEWIDTH = 1;
unsigned long int PATTERN = 0xFFFFFFFF;

void main()
{
    float r=.95,x,delta_r;
    int i,j, row, col;

    setMode(16);

    for (j=0; j<2; j++)
    {
        delta_r = 0.005;
        if (j == 1)
        {
            cls();
            r = 3.55;
            delta_r = 0.0005;
        }
        for (col=0; col<719; col++)
        {
```

453

```
            x = .5;
            r += delta_r;
            for (i=0; i<256; i++)
            {
                x = r*x*(1-x);
                if ((x>1000000) || (x<-1000000))
                    break;
/*  COMPUTATION FOR rx(1-x)   */

                row = 347 -(x*350);
/*  COMPUTATION FOR x(1-x)
                row = 347 -((x/r)*700);
*/
                if ((i>64) && (row<347) && (row>=0) &&
                    (col>=0) && (col<719))
                {
                    plot(col,row,1);
                }
            }
        }
        getch();
    }
    setMode(0);
}




/*

        bindecom = program for binary decomposition

*/

#include <stdio.h>
#include <stdlib.h>
#include <math.h>
#include <dos.h>
#include <process.h>
#include "tools.h"

const int maxcol = 719;
const int maxrow = 347;

char strings[80];
int col,row,i;
int max_iterations = 64;
int max_size = 4;
int LINEWIDTH=1, OPERATOR=0;
int CURSOR_X=0,CURSOR_Y=0;
unsigned long int PATTERN=0xFFFFFFFF;
```

```
float P,Q,Xmax= 2.0, Xmin=-2.0, Ymax=1.50, Ymin=-1.50,theta;

main()
{
    float deltaX, deltaY, X, Y, Xsquare,Ysquare,Ytemp,temp1,temp2;
    int color, j, row, col;

    setMode(1);
    P = 0;
    Q = 0;

    for (j=0; j<2; j++)
    {
        cls();
        deltaX = (Xmax - Xmin)/(maxcol);
        deltaY = (Ymax - Ymin)/(maxrow);
        for (col=0; col<=maxcol; col++)
        {
            if (kbhit() != 0) break;
            for (row=0; row<=maxrow; row++)
            {
                X = Xmin + col * deltaX;
                Y = Ymax - row * deltaY;
                Xsquare = 0;
                Ysquare = 0;
                i = 0;
                while ((i<max_iterations) && ((Xsquare +
                    Ysquare) < max_size))
                {
                    Xsquare = X*X;
                    Ysquare = Y*Y;
                    Ytemp = 2*X*Y;
                    X = Xsquare - Ysquare + P;
                    Y = Ytemp + Q;
                    i++;
                }
                if (X == 0)
                    color = 1;
                else
                {
                    theta = acos(fabs(X)/(sqrt(X*X +
                        Y*Y)));
                    if ((X<0) && (Y>=0))
                        theta += 1.5707963;
                    if ((X<0) && (Y<0))
                        theta += 3.14159625;
                    if ((X>0) && (Y<0))
                        theta += 4.7123889;
                    if ((theta>=0) &&
                        (theta<=3.14159625))
                        color = 1;
```

```
                   else
                        color = 0;
                 }

                 plot(col, row, color);
           }
       }
       getch();
       P = .318623;
       Q = .0429799;
    }
    setMode(0);
}

/*

    brown2d = PROGRAM TO GENERATE TWO DIMENSIONAL BROWNIAN
              FRACTALS

*/

#include <stdio.h>
#include <math.h>
#include <dos.h>
#include "tools.h"

float gauss(unsigned seed);
void subdivide (int f1, int f2, float std);

float Fh[2049],Fw[2049],ratio;
char combination= 0x00;
unsigned long int PATTERN=0xFFFFFFFF;
unsigned int seed=3245;
int LINEWIDTH = 1;

main()
{
    float scale=2000,h=.87,std;
    int i,px1,px2,py1,py2;

    while (seed != 0)
    {
        setMode(0);
        printf("Enter seed (0 to quit): ");
        scanf("%d",&seed);
        Fh[0] = 0;
        Fh[2048] = gauss(seed) * scale;
        Fw[0] = 0;
        Fw[2048] = gauss(0) * scale;
        ratio = pow(2,-h);
        std = scale*ratio;
```

```
        subdivide(0,2048,std);
        setMode(1);
        for (i=0; i<2048; i++)
        {
            px1 = Fw[i];
            py1 = Fh[i];
            px2 = Fw[i+1];
            py2 = Fh[i+1];
            drawLine(px1,py1,px2,py2,1);
        }
        PATTERN = 0x0F0F0F0F;
        drawLine(-260,0,252,0,1);
        drawLine(0,-220,0,220,1);
        PATTERN = 0xFFFFFFFF;
        getch();
    }
    setMode(0);
}

void subdivide (int f1, int f2, float std)
{
    int fmid;
    float stdmid;

    fmid = (f1 + f2)/2;
    if (( fmid != f1) && (fmid != f2))
    {
        Fh[fmid] = (Fh[f1] + Fh[f2])/2.0 + gauss(0) * std;
        Fw[fmid] = (Fw[f1] + Fw[f2])/2.0 + gauss(0) * std;
        stdmid = std*ratio;
        subdivide(f1,fmid,stdmid);
        subdivide(fmid,f2,stdmid);
    }
}

float gauss(unsigned seed)
{
    int k;
    float value,exponent,gauss;

    if (seed != 0)
        srand(seed);
    k = rand() - 16383;
    value = k/5461.0;
    exponent = -(value*value)/2.;
    gauss = .15915494*exp(exponent);
    k = rand();

    if (k > 16383)
        gauss *= -1;
    return(gauss);
```

```
}

/*

        brownian = PROGRAM TO GENERATE BROWNIAN FRACTALS

*/


#include <stdio.h>
#include <math.h>
#include <dos.h>
#include "tools.h"

float gauss(unsigned seed);
void subdivide (int f1, int f2, float std);

float Fh[257],ratio;
char combination= 0x00;
unsigned long int PATTERN=0xFFFFFFFF;
unsigned int seed=3245;
int LINEWIDTH = 1;

main()
{
    float scale=1000,h=.87,std;
    int i,px1,px2;

    while (seed != 0)
    {
        setMode(0);
        printf("Enter seed (0 to quit): ");
        scanf("%d",&seed);
        Fh[0] = gauss(seed) * scale;
        Fh[256] = gauss(0) * scale;
        ratio = pow(2,-h);
        std = scale*ratio;
        subdivide(0,256,std);
        setMode(1);
        for (i=0; i<256; i++)
        {
            px1 = Fh[i];
            px2 = Fh[i+1];
            drawLine(2*i-260,px1,2*(i+1)-260,px2,1);
        }
        PATTERN = 0x0F0F0F0F;
        drawLine(-260,0,252,0,1);
        PATTERN = 0xFFFFFFFF;
        getch();
    }
}
```

```
void subdivide (int f1, int f2, float std)
{
    int fmid;
    float stdmid;

    fmid = (f1 + f2)/2;
    if (( fmid != f1) && (fmid != f2))
    {
        Fh[fmid] = (Fh[f1] + Fh[f2])/2.0 + gauss(0) * std;
        stdmid = std*ratio;
        subdivide(f1,fmid,stdmid);
        subdivide(fmid,f2,stdmid);
    }
}

float gauss(unsigned seed)
{
    int k;
    float value,exponent,gauss;

    if (seed != 0)
        srand(seed);
    k = rand() - 16383;
    value = k/5461.0;
    exponent = -(value*value)/2.;
    gauss = .15915494*exp(exponent);
    k = rand();

    if (k > 16383)
        gauss *= -1;
    return(gauss);
}

/*

        cdragon = ADVANCED PROGRAM TO MAP THE DRAGON CURVES

*/

#include <ctype.h>
#include <conio.h>
#include <stdio.h>
#include <math.h>
#include <dos.h>
#include <process.h>
#include "tools.h"

int plot_point(int x, int y, int color);

const int maxcol = 719;
const int maxrow = 347;
```

```
int CURSOR_X=0,CURSOR_Y=0,col,row;
int max_iterations;
int max_size = 4;
int LINEWIDTH=1, OPERATOR=0x00;
unsigned long int PATTERN=0xFFFFFFFF;
float P,Q;
union LIMIT XMax,YMax,XMin,YMin,Pval,Qval;

main()
{
    float deltaX, deltaY, X, Y, Xsquare, Ysquare,Ytemp,temp_sq,
        temp_xy;
    int i, row, col,error,response;

    printf("values for P and Q sep[arated by a comma: ");
    scanf("%f,%f",&P,&Q);
    printf("\nEnter number of iterations: ");
    scanf("%d",&max_iterations);
    XMax.f = 1.4;
    XMin.f = -.4;
    YMax.f = .8;
    YMin.f = -.8;
    setMode(1);
    cls();
    deltaX = (XMax.f - XMin.f)/(maxcol);
    deltaY = (YMax.f - YMin.f)/(maxrow);
    for (col=0; col<=maxcol; col++)
    {
        if (kbhit() != 0)
        {
            setMode(0);
            exit(0);
        }
        for (row=0; row<=maxrow; row++)
        {
            X = XMin.f + col * deltaX;
            Y = YMax.f - row * deltaY;
            Xsquare = 0;
            Ysquare = 0;
            i = 0;
            while ((i<max_iterations) &&
                ((Xsquare + Ysquare) < max_size))
            {
                Xsquare = X*X;
                Ysquare = Y*Y;
                temp_sq = Ysquare - Xsquare;
                temp_xy = X*Y;
                temp_xy += temp_xy;
                Ytemp = Q*(temp_sq + X)-
                    P*(temp_xy - Y);
                X = P*(temp_sq + X)
```

```
                            + Q*(temp_xy - Y);
                  Y = Ytemp;
                  i++;
            }
            if (i >= max_iterations)
                plot(col, row, 1);
         }
     }
     getch();
     setMode(0);
}


/*

      cesaro1 = PROGRAM TO GENERATE ORIGINAL CESARO CURVE

*/

#include <stdio.h>
#include <math.h>
#include <dos.h>
#include "tools.h"

void generate (float X1, float Y1, float X2, float Y2,
    int level,int sign);

int generator_size = 3;
int level;
int init_size = 1;
int initiator_x1[10] = {-150},initiator_x2[10]={150},
    initiator_y1[10]={0}, initiator_y2[10]={0};
int combination = 0,LINEWIDTH=1, OPERATOR=0;
unsigned long int PATTERN=0xFFFFFFFF;
float turtle_theta;
int i,sign=1;
float Xpoints[25], Ypoints[25];
float turtle_x,turtle_y,turtle_r;

main()
{

    printf("\nEnter level (1 - 16): ");
    scanf("%d",&level);
    if (level < 1)
        level = 1;
    setMode(1);
    cls();

    for (i=0; i<init_size; i++)
        generate(initiator_x1[i], initiator_y1[i],
```

```
                initiator_x2[i], initiator_y2[i], level,sign);
    getch();
    setMode(0);
}

/*

                    generate() = Generates curve

*/

void generate (float X1, float Y1, float X2, float Y2,
    int level, int sign)
{
    int j,k,line,px1,px2,py1,py2;
        float a, b, Xpoints[25], Ypoints[25];

    level--;
    turtle_r = sqrt((((X2 - X1)*(X2 - X1) + (Y2 - Y1)*
        (Y2 - Y1)))/2.0;
    Xpoints[0] = X1;
    Ypoints[0] = Y1;
    Xpoints[2] = X2;
    Ypoints[2] = Y2;
    turtle_theta = point(X1,Y1,X2,Y2);
    turtle_x = X1;
    turtle_y = Y1;
    step();
    Xpoints[3] = turtle_x;
    Ypoints[3] = turtle_y;
    turn(90*sign);
    step();
    Xpoints[1] = turtle_x;
    Ypoints[1] = turtle_y;
    sign = -1;
    if (level > 0)
    {
        for (j=0; j<generator_size-1; j++)
        {
                X1 = Xpoints[j];
                X2 = Xpoints[j+1];
                Y1 = Ypoints[j];
                Y2 = Ypoints[j+1];
            generate (X1,Y1,X2,Y2,level,sign);
        }
    }
    else
    {
        px1 = Xpoints[0];
        py1 = Ypoints[0];
        px2 = Xpoints[2];
```

```
        py2 = Ypoints[2];
        drawLine(px1,py1,px2,py2,1);
        px1 = Xpoints[1];
        py1 = Ypoints[1];
        px2 = Xpoints[3];
        py2 = Ypoints[3];
        drawLine(px1,py1,px2,py2,1);
    }
}


/*

        cesaro2 = PROGRAM TO GENERATE MODIFIED CESARO CURVE

*/

#include <stdio.h>
#include <math.h>
#include <dos.h>
#include "tools.h"

void generate (float X1, float Y1, float X2, float Y2,
    int level,int sign);

int generator_size = 3;
int level;
int init_size = 1;
int initiator_x1[10] = {-150},initiator_x2[10]={150},
    initiator_y1[10]={0}, initiator_y2[10]={0};
int combination = 0,LINEWIDTH=1, OPERATOR=0;
unsigned long int PATTERN=0xFFFFFFFF;
float turtle_theta;
int i,sign=1;
float Xpoints[25], Ypoints[25];
float turtle_x,turtle_y,turtle_r;

main()
{

    printf("\nEnter level (1 - 8): ");
    scanf("%d",&level);
    if (level < 1)
        level = 1;
    setMode(1);
    cls();

    for (i=0; i<init_size; i++)
        generate(initiator_x1[i], initiator_y1[i],
            initiator_x2[i],initiator_y2[i], level,sign);
    getch();
```

```
    setMode(0);
}

/*

                    generate() = Generates curve
*/

void generate (float X1, float Y1, float X2, float Y2,
    int level, int sign)
{
    int j,k,line,px1,px2,py1,py2;
    float a, b, Xpoints[25], Ypoints[25];

    level--;
    a = sqrt(((X2 - X1)*(X2 - X1) + (Y2 - Y1)*(Y2 - Y1)))/2.0;
    b = a * 0.9128442;
    turtle_r = b;
    Xpoints[0] = X1;
    Ypoints[0] = Y1;
    Xpoints[2] = X2;
    Ypoints[2] = Y2;
    turtle_theta = point(X1,Y1,X2,Y2);
    turtle_x = X1;
    turtle_y = Y1;
    step();
    Xpoints[3] = turtle_x;
    Ypoints[3] = turtle_y;
    turn(85*sign);
    turtle_r = a;
    step();
    Xpoints[1] = turtle_x;
    Ypoints[1] = turtle_y;
    turn(-170*sign);
    step();
    Xpoints[4] = turtle_x;
    Ypoints[4] = turtle_y;

    sign = -1;
    if (level > 0)
    {
        for (j=0; j<generator_size-1; j++)
        {
                X1 = Xpoints[j];
                X2 = Xpoints[j+1];
                Y1 = Ypoints[j];
                Y2 = Ypoints[j+1];
            generate (X1,Y1,X2,Y2,level,sign);
        }
    }
```

```
    else
    {
        px1 = Xpoints[0];
        py1 = Ypoints[0];
        px2 = Xpoints[3];
        py2 = Ypoints[3];
        drawLine(px1,py1,px2,py2,1);
        px1 = Xpoints[2];
        py1 = Ypoints[2];
        px2 = Xpoints[4];
        py2 = Ypoints[4];
        drawLine(px1,py1,px2,py2,1);
        px1 = Xpoints[3];
        py1 = Ypoints[3];
        px2 = Xpoints[1];
        py2 = Ypoints[1];
        drawLine(px1,py1,px2,py2,1);
        px1 = Xpoints[4];
        py1 = Ypoints[4];
        drawLine(px1,py1,px2,py2,1);
    }
}

/*


        cesaro3 = PROGRAM TO GENERATE ORIGINAL CESARO CURVE

*/

#include <stdio.h>
#include <math.h>
#include <dos.h>
#include "tools.h"

void generate (float X1, float Y1, float X2, float Y2,
    int level);

int generator_size = 3;
int level;
int init_size = 1;
int initiator_x1[10] = {-150},initiator_x2[10]={150},
    initiator_y1[10]={0},initiator_y2[10]={0};
int combination = 0,LINEWIDTH=1, OPERATOR=0;
unsigned long int PATTERN=0xFFFFFFFF;
float turtle_theta;
int i,sign[16],sign1=-1;
float Xpoints[25], Ypoints[25];
float turtle_x,turtle_y,turtle_r;

main()
{
```

```
    printf("\nEnter level (1 - 16): ");
    scanf("%d",&level);
    if (level < 1)
        level = 1;
    setMode(1);
    cls();
    for (i=level; i>=0; i--)
    {
        sign[i] = sign1;
        sign1 *= -1;
    }
    for (i=0; i<init_size; i++)
        generate(initiator_x1[i], initiator_y1[i],
            initiator_x2[i], initiator_y2[i], level);
    getch();
    setMode(0);
}

/*

                    generate() = Generates curve

*/

void generate (float X1, float Y1, float X2, float Y2,
    int level)
{
    int j,k,line,px1,px2,py1,py2;
        float a, b, Xpoints[25], Ypoints[25];

    level--;
    turtle_r = sqrt((((X2 - X1)*(X2 - X1) + (Y2 - Y1)*(Y2 -
        Y1)))/2.0;
    Xpoints[0] = X1;
    Ypoints[0] = Y1;
    Xpoints[2] = X2;
    Ypoints[2] = Y2;
    turtle_theta = point(X1,Y1,X2,Y2);
    turtle_x = X1;
    turtle_y = Y1;
    step();
    Xpoints[3] = turtle_x;
    Ypoints[3] = turtle_y;
    turn(90*sign[level]);
    step();
    Xpoints[1] = turtle_x;
    Ypoints[1] = turtle_y;
    if (level > 0)
    {
        for (j=0; j<generator_size-1; j++)
```

```
        {
                X1 = Xpoints[j];
                X2 = Xpoints[j+1];
                Y1 = Ypoints[j];
                Y2 = Ypoints[j+1];
            generate (X1,Y1,X2,Y2,level);
        }
    }
    else
    {
        px1 = Xpoints[0];
        py1 = Ypoints[0];
        px2 = Xpoints[2];
        py2 = Ypoints[2];
        drawLine(px1,py1,px2,py2,1);
        px1 = Xpoints[1];
        py1 = Ypoints[1];
        px2 = Xpoints[3];
        py2 = Ypoints[3];
        drawLine(px1,py1,px2,py2,1);
    }
}

/*


        cesaro4 = PROGRAM TO GENERATE MODIFIRD CESARO CURVE

*/

#include <stdio.h>
#include <math.h>
#include <dos.h>
#include "tools.h"

void generate (float X1, float Y1, float X2, float Y2,
    int level);

int generator_size = 3;
int level;
int init_size = 1;
int initiator_x1[10] = {-150},initiator_x2[10]={150},
    initiator_y1[10]={0}, initiator_y2[10]={0};
int combination = 0,LINEWIDTH=1, OPERATOR=0;
unsigned long int PATTERN=0xFFFFFFFF;
float turtle_theta;
int i,sign[17],sign1=-1;
float Xpoints[25], Ypoints[25];
float turtle_x,turtle_y,turtle_r;

main()
{
```

```
    printf("\nEnter level (1 - 16): ");
    scanf("%d",&level);
    if (level < 1)
        level = 1;
    setMode(1);
    cls();
    for (i=level; i>=0; i--)
    {
        sign[i] = sign1;
        sign1 *= -1;
    }
    for (i=0; i<init_size; i++)
        generate(initiator_x1[i], initiator_y1[i],
            initiator_x2[i],initiator_y2[i], level);
    getch();
    setMode(0);
}


/*

                    generate() = Generates curve

*/

void generate (float X1, float Y1, float X2, float Y2,
    int level)
{
    int j,k,line,px1,px2,py1,py2;
    float a, b, Xpoints[25], Ypoints[25];

    level--;
    a = sqrt((((X2 - X1)*(X2 - X1) + (Y2 - Y1)*(Y2 - Y1)))/2.0;
    b = a * 0.9128442;
    turtle_r = b;
    Xpoints[0] = X1;
    Ypoints[0] = Y1;
    Xpoints[2] = X2;
    Ypoints[2] = Y2;
    turtle_theta = point(X1,Y1,X2,Y2);
    turtle_x = X1;
    turtle_y = Y1;
    step();
    Xpoints[3] = turtle_x;
    Ypoints[3] = turtle_y;
    turn(85*sign[level]);
    turtle_r = a;
    step();
    Xpoints[1] = turtle_x;
    Ypoints[1] = turtle_y;
```

```
        turn(-170*sign[level]);
        step();
        Xpoints[4] = turtle_x;
        Ypoints[4] = turtle_y;
        if (level > 0)
        {
            for (j=0; j<generator_size-1; j++)
            {
                    X1 = Xpoints[j];
                    X2 = Xpoints[j+1];
                    Y1 = Ypoints[j];
                    Y2 = Ypoints[j+1];
                generate (X1,Y1,X2,Y2,level);
            }
        }
        else
        {
            px1 = Xpoints[0];
            py1 = Ypoints[0];
            px2 = Xpoints[3];
            py2 = Ypoints[3];
            drawLine(px1,py1,px2,py2,1);
            px1 = Xpoints[2];
            py1 = Ypoints[2];
            px2 = Xpoints[4];
            py2 = Ypoints[4];
            drawLine(px1,py1,px2,py2,1);
            px1 = Xpoints[3];
            py1 = Ypoints[3];
            px2 = Xpoints[1];
            py2 = Ypoints[1];
            drawLine(px1,py1,px2,py2,1);
            px1 = Xpoints[4];
            py1 = Ypoints[4];
            px2 = Xpoints[1];
            py2 = Ypoints[1];
            drawLine(px1,py1,px2,py2,1);
        }
}

/*

        cjulia = ADVANCED PROGRAM TO MAP THE JULIA SETS

*/
#include <conio.h>
#include <stdio.h>
#include <math.h>
#include <dos.h>
#include <process.h>
#include "tools.h"
```

```c
#include <ctype.h>

const int maxcol = 719;
const int maxrow = 347;
int CURSOR_X=0,CURSOR_Y=0,col,row;
int max_iterations;
int max_size = 4;
int LINEWIDTH=1, OPERATOR=0x00;
unsigned long int PATTERN=0xFFFFFFFF;
float P,Q;
float TXMax,TXMin,TYMax,TYMin;
union LIMIT XMax,YMax,XMin,YMin,Pval,Qval;

main()
{
    float deltaX, deltaY, X, Y, Xsquare, Ysquare;
    int i,color, row, col,error,response;

    setMode(0);
    printf("\nEnter values for P and Q, separated by a "
        "comma: ");
    scanf("%f,%f",&P,&Q);
    printf("\nEnter number of iterations: ");
    scanf("%d",&max_iterations);
    setMode(1);
    XMax.f = 1.8;
    XMin.f = -1.8;
    YMax.f = 1.2;
    YMin.f = -1.2;
    cls();
    deltaX = (XMax.f - XMin.f)/(maxcol);
    deltaY = (YMax.f - YMin.f)/(maxrow);
    for (col=1; col<=maxcol; col++)
    {
        if (kbhit() != 0)
        {
            setMode(0);
            exit(0);
        }
        for (row=0; row<=maxrow; row++)
        {
            X = XMin.f + col * deltaX;
            Y = YMax.f - row * deltaY;
            Xsquare = 0;
            Ysquare = 0;
            i = 0;
            while ((i<max_iterations) &&
                ((Xsquare + Ysquare) < max_size))
            {
                Xsquare = X*X;
                Ysquare = Y*Y;
```

```
                Y = 2*X*Y + Q;
                X = Xsquare - Ysquare + P;
                i++;
            }
            if (i >= max_iterations)
                plot(col, row, 1);
        }
    }
    getch();
    setMode(0);
}

/*

      cmandel = ADVANCED PROGRAM TO MAP THE MANDELBROT SET
*/
#include <stdio.h>
#include <math.h>
#include <dos.h>
#include <process.h>
#include "tools.h"

const int maxcol = 719;
const int maxrow = 347;
const int max_colors = 2;
int CURSOR_X=0,CURSOR_Y=0,col,row;
int max_iterations = 512;
int max_size = 4;
int LINEWIDTH=1, OPERATOR=0x00;
unsigned long int PATTERN=0xFFFFFFFF;
double Q[350];
float TXMax,TXMin,TYMax,TYMin;
union LIMIT XMax,YMax,XMin,YMin,Pval,Qval;


main()
{
    double P,deltaP, deltaQ, X, Y, Xsquare, Ysquare;
    int i,color, row, col,error,response,repeat=0x30,start_col;

    XMax.f = 1.2;
    XMin.f = -2.0;
    YMax.f = 1.2;
    YMin.f = -1.2;
    start_col = 0;
    setMode(1);
    cls();
    while (repeat == 0x30)
    {
        deltaP = (XMax.f - XMin.f)/(maxcol);
```

```
        deltaQ = (YMax.f - YMin.f)/(maxrow);
        Q[0] = YMax.f;
        for (row=1; row<=maxrow; row++)
            Q[row] = Q[row-1] - deltaQ;
        P = XMin.f + start_col * deltaP;

        for (col=start_col; col<maxcol; col++)
        {
            if (kbhit() != 0)
            {
                exit(0);
            }
            for (row=0; row<=maxrow; row++)
            {
                X = Y = Xsquare = Ysquare = 0.0;
                color = 1;
                while ((color<max_iterations) && ((Xsquare +
                Ysquare) < max_size))
                {
                    Xsquare = X*X;
                    Ysquare = Y*Y;
                    Y = 2*X*Y + Q[row];
                    X = Xsquare - Ysquare + P;
                    color ++;
                }
                plot(col, row, (color % max_colors));
            }
            P += deltaP;
        }
        getch();

        write_horz_str(-300,-220,"Enter '0' to run another "
            "plot, '1' to quit: ",1);
        repeat = getche();
        if (repeat == 0x30)
        {
            move_cursor(0,15,0,0);
            move_cursor(1,15,CURSOR_X,CURSOR_Y);
            XMax.f = TXMax;
            XMin.f = TXMin;
            YMax.f = TYMax;
            YMin.f = TYMin;
            start_col = 0;
            cls();
        }
    }
    setMode(0);
}

/*
```

3

```
      cnewton = MAP OF NEWTON'S METHOD FOR SOLVING Z -2Z-5=0

*/
#include <stdio.h>
#include <math.h>
#include <dos.h>
#include <process.h>
#include "tools.h"

const int maxcol = 719;
const int maxrow = 347;
const int max_colors = 2;


char strings[80];
int col,row,i;
int max_iterations = 64;
int max_size = 4;
int LINEWIDTH=1, OPERATOR=0;
int CURSOR_X=0,CURSOR_Y=0;
unsigned long int PATTERN=0xFFFFFFFF;
/*float P=-.5,Q=0,Xmax= 1.5, Xmin=-1.5, Ymax=1.20,
    Ymin=-1.20;*/
float  Xmax = 3.5, Xmin=-3.5, Ymax=2.50, Ymin=-2.50;

main()
{
    double deltaX, deltaY, X, Y, Xsquare,
        Ysquare,Ytemp,temp1,temp2,temp3,denom,numer,theta;
    int color, row, col;
    float Xold,Yold,Xnew,Ynew;

    setMode(1);
    cls();
    deltaX = (Xmax - Xmin)/(maxcol);
        deltaY = (Ymax - Ymin)/(maxrow);
    for (col=0; col<=maxcol; col++)
        {
        if (kbhit() != 0)
        {
            setMode(0);
            break;
        }
        for (row=0; row<=maxrow; row++)
            {
                    X = Xmin + col * deltaX;
            Y = Ymax - row * deltaY;
            Xsquare = 0;
            Ysquare = 0;
            Xold = 42;
            Yold = 42;
```

```
            for (i=0; i<max_iterations; i++)
            {
                        Xsquare = X*X;
                            Ysquare = Y*Y;
                denom = (3*Xsquare - 3*Ysquare - 2);
                denom = denom*denom + 36*Xsquare*Ysquare;
                if (denom == 0)
                    denom = .00000001;
                temp1 = X*Xsquare - 3*X*Ysquare - 2*X -5;
                temp2 = 3*Xsquare - 3*Ysquare - 2;
                temp3 = 3*Xsquare*Y - Ysquare*Y - 2*Y;
                X = X - (temp1 * temp2 - 6*X*Y*temp3)/denom;
                Y = Y - (temp1 * (-6*X*Y) + temp3 * temp2)
                    /denom;
                Xnew = X;
                Ynew = Y;
                if ((Xold == Xnew) && (Yold == Ynew))
                    break;
                Xold = X;
                Yold = Y;
            }
            color = i%max_colors;
            plot(col, row, color);
        }
    }
    getch();
    setMode(0);
}

/*
```

$$\text{cnewton} = \text{MAP OF NEWTON'S METHOD FOR SOLVING } Z^3 = 1$$

```
*/
#include <stdio.h>
#include <math.h>
#include <dos.h>
#include <process.h>
#include "tools.h"

const int maxcol = 719;
const int maxrow = 347;
const int max_colors = 2;

char strings[80];
int col,row,i;
int max_iterations = 64;
int max_size = 4;
int LINEWIDTH=1, OPERATOR=0;
int CURSOR_X=0,CURSOR_Y=0;
unsigned long int PATTERN=0xFFFFFFFF;
```

```
float   Xmax = 3.5, Xmin=-3.5, Ymax=2.50, Ymin=-2.50;

main()
{
    double deltaX, deltaY, X, Y, Xsquare,Xold,Yold,
          Ysquare,Ytemp,temp1,temp2,denom,theta;
    int color, row, col;

    setMode(1);
    cls();
    deltaX = (Xmax - Xmin)/(maxcol);
        deltaY = (Ymax - Ymin)/(maxrow);
        for (col=0; col<=maxcol; col++)
        {
        if (kbhit() != 0)
        {
            setMode(0);
            break;
        }
        for (row=0; row<=maxrow; row++)
              {
                    X = Xmin + col * deltaX;
            Y = Ymax - row * deltaY;
            Xsquare = 0;
            Ysquare = 0;
            Xold = 42;
            Yold = 42;
            for (i=0; i<max_iterations; i++)
            {
                          Xsquare = X*X;
                              Ysquare = Y*Y;
                denom = 3*((Xsquare - Ysquare)*(Xsquare -
                    Ysquare) + 4*Xsquare*Ysquare);
                if (denom == 0)
                    denom = .00000001;
                X = .6666667*X + (Xsquare - Ysquare)/denom;

                Y = .6666667*Y - 2*X*Y/denom;
                if ((Xold == X) && (Yold == Y))
                    break;
                Xold = X;
                Yold = Y;
                      }
            color = i%2;
            plot(col, row, color);
        }
    }
        getch();
    setMode(0);
}
```

```c
/*

    cphoenix = ADVANCED PROGRAM TO MAP THE PHOENIX CURVES

*/

#include <ctype.h>
#include <conio.h>
#include <stdio.h>
#include <math.h>
#include <dos.h>
#include <process.h>
#include "tools.h"

const int maxcol = 719;
const int maxrow = 347;
const int max_colors = 16;
int CURSOR_X=0,CURSOR_Y=0,col,row;
int max_iterations;
int max_size = 4;
int LINEWIDTH=1, OPERATOR=0x00, ANGLE, XCENTER, YCENTER;
unsigned long int PATTERN=0xFFFFFFFF;
int colors[7]={88};
float P,Q;
float TXMax,TXMin,TYMax,TYMin;
union LIMIT XMax,YMax,XMin,YMin,Pval,Qval;

main()
{

    float deltaX, deltaXi, X, Y, Xsquare, Ysquare,Ytemp,
        temp_sq,temp_xy,Xi,Xisquare,Yi,Xtemp,Xitemp;
    int i,color, row, col,error,response,repeat=0x32,start_col;
    printf("Enter P and Q separated by a comma: ");
    scanf("%f,%f",&P,&Q);
    printf("\nEnter number of iterations: ");
    scanf("%d",&max_iterations);
    XMax.f = 1.5;
    XMin.f = -1.5;
    YMax.f = 1.2;
    YMin.f = -1.2;
    setMode(1);
    cls();
    deltaX = (YMax.f - YMin.f)/(maxrow - 1);
    deltaXi = (XMax.f - XMin.f)/(maxcol - 1);
    for (col=0; col<=maxcol; col++)
    {
        if (kbhit() != 0)
        {
            setMode(0);
            exit(0);
```

```
        }
        for (row=0; row<=maxrow; row++)
        {
            Y = 0;
            Yi = 0;
            X = YMax.f - row * deltaX;
            Xi = XMin.f + col * deltaXi;
            color = 0;
            Xsquare = Xisquare = 0;
            while ((color<max_iterations) && ((Xsquare +
                Xisquare) < max_size))
            {
                Xsquare = X*X;
                Xisquare = Xi*Xi;
                Xtemp = Xsquare - Xisquare + P + Q*Y;
                Xitemp = 2*X*Xi + Q*Yi;
                Y = X;
                Yi = Xi;
                X = Xtemp;
                Xi = Xitemp;
                color++;
            }
            if (color > 32)
                plot(col, row, 1);
        }
    }
    getch();
    setMode(0);
}

/*

        csdragon = ADVANCED PROGRAM TO MAP THE DRAGON SET

*/
#include <stdio.h>
#include <math.h>
#include <dos.h>
#include <process.h>
#include "tools.h"

const int maxcol = 719;
const int maxrow = 347;
const int max_colors = 2;
int max_iterations = 256;
int max_size = 4;
int LINEWIDTH=1, OPERATOR=0x00;
unsigned long int PATTERN=0xFFFFFFFF;
float Q[350];
union LIMIT XMax,YMax,XMin,YMin;
```

```
main()
{
    float P,deltaP, deltaQ, X, Y, Xsquare, Ysquare,Xtemp,Ytemp;
    int i,color, row, col,error,response;

    XMax.f = 4.2;
    XMin.f = -2.2;
    YMax.f = 1.5;
    YMin.f = -1.5;
    setMode(1);
    cls();
    deltaP = (XMax.f - XMin.f)/(maxcol);
    deltaQ = (YMax.f - YMin.f)/(maxrow);
    Q[0] = YMax.f;
    for (row=1; row<=maxrow; row++)
    Q[row] = Q[row-1] - deltaQ;
    P = XMin.f;
    for (col=0; col<maxcol; col++)
    {
        if (kbhit() != 0)
        {
            setMode(0);
            exit(0);
        }
        for (row=0; row<=maxrow; row++)
        {
            X = 0.50;
            Y = 0.0;
            color = 0;
            while (((X*X + Y*Y) < max_size) &&
                (color<max_iterations))
            {
                Xtemp = (Y - X)*(Y + X) + X;
                Ytemp = X * Y;
                Ytemp = Ytemp + Ytemp - Y;
                X = P * Xtemp + Q[row] * Ytemp;
                Y = Q[row] * Xtemp - P * Ytemp;
                color++;
            }
            plot(col, row, (color % max_colors));
        }
        P += deltaP;
    }
    getch();
    setMode(0);
}

/*
    csphemix = ADVANCED PROGRAM TO MAP THE SET FOR PHOENIX
*/
```

```c
#include <stdio.h>
#include <math.h>
#include <dos.h>
#include <process.h>
#include "tools.h"

const int maxcol = 719;
const int maxrow = 347;
const int max_colors = 2;
int CURSOR_X=0,CURSOR_Y=0,col,row;
int max_iterations = 32;
int max_size = 4;
int LINEWIDTH=1, OPERATOR=0x00;
unsigned long int PATTERN=0xFFFFFFFF;
float P,Q[350],Qval,Pval;
union LIMIT XMax,YMax,XMin,YMin;

main()
{
    float P,deltaP, deltaQ, X, Y, Xsquare, Xisquare,Xtemp,
        Xitemp,Xi,Yi;
    int i,color, row, col,error,response;

    XMax.f = 1.5;
    XMin.f = -2.1;
    YMax.f = 2.0;
    YMin.f = -2.0;
    setMode(1);
    cls();
    deltaP = (XMax.f - XMin.f)/(maxcol);
    deltaQ = (YMax.f - YMin.f)/(maxrow);
    Q[0] = YMax.f;
    for (row=1; row<=maxrow; row++)
        Q[row] = Q[row-1] - deltaQ;
    P = XMin.f;
    for (col=0; col<maxcol; col++)
    {
        if (kbhit() != 0)
        {
            setMode(0);
            exit(0);
        }
        for (row=0; row<=maxrow; row++)
        {
            Y = 0;
            Yi = 0;
            X = 0;
            Xi = 0;
            color = 0;
            Xsquare = Xisquare = 0;
            while ((color<max_iterations) &&
```

```
                        ((Xsquare + Xisquare) < max_size))
                {
                    Xsquare = X*X;
                    Xisquare = Xi*Xi;
                    Xtemp = Xsquare - Xisquare + P
                        + Q[row]*Y;
                    Xitemp = 2*X*Xi + Q[row]*Yi;
                    Y = X;
                    Yi = Xi;
                    X = Xtemp;
                    Xi = Xitemp;
                    color++;
                }
                plot(col, row, color%max_colors);
            }
            P += deltaP;
        }
        getch();
        setMode(0);
}

/*

        dragout = PROGRAM TO GENERATE DRAGON OUTLINES

*/

#include <stdio.h>
#include <math.h>
#include <dos.h>
#include "tools.h"

int i, OPERATOR = 0x00,row,col;
int x_center = 320, y_center = 175;
float x = .50001, y = 0,P,Q,magnitude,scale,temp,temp_x,temp_y;

main()
{
    printf("Enter P and Q (real and imaginary parameters) "
        "separated by comma): ");
    scanf("%f,%f",&P,&Q);
    magnitude = P*P + Q*Q;
    P = 4*P/magnitude;
    Q = -4*Q/magnitude;
    printf("\nEnter Scale: ");
    scanf("%f",&scale);
    scale = x_center*scale;
    setMode(1);
    cls();
    for (i=0; i<12000; i++)
    {
        temp_x = x*P - y*Q;
```

```
        y = x*Q + y*P;
        temp_y = y;
        x = 1 - temp_x;
        magnitude = sqrt(x*x + y*y);
        y = sqrt((-x + magnitude)/2);
        x = sqrt((x + magnitude) /2);
        if (temp_y < 0)
            x = -x;
        if (rand() < 16163)
        {
            x = -x;
            y = -y;
        }
        x = (1 - x)/2;
        y = y/2;


        col = scale*(x-.5) + x_center;
        row = y_center - scale*y;
        if ((i > 10) && (col >= 0) && (col < 720) && (row >= 0)
            && (row < 348))
            plot (col,row,1);
    }
    getch();
    setMode(0);
}

/*

        feigenbm = PROGRAM TO GENERATE FEIGENBAUM NUMBER

*/

#include <stdio.h>
#include <stdlib.h>
#include <math.h>
#include "tools.h"

long double x,lambda,f,step_size,old_x,test,lambda_1,lambda_2,
    delta,init_step,old_lambda;
double new_step, old_step;
long int i,iterations;
int j,sign;

main()
{
    setMode(3);
    lambda = 3.0;
    printf("\n n          Lambda                 Delta\n");
    init_step = 1;
```

```
for (j=1; j<20; j++)
{
    if (j%2 == 0)
        sign = -1;
    else
        sign = 1;
    gotoxy(0,15+j);
    init_step /= 4.67;
    step_size = init_step;
    iterations = pow(2,j);
    old_x = 0.5;
    lambda += step_size;
    for (;;)
    {
        x = old_x;
        for (i=0; i<iterations; i++)
            x = lambda*x*(1-x);
        test = (x - old_x)*sign;
        if (test < 0)
        {
            lambda -= step_size;
            step_size = step_size/2;
        }
        old_lambda = lambda;
        lambda += step_size;
        if (old_lambda >= lambda)
            break;
        gotoxy(1,j+3);
        printf(" %2d    %18.15Lf",j,lambda);
    }
    if (j > 2)
    {
        delta = (lambda_1 - lambda_2)/(lambda - lambda_1);
        printf("    %20.17Lf",delta);
    }
    lambda_2 = lambda_1;
    lambda_1 = lambda;
}
}

/*


           gosp7 = PROGRAM TO GENERATE GOSPER CURVES

*/

#include <stdio.h>
#include <math.h>
#include <dos.h>
#include "tools.h"
```

482

```c
void generate (float X1, float Y1, float X2, float Y2,
    int level);

int generator_size = 3;
int init_size = 6;
int level;
int initiator_x1[10] = {0,130,130,0,-130,-130},
    initiator_x2[10]={130,130,0,-130,-130,0},
    initiator_y1[10]={150,75,-75,-150,-75,75},
    initiator_y2[10]={75,-75,-150,-75,75,150};
int combination = 0,LINEWIDTH=1, OPERATOR=0;
unsigned long int PATTERN=0xFFFFFFFF;
float turtle_theta;
int i;
float Xpoints[25], Ypoints[25];
float turtle_x,turtle_y,turtle_r;

main()
{

    printf("\nEnter level (1 - 8): ");
    scanf("%d",&level);
    if (level < 1)
        level = 1;
    setMode(1);
    cls();

    for (i=0; i<init_size; i++)
        generate(initiator_x1[i], initiator_y1[i],
            initiator_x2[i], initiator_y2[i], level);
    getch();
    setMode(0);
}

/*

                generate() = Generates curve

*/

void generate (float X1, float Y1, float X2, float Y2,
    int level)
{
    int j,k,line,set_type,px1,py1,px2,py2;
        float a, b, Xpoints[25], Ypoints[25], temp,temp_r;

    level--;
    turtle_r = sqrt((((X2 - X1)*(X2 - X1) + (Y2 - Y1)*(Y2 - Y1))
        /7.0);
    turtle_x = X1;
    turtle_y = Y1;
```

```
        Xpoints[0] = X1;
        Ypoints[0] = Y1;
        Xpoints[3] = X2;
        Ypoints[3] = Y2;
        turtle_theta = point(X1,Y1,X2,Y2);
        turn(19.1);
        step();
        Xpoints[1] = turtle_x;
        Ypoints[1] = turtle_y;
        turn(-60);
        step();
        Xpoints[2] = turtle_x;
        Ypoints[2] = turtle_y;
        if (level == 0)
        {
            for (k=0; k<generator_size; k++)
            {
                px1 = Xpoints[k];
                py1 = Ypoints[k];
                px2 = Xpoints[k+1];
                py2 = Ypoints[k+1];
                drawLine(px1,py1,px2,py2,1);
            }
        }
        else
        {
            for (j=0; j<generator_size; j++)
            {
                X1 = Xpoints[j];
                X2 = Xpoints[j+1];
                Y1 = Ypoints[j];
                    Y2 = Ypoints[j+1];
                generate (X1,Y1,X2,Y2,level);
            }
        }
}

/*

            gosper = PROGRAM TO PEANO-GOSPER CURVES

*/

#include <stdio.h>
#include <math.h>
#include <dos.h>
#include "tools.h"

void generate (float X1, float Y1, float X2, float Y2,
    int level,int type);
```

```c
int combination = 0,LINEWIDTH=1, OPERATOR=0;
unsigned long int PATTERN=0xFFFFFFFF;
float turtle_theta;
int i;
int generator_size = 8;
int level;
int init_size = 1;
int initiator_x1[10] = {-150,150},initiator_x2[10]={150,-150},
    initiator_y1[10]={-50}, initiator_y2[10]={-50};
float Xpoints[25], Ypoints[25];
int px1,px2,py1,py2;
float turtle_x,turtle_y,turtle_r;

main()
{


    printf("\nEnter level (1 - 8): ");
    scanf("%d",&level);
    if (level < 1)
        level = 1;
    setMode(1);
    cls();
    for (i=0; i<init_size; i++)
    {
        generate(initiator_x1[i], initiator_y1[i],
            initiator_x2[i], initiator_y2[i], level,0);
    }
    getch();
    setMode(0);
}

/*

                generate() = Generates curve

*/

void generate (float X1, float Y1, float X2, float Y2,
    int level, int type)
{
    int j,k,line,set_type;
        float a, b, Xpoints[25], Ypoints[25],sign=1, temp;


    switch (type)
    {
        case 0: break;

        case 1: sign *= -1;
            break;
```

485

```
          case 2: sign *= -1;
          case 3: temp = X1;
              X1 = X2;
              X2 = temp;
              temp = Y1;
              Y1 = Y2;
              Y2 = temp;
              break;
      }
  level--;
  turtle_r = (sqrt((X2 - X1)*(X2 - X1) + (Y2 - Y1)*(Y2 -
      Y1)))/2.6457513;
  Xpoints[0] = X1;
  Ypoints[0] = Y1;
  Xpoints[7] = X2;
  Ypoints[7] = Y2;
  turtle_theta = point(X1,Y1,X2,Y2);
  turn(-19*sign);
  turtle_x = X1;
  turtle_y = Y1;
  step();
  Xpoints[1] = turtle_x;
  Ypoints[1] = turtle_y;
      turn(60*sign);
  step();
  Xpoints[2] = turtle_x;
  Ypoints[2] = turtle_y;
  turn(120*sign);
  step();
  Xpoints[3] = turtle_x;
  Ypoints[3] = turtle_y;
      turn(-60*sign);
  step();
  Xpoints[4] = turtle_x;
  Ypoints[4] = turtle_y;
  turn(-120*sign);
  step();
  Xpoints[5] = turtle_x;
  Ypoints[5] = turtle_y;
  step();
  Xpoints[6] = turtle_x;
  Ypoints[6] = turtle_y;
  if (level > 0)
  {
      for (j=0; j<generator_size-1; j++)
      {
          switch(j)
          {
              case 0:
              case 3:
```

```
                    case 4:
                    case 5:
                        set_type = 0;
                        break;
                    case 2:
                    case 1:
                    case 6:
                        set_type = 3;
                        break;
                }
                    X1 = Xpoints[j];
                    X2 = Xpoints[j+1];
                    Y1 = Ypoints[j];
                    Y2 = Ypoints[j+1];
                generate (X1,Y1,X2,Y2,level,set_type);
            }
        }
        else
        {
            for (k=0; k<generator_size-1; k++)
            {
                px1 = Xpoints[k];
                py1 = Ypoints[k];
                px2 = Xpoints[k+1];
                py2 = Ypoints[k+1];
                drawLine(px1,py1,px2,py2,1);
            }
        }
}

/*


            hil3d = PROGRAM TO GENERATE 3D HILBERT CURVES

*/

#include <stdio.h>
#include <math.h>
#include <dos.h>
#include <stdlib.h>
#include "tools.h"
void generate (int a, int b, int c);

int level,max_level;
int combination = 0,LINEWIDTH=1, OPERATOR=0;
unsigned long int PATTERN=0xFFFFFFFF;
int i;
float points[3],x1,x2,y_one,y2,r;
int px1,py1,px2,py2;
float x_angle = -55, y_angle = 90, z_angle = 0,cx,cy,cz,sx,sy,
    sz;
```

```
main()
{
    printf("Enter level: ");
    scanf ("%d",&level);
    max_level = level;
    setMode(1);
    cls();
    sx = sin(x_angle*.017453292);
    sy = sin(y_angle*.017453292);
    sz = sin(z_angle*.017453292);
    cx = cos(x_angle*.017453292);
    cy = cos(y_angle*.017453292);
    cz = cos(z_angle*.017453292);

    r = 300/(pow(2,level));
    points[0] = -200;
    points[1] = 50;
    points[2] = 0;
    generate(3,-2,1);
    getch();
    setMode(0);
}

/*

                generate() = Generates curve

*/

void generate (int a, int b, int c)
{
    int sign[3];
    sign[0] = 1;
    sign[1] = 1;
    sign[2] = 1;

    level--;
    if (a < 0)
        sign[0] = -1;
    a = abs(a)-1;
    if (b < 0)
        sign[1] = -1;
    b = abs(b)-1;
    if (c < 0)
        sign[2] = -1;
    c = abs(c)-1;

    x1 = points[0]*cx + points[1]*cy + points[2]*cz;
    y_one = points[0]*sx + points[1]*sy + points[2]*sz;
    if (level > 0)
```

```
    generate(-2,1,3);
points[a] += (r*sign[0]);
x2 = points[0]*cx + points[1]*cy + points[2]*cz;
y2 = points[0]*sx + points[1]*sy + points[2]*sz;
px1 = x1;
py1 = y_one;
px2 = x2;
py2 = y2;
drawLine(px1,py1,px2,py2,1);
x1 = points[0]*cx + points[1]*cy + points[2]*cz;
y_one = points[0]*sx + points[1]*sy + points[2]*sz;
if (level > 0)
    generate(3,1,-2);
points[b] += (r*sign[1]);
x2 = points[0]*cx + points[1]*cy + points[2]*cz;
y2 = points[0]*sx + points[1]*sy + points[2]*sz;
px1 = x1;
py1 = y_one;
px2 = x2;
py2 = y2;
drawLine(px1,py1,px2,py2,1);
x1 = points[0]*cx + points[1]*cy + points[2]*cz;
y_one = points[0]*sx + points[1]*sy + points[2]*sz;
if (level > 0)
    generate(3,1,-2);
points[a] -= (r*sign[0]);
x2 = points[0]*cx + points[1]*cy + points[2]*cz;
y2 = points[0]*sx + points[1]*sy + points[2]*sz;
px1 = x1;
py1 = y_one;
px2 = x2;
py2 = y2;
drawLine(px1,py1,px2,py2,1);
x1 = points[0]*cx + points[1]*cy + points[2]*cz;
y_one = points[0]*sx + points[1]*sy + points[2]*sz;
if (level > 0)
    generate(2,-3,1);
points[c] += (r*sign[2]);
x2 = points[0]*cx + points[1]*cy + points[2]*cz;
y2 = points[0]*sx + points[1]*sy + points[2]*sz;
px1 = x1;
py1 = y_one;
px2 = x2;
py2 = y2;
drawLine(px1,py1,px2,py2,1);
x1 = points[0]*cx + points[1]*cy + points[2]*cz;
y_one = points[0]*sx + points[1]*sy + points[2]*sz;
if (level > 0)
    generate(-3,1,2);
points[a] += (r*sign[0]);
x2 = points[0]*cx + points[1]*cy + points[2]*cz;
```

```
        y2 = points[0]*sx + points[1]*sy + points[2]*sz;
        px1 = x1;
        py1 = y_one;
        px2 = x2;
        py2 = y2;
        drawLine(px1,py1,px2,py2,1);
        x1 = points[0]*cx + points[1]*cy + points[2]*cz;
        y_one = points[0]*sx + points[1]*sy + points[2]*sz;
        if (level > 0)
            generate(-2,3,1);
        points[b] -= (r*sign[1]);
        x2 = points[0]*cx + points[1]*cy + points[2]*cz;
        y2 = points[0]*sx + points[1]*sy + points[2]*sz;
        px1 = x1;
        py1 = y_one;
        px2 = x2;
        py2 = y2;
        drawLine(px1,py1,px2,py2,1);
        x1 = points[0]*cx + points[1]*cy + points[2]*cz;
        y_one = points[0]*sx + points[1]*sy + points[2]*sz;
        if (level > 0)
            generate(3,-1,2);
        points[a] -= (r*sign[0]);
        x2 = points[0]*cx + points[1]*cy + points[2]*cz;
        y2 = points[0]*sx + points[1]*sy + points[2]*sz;
        px1 = x1;
        py1 = y_one;
        px2 = x2;
        py2 = y2;
        drawLine(px1,py1,px2,py2,1);
        x1 = points[0]*cx + points[1]*cy + points[2]*cz;
        y_one = points[0]*sx + points[1]*sy + points[2]*sz;
        if (level > 0)
            generate(-2,-1,-3);
        level++;
}

/*


        hilbert = PROGRAM TO GENERATE HILBERT CURVES

*/

#include <stdio.h>
#include <math.h>
#include <dos.h>
#include "tools.h"

void generate (float r1, float r2);

int level,sign=-1;
```

```
int combination = 0,LINEWIDTH=1, OPERATOR=0;
unsigned long int PATTERN=0xFFFFFFFF;
int i,px1,px2,py1,py2;
float x1,x2,y_one,y2,r;

main()
{
    float temp;

    printf("Enter level: ");
    scanf ("%d",&level);
    setMode(1);
    cls();
    r = 400/(pow(2,level));
    x1 = -200;
    y_one = -200;
    x2 = -200;
    y2 = -200;
    generate(r,0);
    getch();
    setMode(0);
}

/*

                    generate() = Generates curve

*/

void generate (float r1, float r2)
{

    level--;
    if (level > 0)
        generate(r2,r1);
    x2 += r1;
    y2 += r2;
    px1 = x1;
    py1 = y_one;
    px2 = x2;
    py2 = y2;
    drawLine(px1,py1,px2,py2,1);
    x1 = x2;
    y_one = y2;
    if (level > 0)
        generate(r1,r2);
    x2 += r2;
    y2 += r1;
    px1 = x1;
    py1 = y_one;
    px2 = x2;
```

```
        py2 = y2;
        drawLine(px1,py1,px2,py2,1);
        x1 = x2;
        y_one = y2;
        if (level > 0)
            generate(r1,r2);
        x2 -= r1;
        y2 -= r2;
        px1 = x1;
        py1 = y_one;
        px2 = x2;
        py2 = y2;
        drawLine(px1,py1,px2,py2,1);
        x1 = x2;
        y_one = y2;
        if (level > 0)
            generate(-r2,-r1);
        level++;
}

/*

            hilbert = PROGRAM TO GENERATE HILBERT CURVES

*/

#include <stdio.h>
#include <math.h>
#include <dos.h>
#include "tools.h"

void gen1(int i);
void gen2(int i);
void gen3(int i);
void gen4(int i);

int combination = 0,LINEWIDTH=1, OPERATOR=0;
unsigned long int PATTERN=0xFFFFFFFF;
int xa=0,ya=0, x,y,old_x,old_y, i,j,h=448;
int level;

main()
{
    printf("\nEnter level (1 - 8): ");
    scanf("%d",&level);
    if (level < 1)
        level = 1;
    setMode(1);
    cls();

    for (i=1; i<=level; i++)
```

```
    {
        h /=2;
        x += h/2;
        y += h/2;
        old_x = x;
        old_y = y;
    }
    gen1(level);
    getch();
    setMode(0);
}

void gen1(int i)
{
    if(i > 0)
    {
        gen4(i-1);
        x -= h;
        drawLine(old_x,old_y,x,y,1);
        old_x = x;
        old_y = y;
        gen1(i-1);
        y -= h;
        drawLine(old_x,old_y,x,y,1);
        old_x = x;
        old_y = y;
        gen1(i-1);
        x += h;
        drawLine(old_x,old_y,x,y,1);
        old_x = x;
        old_y = y;
        gen2(i-1);
    }
}

void gen2(int i)
{
    if (i > 0)
    {
        gen3(i-1);
        y += h;
        drawLine(old_x,old_y,x,y,1);
        old_x = x;
        old_y = y;
        gen2(i-1);
        x += h;
        drawLine(old_x,old_y,x,y,1);
        old_x = x;
        old_y = y;
        gen2(i-1);
        y -= h;
```

```
         drawLine(old_x,old_y,x,y,1);
         old_x = x;
         old_y = y;
         gen1(i-1);
      }
}

void gen3(int i)
{
   if (i > 0)
   {
      gen2(i-1);
      x += h;
      drawLine(old_x,old_y,x,y,1);
      old_x = x;
      old_y = y;
      gen3(i-1);
      y += h;
      drawLine(old_x,old_y,x,y,1);
      old_x = x;
      old_y = y;
      gen3(i-1);
      x -= h;
      drawLine(old_x,old_y,x,y,1);
      old_x = x;
      old_y = y;
      gen4(i-1);
   }
}

void gen4(int i)
{
   if (i > 0)
   {
      gen1(i-1);
      y -= h;
      drawLine(old_x,old_y,x,y,1);
      old_x = x;
      old_y = y;
      gen4(i-1);
      x -= h;
      drawLine(old_x,old_y,x,y,1);
      old_x = x;
      old_y = y;
      gen4(i-1);
      y += h;
      drawLine(old_x,old_y,x,y,1);
      old_x = x;
      old_y = y;
      gen3(i-1);
   }
```

494

```
}



/*

      hkoch8 = PROGRAM TO GENERATE 8 SEGMENT HEXAGONAL KOCH
               CURVE

*/

#include <stdio.h>
#include <math.h>
#include <dos.h>
#include "tools.h"

void generate (float X1, float Y1, float X2, float Y2,
     int level);

int generator_size = 8;
int init_size = 6;
int level;
int initiator_x1[10] = {-75,75,150,75,-75,-150},
     initiator_x2[10]={75,150,75,-75,-150,-75},
     initiator_y1[10]={115,115,0,-115,-115,0},
     initiator_y2[10]={115,0,-115,-115,0,115};
int combination = 0,LINEWIDTH=1, OPERATOR=0;
unsigned long int PATTERN=0xFFFFFFFF;
float turtle_theta;
int i;
float Xpoints[25], Ypoints[25];
float turtle_x,turtle_y,turtle_r;
int px1,px2,py1,py2;

main()
{

    printf("\nEnter level (1 - 8): ");
    scanf("%d",&level);
    if (level < 1)
        level = 1;
    setMode(1);
    cls();

    for (i=0; i<init_size; i++)
        generate(initiator_x1[i], initiator_y1[i],
             initiator_x2[i],initiator_y2[i], level);
    getch();
    setMode(0);
}
```

```
/*

                    generate() = Generates curve

*/

void generate (float X1, float Y1, float X2, float Y2,
    int level)
{
    int j,k,line,set_type;
        float a, b, Xpoints[25], Ypoints[25], temp,temp_r;

    level--;
    turtle_r = sqrt((X2 - X1)*(X2 - X1) + (Y2 - Y1)*(Y2 -
        Y1))/4.0;
    turtle_x = X1;
    turtle_y = Y1;
    Xpoints[0] = X1;
    Ypoints[0] = Y1;
    Xpoints[8] = X2;
    Ypoints[8] = Y2;
    turtle_theta = point(X1,Y1,X2,Y2);
    step();
    Xpoints[1] = turtle_x;
    Ypoints[1] = turtle_y;
    turn(90);
    step();
    Xpoints[2] = turtle_x;
    Ypoints[2] = turtle_y;
    turn(-90);
    step();
    Xpoints[3] = turtle_x;
    Ypoints[3] = turtle_y;
    turn(-90);
    step();
    Xpoints[4] = turtle_x;
    Ypoints[4] = turtle_y;
    step();
    Xpoints[5] = turtle_x;
    Ypoints[5] = turtle_y;
    turn(90);
    step();
    Xpoints[6] = turtle_x;
    Ypoints[6] = turtle_y;
    turn(90);
    step();
    Xpoints[7] = turtle_x;
    Ypoints[7] = turtle_y;
    if (level == 0)
    {
        for (k=0; k<generator_size; k++)
```

496

```
            {
                px1 = Xpoints[k];
                py1 = Ypoints[k];
                px2 = Xpoints[k+1];
                py2 = Ypoints[k+1];
                drawLine(px1,py1,px2,py2,1);
            }
        }
        else
        {
            for (j=0; j<generator_size; j++)
            {
                X1 = Xpoints[j];
                X2 = Xpoints[j+1];
                Y1 = Ypoints[j];
                    Y2 = Ypoints[j+1];
                generate (X1,Y1,X2,Y2,level);
            }
        }
}

/*

        image = PROGRAM TO GENERATE ITERATED FUNCTION SYSTEMS

*/

#include <stdio.h>
#include <math.h>
#include <dos.h>

/* USER WRITTEN INCLUDES */
#include "tools.h"

/* GLOBALS */


int LINEWIDTH,OPERATOR;
unsigned long int PATTERN;

void image_draw(int color);
void plots(int x, int y, int color);

int adapt,mode;
int j, k, xscale,yscale,xoffset,yoffset,pr,p[4],pk[4];
long unsigned int i;
float a[4],b[4],c[4],d[4],e[4],f[4],x,y,newx;

main()
{
    setMode(1);
```

```
a[0] =0; a[1] = .2; a[2] = -.15; a[3] = .85;
b[0] = 0; b[1] = -.26; b[2] = .28; b[3] = .04;
c[0] = 0; c[1] = .23; c[2] =.26; c[3] = -.04;
d[0] = .16; d[1] = .22; d[2] = .24; d[3] = .85;
e[0] = 0; e[1] = 0; e[2] = 0; e[3] = 0;
f[0] = 0; f[1] = .2; f[2] = .2; f[3] = .2;
p[0] = 328; p[1] = 2621; p[2] = 4915; p[3] = 32767;
xscale = 300;
yscale = 300;
xoffset = -50;
yoffset = -180;
cls ();
image_draw(1);
getch();

a[0] = 0; a[1] = .1; a[2] = .42; a[3] = .42;
b[0] = 0; b[1] = 0; b[2] = -.42; b[3] = .42;
c[0] = 0; c[1] = 0; c[2] = .42; c[3] = -.42;
d[0] = .5; d[1] = .1; d[2] = .42; d[3] = .42;
e[0] = 0; e[1] = 0; e[2] = 0; e[3] = 0;
f[0] = 0; f[1] = .2; f[2] = .2; f[3] = .2;
p[0] = 1638; p[1] = 6553; p[2] = 19660; p[3] = 32767;
xscale = 750;
yscale = 750;
xoffset = 0;
yoffset = -160;
cls();
image_draw(1);
getch();

a[0] = .5; a[1] = .5; a[2] = .5; a[3] = 0;
b[0] = 0; b[1] = 0; b[2] = 0; b[3] = 0;
c[0] = 0; c[1] = 0; c[2] = 0; c[3] = 0;
d[0] = .5; d[1] = .5; d[2] = .5; d[3] = 0;
e[0] = 0; e[1] = 1.; e[2] = .5; e[3] = 0;
f[0] = 0; f[1] = 0; f[2] = .5; f[3] = 0;
p[0] = 10813; p[1] = 21626; p[2] = 32767; p[3] = 32767;
xscale = 200;
yscale = 200;
xoffset = -200;
yoffset = -160;
cls();
image_draw(1);
getch();

cls();
a[0] = .333; a[1] = .333; a[2] = .667; a[3] = 0;
b[0] = 0; b[1] = 0; b[2] = 0; b[3] = 0;
c[0] = 0; c[1] = 0; c[2] = 0; c[3] = 0;
d[0] = .333; d[1] = .333; d[2] = .667; d[3] = 0;
e[0] = 0; e[1] = 1.; e[2] = .5; e[3] = 0;
```

```
    f[0] = 0; f[1] = 0; f[2] = .5; f[3] = 0;
    p[0] = 10813; p[1] = 21626; p[2] = 32767; p[3] = 32767;
    xscale = 120;
    yscale = 140;
    xoffset = -100;
    yoffset = -160;
    image_draw(1);
    getch();
    setMode(0);

}

void image_draw(int color)
{

    int px,py;

    x = 0;
    y = 0;
    for (i=1; i<=10000; i++)
    {
        j = rand();
        k = (j < p[0]) ? 0 : ((j < p[1]) ? 1 :
            ((j < p[2]) ? 2 : 3));
        newx = (a[k]* x + b[k] * y + e[k]);
        y = (c[k] * x + d[k] * y + f[k]);
        x = newx;
                px = x*xscale + xoffset;
                py = (y*yscale + yoffset);
        if ((px>=-320) && (px<320)  && (py>=-240) && (py<240))
            plots (px,py,color);
    }
}

void plots(int x, int y, int color)
{

    #define convert(x,y)    {x = (x + 319);
                            y = (175 - ((93*y) >> 7));}

    convert(x,y);
    plot(x,y,color);
}

/*

        image3d = PROGRAM TO GENERATE THREE DIMENSIONAL
                  ITERATED FUNCTION SYSTEMS

*/
```

```c
#include <stdio.h>
#include <math.h>
#include <dos.h>
#include "tools.h"

int LINEWIDTH,OPERATOR;
unsigned long int PATTERN;

void image_draw(void);
float degrees_to_radians(float degrees);

int adapt,mode;
int j, k, index, xscale,yscale,xoffset,yoffset,pr,p[4],pk[4];
int hues[8] = {2,10,11,14};
long unsigned int i;
float a[4],b[4],c[4],d[4],e[4],f[4],g[4],h[4],m[4],n[4],q[4],
    r[4],ca,cb,cg,sa,sb,sg,x,y,z,newx,newy,alpha[4] =
    {30,45,15,95},beta[4] = {115,105,70,40},gamma[4]=
    {25,70,20,-30};
float rad_per_degree=0.0174533;
main()
{
    setMode(1);
    a[0] =0; a[1] = .83; a[2] = .22; a[3] = -.22;
    b[0] = 0; b[1] = 0; b[2] = -.23; b[3] = .23;
    c[0] = 0; c[1] = 0; c[2] = 0; c[3] = 0;
    d[0] = 0; d[1] = 0; d[2] = .24; d[3] = .24;
    e[0] = .18; e[1] = .86; e[2] = .22; e[3] = .22;
    f[0] = 0; f[1] = .1; f[2] = 0; f[3] = 0;
    g[0] = 0; g[1] = 0; g[2] = 0; g[3] = 0;
    h[0] = 0; h[1] = -.12; h[2] = 0; h[3] = 0;
    m[0] = 0; m[1] = .84; m[2] = .32; m[3] = .32;
    n[0] = 0; n[1] = 0; n[2] = 0; n[3] = 0;
    q[0] = 0; q[1] = 1.62; q[2] = .82; q[3] = .82;
    r[0] = 0; r[1] = 0; r[2] = 0; r[3] = 0;
    p[0] = 328; p[1] = 27879 ; p[2] = 30173; p[3] = 32767;
    xscale = 40;
    yscale = 50;
    xoffset = 60;
    yoffset = -180;
    cls ();
    for (index=0; index<4; index++)
    {
        ca = cos(alpha[index]*0.0174533);
        cb = cos(beta[index]*0.0174533);
        cg = cos(gamma[index]*0.0174533);
        sa = sin(alpha[index]*0.0174533);
        sb = sin(beta[index]*0.0174533);
        sg = sin(gamma[index]*0.0174533);
        image_draw();
    }
```

```
    getch();
    setMode(0);
}

void image_draw(void)
{

    int px,py;
    float vx,vy;

    x = 0;
    y = 0;
    z = 0;
    for (i=1; i<=10000; i++)
    {
        j = rand();
        k = (j < p[0]) ? 0 : ((j < p[1]) ? 1 :
            ((j < p[2]) ? 2 : 3));
        newx = (a[k]* x + b[k] * y + c[k] * z + n[k]);
        newy = (d[k] * x + e[k] * y + f[k] * z + q[k]);
        z = g[k] * x + h[k] * y + m[k] * z + r[k];
        x = newx;
        y = newy;
        vx = x*ca + y*cb + z*cg;
        px = vx*xscale + xoffset;
        vy = x*sa + y*sb + z*sg;
        py = (vy*yscale + yoffset);
        if ((px>=-320) && (px<320)  && (py>=-240) && (py<240))
            plots (px,py,1);
    }
}

float degrees_to_radians(float degrees)
{
    float angle;

    while (degrees >= 360)
        degrees -= 360;
    while (degrees < 0)
        degrees += 360;
    angle = rad_per_degree*degrees;
    return angle;
}

/*

            lorenz = PROGRAM TO PLOT LORENZ ATTRACTOR

*/

#include <dos.h>
```

```c
#include <stdio.h>
#include <math.h>
#include "tools.h"

float radians_to_degrees(float degrees);;

const int maxcol = 719;
const int maxrow = 347;

int LINEWIDTH = 3, OPERATOR = 0;
unsigned long int PATTERN = 0xFFFFFFFF;
float rad_per_degree=0.0174533,x_angle=45,y_angle=0,z_angle=90;
union LIMIT XMax,YMax,XMin,YMin,Pval,Qval;

main()
{
    double x,y,z,d0_x,d0_y,d0_z,d1_x,d1_y,d1_z,d2_x,d2_y,d2_z,
        d3_x,d3_y,d3_z,xt,yt,zt,dt,dt2,third=0.333333333,
        sx,sy,sz,cx,cy,cz,temp_x,temp_y,old_y;
    int i, j, row, col, old_row, old_col;

    x_angle = radians_to_degrees(x_angle);
    sx = sin(x_angle);
    cx = cos(x_angle);
    y_angle = radians_to_degrees(y_angle);
    sy = sin(y_angle);
    cy = cos(y_angle);
    z_angle = radians_to_degrees(z_angle);
    sz = sin(z_angle);
    cz = cos(z_angle);
    for (j=0; j<3; j++)
        {
        LINEWIDTH = 3;
        x = 0;
        y = 1;
        z = 0;
        setMode(1);
        if (j == 0)
        {
            old_col = y*9;
            old_row = 9*z - 240;
            drawLine(-320,-238,319,-238,1);
            drawLine(0,-238,0,239,1);
        }
        if (j == 1)
        {
            old_col = y*10;
            old_row = 10*x;
            drawLine(-320,0,319,0,1);
            drawLine(0,-238,0,238,1);
        }
```

```
        if (j == 2)
        {
    old_col = y*9;
    old_row = 9*z - 240;
    drawLine(-320,-238,319,-238,1);
    drawLine(0,-238,0,239,1);
    drawLine(0,-238,319,82,1);
        }

        LINEWIDTH = 1;
dt = 0.01;
dt2 = dt/2;
for (i=0; i<8000; i++)
{
    d0_x = 10*(y-x)*dt2;
    d0_y = (-x*z + 28*x - y)*dt2;
    d0_z  = (x*y - 8*z/3)*dt2;
    xt = x + d0_x;
    yt = y + d0_y;
    zt = z + d0_z;
    d1_x = (10*(yt-xt))*dt2;
    d1_y = (-xt*zt + 28*xt - yt)*dt2;
    d1_z  =(xt*yt - 8*zt/3)*dt2;
    xt = x + d1_x;
    yt = y + d1_y;
    zt = z + d1_z;
    d2_x = (10*(yt-xt))*dt;
    d2_y = (-xt*zt + 28*xt - yt)*dt;
    d2_z  =(xt*yt - 8*zt/3)*dt;
    xt = x + d2_x;
    yt = y + d2_y;
    zt = z + d2_z;
    d3_x = (10*(yt - xt))*dt2;
    d3_y = (-xt*zt + 28*xt - yt)*dt2;
    d3_z = (xt*yt - 8*zt/3)*dt2;
                old_y = y;
    x += (d0_x + d1_x + d1_x + d2_x + d3_x) * third;
    y += (d0_y + d1_y + d1_y + d2_y + d3_y) * third;
    z += (d0_z + d1_z + d1_z + d2_z + d3_z) * third;
    if (j == 0)
    {
        col = y*9;
        row = 9*z - 240;
    }
    if (j == 1)
    {
        col = y*10;
        row = 10*x;
                }
                if (j == 2)
                {
```

```
                    temp_x = x*cx + y*cy + z*cz;
                    temp_y = x*sx + y*sy + z*sz;
                    col = temp_x*8;
                    row = temp_y*7-240;
                    }
            drawLine(old_col,old_row,col,row,1);
            old_row = row;
            old_col = col;
            }
        getch();
        }
        setMode(0);
}



float radians_to_degrees(float degrees)
{
        float angle;

        while (degrees >= 360)
            degrees -= 360;
        while (degrees < 0)
            degrees += 360;
        angle = rad_per_degree*degrees;
        return angle;
}

/*

        peano1 = PROGRAM TO GENERATE ORIGINAL PEANO CURVE

*/

#include <stdio.h>
#include <math.h>
#include <dos.h>
#include "tools.h"

void generate (float X1, float Y1, float X2, float Y2,
    int level);

int generator_size = 9;
int level;
int init_size = 1;
int initiator_x1[10] = {0},initiator_x2[10]={0},
    initiator_y1[10]={-100}, initiator_y2[10]={100};
int combination = 0,LINEWIDTH=1, OPERATOR=0;
unsigned long int PATTERN=0xFFFFFFFF;
float turtle_theta;
int i,px1,px2,py1,py2;
```

```
float Xpoints[25], Ypoints[25];
float turtle_x,turtle_y,turtle_r;

main()
{

    printf("\nEnter level (1 - 8): ");
    scanf("%d",&level);
    if (level < 1)
        level = 1;
    setMode(1);
    cls();

    for (i=0; i<init_size; i++)
        generate(initiator_x1[i], initiator_y1[i],
            initiator_x2[i], initiator_y2[i], level);
    getch();
    setMode(0);
}

/*


                    generate() = Generates curve

*/

void generate (float X1, float Y1, float X2, float Y2, int level)
{
    int j,k,line;
        float a, b, Xpoints[25], Ypoints[25];

    level--;
    turtle_r = (sqrt((X2 - X1)*(X2 - X1) + (Y2 - Y1)*(Y2 -
        Y1)))/3.0;
    Xpoints[0] = X1;
    Ypoints[0] = Y1;
    Xpoints[9] = X2;
    Ypoints[9] = Y2;
    turtle_theta = point(X1,Y1,X2,Y2);
    turtle_x = X1;
    turtle_y = Y1;
    step();
    Xpoints[1] = turtle_x;
    Ypoints[1] = turtle_y;
    turn(90);
    step();
    Xpoints[2] = turtle_x;
    Ypoints[2] = turtle_y;
        turn(-90);
    step();
    Xpoints[3] = turtle_x;
```

```
    Ypoints[3] = turtle_y;
    turn(-90);
    step();
    Xpoints[4] = turtle_x;
    Ypoints[4] = turtle_y;
        turn(-90);
    step();
    Xpoints[5] = turtle_x;
    Ypoints[5] = turtle_y;
    turn(90);
    step();
    Xpoints[6] = turtle_x;
    Ypoints[6] = turtle_y;
        turn(90);
    step();
    Xpoints[7] = turtle_x;
    Ypoints[7] = turtle_y;
    turn(90);
    step();
    Xpoints[8] = turtle_x;
    Ypoints[8] = turtle_y;
    if (level > 0)
    {
        for (j=0; j<generator_size; j++)
        {
                X1 = Xpoints[j];
                X2 = Xpoints[j+1];
                Y1 = Ypoints[j];
                Y2 = Ypoints[j+1];
            generate (X1,Y1,X2,Y2,level);
        }
    }
    else
    {
        for (k=0; k<generator_size; k++)
        {
            px1 = Xpoints[k];
            py1 = Ypoints[k];
            px2 = Xpoints[k+1];
            py2 = Ypoints[k+1];
            drawLine(px1,py1,px2,py2,1);
        }
    }
}

/*

    peano2 = PROGRAM TO GENERATE MODIFIED PEANO CURVE

*/
```

```c
#include <stdio.h>
#include <math.h>
#include <dos.h>
#include "tools.h"

void generate (float X1, float Y1, float X2, float Y2, int level);

int generator_size = 19;
int level;
int init_size = 1;
int initiator_x1[10] = {0},initiator_x2[10]={0},
    initiator_y1[10]={-200}, initiator_y2[10]={200};
int combination = 0,LINEWIDTH=1, OPERATOR=0;
unsigned long int PATTERN=0xFFFFFFFF;
float turtle_theta;
int i,px1,px2,py1,py2;
float Xpoints[25], Ypoints[25],Xptemp,Yptemp;
float turtle_x,turtle_y,turtle_r;

main()
{

    printf("\nEnter level (1 - 8): ");
    scanf("%d",&level);
    if (level < 1)
        level = 1;
    setMode(1);
    cls();

    Xptemp = initiator_x1[0];
    Yptemp = initiator_y1[0];
    for (i=0; i<init_size; i++)
        generate(initiator_x1[i], initiator_y1[i],
            initiator_x2[i], initiator_y2[i], level);
    getch();
    setMode(0);
}

/*

                 generate() = Generates curve

*/

void generate (float X1, float Y1, float X2, float Y2,
    int level)
{
    int j,k,line;
        float a, b, Xpoints[25], Ypoints[25];

    level--;
```

```
Xpoints[0] = X1;
Ypoints[0] = Y1;
turtle_theta = point(X1,Y1,X2,Y2);
turtle_x = X1;
turtle_y = Y1;
if (level != 0)
{
    turtle_r = (sqrt((X2 - X1)*(X2 - X1) + (Y2 - Y1)*(Y2
        - Y1)))/3.0;
    Xpoints[9] = X2;
    Ypoints[9] = Y2;
    step();
    Xpoints[1] = turtle_x;
    Ypoints[1] = turtle_y;
    turn(90);
    step();
    Xpoints[2] = turtle_x;
    Ypoints[2] = turtle_y;
        turn(-90);
    step();
    Xpoints[3] = turtle_x;
    Ypoints[3] = turtle_y;
    turn(-90);
    step();
    Xpoints[4] = turtle_x;
    Ypoints[4] = turtle_y;
        turn(-90);
    step();
    Xpoints[5] = turtle_x;
    Ypoints[5] = turtle_y;
    turn(90);
    step();
    Xpoints[6] = turtle_x;
    Ypoints[6] = turtle_y;
        turn(90);
    step();
    Xpoints[7] = turtle_x;
    Ypoints[7] = turtle_y;
    turn(90);
    step();
    Xpoints[8] = turtle_x;
    Ypoints[8] = turtle_y;
    for (j=0; j<9; j++)
    {
            X1 = Xpoints[j];
            X2 = Xpoints[j+1];
            Y1 = Ypoints[j];
            Y2 = Ypoints[j+1];
        generate (X1,Y1,X2,Y2,level);
    }
}
```

```
else
{
    turtle_r = (sqrt((X2 - X1)*(X2 - X1) + (Y2 - Y1)*(Y2
        - Y1)))/18.0;
    Xpoints[0] = Xptemp;
    Ypoints[0] = Yptemp;
    Xpoints[19] = X2;
    Ypoints[19] = Y2;
    step();
    Xpoints[1] = turtle_x;
    Ypoints[1] = turtle_y;
    step();
    step();
    step();
    step();
    Xpoints[2] = turtle_x;
    Ypoints[2] = turtle_y;
    step();
    turn(90);
    step();
    Xpoints[3] = turtle_x;
    Ypoints[3] = turtle_y;
    step();
    step();
    step();
    step();
    Xpoints[4] = turtle_x;
    Ypoints[4] = turtle_y;
    step();
        turn(-90);
    step();
    Xpoints[5] = turtle_x;
    Ypoints[5] = turtle_y;
    step();
    step();
    step();
    step();
    Xpoints[6] = turtle_x;
    Ypoints[6] = turtle_y;
    step();
    turn(-90);
    step();
    Xpoints[7] = turtle_x;
    Ypoints[7] = turtle_y;
    step();
    step();
    step();
    step();
    Xpoints[8] = turtle_x;
    Ypoints[8] = turtle_y;
    step();
```

```
        turn(-90);
    step();
    Xpoints[9] = turtle_x;
    Ypoints[9] = turtle_y;
    step();
    step();
    step();
    step();
    Xpoints[10] = turtle_x;
    Ypoints[10] = turtle_y;
    step();
    turn(90);
    step();
    Xpoints[11] = turtle_x;
    Ypoints[11] = turtle_y;
    step();
    step();
    step();
    step();
    Xpoints[12] = turtle_x;
    Ypoints[12] = turtle_y;
    step();
        turn(90);
    step();
    Xpoints[13] = turtle_x;
    Ypoints[13] = turtle_y;
    step();
    step();
    step();
    step();
    Xpoints[14] = turtle_x;
    Ypoints[14] = turtle_y;
    step();
    turn(90);
    step();
    Xpoints[15] = turtle_x;
    Ypoints[15] = turtle_y;
    step();
    step();
    step();
    step();
    Xpoints[16] = turtle_x;
    Ypoints[16] = turtle_y;
    step();
    turn(-90);
    step();
    Xpoints[17] = turtle_x;
    Ypoints[17] = turtle_y;
    step();
    step();
    step();
```

```
        step();
        Xpoints[18] = turtle_x;
        Ypoints[18] = turtle_y;
        Xptemp = Xpoints[18];
        Yptemp = Ypoints[18];
        for (k=0; k<generator_size-1; k++)
        {
            px1 = Xpoints[k];
            py1 = Ypoints[k];
            px2 = Xpoints[k+1];
            py2 = Ypoints[k+1];
            drawLine(px1,py1,px2,py2,1);
        }
    }
}

/*

        pharaoh = PROGRAM TO GENERATE PHARAOH'S BREASTPLATE

*/

#include <stdio.h>
#include <math.h>
#include "tools.h"
#include <stdlib.h>
#include <dos.h>

void drawOval(int x, int y, int b, int color, float aspect);
void inverseOval(float x, float y, float b, int color, float
    aspect);
void gen_circle(float x,float y,float radius);

unsigned long int PATTERN = 0xFFFFFFFF;
int i,j,LINEWIDTH = 1,OPERATOR=0;
double a_line,b_line,x_o,y_o,radius,r_sq,height;

main()
{

    float xbig,ybig,rbig,xtan,ytan,rtan;

    setMode(1);
    cls();
    r_sq = 400000;
    xbig = 0;
    ybig = 0;
    rbig = 220;
    rtan = 140;
    xtan = 0;
    ytan = ybig + rbig - rtan;
```

```
    y_o = ybig - rbig;
    x_o = xbig;
    drawOval(xbig, ybig,rbig,1,1.0);
    drawOval(xtan,ytan,rtan,1,1.0);
    a_line = r_sq/(2*rbig);
    b_line = r_sq/(2*rtan);
    height = (b_line - a_line);
    radius = height/2;
    height = radius*sqrt(2.0);
    for (i=0; i<20; i++)
    {
        gen_circle(x_o + height*i,y_o + a_line + radius,
            radius);
        gen_circle(x_o + height*i,y_o + a_line + radius/2,
            radius/2);
        gen_circle(x_o + height*i,y_o + b_line - radius/2,
            radius/2);
        gen_circle(x_o + height*i + height/2,y_o + a_line +
            3*radius/4,radius/4);
        gen_circle(x_o + height*i + height/2,y_o + b_line -
            3*radius/4,radius/4);
        gen_circle(x_o + height*i + height/2,y_o + a_line +
            radius/8, radius/8);
        gen_circle(x_o + height*i + height/2,y_o + b_line -
            radius/8, radius/8);
        gen_circle(x_o + height*i + height/2,y_o + a_line +
            5*radius/12,radius/12);
        gen_circle(x_o + height*i + height/2,y_o + b_line -
            5*radius/12,radius/12);
        gen_circle(x_o + height*i + 0.4*height,y_o + a_line +
            0.3*radius,radius/10);
        gen_circle(x_o + height*i + 0.6*height,y_o + a_line +
            0.3*radius,radius/10);
        gen_circle(x_o + height*i + 0.4*height,y_o + b_line -
            0.3*radius,radius/10);
        gen_circle(x_o + height*i + 0.6*height,y_o + b_line -
            0.3*radius,radius/10);
    }
    getch();
    setMode(0);
}

/*

        gen_circle() = performs two inversions

*/

void gen_circle(float x,float y,float radius)
{
    inverseOval(x,y,radius,1,1.0);
```

```
    inverseOval(-x,y,radius,1,1.0);
}

/*

    inverseOval() = draws the inverse of an oval with
                    specified center, radius, color and
                    aspect ratio.

*/

void inverseOval(float x, float y, float b, int color,
    float aspect)
{

    union REGS reg;

    int i, bnew,new_col, new_row;
    float length,new_length;
    long a,a_square, b_square, two_a_square, two_b_square,
        four_a_square, four_b_square,d,row,col;

    b -= LINEWIDTH/2;
    a = b/aspect;

    for (i=1; i<=LINEWIDTH; i++)
    {
        b_square = (long)b*b;
        a_square = (a*a);
        row = b;
        col = 0;
        two_a_square = a_square << 1;
        four_a_square = a_square << 2;
        four_b_square = b_square << 2;
        two_b_square = b_square << 1;
        d = two_a_square * (((long)row  -1)*(row )) + a_square
            + two_b_square*(1-a_square);
        while (a_square*(row ) > b_square * (col))
        {
            length = sqrt((x_o - col - x)*(x_o - col - x) +
                (y_o - row - y)*(y_o - row - y));
            new_length = r_sq/length;
            new_col = x_o - (x_o - col - x)*new_length/length;
            new_row = -y_o + (y_o - row - y)*new_length/length;
            plots(new_col,new_row,color);
            length = sqrt((x_o + col - x)*(x_o + col - x) +
                (y_o - row - y)*(y_o - row - y));
            new_length = r_sq/length;
            new_col = x_o - (x_o + col - x)*new_length/length;
            new_row = -y_o + (y_o - row - y)*new_length/length;
```

```
        plots(new_col,new_row,color);
        length = sqrt((x_o - col - x)*(x_o - col - x) +
            (y_o + row - y)*(y_o + row - y));
        new_length = r_sq/length;
        new_col = x_o - (x_o - col - x)*new_length/length;
        new_row = -y_o + (y_o + row - y)*new_length/length;
        plots(new_col,new_row,color);
        length = sqrt((x_o + col - x)*(x_o + col - x) +
            (y_o + row - y)*(y_o + row - y));
        new_length = r_sq/length;
        new_col = x_o - (x_o + col - x)*new_length/length;
        new_row = -y_o + (y_o + row - y)*new_length/length;
        plots(new_col,new_row,color);
        if (d>= 0)
        {
            row--;
            d -= four_a_square*(row);
        }
        d += two_b_square*(3 + (col<<1));
        col++;
    }

    d = two_b_square * (col + 1)*col + two_a_square*(row *
            (row  -2) +1) + (1-two_a_square)*b_square;
    while ((row) + 1)
    {
        length = sqrt((x_o - col - x)*(x_o - col - x) +
            (y_o - row - y)*(y_o - row - y));
        new_length = r_sq/length;
        new_col = x_o - (x_o - col - x)*new_length/length;
        new_row = -y_o + (y_o - row - y)*new_length/length;
        plots(new_col,new_row,color);
        length = sqrt((x_o + col - x)*(x_o + col - x) +
            (y_o - row - y)*(y_o - row - y));
        new_length = r_sq/length;
        new_col = x_o - (x_o + col - x)*new_length/length;
        new_row = -y_o + (y_o - row - y)*new_length/length;
        plots(new_col,new_row,color);
        length = sqrt((x_o - col - x)*(x_o - col - x) +
            (y_o + row - y)*(y_o + row - y));
        new_length = r_sq/length;
        new_col = x_o - (x_o - col - x)*new_length/length;
        new_row = -y_o + (y_o + row - y)*new_length/length;
        plots(new_col,new_row,color);
        length = sqrt((x_o + col - x)*(x_o + col - x) +
            (y_o + row - y)*(y_o + row - y));
        new_length = r_sq/length;
        new_col = x_o - (x_o + col - x)*new_length/length;
        new_row = -y_o + (y_o + row - y)*new_length/length;
        plots(new_col,new_row,color);
        if (d<= 0)
```

```
        {
            col++;
            d += four_b_square*col;
        }
        row--;
        d += two_a_square * (3 - (row<<1));
    }
    b++;
    }
}

/*

    pikespk = PROGRAM TO GENERATE PIKE'S PEAK LANDSCAPE

*/

#include <stdio.h>
#include <math.h>
#include <dos.h>
#include <stdlib.h>
#include <time.h>
#include "tools.h"

void generate(int x1, int y_one, int x2, int y2, int x3,
    int y3, int level,int color1, int color2);
void midpoint();
void node(int x1, int y_one, int x2, int y2, int x3, int y3,
    int x4,int y4, int x5, int y5, int x6, int y6, int level,
    int color1, int color2);
void plot_triangle(int x1, int y_one, int x2, int y2, int x3,
    int y3,int color1, int color2);
float random_no (float limit_start, float limit_end);

int combination = 0,LINEWIDTH=1, OPERATOR=0;
unsigned long int PATTERN=0xFFFFFFFF;
int interim;
int i,j;
int y_max = 180;
int level[12] = {6,6,5,5,5,5,4,4,4,4};
int x1[12] = {-220,-780,-480,-100,-770,-550,-220,-200};
int y_one[12] = {-240,-200,0,-260,-300,-280,-280,-280};
int x2[12] = {120,40,-240,240,-250,-60,80,230};
int y2[12] = {100,130,60,40,-110,-140,-130,-120};
int x3[12] = {500,420,0,500,600,400,340,580};
int y3[12] = {-40,-120,-60,-180,-300,-300,-300,-300};
int colors[16] = {0,1,2,11,10,10,34,31,47,58,18,2,6,27,62,63};
float xz,yz,xp,yp;
int color_value=2;
float x,y;
```

```
main()
{
    setMode(1);
    cls();
    i=0;
    for (i=0; i<4; i++)
    {
        if (i==1)
            y_max = 160;
        else
            y_max = 180;
        generate(x1[i],y_one[i],x2[i],y2[i],x3[i],y3[i],
            level[i],1,0);
    }
    fillTriangle(-320,-200,-320,-110,319,-110,1);
    fillTriangle(319,-110,319,-200,-320,-200,1);
    y_max = -100;
    for (i=4; i<8; i++)
        generate(x1[i],y_one[i],x2[i],y2[i],x3[i],y3[i],
            level[i],1,0);
    getch();
    setMode(0);
}

void midpoint()
{
    float r,w;
    unsigned int seed;
    unsigned long int seed_gen;

    seed_gen = 350*(y+240) + x + 320;
    seed = seed_gen%32760 + 2;
    srand(seed);
    r = 0.5 + random_no(0,.16666);
    w = random_no(.015,.035);
    xz = r*x - (w+.05)*y;
    yz = r*y + (w + .05)*x;
}


/*

        generate() = Finds coordinates of four triangles
                     making up a larger triangle.

*/

void generate(int x1, int y_one, int x2, int y2, int x3,
    int y3, int level,int color1, int color2)
{
    int x4,x5,x6,y4,y5,y6,ax,bx,cx,ay,by,cy;
```

```
    x = (x2-x1);
    y = (y2-y_one);
    midpoint(x,y);
    x4 = x1 + xz;
    y4 = y_one + yz;
    x = x1-x3;
    y = y_one-y3;
    midpoint(x,y);
    x6 = x3 + xz;
    y6 = y3 + yz;
    x = (x3-x2);
    y = (y3-y2);
    midpoint(x,y);
    x5 = x2 + xz;
    y5 = y2 + yz;
    if (level == 0)
    {
        plot_triangle(x1,y_one,x6,y6,x4,y4,color1,color2);
        plot_triangle(x2,y2,x4,y4,x5,y5,color1,color2);
        plot_triangle(x3,y3,x5,y5,x6,y6,color1,color2);
        plot_triangle(x4,y4,x5,y5,x6,y6,color1,color2);
    }
    else
        node(x1,y_one,x2,y2,x3,y3,x4,y4,x5,y5,x6,y6,level,
            color1,color2); }

/*

        random_no() = Gets a floating point random number
                      between two limits.

*/

float random_no (float limit_start, float limit_end)
{
    float result;

    limit_end -= limit_start;
    limit_end = 16383.0/limit_end;
    result = (rand() - 16383)/limit_end;
    if (result >= 0)
        result += limit_start;
    else
        result -= limit_start;
    return(result);
}


/*
```

```
          node() = Runs 'generate' for four triangles

*/

void node(int x1, int y_one, int x2, int y2, int x3, int y3,
     int x4, int y4, int x5, int y5, int x6, int y6, int level,
     int color1, int color2)
{
     int x_ret1, y_ret1, x_ret2, y_ret2, x_ret3, y_ret3;
     if (level == 0)
        return;
     generate (x1,y_one,x6,y6,x4,y4,level-1,color1,color2);
     generate (x2,y2,x4,y4,x5,y5,level-1,color1,color2);
     generate (x3,y3,x5,y5,x6,y6,level-1,color1,color2);
     generate (x4,y4,x5,y5,x6,y6,level-1,color1,color2);
}


/*

     plot_triangle() = Determines colors to use to fill a
                       triangle.

*/

void plot_triangle(int x1, int y_one, int x2, int y2, int x3,
     int y3,int color1, int color2)
{
     int ytt,color,temp;
     float zt;

     if (y_one > y2)
        ytt = y_one;
     else
        ytt = y2;
     if (ytt < y3)
        ytt = y3;
     zt = (y_max+240)*(1-(float)(ytt+240)/(y_max+240)*
        (float)(ytt+240)/(y_max+240));
     temp = 32767/(y_max+240);
     temp = rand()/temp;
     if (temp <= zt)
        color = color1;
     else
        color = color2;
     if (ytt + 240 < (.25 * (y_max + 240)))
        color = color1;
     if (ytt+240 > (.98 * (y_max+240)))
        color = color2;
     fillTriangle(x1,y_one,x2,y2,x3,y3,color);
}
```

```
/*

                polya = PROGRAM TO GENERATE POLYA CURVE

*/

#include <stdio.h>
#include <math.h>
#include <dos.h>
#include "tools.h"

void generate (float X1, float Y1, float X2, float Y2,
    int level);

int combination = 0,LINEWIDTH=1, OPERATOR=0;
unsigned long int PATTERN=0xFFFFFFFF;
float turtle_theta;
int i, sign1 =1,px1,px2,py1,py2;
int generator_size = 3;
int level;
int init_size = 2;
int sign[17];
int initiator_x1[10] = {-150},initiator_x2[10]={150},
    initiator_y1[10]={-75},
    initiator_y2[10]={-75};
float Xpoints[25], Ypoints[25];
float turtle_x,turtle_y,turtle_r;

main()
{

    printf("\nEnter level (1 - 16): ");
    scanf("%d",&level);
    if (level < 1)
        level = 1;

    setMode(1);
    cls();
    for (i=level; i>0; i--)
    {
        sign[i] = sign1;
        sign1 *= -1;
    }
    for (i=0; i<init_size-1; i++)
    {
        generate(initiator_x1[i], initiator_y1[i],
            initiator_x2[i], initiator_y2[i], level);
    }
    getch();
    setMode(0);
}
```

```
/*

                generate() = Generates curve

*/

void generate (float X1, float Y1, float X2, float Y2,
    int level)
{
    int j,k,line;
        float a, b, Xpoints[25], Ypoints[25];

    turtle_r = (sqrt((X2 - X1)*(X2 - X1) + (Y2 - Y1)*(Y2 -
        Y1)))/1.41421;
    Xpoints[0] = X1;
    Ypoints[0] = Y1;
    Xpoints[2] = X2;
    Ypoints[2] = Y2;
    turtle_theta = point(X1,Y1,X2,Y2);
    turtle_x = X1;
    turtle_y = Y1;
    turn(sign[level]*(45));
    step();
    Xpoints[1] = turtle_x;
    Ypoints[1] = turtle_y;
    level--;
    if (level > 0)
    {
        for (j=0; j<generator_size-1; j++)
        {
            X1 = Xpoints[j];
                X2 = Xpoints[j+1];
                Y1 = Ypoints[j];
                Y2 = Ypoints[j+1];
            generate (X1,Y1,X2,Y2,level);
            sign[level] *= -1;
        }

    }
    else
    {
        for (k=0; k<generator_size-1; k++)
        {
            px1 = Xpoints[k];
            py1 = Ypoints[k];
            px2 = Xpoints[k+1];
            py2 = Ypoints[k+1];
            drawLine(px1,py1,px2,py2,1);
        }
    }
```

```
}

/*

            qkoch18 = PROGRAM TO GENERATE KOCH CURVES

*/

#include <stdio.h>
#include <math.h>
#include <dos.h>
#include "tools.h"
void generate (float X1, float Y1, float X2, float Y2,
    int level);

int generator_size = 18;
int init_size = 4;
int level;
int initiator_x1[10] = {-130,130,130,-130},initiator_x2[10]=
    {130,130,-130,-130},initiator_y1[10]={130,130,-130,-130},
    initiator_y2[10]={130,-130,-130,130};
int combination = 0,LINEWIDTH=1, OPERATOR=0;
unsigned long int PATTERN=0xFFFFFFFF;
float turtle_theta;
int i,px1,px2,py1,py2;
float Xpoints[25], Ypoints[25];
float turtle_x,turtle_y,turtle_r;

main()
{

    printf("\nEnter level (1 - 8): ");
    scanf("%d",&level);
    if (level < 1)
        level = 1;
    setMode(1);
    cls();

    for (i=0; i<init_size; i++)
        generate(initiator_x1[i], initiator_y1[i],
            initiator_x2[i],initiator_y2[i], level);
    getch();
    setMode(0);
}


/*

                generate() = Generates curve

*/
```

```
void generate (float X1, float Y1, float X2, float Y2,
    int level)
{
    int j,k,line,set_type;
        float a, b, Xpoints[25], Ypoints[25], temp,temp_r;

    level--;
    turtle_r = sqrt((((X2 - X1)*(X2 - X1) + (Y2 - Y1)*(Y2 -
        Y1)))/6.0;
    turtle_x = X1;
    turtle_y = Y1;
    Xpoints[0] = X1;
    Ypoints[0] = Y1;
    Xpoints[18] = X2;
    Ypoints[18] = Y2;
    turtle_theta = point(X1,Y1,X2,Y2);
    step();
    Xpoints[1] = turtle_x;
    Ypoints[1] = turtle_y;
    turn(90);
    step();
    Xpoints[2] = turtle_x;
    Ypoints[2] = turtle_y;
    step();
    Xpoints[3] = turtle_x;
    Ypoints[3] = turtle_y;
    turn(-90);
    step();
    Xpoints[4] = turtle_x;
    Ypoints[4] = turtle_y;
    step();
    Xpoints[5] = turtle_x;
    Ypoints[5] = turtle_y;
    turn(-90);
    step();
    Xpoints[6] = turtle_x;
    Ypoints[6] = turtle_y;
    turn(-90);
    step();
    Xpoints[7] = turtle_x;
    Ypoints[7] = turtle_y;
    turn(90);
    step();
    Xpoints[8] = turtle_x;
    Ypoints[8] = turtle_y;
    turn(90);
    step();
    Xpoints[9] = turtle_x;
    Ypoints[9] = turtle_y;
    step();
```

```
Xpoints[10] = turtle_x;
Ypoints[10] = turtle_y;
turn(-90);
step();
Xpoints[11] = turtle_x;
Ypoints[11] = turtle_y;
turn(-90);
step();
Xpoints[12] = turtle_x;
Ypoints[12] = turtle_y;
turn(90);
step();
Xpoints[13] = turtle_x;
Ypoints[13] = turtle_y;
turn(90);
step();
Xpoints[14] = turtle_x;
Ypoints[14] = turtle_y;
step();
Xpoints[15] = turtle_x;
Ypoints[15] = turtle_y;
turn(90);
step();
Xpoints[16] = turtle_x;
Ypoints[16] = turtle_y;
step();
Xpoints[17] = turtle_x;
Ypoints[17] = turtle_y;
if (level == 0)
{
    for (k=0; k<generator_size; k++)
    {
        px1 = Xpoints[k];
        py1 = Ypoints[k];
        px2 = Xpoints[k+1];
        py2 = Ypoints[k+1];
        drawLine(px1,py1,px2,py2,1);
    }
}
else
{
    for (j=0; j<generator_size; j++)
    {
        X1 = Xpoints[j];
        X2 = Xpoints[j+1];
        Y1 = Ypoints[j];
            Y2 = Ypoints[j+1];
        generate (X1,Y1,X2,Y2,level);
    }
    }
}
```

```
/*

        qkoch3 = PROGRAM TO GENERATE THREE SEGMENT KOCH CURVE

*/

#include <stdio.h>
#include <math.h>
#include <dos.h>
#include "tools.h"

void generate (float X1, float Y1, float X2, float Y2,
    int level);

int generator_size = 3;
int init_size = 4;
int level;
int initiator_x1[10] = {-130,130,130,-130},initiator_x2[10]=
    {130,130,-130,-130},initiator_y1[10]={130,130,-130,-130},
    initiator_y2[10]={130,-130,-130,130};
int combination = 0,LINEWIDTH=1, OPERATOR=0;
unsigned long int PATTERN=0xFFFFFFFF;
float turtle_theta;
int i;
float Xpoints[25], Ypoints[25];
float turtle_x,turtle_y,turtle_r;

main()
{

    printf("\nEnter level (1 - 8): ");
    scanf("%d",&level);
    if (level < 1)
        level = 1;
    setMode(16);
    cls(0);

    for (i=0; i<init_size; i++)
        generate(initiator_x1[i], initiator_y1[i],
            initiator_x2[i],initiator_y2[i], level);
    getch();
    setMode(0);
}

/*

                generate() = Generates curve

*/
```

```
void generate (float X1, float Y1, float X2, float Y2,
    int level)
{
    int j,k,line,set_type;
        float a, b, Xpoints[25], Ypoints[25], temp,temp_r;

    level--;
    turtle_r = sqrt((((X2 - X1)*(X2 - X1) + (Y2 - Y1)*(Y2 -
        Y1))/5.0);
    turtle_x = X1;
    turtle_y = Y1;
    Xpoints[0] = X1;
    Ypoints[0] = Y1;
    Xpoints[3] = X2;
    Ypoints[3] = Y2;
    turtle_theta = point(X1,Y1,X2,Y2);
    turn(26.56);
    step();
    Xpoints[1] = turtle_x;
    Ypoints[1] = turtle_y;
    turn(-90);
    step();
    Xpoints[2] = turtle_x;
    Ypoints[2] = turtle_y;
    if (level == 0)
    {
        for (k=0; k<generator_size; k++)
        {
            drawLine(Xpoints[k],Ypoints[k],
                Xpoints[k+1],Ypoints[k+1],15);
        }
    }
    else
    {
        for (j=0; j<generator_size; j++)
        {
            X1 = Xpoints[j];
            X2 = Xpoints[j+1];
            Y1 = Ypoints[j];
                Y2 = Ypoints[j+1];
            generate (X1,Y1,X2,Y2,level);
        }
    }
}


/*


                qkoch32 = PROGRAM TO GENERATE KOCH CURVES
```

```
*/

#include <stdio.h>
#include <math.h>
#include <dos.h>
#include "tools.h"

void generate (float X1, float Y1, float X2, float Y2,
    int level);

int generator_size = 32;
int init_size = 4;
int level;
int initiator_x1[10] = {-100,100,100,-100},
    initiator_x2[10]={100,100,-100,-100},initiator_y1[10]=
    {100,100,-100,-100}, initiator_y2[10]={100,-100,-100,100};
int combination = 0,LINEWIDTH=1, OPERATOR=0;
unsigned long int PATTERN=0xFFFFFFFF;
float turtle_theta;
int i,px1,px2,py1,py2;
float Xpoints[25], Ypoints[25];
float turtle_x,turtle_y,turtle_r;

main()
{

    printf("\nEnter level (1 - 8): ");
    scanf("%d",&level);
    if (level < 1)
        level = 1;
    setMode(1);
    cls();

    for (i=0; i<init_size; i++)
        generate(initiator_x1[i], initiator_y1[i],
            initiator_x2[i], initiator_y2[i], level);
    getch();
    setMode(0);
}

/*

                generate() = Generates curve

*/

void generate (float X1, float Y1, float X2, float Y2,
    int level)
{
    int j,k,line,set_type;
    float a, b, Xpoints[55], Ypoints[55], temp,temp_r;
```

```
level--;
turtle_r = sqrt((X2 - X1)*(X2 - X1) + (Y2 - Y1)*(Y2 -
    Y1))/8.0;
turtle_x = X1;
turtle_y = Y1;
Xpoints[0] = X1;
Ypoints[0] = Y1;
Xpoints[32] = X2;
Ypoints[32] = Y2;
turtle_theta = point(X1,Y1,X2,Y2);
turn(90);
step();
Xpoints[1] = turtle_x;
Ypoints[1] = turtle_y;
turn(-90);
step();
Xpoints[2] = turtle_x;
Ypoints[2] = turtle_y;
turn(90);
step();
Xpoints[3] = turtle_x;
Ypoints[3] = turtle_y;
turn(90);
step();
Xpoints[4] = turtle_x;
Ypoints[4] = turtle_y;
turn(-90);
step();
Xpoints[5] = turtle_x;
Ypoints[5] = turtle_y;
turn(-90);
step();
Xpoints[6] = turtle_x;
Ypoints[6] = turtle_y;
step();
Xpoints[7] = turtle_x;
Ypoints[7] = turtle_y;
turn(90);
step();
Xpoints[8] = turtle_x;
Ypoints[8] = turtle_y;
turn(-90);
step();
Xpoints[9] = turtle_x;
Ypoints[9] = turtle_y;
turn(-90);
step();
Xpoints[10] = turtle_x;
Ypoints[10] = turtle_y;
step();
```

```
Xpoints[11] = turtle_x;
Ypoints[11] = turtle_y;
turn(-90);
step();
Xpoints[12] = turtle_x;
Ypoints[12] = turtle_y;
turn(90);
step();
Xpoints[13] = turtle_x;
Ypoints[13] = turtle_y;
turn(90);
step();
Xpoints[14] = turtle_x;
Ypoints[14] = turtle_y;
step();
Xpoints[15] = turtle_x;
Ypoints[15] = turtle_y;
turn(-90);
step();
Xpoints[16] = turtle_x;
Ypoints[16] = turtle_y;
step();
Xpoints[17] = turtle_x;
Ypoints[17] = turtle_y;
turn(90);
step();
Xpoints[18] = turtle_x;
Ypoints[18] = turtle_y;
step();
Xpoints[19] = turtle_x;
Ypoints[19] = turtle_y;
turn(-90);
step();
Xpoints[20] = turtle_x;
Ypoints[20] = turtle_y;
turn(-90);
step();
Xpoints[21] = turtle_x;
Ypoints[21] = turtle_y;
turn(90);
step();
Xpoints[22] = turtle_x;
Ypoints[22] = turtle_y;
step();
Xpoints[23] = turtle_x;
Ypoints[23] = turtle_y;
turn(90);
step();
Xpoints[24] = turtle_x;
Ypoints[24] = turtle_y;
turn(90);
```

```
step();
Xpoints[25] = turtle_x;
Ypoints[25] = turtle_y;
turn(-90);
step();
Xpoints[26] = turtle_x;
Ypoints[26] = turtle_y;
step();
Xpoints[27] = turtle_x;
Ypoints[27] = turtle_y;
turn(90);
step();
Xpoints[28] = turtle_x;
Ypoints[28] = turtle_y;
turn(90);
step();
Xpoints[29] = turtle_x;
Ypoints[29] = turtle_y;
turn(-90);
step();
Xpoints[30] = turtle_x;
Ypoints[30] = turtle_y;
turn(-90);
step();
Xpoints[31] = turtle_x;
Ypoints[31] = turtle_y;
if (level == 0)
{
    for (k=0; k<generator_size; k++)
    {
        px1 = Xpoints[k];
        py1 = Ypoints[k];
        px2 = Xpoints[k+1];
        py2 = Ypoints[k+1];
        drawLine(px1,py1,px2,py2,1);
    }
}
else
{
    for (j=0; j<generator_size; j++)
    {
        X1 = Xpoints[j];
        X2 = Xpoints[j+1];
        Y1 = Ypoints[j];
            Y2 = Ypoints[j+1];
        generate (X1,Y1,X2,Y2,level);
    }
    }
}

/*
```

```
               qkoch50 = PROGRAM TO GENERATE KOCH CURVES
*/
```

```c
#include <stdio.h>
#include <math.h>
#include <dos.h>
#include "tools.h"

void generate (float X1, float Y1, float X2, float Y2,
    int level);

int generator_size = 50;
int init_size = 4;
int level;
int initiator_x1[10] = {-120,120,120,-120},initiator_x2[10]=
    {120,120,-120,-120},initiator_y1[10]={120,120,-120,-120},
    initiator_y2[10]={120,-120,-120,120};
int combination = 0,LINEWIDTH=1, OPERATOR=0;
unsigned long int PATTERN=0xFFFFFFFF;
float turtle_theta;
int i,px1,py1,px2,py2;
float Xpoints[25], Ypoints[25];
float turtle_x,turtle_y,turtle_r;

main()
{

    printf("\nEnter level (1 - 8): ");
    scanf("%d",&level);
    if (level < 1)
        level = 1;
    setMode(1);
    cls();

    for (i=0; i<init_size; i++)
        generate(initiator_x1[i], initiator_y1[i],
            initiator_x2[i], initiator_y2[i], level);
    getch();
    setMode(0);
}

/*

                  generate() = Generates curve

*/

void generate (float X1, float Y1, float X2, float Y2,
    int level)
```

```
{
    int j,k,line,set_type;
    float a, b, Xpoints[55], Ypoints[55], temp,temp_r;

    level--;
    turtle_r = sqrt((X2 - X1)*(X2 - X1) + (Y2 - Y1)*(Y2 -
        Y1))/10.0;
    turtle_x = X1;
    turtle_y = Y1;
    Xpoints[0] = X1;
    Ypoints[0] = Y1;
    Xpoints[50] = X2;
    Ypoints[50] = Y2;
    turtle_theta = point(X1,Y1,X2,Y2);
    step();
    Xpoints[1] = turtle_x;
    Ypoints[1] = turtle_y;
    turn(90);
    step();
    Xpoints[2] = turtle_x;
    Ypoints[2] = turtle_y;
    turn(-90);
    step();
    Xpoints[3] = turtle_x;
    Ypoints[3] = turtle_y;
    turn(-90);
    step();
    Xpoints[4] = turtle_x;
    Ypoints[4] = turtle_y;
    step();
    Xpoints[5] = turtle_x;
    Ypoints[5] = turtle_y;
    step();
    Xpoints[6] = turtle_x;
    Ypoints[6] = turtle_y;
    turn(90);
    step();
    Xpoints[7] = turtle_x;
    Ypoints[7] = turtle_y;
    step();
    Xpoints[8] = turtle_x;
    Ypoints[8] = turtle_y;
    turn(-90);
    step();
    Xpoints[9] = turtle_x;
    Ypoints[9] = turtle_y;
    step();
    Xpoints[10] = turtle_x;
    Ypoints[10] = turtle_y;
    turn(90);
    step();
```

```
Xpoints[11] = turtle_x;
Ypoints[11] = turtle_y;
turn(90);
step();
Xpoints[12] = turtle_x;
Ypoints[12] = turtle_y;
step();
Xpoints[13] = turtle_x;
Ypoints[13] = turtle_y;
step();
Xpoints[14] = turtle_x;
Ypoints[14] = turtle_y;
turn(90);
step();
Xpoints[15] = turtle_x;
Ypoints[15] = turtle_y;
step();
Xpoints[16] = turtle_x;
Ypoints[16] = turtle_y;
turn(-90);
step();
Xpoints[17] = turtle_x;
Ypoints[17] = turtle_y;
step();
Xpoints[18] = turtle_x;
Ypoints[18] = turtle_y;
step();
Xpoints[19] = turtle_x;
Ypoints[19] = turtle_y;
step();
Xpoints[20] = turtle_x;
Ypoints[20] = turtle_y;
turn(-90);
step();
Xpoints[21] = turtle_x;
Ypoints[21] = turtle_y;
turn(-90);
step();
Xpoints[22] = turtle_x;
Ypoints[22] = turtle_y;
step();
Xpoints[23] = turtle_x;
Ypoints[23] = turtle_y;
step();
Xpoints[24] = turtle_x;
Ypoints[24] = turtle_y;
turn(90);
step();
Xpoints[25] = turtle_x;
Ypoints[25] = turtle_y;
step();
```

```
Xpoints[26] = turtle_x;
Ypoints[26] = turtle_y;
turn(-90);
step();
Xpoints[27] = turtle_x;
Ypoints[27] = turtle_y;
step();
Xpoints[28] = turtle_x;
Ypoints[28] = turtle_y;
step();
Xpoints[29] = turtle_x;
Ypoints[29] = turtle_y;
turn(90);
step();
Xpoints[30] = turtle_x;
Ypoints[30] = turtle_y;
turn(90);
step();
Xpoints[31] = turtle_x;
Ypoints[31] = turtle_y;
step();
Xpoints[32] = turtle_x;
Ypoints[32] = turtle_y;
step();
Xpoints[33] = turtle_x;
Ypoints[33] = turtle_y;
step();
Xpoints[34] = turtle_x;
Ypoints[34] = turtle_y;
turn(90);
step();
Xpoints[35] = turtle_x;
Ypoints[35] = turtle_y;
step();
Xpoints[36] = turtle_x;
Ypoints[36] = turtle_y;
turn(-90);
step();
Xpoints[37] = turtle_x;
Ypoints[37] = turtle_y;
step();
Xpoints[38] = turtle_x;
Ypoints[38] = turtle_y;
step();
Xpoints[39] = turtle_x;
Ypoints[39] = turtle_y;
turn(-90);
step();
Xpoints[40] = turtle_x;
Ypoints[40] = turtle_y;
turn(-90);
```

```
step();
Xpoints[41] = turtle_x;
Ypoints[41] = turtle_y;
step();
Xpoints[42] = turtle_x;
Ypoints[42] = turtle_y;
turn(90);
step();
Xpoints[43] = turtle_x;
Ypoints[43] = turtle_y;
step();
Xpoints[44] = turtle_x;
Ypoints[44] = turtle_y;
turn(-90);
step();
Xpoints[45] = turtle_x;
Ypoints[45] = turtle_y;
step();
Xpoints[46] = turtle_x;
Ypoints[46] = turtle_y;
step();
Xpoints[47] = turtle_x;
Ypoints[47] = turtle_y;
turn(90);
step();
Xpoints[48] = turtle_x;
Ypoints[48] = turtle_y;
turn(90);
step();
Xpoints[49] = turtle_x;
Ypoints[49] = turtle_y;
if (level == 0)
{
    for (k=0; k<generator_size; k++)
    {
        px1 = Xpoints[k];
        py1 = Ypoints[k];
        px2 = Xpoints[k+1];
        py2 = Ypoints[k+1];
        drawLine(px1,py1,px2,py2,1);
    }
}
else
{
    for (j=0; j<generator_size; j++)
    {
        X1 = Xpoints[j];
        X2 = Xpoints[j+1];
        Y1 = Ypoints[j];
            Y2 = Ypoints[j+1];
        generate (X1,Y1,X2,Y2,level);
```

```
            }
            }
    }

    /*

         qkoch8 = PROGRAM TO GENERATE THREE SEGMENT KOCH CURVE

    */

    #include <stdio.h>
    #include <math.h>
    #include <dos.h>
    #include "tools.h"

    void generate (float X1, float Y1, float X2, float Y2,
        int level);

    int generator_size = 8;
    int init_size = 4;
    int level;
    int initiator_x1[10] = {-130,130,130,-130},initiator_x2[10]=
        {130,130,-130,-130},initiator_y1[10]={130,130,-130,-130},
        initiator_y2[10]={130,-130,-130,130};
    int combination = 0,LINEWIDTH=1, OPERATOR=0;
    unsigned long int PATTERN=0xFFFFFFFF;
    float turtle_theta;
    int i,px1,py1,px2,py2;
    float Xpoints[25], Ypoints[25];
    float turtle_x,turtle_y,turtle_r;

    main()
    {

        printf("\nEnter level (1 - 8): ");
        scanf("%d",&level);
        if (level < 1)
            level = 1;
        setMode(1);
        cls();

        for (i=0; i<init_size; i++)
            generate(initiator_x1[i], initiator_y1[i],
                initiator_x2[i], initiator_y2[i], level);
        getch();
        setMode(0);
    }

    /*

                    generate() = Generates curve
```

```
*/

void generate (float X1, float Y1, float X2, float Y2,
        int level)
{
    int j,k,line,set_type;
        float a, b, Xpoints[25], Ypoints[25], temp,temp_r;

    level--;
    turtle_r = sqrt((X2 - X1)*(X2 - X1) + (Y2 - Y1)*(Y2 -
        Y1))/4.0;
    turtle_x = X1;
    turtle_y = Y1;
    Xpoints[0] = X1;
    Ypoints[0] = Y1;
    Xpoints[8] = X2;
    Ypoints[8] = Y2;
    turtle_theta = point(X1,Y1,X2,Y2);
    step();
    Xpoints[1] = turtle_x;
    Ypoints[1] = turtle_y;
    turn(90);
    step();
    Xpoints[2] = turtle_x;
    Ypoints[2] = turtle_y;
    turn(-90);
    step();
    Xpoints[3] = turtle_x;
    Ypoints[3] = turtle_y;
    turn(-90);
    step();
    Xpoints[4] = turtle_x;
    Ypoints[4] = turtle_y;
    step();
    Xpoints[5] = turtle_x;
    Ypoints[5] = turtle_y;
    turn(90);
    step();
    Xpoints[6] = turtle_x;
    Ypoints[6] = turtle_y;
    turn(90);
    step();
    Xpoints[7] = turtle_x;
    Ypoints[7] = turtle_y;
    if (level == 0)
    {
        for (k=0; k<generator_size; k++)
        {
            px1 = Xpoints[k];
            py1 = Ypoints[k];
```

```
            px2 = Xpoints[k+1];
            py2 = Ypoints[k+1];
            drawLine(px1,py1,px2,py2,1);
        }
    }
    else
    {
        for (j=0; j<generator_size; j++)
        {
            X1 = Xpoints[j];
            X2 = Xpoints[j+1];
            Y1 = Ypoints[j];
                Y2 = Ypoints[j+1];
            generate (X1,Y1,X2,Y2,level);
        }
        }
}

/*

        sanmarco = PROGRAM TO GENERATE SAN MARCOS   DRAGON

*/

#include <stdio.h>
#include <math.h>
#include <dos.h>
#include <string.h>
#include "tools.h"

const int maxcol = 719;
const int maxrow = 347;
const int combination = 0;

int max_iterations = 64;
int max_size = 4;
int LINEWIDTH=1, OPERATOR=0;
unsigned long int PATTERN=0xFFFFFFFF;
int i,x,y,limit=0;

main()
{
    float Xmax= 1.2, Xmin=-.3, Ymax=.60, Ymin=-.60, P=3.0, Q=0,
        deltaX, deltaY, X, Y, Xtemp, Ytemp,Xstart,Ystart;
    int col,row;
        char ch;

    setMode(1);
    cls();
    deltaX = (Xmax - Xmin)/(maxcol);
        deltaY = (Ymax - Ymin)/(maxrow);
```

```
            for (col=0; col<=maxcol; col++)
            {
            if (kbhit() != 0) break;
                    Xstart = Xmin + col * deltaX;
        Ystart = Ymax;
            for (row=0; row<=maxrow; row++)
                    {
                            X = Xstart;
            Y = Ystart;
            for (i=0; i<max_iterations && (X*X + Y*Y <
                max_size); i++)
            {
                Ytemp = X+X-1;
                Ytemp *= Y;
                X += (Y+X)*(Y-X);
                Y = Q*X - P*Ytemp;
                X = P*X + Q*Ytemp;
            }
            if (i >= max_iterations)
                plot(col, row, 1);
            Ystart -= deltaY;
        }
    }
    getch();
    setMode(0);
}

/*

    sierbox = PROGRAM TO GENERATE RECTANGULAR SIERPINSKI
             GASKET

*/

#include <stdio.h>
#include <math.h>
#include <dos.h>
#include "tools.h"

void fillRect(int x1, int y01, int x2, int y2,int color);
void node(int x1, int y01, int x2, int y2, int x3, int y3,
    int x4,int y4, int level,int length);
void generate (int x1, int y01, int x2, int y2, int level,
    int length);

int x1,y01,x2,y2,x3,y3;
int level = 3;
int combination = 0,LINEWIDTH=1, OPERATOR=0;
unsigned long int PATTERN=0xFFFFFFFF;

main()
```

```
{
    int x1,x2,x3,x4,y01,y2,y3,y4,length;
    x1 = -220;
    y01 = -220;
    x2 = 220;
    y2 = 220;
    length = 440;

    setMode(1);
    cls();
    fillRect(x1,y01,x2,y2,1);
    generate(x1,y01,x2,y2,level,length);
    getch();
    setMode(0);
}

/*

        generate() = Divides box into nine smaller boxes

*/

void generate (int x1,int y01, int x2, int y2, int level,
    int length)
{
    int line_length,x3,y3,x4,y4;

    line_length = length/3;
    x3 = x1 + line_length;
    y3 = y01 + line_length;
    x4 = x2 - line_length;
    y4 = y2 - line_length;
    node (x1,y01,x2,y2,x3,y3,x4,y4,level,line_length);
}

/*

        node() = blanks middle boxe and calls 'generate'
                for   eight surrounding boxes

*/

void node(int x1, int y01, int x2, int y2, int x3, int y3,
    int x4, int y4, int level,int length)
{
    fillRect(x3,y3,x4,y4,0);
    if (level == 0)
        return(0);
    generate (x1,y01,x3,y3,level-1,length);
    generate (x3,y01,x4,y3,level-1,length);
    generate (x4,y01,x2,y3,level-1,length);
```

```
        generate (x1,y3,x3,y4,level-1,length);
        generate (x4,y3,x2,y4,level-1,length);
        generate (x1,y4,x3,y2,level-1,length);
        generate (x3,y4,x4,y2,level-1,length);
        generate (x4,y4,x2,y2,level-1,length);
}

/*

        fillRect() = fills a rectangle with a specified color

*/

void fillRect(int x1, int y01, int x2, int y2,int color)
{
    int i,j;

        x1 = ((x1 + 319)*18) >> 4;
    y01 = 174 - ((93*y01) >> 7);
        x2 = ((x2 + 319)*18) >> 4;
    y2 = 174 - ((93*y2) >> 7);

    for (i=y2; i<=y01; i++)
    {
        for (j=x1; j<= x2; j++)
            plot(j,i,color);
    }
}

/*

        sierchet = GENERATES SIERPINSKI TRIANGLE WITH 1/3
                   AND 2/3 MULTIPLIERS

*/

#include <stdio.h>
#include <math.h>
#include <stdlib.h>
#include "tools.h"

int  x,y;
int switcher;
long int i;

main()
{
    setMode(1);
    x = 32767/719;
    x = rand()/x;
    y = 32767/347;
```

```
    y = rand()/y;
    for (i=0; i<120000; i++)
    {
        switcher = 32767/4;
        switcher = rand()/switcher;
        switch(switcher)
        {
            case 0: x /= 3;
                y /= 3;
                break;

            case 1: x = (x + 719)*2/3;
                y /= 3;
                break;

            case 2: x = (x + 719)/3;
                y = (y + 347)*2/3;
                break;
            case 3: x /= 3;
                y = (y + 347)*2/3;
        }
        if ((x>=0) && (x<720) && (y>=0) && (y<348))
            plot(x,y,1);
    }
    getch();
    setMode(0);
}

/*

    siergask = PROGRAM TO GENERATE SIERPINSKI TRIANGLE GASKET

*/

#include <stdio.h>
#include <math.h>
#include <dos.h>
#include "tools.h"

void node(int x1, int y01, int x2, int y2, int x3, int y3,
    int x4,int y4, int x5, int y5, int x6, int y6, int level,
    int length);
void sort(int index, int x_coord[], int y_coord[]);
void fillTriangle (int x1, int y01, int x2, int y2, int x3,
    int y3, int color);
void generate (int x1, int y01, int x2, int y2, int x3, int y3,
    int level, int length);

int x1,y01,x2,y2,x3,y3;
int level = 5;
int combination = 0,LINEWIDTH=1, OPERATOR=0;
```

```
unsigned long int PATTERN=0xFFFFFFFF;
float turtle_theta;
int i, sign;

main()
{
    int x1,x2,x3,y01,y2,y3,length;
    x1 = -256;
    y01 = -220;
    x2 = 256;
    y2 = -220;
    x3 = 0;
    y3 = 223;
    length = 512;

    setMode(1);
    cls();
    fillTriangle(x1,y01,x2,y2,x3,y3,1);
    generate(x1,y01,x2,y2,x3,y3,level,length);
    getch();
    setMode(0);
}

/*

        generate() = splits triangle into four small
                     small triangles

*/

void generate (int x1,int y01, int x2, int y2, int x3, int y3,
    int level, int length)
{
    int line_length,x4,y4,x5,y5,x6,y6;

    line_length = length/2;
    x4 = x1 + line_length;
    y4 = y01;
    x5 = x1 + line_length/2;
    y5 = y01 + 1.732*line_length/2;
    x6 = x5 + line_length;
    y6 = y5;
    node (x1,y01,x2,y2,x3,y3,x4,y4,x5,y5,x6,y6,level,
        line_length);
}

/*

    fillTriangle() = fills a triangle in specified color

*/
```

```
void fillTriangle (int x1, int y01, int x2, int y2, int x3,
    int y3, int color)
{

    #define sign(x) ((x) > 0 ? 1:  ((x) == 0 ? 0:  (-1)))

    int dx, dy, dxabs, dyabs, i, index=0, j, k, px, py, sdx,
        sdy, x, y, xpoint[4], ypoint[4], toggle, old_sdy,sy0;
        long int check;
    int *x_coord, *y_coord;

    x_coord = (int *) malloc(4000 * sizeof(int));
    y_coord = (int *) malloc(4000 * sizeof(int));
    xpoint[0] = ((x1 + 319)*18) >> 4;
    ypoint[0] = 174 - ((93*y01) >> 7);
    xpoint[1] = ((x2 + 319)*18) >> 4;
    ypoint[1] = 174 - ((93*y2) >> 7);
    xpoint[2] = ((x3 + 319)*18) >> 4;
    ypoint[2] = 174 - ((93*y3) >> 7);
    xpoint[3] = xpoint[0];
    ypoint[3] = ypoint[0];
    i = 3;
    px = xpoint[0];
    py = ypoint[0];
    if (ypoint[1] == ypoint[0])
    {
        x_coord[index] = px;
        y_coord[index++] = py;
    }
    for (j=0; j<i; j++)
    {
        dx = xpoint[j+1] - xpoint[j];
        dy = ypoint[j+1] - ypoint[j];
        sdx = sign(dx);
        sdy = sign(dy);
        if (j==0)
        {
            old_sdy = sdy;
            sy0 = sdy;
        }
        dxabs = abs(dx);
        dyabs = abs(dy);
        x = 0;
        y = 0;
        if (dxabs >= dyabs)
        {
            for (k=0; k<dxabs; k++)
            {
                y += dyabs;
                if (y>=dxabs)
```

```
                {
                    y -= dxabs;
                    py += sdy;
                    if (old_sdy != sdy)
                    {
                        old_sdy = sdy;
                        index--;
                    }
                    x_coord[index] = px+sdx;
                    y_coord[index++] = py;
                }
                px += sdx;
            }
        }
        else
        {
            for (k=0; k<dyabs; k++)
            {
                x += dxabs;
                if (x>=dyabs)
                {
                    x -= dyabs;
                    px += sdx;
                }
                py += sdy;
                if (old_sdy != sdy)
                {
                    old_sdy = sdy;
                    if (sdy != 0)
                        index--;
                }

                x_coord[index] = px;
                y_coord[index++] = py;
            }
        }
        }
index--;
if (sy0 + sdy== 0)
    index--;
sort(index,x_coord,y_coord);
toggle = 0;
        if (x_coord[0] < 0)
            x_coord[0] = 0;
        if (x_coord[0] > 639)
            x_coord[0] = 639;
for (i=0; i<index; i++)
{
    if (x_coord[i+1] < 0)
        x_coord[i+1] = 0;
    if (x_coord[i+1] > 719)
```

```
            x_coord[i+1] = 719;
        if ((y_coord[i] == y_coord[i+1]) && (toggle == 0) &&
            (y_coord[i] >= 0) && (y_coord[i] < 348))
        {
            for (j=x_coord[i]; j<=x_coord[i+1]; j++)
                plot(j,y_coord[i],color);
            toggle = 1;
        }
        else
            toggle = 0;
    }

    free(x_coord);
    free(y_coord);
}

/*

    sort() = sorts coordinate pairs for drawing and
             filling polygons.

*/

void sort(int index, int x_coord[], int y_coord[])
{
    int d=4,i,j,k,temp;

    while (d<=index)
        d*=2;
    d-=1;
    while (d>1)
    {
        d/=2;
            for (j=0; j<=(index-d); j++)
        {
            for (i=j; i>=0; i-=d)
            {
                if ((y_coord[i+d] < y_coord[i]) ||
                    ((y_coord[i+d] == y_coord[i]) &&
                    (x_coord[i+d] <= x_coord[i])))
                {
                    temp = y_coord[i];
                    y_coord[i] = y_coord[i+d];
                    y_coord[i+d] = temp;
                    temp = x_coord[i];
                    x_coord[i] = x_coord[i+d];
                    x_coord[i+d] = temp;
                }
            }
        }
    }
}
```

```
}

/*

    node() = blanks center triangle and calls 'generate'
             for three surrounding triangles

*/

void node(int x1, int y01, int x2, int y2, int x3, int y3,
    int x4,int y4, int x5, int y5, int x6, int y6, int level,
    int length)
{
    fillTriangle(x4,y4,x5,y5,x6,y6,0);
    if (level == 0)
        return(0);
    generate (x1,y01,x4,y4,x5,y5,level-1,length);
    generate (x4,y4,x2,y2,x6,y6,level-1,length);
    generate (x5,y5,x6,y6,x3,y3,level-1,length);
}


/*

            sierp = PROGRAM TO GENERATE SIERPINSKI CURVES

*/

#include <stdio.h>
#include <math.h>
#include <dos.h>
#include "tools.h"

void generate (float X1, float Y1, float X2, float Y2,
    int level,int sign);
int generator_size = 3;
int init_size = 1;
int level;
int initiator_x1[10] = {-130,130,130,-130},initiator_x2[10]=
    {130,130,-130,-130},initiator_y1[10]={0,130,130,-130,-130},
    initiator_y2[10]={0,130,-130,-130,130};
int combination = 0,LINEWIDTH=1, OPERATOR=0;
unsigned long int PATTERN=0xFFFFFFFF;
float turtle_theta;
int i, sign,px1,px2,py1,py2;
float Xpoints[25], Ypoints[25];
float turtle_x,turtle_y,turtle_r,angle;

main()
{
    setMode(0);
```

```
    printf("\nEnter level (1 - 12): ");
    scanf("%d",&level);
    if (level < 1)
        level = 1;
    setMode(1);
    cls();
    for (i=0; i<init_size; i++)
        generate(initiator_x1[i], initiator_y1[i],
            initiator_x2[i], initiator_y2[i], level,1);
    getch();
    setMode(0);
}

/*

                    generate() = Generates curve

*/

void generate (float X1, float Y1, float X2, float Y2,
    int level,int sign)
{
    int j,k,line,int_sign;
        float a, b, Xpoints[25], Ypoints[25], temp,temp_r;

    turtle_r = sqrt((X2 - X1)*(X2 - X1) + (Y2 - Y1)*(Y2 -
        Y1))/2.0;
    turtle_x = X1;
    turtle_y = Y1;
    Xpoints[0] = X1;
    Ypoints[0] = Y1;
    Xpoints[3] = X2;
    Ypoints[3] = Y2;
    turtle_theta = point(X1,Y1,X2,Y2);
    turn(60*sign);
    step();
    Xpoints[1] = turtle_x;
    Ypoints[1] = turtle_y;
    turn(-60*sign);
    step();
    Xpoints[2] = turtle_x;
    Ypoints[2] = turtle_y;
    level--;
    sign *= -1;
    if (level == 0)
    {
        for (k=0; k<generator_size; k++)
        {
            px1 = Xpoints[k];
            py1 = Ypoints[k];
            px2 = Xpoints[k+1];
```

```
                py2 = Ypoints[k+1];
                drawLine(px1,py1,px2,py2,1);
            }
        }
    else
        {
        int_sign = sign;
        for (j=0; j<generator_size; j++)
            {
            X1 = Xpoints[j];
            X2 = Xpoints[j+1];
            Y1 = Ypoints[j];
                Y2 = Ypoints[j+1];
            generate (X1,Y1,X2,Y2,level,int_sign);
            int_sign *= -1;
            }
            }
}

/*
    sirchet2 = PROGRAM TO GENERATE SIERPINSKI TRIANGLE
*/

#include <stdio.h>
#include <math.h>
#include <stdlib.h>
#include "tools.h"

float s2,x,y;
int switcher;
long int i;

main()
{
    setMode(1);
    s2 = sqrt(0.5);
    x = 32767/719;
    x = rand()/x;
    y = 32767/347;
    y = rand()/y;
    for (i=0; i<120000; i++)
        {
        switcher = 32767/3;
        switcher = rand()/switcher;
        switch(switcher)
            {
            case 0: x *= s2;
                y *= s2;
                break;

            case 1: x = sqrt((719.*719. + x*x)/2);
```

```
            y *= s2;
            break;

        case 2: x = sqrt((340.*340. + x*x)/2.);
                y = sqrt((347.*347. + y*y)/2.);
        }
        plot(x,y,1);
    }
    getch();
    setMode(0);
}

/*

sirchet3 = PROGRAM TO GENERATE SIERPINSKI TRIANGLE

*/

#include <stdio.h>
#include <math.h>
#include <stdlib.h>
#include "tools.h"

float s2,x,y;
int switcher;
long int i;
main()
{
    setMode(16);
    x = 32767/719;
    x = rand()/x;
    y = 32767/347;
    y = rand()/y;
    for (i=0; i<120000; i++)
    {
        switcher = 32767/3;
        switcher = rand()/switcher;
        switch(switcher)
        {
            case 0: x /= 2;
                y /= 2;
                break;

            case 1: x = (x + 719)/2;
                y /= 2;
                break;

            case 2: x = (x + 340)/2;
                y = (y + 347)/2;
        }
        plot(x,y,1);
```

```
        }
    getch();
    setMode(0);
}

/*

        snoflake() = PROGRAM TO GENERATE KOCH SNOWFLAKE

*/

#include <stdio.h>
#include <math.h>
#include <dos.h>
#include "tools.h"

void generate (float X1, float Y1, float X2, float Y2,
    int level);

int combination = 0,LINEWIDTH=1, operator=0;
unsigned long int PATTERN=0xFFFFFFFF;
float turtle_theta;
int i;
int generator_size = 5;
int level;
int init_size = 3,px1,px2,py1,py2;
int initiator_x1[10] = {-150,0,150},initiator_x2[10]={0,
    150,-150},initiator_y1[10]={-75,185,-75},
    initiator_y2[10]={185,-75,-75};
float Xpoints[25], Ypoints[25];
float turtle_x,turtle_y,turtle_r;

main()
{

    printf("\nEnter level (1 - 8): ");
    scanf("%d",&level);
    if (level < 1)
        level = 1;
    setMode(1);
    cls();

    for (i=0; i<init_size; i++)
    {
        generate(initiator_x1[i], initiator_y1[i],
            initiator_x2[i], initiator_y2[i], level);
    }
    getch();
    setMode(0);
}
```

```
/*

                    generate() = Generates curve

*/

void generate (float X1, float Y1, float X2, float Y2,
    int level)
{
    int j,k,line;
        float a, b, Xpoints[25], Ypoints[25];

    level--;
    turtle_r = (sqrt((X2 - X1)*(X2 - X1) + (Y2 - Y1)*(Y2 -
        Y1)))/3.0;
    Xpoints[0] = X1;
    Ypoints[0] = Y1;
    Xpoints[4] = X2;
    Ypoints[4] = Y2;
    turtle_theta = point(X1,Y1,X2,Y2);
    turtle_x = X1;
    turtle_y = Y1;
    step();
    Xpoints[1] = turtle_x;
    Ypoints[1] = turtle_y;
    turn(60);
    step();
    Xpoints[2] = turtle_x;
    Ypoints[2] = turtle_y;
        turn(-120);
    step();
    Xpoints[3] = turtle_x;
    Ypoints[3] = turtle_y;
    if (level > 0)
    {
        for (j=0; j<generator_size-1; j++)
        {
                X1 = Xpoints[j];
                X2 = Xpoints[j+1];
                Y1 = Ypoints[j];
                Y2 = Ypoints[j+1];
            generate (X1,Y1,X2,Y2,level);
        }
    }
    else
    {
        for (k=0; k<generator_size-1; k++)
        {
            px1 = Xpoints[k];
            py1 = Ypoints[k];
            px2 = Xpoints[k+1];
```

```
                py2 = Ypoints[k+1];
                drawLine(px1,py1,px2,py2,1);
            }
        }
    }


/*

        snow13 = generates snowflake with 13 segment generator

*/

#include <stdio.h>
#include <math.h>
#include <dos.h>
#include "tools.h"

void generate (float X1, float Y1, float X2, float Y2,
    int level, int type, int sign);

int combination = 0,LINEWIDTH=1, OPERATOR=0;
unsigned long int PATTERN=0xFFFFFFFF;
int color,flag = 0,i,start_level;
int generator_size = 13;
int start_level,level,px1,px2,py1,py2;
int init_size = 1,sign = 1;
int initiator_x1[10] = {-125},initiator_x2[10]={125},
    initiator_y1[10]={0},initiator_y2[10]={0};
float Xpoints[25], Ypoints[25];
float turtle_x,turtle_y,turtle_r,turtle_theta;

main()
{
    printf("\nEnter level (1 - 8): ");
    scanf("%d",&level);
    if (level < 1)
        level = 1;
    start_level = level;
    setMode(1);
    cls();

    for (i=0; i<init_size; i++)
    {
        generate(initiator_x1[i], initiator_y1[i],
            initiator_x2[i], initiator_y2[i], level,0,sign);
    }
    getch();
    setMode(0);
}
```

```
/*

                    generate() = Generates curve

*/

void generate (float X1, float Y1, float X2, float Y2,
    int level, int type, int sign)
{
    int j,k,line,set_type;
        float a, b, Xpoints[25], Ypoints[25], temp,temp_r;


    switch (type)
    {
        case 0: break;

        case 1: sign *= -1;
            break;

        case 2: sign *= -1;
        case 3: temp = X1;
            X1 = X2;
            X2 = temp;
            temp = Y1;
            Y1 = Y2;
            Y2 = temp;
            break;
    }
    level--;
    turtle_r = (sqrt((X2 - X1)*(X2 - X1) + (Y2 - Y1)*(Y2 -
        Y1)))/3.0;
    Xpoints[0] = X1;
    Ypoints[0] = Y1;
    Xpoints[13] = X2;
    Ypoints[13] = Y2;
    turtle_theta = point(X1,Y1,X2,Y2);
    turtle_x = X1;
    turtle_y = Y1;
    turn(60*sign);
    step();
    Xpoints[1] = turtle_x;
    Ypoints[1] = turtle_y;
    step();
    Xpoints[2] = turtle_x;
    Ypoints[2] = turtle_y;
    turn(-60*sign);
    step();
    Xpoints[3] = turtle_x;
    Ypoints[3] = turtle_y;
        turn(-60*sign);
```

```
step();
Xpoints[4] = turtle_x;
Ypoints[4] = turtle_y;
    turn(-60*sign);
step();
Xpoints[12] = turtle_x;
Ypoints[12] = turtle_y;
    turn(-60*sign);
step();
Xpoints[11] = turtle_x;
Ypoints[11] = turtle_y;
turtle_r = (sqrt((Xpoints[11] - Xpoints[4])*(Xpoints[11] -
    Xpoints[4]) + (Ypoints[11] - Ypoints[4])*(Ypoints[11]
    - Ypoints[4])))/3.0;
turtle_theta = point(Xpoints[4],Ypoints[4],Xpoints[11],
    Ypoints[11]);
turtle_x = Xpoints[4];
turtle_y = Ypoints[4];
turn(-60*sign);
step();
Xpoints[5] = turtle_x;
Ypoints[5] = turtle_y;
step();
Xpoints[6] = turtle_x;
Ypoints[6] = turtle_y;
turn(60*sign);
step();
Xpoints[7] = turtle_x;
Ypoints[7] = turtle_y;
turn(60*sign);
step();
Xpoints[8] = turtle_x;
Ypoints[8] = turtle_y;
turn(60*sign);
step();
Xpoints[10] = turtle_x;
Ypoints[10] = turtle_y;
turn(60*sign);
step();
Xpoints[9] = turtle_x;
Ypoints[9] = turtle_y;
if (level == 0)
{
    for (k=0; k<generator_size; k++)
    {
        px1 = Xpoints[k];
        py1 = Ypoints[k];
        px2 = Xpoints[k+1];
        py2 = Ypoints[k+1];
        drawLine(px1,py1,px2,py2,1);
    }
```

```
    }
    else
    {
        for (j=0; j<generator_size; j++)
        {
            switch(j)
            {
                case 1:
                case 2:
                case 3:
                case 4:
                case 8:
                case 9:
                case 12:
                    set_type = 0;
                    break;
                case 0:
                case 5:
                case 6:
                case 7:
                case 10:
                case 11:
                    set_type = 1;
                    break;
            }
            X1 = Xpoints[j];
            X2 = Xpoints[j+1];
            Y1 = Ypoints[j];
            Y2 = Ypoints[j+1];
            generate (X1,Y1,X2,Y2,level,set_type,sign);
        }
    }
}


/*

    snow7 = generates snowflake with 7 segment generator

*/

#include <stdio.h>
#include <math.h>
#include <dos.h>
#include "tools.h"

void generate (float X1, float Y1, float X2, float Y2,
    int level, int type, int sign);

int combination = 0,LINEWIDTH=1, OPERATOR=0;
unsigned long int PATTERN=0xFFFFFFFF;
```

```
int color,flag = 0,i,start_level;
int generator_size = 7;
int start_level,level;
int init_size = 1,sign = 1,px1,px2,py1,py2;
int initiator_x1[10] = {-125},initiator_x2[10]={125},
    initiator_y1[10]={0},initiator_y2[10]={0};
float Xpoints[25], Ypoints[25];
float turtle_x,turtle_y,turtle_r,turtle_theta;

main()
{
    printf("\nEnter level (1 - 8): ");
    scanf("%d",&level);
    if (level < 1)
        level = 1;
    start_level = level;
    setMode(1);
    cls();

    for (i=0; i<init_size; i++)
    {
        generate(initiator_x1[i], initiator_y1[i],
            initiator_x2[i], initiator_y2[i], level,0,sign);
    }
    getch();
    setMode(0);
}

/*

                    generate() = Generates curve

*/

void generate (float X1, float Y1, float X2, float Y2,
    int level, int type, int sign)
{
    int j,k,line,set_type;
        float a, b, Xpoints[25], Ypoints[25], temp,temp_r;


    switch (type)
    {
        case 0: break;

        case 1: sign *= -1;
            break;

        case 2: sign *= -1;
        case 3: temp = X1;
            X1 = X2;
```

```
        X2 = temp;
        temp = Y1;
        Y1 = Y2;
        Y2 = temp;
        break;
}
level--;
turtle_r = (sqrt((X2 - X1)*(X2 - X1) + (Y2 - Y1)*(Y2 -
    Y1)))/3.0;
Xpoints[0] = X1;
Ypoints[0] = Y1;
Xpoints[7] = X2;
Ypoints[7] = Y2;
turtle_theta = point(X1,Y1,X2,Y2);
turtle_x = X1;
turtle_y = Y1;
turn(60*sign);
step();
Xpoints[1] = turtle_x;
Ypoints[1] = turtle_y;
step();
Xpoints[2] = turtle_x;
Ypoints[2] = turtle_y;
turn(-60*sign);
step();
Xpoints[3] = turtle_x;
Ypoints[3] = turtle_y;
    turn(-60*sign);
step();
Xpoints[4] = turtle_x;
Ypoints[4] = turtle_y;
    turn(-60*sign);
step();
Xpoints[6] = turtle_x;
Ypoints[6] = turtle_y;
    turn(-60*sign);
step();
Xpoints[5] = turtle_x;
Ypoints[5] = turtle_y;
if (level == 0)
{
    for (k=0; k<generator_size; k++)
    {
        px1 = Xpoints[k];
        py1 = Ypoints[k];
        px2 = Xpoints[k+1];
        py2 = Ypoints[k+1];
        drawLine(px1,py1,px2,py2,1);
    }
}
else
```

```
        {
        for (j=0; j<generator_size; j++)
        {
            switch(j)
            {
                case 5:
                case 0:
                    set_type = 1;
                    break;
                case 1:
                case 2:
                case 3:
                case 6:
                    set_type = 2;
                    break;
                case 4:
                    set_type = 3;
                    break;
            }
            X1 = Xpoints[j];
            X2 = Xpoints[j+1];
            Y1 = Ypoints[j];
            Y2 = Ypoints[j+1];
            generate (X1,Y1,X2,Y2,level,set_type,sign);
        }
        }
}


/*

        snowhall = PROGRAM TO GENERATE SNOWFLAKE HALLS

*/

#include <stdio.h>
#include <math.h>
#include <dos.h>
#include "tools.h"

void generate (float X1, float Y1, float X2, float Y2,
    int level,int type, int sign);

int combination = 0,LINEWIDTH=1, OPERATOR=0;
unsigned long int PATTERN=0xFFFFFFFF;
float turtle_theta;
int i,px1,px2,py1,py2;
int generator_size = 11;
int level = 4;
int init_size = 1;
int initiator_x1[10] = {-150},initiator_x2[10]={150},
```

```
    initiator_y1[10]={-75},
    initiator_y2[10]={-75};
float Xpoints[25], Ypoints[25];
float turtle_x,turtle_y,turtle_r;

main()
{

    int sign=1;
    int set_type=0;

    printf("\nEnter level (1 - 8): ");
    scanf("%d",&level);
    if (level < 1)
        level = 1;
    setMode(1);
    cls();
    for (i=0; i<init_size; i++)
        generate(initiator_x1[i], initiator_y1[i],
            initiator_x2[i], initiator_y2[i], level,set_type,
            sign);
    getch();
    setMode(0);
}


/*

                  generate() = Generates curve

*/

void generate (float X1, float Y1, float X2, float Y2,
    int level, int type, int sign)
{
    int j,k,line,set_type;
        float a, b, Xpoints[25], Ypoints[25], temp,temp_r;


    switch (type)
    {
        case 0: break;

        case 1: sign *= -1;
            break;

        case 2: sign *= -1;
        case 3: temp = X1;
            X1 = X2;
            X2 = temp;
            temp = Y1;
```

```
            Y1 = Y2;
            Y2 = temp;
            break;
    }
    level--;
    turtle_r = (sqrt((X2 - X1)*(X2 - X1) + (Y2 - Y1)*(Y2 -
        Y1)))/3.0;
    Xpoints[0] = X1;
    Ypoints[0] = Y1;
    Xpoints[11] = X2;
    Ypoints[11] = Y2;
    turtle_theta = point(X1,Y1,X2,Y2);
    turtle_x = X1;
    turtle_y = Y1;
    turn(60*sign);
    step();
    Xpoints[1] = turtle_x;
    Ypoints[1] = turtle_y;
    step();
    Xpoints[2] = turtle_x;
    Ypoints[2] = turtle_y;
    turn(-60*sign);
    step();
    Xpoints[3] = turtle_x;
    Ypoints[3] = turtle_y;
        turn(-60*sign);
    step();
    Xpoints[4] = turtle_x;
    Ypoints[4] = turtle_y;
        turn(-60*sign);
    step();
    Xpoints[10] = turtle_x;
    Ypoints[10] = turtle_y;
        turn(-60*sign);
    step();
    Xpoints[9] = turtle_x;
    Ypoints[9] = turtle_y;
    turtle_r = (sqrt((Xpoints[9] - Xpoints[4])*(Xpoints[9] -
        Xpoints[4]) + (Ypoints[9] - Ypoints[4])*(Ypoints[9]
        - Ypoints[4])))/3.0;
    turtle_theta = point(Xpoints[4],Ypoints[4],Xpoints[9],
        Ypoints[9]);
    turtle_x = Xpoints[4];
    turtle_y = Ypoints[4];
    turn(-60*sign);
    step();
    Xpoints[5] = turtle_x;
    Ypoints[5] = turtle_y;
    step();
    Xpoints[6] = turtle_x;
    Ypoints[6] = turtle_y;
```

```
turn(60*sign);
step();
Xpoints[7] = turtle_x;
Ypoints[7] = turtle_y;
turn(60*sign);
step();
Xpoints[8] = turtle_x;
Ypoints[8] = turtle_y;
if (level == 0)
{
    for (k=0; k<generator_size; k++)
    {
        px1 = Xpoints[k];
        py1 = Ypoints[k];
        px2 = Xpoints[k+1];
        py2 = Ypoints[k+1];
        drawLine(px1,py1,px2,py2,1);
    }
}
else
{
    for (j=0; j<generator_size; j++)
    {
        switch(j)
        {
            case 2:
            case 8:
            case 10:
            case 12:
                set_type = 0;
                break;
            case 0:
            case 5:
                set_type = 1;
                break;
            case 1:
            case 3:
            case 4:
                set_type = 2;
                break;
            case 6:
            case 7:
            case 9:
                set_type = 3;
        }
        X1 = Xpoints[j];
        X2 = Xpoints[j+1];
        Y1 = Ypoints[j];
        Y2 = Ypoints[j+1];
        generate (X1,Y1,X2,Y2,level,set_type,sign);
    }
```

```
        }
    }

/*


            strange = PROGRAM GENERATES STRANGE ATTRACTORS

*/

#include <stdio.h>
#include <math.h>
#include <dos.h>
#include "tools.h"

float Xmax = 2.8,Xmin = -2.8,Ymax = 2,Ymin = -2, X = 0, Y = 0,
    Z = 0;
float deltaX,deltaY,Xtemp,Ytemp,Ztemp;
int col,row,j,max_row = 347, max_col = 719,color;
float a = 2.24, b = .43, c = -.65, d = -2.43, e = 1;
long int max_iterations=50000,i;
int OPERATOR = 0;
char ch;
main()
{
    setMode(1);
    deltaX = max_col/(Xmax - Xmin);
    deltaY = max_row/(Ymax - Ymin);
    for (j=0; j<2; j++)
    {
        cls();
        for (i=0; i<max_iterations; i++)
        {
            Xtemp = sin(a*Y) - Z*cos(b*X);
            Ytemp = Z*sin(c*X) - cos(d*Y);
            Z = e*sin(X);
            X = Xtemp;
            Y = Ytemp;
            if (j==0)
            {
                col = (X - Xmin)*deltaX;
                row = (Y - Ymin)*deltaY;
            }
            else
            {
                col = (Y - Xmin)*deltaX;
                row = (Z - Ymin)*deltaY;
            }
            if ((col>0) && (col<=max_col) &&
                (row>0) && (row<=max_row))
            {
                plot(col,row,1);
```

```
            }
        }
        getch();
    }
    setMode(0);
}

/*

                trees = PROGRAM TO GENERATE TREES

*/

#include <stdio.h>
#include <math.h>
#include <dos.h>
#include <stdlib.h>
#include <time.h>
#include "tools.h"

int combination = 0,LINEWIDTH=1, OPERATOR=0;
unsigned long int PATTERN=0xFFFFFFFF;
int i,j;

float height,width,left_alpha,right_alpha,left_angle,
    right_angle,left_width_factor,left_height_factor,
    right_width_factor,right_height_factor;
float x,y,x1,y01,x2,y2;
float turtle_x,turtle_y,turtle_r,turtle_theta;
int level,px1,px2,py1,py2;

void generate(float x, float y, float width, float height,
    float angle, int level);

main()
{
    printf("\nEnter stem height: ");
    scanf("%f",&height);
    printf("\nEnter stem width: ");
    scanf("%f",&width);
    printf("\nEnter left alpha: ");
    scanf("%f",&left_alpha);
    printf("\nEnter right alpha: ");
    scanf("%f",&right_alpha);
    printf("\nEnter left branch angle: ");
    scanf("%f",&left_angle);
    printf("\nEnter right branch angle: ");
    scanf("%f",&right_angle);
    printf("\nEnter recursion level: ");
    scanf("%d",&level);
    left_width_factor = pow(2,-1/left_alpha);
```

```
        left_height_factor = pow(2,-2/(3*left_alpha));
        right_width_factor = pow(2,-1/right_alpha);
        right_height_factor = pow(2,-2/(3*right_alpha));
        x = 0;
        y = -235;
        LINEWIDTH = width;
        setMode(1);
        cls();
        x1 = 0;
        y01 = y + height;
        px1 = x;
        py1 = y;
        px2 = x1;
        py2 = y01;
        drawLine(px1,py1,px2,py2,1);
        turtle_theta = point(x,y,x1,y01);
        turn(left_angle);
        generate(x1,y01,left_width_factor*width,
            left_height_factor*height,left_angle,level);
        turtle_theta = point(x,y,x1,y01);
        turn(-right_angle);
        generate(x1,y01,right_width_factor*width,
            right_height_factor*height,right_angle,level);
        getch();
        setMode(0);
}

void generate(float x, float y, float width, float height,
    float angle, int level)
{
    float x1,y01;

    turtle_x = x;
    turtle_y = y;
    turtle_r = height;
    step();
    x1 = turtle_x;
    y01 = turtle_y;
    LINEWIDTH = width;
    level--;
    px1 = x;
    py1 = y;
    px2 = x1;
    py2 = y01;
    drawLine(px1,py1,px2,py2,1);
    if (level > 0)
    {
        turtle_theta = point(x,y,x1,y01);
        turn(left_angle);
        generate(x1,y01,left_width_factor*width,
            left_height_factor*height,left_angle,level);
```

```
        turtle_theta = point(x,y,x1,y01);
        turn(-right_angle);
        generate(x1,y01,right_width_factor*width,
            right_height_factor*height,right_angle,level);
    }
}

/*


        twindrag = PROGRAM TO GENERATE A TWIN DRAGON

*/

#include <stdio.h>
#include <math.h>
#include <dos.h>
#include "tools.h"

void generate (float X1, float Y1, float X2, float Y2, int level,
    int sign);

int combination = 0,LINEWIDTH=1, OPERATOR=0;
unsigned long int PATTERN=0xFFFFFFFF;
float turtle_theta;
int i,flag[24],px1,px2,py1,py2;
int generator_size = 3;
int level = 16;
int init_size = 2;
int initiator_x1[10] = {-150,150},initiator_x2[10]={150,-150},
    initiator_y1[10]={-25,-25},
    initiator_y2[10]={-25,-25};
float Xpoints[25], Ypoints[25];
float turtle_x,turtle_y,turtle_r;

main()
{

    int sign = 1;

    setMode(1);
    cls();

    for (i=0; i<init_size; i++)
    {
        generate(initiator_x1[i], initiator_y1[i],
            initiator_x2[i], initiator_y2[i], level, sign);
    }
    getch();
    setMode(0);
}
```

```
/*

                 generate() = Generates curve

*/

void generate (float X1, float Y1, float X2, float Y2,
    int level, int sign)
{
    int j,k,line,sign2=-1;
    float a, b, Xpoints[25], Ypoints[25];

    turtle_r = (sqrt((X2 - X1)*(X2 - X1) + (Y2 - Y1)*(Y2 -
        Y1)))/1.41421;
    Xpoints[0] = X1;
    Ypoints[0] = Y1;
    Xpoints[2] = X2;
    Ypoints[2] = Y2;
    turtle_theta = point(X1,Y1,X2,Y2);
    turtle_x = X1;
    turtle_y = Y1;
    turn(sign*(45));
    step();
    Xpoints[1] = turtle_x;
    Ypoints[1] = turtle_y;
    level--;
    if (level > 0)
    {
        for (j=0; j<generator_size-1; j++)
        {
                X1 = Xpoints[j];
                X2 = Xpoints[j+1];
                Y1 = Ypoints[j];
                Y2 = Ypoints[j+1];
            generate (X1,Y1,X2,Y2,level,sign2);
            sign2 *= -1;
        }
    }
    else
    {
        for (k=0; k<generator_size-1; k++)
        {
            px1 = Xpoints[k];
            py1 = Ypoints[k];
            px2 = Xpoints[k+1];
            py2 = Ypoints[k+1];
            drawLine(px1,py1,px2,py2,1);
        }
    }
}
```

About the Author

Dr. Roger T. Stevens graduated from California Western University, in Santa Ana, California, with a PhD in Electrical Engineering, but not before attaining degrees from three other universities, including: a Masters in Engineering in Systems Engineering at Virginia Polytechnic Institute in Blacksburg, Virginia; a Master of Arts in Mathematics at Boston University in Boston; and a Bachelor of Arts in English at Union College in Schenectady, New York.

Dr. Stevens's engineering career spans over 30 years. He is currently a member of the technical staff of the MITRE Corporation, Bedford, Massachusetts, in charge of system engineering support and development for the Defense Test and Evaluation Suport Agency.

He has written numerous articles for technical magazines and journals, and is the author of Operational Test and Evaluation: A Systems Engineering Process (John Wiley, 1978) and Graphics Programming in C (M&T Books, 1988). Dr. Stevens resides with his wife, Barbara, in Albuquerque, New Mexico.

Bibliography

Ackerman, M., "Hilbert Curves Made Simple," *Byte*, June 1986, pp. 137–138.

Barnsley, M. F., and Sloan, A. D., "A Better Way to Compress Images," *Byte*, January 1988, pp. 215–223.

Barnsley, Michael, *Fractals Everywhere*, Boston, 1988, Academic Press, Inc.

Barnsley, M. and Demko, S., "Iterated Function Systems and the Global Construction of Fractals," *Proceedings R. Soc. Lond*, A 399, 1985, pp. 243–275.

Batty, M., and Longley, P. A., "Fractal-Based Description of Urban Form," *Environment and Planning B: Planning and Design*, Vol. 14, 1987, pp. 123–134.

Batty, M., "Fractals—Geometry Between Dimensions," *New Scientist*, April 1985, pp. 31–35.

Batty, Michael, *Microcomputer Graphics*, London, 1987, Chapman and Hall.

Batty, M. and Longley, P. A., "Urban Shapes as Fractals," *Area*, 19.3, 1987, pp. 215–221.

Bouville, C., "Bounding Ellipsoids for Ray-Fractal Intersection," *SIGGRAPH '85*, Vol. 19, No. 3, pp. 45–52.

Butz, A. R., "Alternative Algorithm for Hilbert's Space-Filling Curve," *IEEE Transactions on Computers*, Vol. C-20, No. 4, April 1971, pp. 424–426.

Collet, P., Eckmann, J.-P., and Lanford, O. E., "Universal Properties of Maps on an Interval," *Communications in Mathematical Physics*, 76, 1980, pp. 211–254.

Demko, S., Hodges, L., and Naylor, B., "Construction of Fractal Objects with Iterated Function Systems," *SIGGRAPH '85*, Vol. 19, No. 3, pp. 271–278.

Dewdney, A. K., "Computer Recreations," *Scientific American*, September 1986, pp. 140–145.

Feigenbaum, M. J., "Quantitative Universality for a Class of Nonlinear Transformations," *Journal of Statistical Physics*, Vol. 19, No. 1, January 1978, pp. 25–52.

Fogg, L., "Drawing the Mandelbrot and Julia Sets," *Micro Cornucopia*, No. 39, January–February 1988, pp. 6–9.

Fogg, L., "Fractal Miscellany," "Micro Cornucopia," No. 43, September–October 1988, pp. 48–51.

Fogg, L., "Introduction to Fractals," *Micro Cornucopia*, No. 33, December–January 1987, pp. 36–40.

Fournier, A., Fussell, D., and Carpenter, L., "Computer Rendering of Stochastic Models," *Communications of the ACM*, Vol. 25, No. 6, June 1982, pp. 371–384.

Gleick, James, *Chaos: Making a New Science*, New York, 1987, Viking.

Hirst, K. E., "The Apollonian Packing of Circles," *Journal London Math Society*, 42, 1967, pp. 281–291.

Land, B. R., "Dragon," *Byte*, April 1986, pp. 137–138.

Lanford, O.E., "A Computer-Assisted Proof of the Feigenbaum Conjectures," *Bulletin of the American Mathematical Society*, Vol. 6, No. 3, May 1982, pp. 427–434.

Li, T.Y., and Yorke, J.A., "Period Three Implies Chaos," *American Mathematical Monthly*, 82, December 1975., pp. 985–992.

Lorenz, E.N., "Deterministic Nonperiodic Flow," *Journal of the Atmospheric Sciences*, Vol. 20, March 1963, pp. 130–141.

Mandelbrot, B., "Comment on Computer Rendering of Fractal Stochastic Models," *Communications of the ACM*, Vol. 25, No. 8, pp. 581–584.

Mandelbrot, B., *The Fractal Geometry of Nature*, New York, 1983, W. H. Freeman and Company.

Mastin, G.A., Watterberg, P.A., and Mareda, J.F., "Fourier Synthesis of Ocean Scenes," *IEEE Computer Graphics and Applications*, March 1987, pp. 16–24.

Mastin, G. A., "From Research into Art," *IEEE Computer Graphics and Applications*, March 1987, pp. 5–8.

Norton, A., "Generation and Display of Geometric Fractals in 3-D," *Computer Graphics*, Vol. 16, No. 3, July 1982, pp. 61–67.

Patrick, E.A., Anderson, D.R., and Bechtel, F.K., "Mapping Multidimensional Space to One Dimension for Computer Output Display," *IEEE Transactions on Computers*, Vol. C-17, No. 10, October 1968, pp. 949–953.

Peitgen, H.O., and Richter, P. H., *The Beauty of Fractals*, Berlin, 1986, Springer-Verlag.

Peitgen, H.O., Saupe, D., *The Science of Fractal Images*, Berlin, 1988, Springer-Verlag.

Pickover, C.A., "A Note on Rendering 3-D Strange Attractors," *Computers and Graphics*, Vol. 12, No. 2, 1988, pp. 263–267.

Preston, F.H., Lehar, A. F., and Stevens, R. J., "Compressing, Ordering and Displaying Image Data," *SPIE Vol 359 Applications of Image Processing IV*, 1982, pp. 302–308.

Robinson, F., "Plotting the Mandelbrot Set with the BGI," *Turbo Techix*, May-June 1988, pp. 28–35.

Sorensen, P., "Fractals," *Byte*, September 1984, pp. 157–171.

Stockman, H. W., "Fast Fractals," *Micro Cornucopia*, No. 43, September–October 1988, pp. 22–29.

Ushiki, S., "Phoenix," *IEEE Transactions on Circuits and Systems*, Vol. 35, No. 7, July 1988, pp. 788–789.

Zorpette, G., "Fractals: Not Just Another Pretty Picture," *IEEE Spectrum*, October 1988, pp. 29–31.

Index

C

P

T

More C Programming Tools from M&T Books

Graphics Programming in C

by Roger T. Stevens

Graphics Programming in C details the fundamentals of graphics processes for the IBM PC family and its clones. All the information you need to program graphics in C, including source code, is presented in this 656-page book. The provided source code will enable you to easily modify graphic functions to suit your own needs.

Written for all levels of programmers, this reference will help you understand the algorithms and techniques necessary to generate graphic images. You'll find complete discussions of ROM BIOS, VGA, EGA, and CGA inherent capabilities; fractals; methods of displaying points on a screen; improved, faster algorithms for drawing and filling lines, rectangles, polygons, ovals, circles, and arcs; graphics cursors; techniques for coordinate transformation; dot matrix characters; and pop-up windows. *Graphics Programming in C* also features 16 pages of sample 4-color figures, includes a complete description of how to put together a graphics library and how to print hard copies of graphics display screens. Both Turbo C and Microsoft C are supported.

Book & Disk (MS-DOS)   *Item #019-2*   *$39.95*
Book only   *Item #018-4*   *$24.95*

Dr. Dobb's Toolbook of C

by the Editors of *Dr. Dobb's Journal*

More than 700 pages of the best of C articles and source code from *Dr. Dobb's Journal of Software Tools* in a single book! Not just a compilation of reprints, this comprehensive volume contains new materials by various C experts as well as updates and revisions of some older articles.

The essays and articles contained within this virtual encyclopedia of information were designed to give the professional programmer a deeper understanding of C by addressing real world programming problems, and how to use C to its fullest.

Some of the highlights include an entire C compiler with support routines, versions of various utility programs such as Grep, and a C program cross-referencer.

Dr. Dobb's Toolbook of C is an invaluable resource that you'll turn to again and again for an in-depth appreciation of C.

Book only   *Item #599-8*   *$29.95*

More C Programming Tools ...

C Programming for MIDI

by Jim Conger

Both musicians and programmers can learn how to create useful programs and libraries of software tools for music applications. Outlined are the features of MIDI and its support of real-time access to musical devices. An introduction to C programming fundamentals as they relate to MIDI is provided. These concepts are fully demonstrated with two MIDI applications: a patch librarian and a simple sequencer. Some of the fundamental MIDI programming elements you'll learn are: full development of a patch librarian program, sequencing applications for the MPU-401 interface, how to create screen displays, and how to write low-level assembly language routines for MIDI. *C Programming for MIDI* shows you how to write customized programs to create the sounds and effects you need. All programs are available on disk with full source code. Supports both Microsoft C and Turbo C.

Book & Disk (MS-DOS)   *Item #90-9*   *$37.95*
Book only   *Item #86-0*   *$22.95*

MIDI Sequencing in C

by Jim Conger

MIDI Sequencing in C picks up where the author's popular book, *C Programming for MIDI,* left off, and approaches the recording and playback of MIDI data from the perspective of both user and programmer. Covered in detail are key topics such as installation, record and editing functions, overviews of block operations and note level edit functions, programming in graphics mode, and much more.

The optional source code disk provides a ready-to-run 8-track MIDI sequencer with full editing features. Programmers will find all source code for the MT sequencer/editor is provided along with full documentation of each function. The MT sequencer runs on IBM PC and AT-type computers using the Roland MPU-401 MIDI interface or equivalent. CGA, EGA, and VGA video standards are supported. Both Microsoft and Turbo C compilers are supported.

Book & Disk (MS-DOS)   *Item #046-X*   *$39.95*
Book only   *Item #045-1*   *$24.95*

More C Programming Tools ...

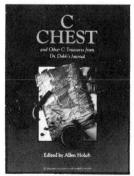

C Chest and Other C Treasures
from *Dr. Dobb's Journal*

edited by Allen Holub

  This comprehensive anthology contains the popular "C Chest" columns by Allen Holub from *Dr. Dobb's Journal of Software Tools*.
  For the novice and experienced C programmer alike, *C Chest and Other C Treasures* will prove to be an invaluable resource, providing hours worth of information to be learned and applied.
  Just some of the many topics detailed are: pipes, wild-card expansion, and quoted arguments; sorting routines; command-line processing; queues and bit maps; ls, make and other utilities; expression parsing; hyphenation; an Fget that edits; redirection; accessing IBM video display memory; trees; an AVL tree database package; directory transversal; sets; shrinking; and .EXE file images.
  The anthology also includes several information-packed articles written by well-known C experts. Learn from the experts about a flexible program that allows you to find the minima of complex, multiple dimension equations; cubic-spline routines that provide an efficient way to do a more restrictive curve-fitting application; an fgrep program that resurrects a very efficient finite-state-machine based algorithm that can be used in any pattern-matching algorithm, and more!
  C Chest and Other C Treasures provides a collection of useful subroutines and practical programs written in C, and are available on disk with full source code.

Book & Disk (MS-DOS) *Item #49-6 $39.95*
Book only   *Item #40-2 $24.95*

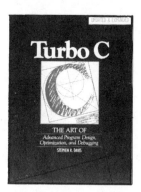

Turbo C: *The Art of Advanced Program Design, Optimization, and Debugging*

by Stephen R. Davis

  Packed with useful example programs, this book details the techniques necessary to skillfully program, optimize, and debug in Turbo C. Every topic and Turbo C feature is fully demonstrated in *Turbo C* source code examples.
  Starting with an overview of the C language, the author advances to topics such as pointers, direct screen I/O; inline statements in *Turbo C*; and how to intercept and redirect BIOS calls, all of which are demonstrated in a RAM resident pop-up program written in Turbo C.
  Fully outlined are the differences between UNIX C and Turbo C; the transition from Turbo Pascal to Turbo C; and the superset of K&R C features implemented in the proposed ANSI C standard.
  Whether you are a C programmer interested in investigating this exciting new dialect of the language or a Turbo Pascal programmer who is curious to learn more of this C language, *Turbo C* is must reading!

Book & Disk (MS-DOS) *Item #45-3 $39.95*
Book only   *Item #38-0 $24.95*

More C Programming Tools ...

A Small C Compiler: *Language, Usage, Theory, and Design*

by James E. Hendrix

For anyone who wants to examine a C compiler from the inside out, *A Small C Compiler* provides all the essential features of a full compiler with the invaluable extra benefit of full source code. All programs are written to be upwardly compatible with full C, and best of all, the book and disk can be yours for only $38.95.

A Small C Compiler contains a full presentation of the design and operation theory of the Small C compiler and programming language. This book provides an excellent example for learning basic compiler theory as well as a full, working Small C compiler. Here is a real compiler that is easy enough to be understood and modified by computer science students, and may be transformed into a cross-compiler or completely ported to other processors. Features include code optimizing, internal use of pseudo code, upward compatibility with full C, recursive descent parsing, a one pass algorithm, and the generation of assembly language code. You'll even learn how the compiler can be used to generate a new version of itself! No other compiler available to the public has ever been so thoroughly documented. The optional diskette includes an executable compiler, fully documented source code, and many sample programs. A Microsoft, IBM Macro Assembler or Jim Hendrix's own Small Assembler is necessary.

Book & Disk (MS-DOS)	*Item #97-6*	*$38.95*
Book only	*Item #88-7*	*$23.95*

Small Assembler: *An 80x86 Macro Assembler Written in Small C*

by James E. Hendrix

Small Assembler is a full macro assembler which was developed primarily for use with the Small C compiler. In addition to being a full assembler that generates standard MASM compatible .OBJ files, the *Small Assembler* is written in Small C. It provides an excellent example for learning the basics of how an assembler works. The *Small Assembler* generates .OBJ files for all 80X86 processors, and will easily adapt to future Intel processors.

The manual provides an overview of the Small Assembler, documents the command lines that invoke programs, and provides appendixes and reference materials for the programmer. The accompanying disk includes both the executable assembler and full source code.

Manual & Disk	*Item #024-9*	*$29.95*

More C Programming Tools ...

Small-Windows: *A Library of Windowing Functions for the C Language*

by James E. Hendrix

    Small-Windows is an extensive library of C language functions for creating and manipulating display windows. The manual and disk package contains 41 windowing functions that allow you to clean, frame, move, hide, show, scroll, push and pop-up menus.

    A file directory illustrates the use of window menu functions and provides file selection, renaming, and deletion capability. Two test programs are provided as examples to show you how to use the library and the window, menu, and directory functions. **Small-Windows** is available for MS-DOS systems, and Microsoft C versions 4.0/5.0, Turbo C 1.5, Small-C, and Lattice C 3.1 compilers. Documentation and full source code included.

Manual & Disk (MS-DOS)   Item #35-6 $29.95
(Microsoft C, Small-C, Lattice C, or Turbo C Compiler)

Small-Tools User's Manual

by James E. Hendrix

    This package of programs performs specific modular operations on text files such as editing, formatting, sorting, merging, listing, printing, searching, changing, transliterating, copying, and concantenating. **Small-Tools** is supplied in source code form. You can select and adapt these tools to your own purposes. Documentation is included. MS-DOS.

Manual & Disk (MS-DOS)   Item #02-X $29.95

More C Programming Tools ...

UNIX Programming on the 80286/80386, 2nd Edition

by Alan Deikman

UNIX Programming on the 80286/80386, 2nd Edition, provides experienced system programmers with an overview of time-saving UNIX features and an informative discussion of the relationship between UNIX and DOS. Included are many helpful techniques specific to programming under the UNIX environment on a PC.

Inside, you'll find complete coverage of the UNIX program environment, file systems, shells, and basic utilities; C programming under UNIX; mass storage programs; 80286 and 80386 architecture; segment register programming; and UNIX administration and documentation.

UNIX Programming on the 80286/80386, 2nd Edition, completely covers the techniques for writing and managing device drivers to accommodate the many PC peripherals available. Many examples of actual code are provided.

Book & Disk (UNIX 5-1/4")   *Item #062-1*   *$39.95*
Book only   *Item #060-5*   *$24.95*

On Command: *Writing a UNIX-Like Shell for MS-DOS*

by Allen Holub

On Command and its ready-to-use program demonstrate how to write a UNIX-like shell for MS-DOS, with techniques applicable to most other programming languages as well. The book and disk include a detailed description and working version of the Shell, complete C source code, a thorough discussion of low-level MS-DOS interfacing, and significant examples of C programming at the system level.

Supported features include: read, aliases, history, redirection and pipes, UNIX-like command syntax, MS-DOS compatible prompt support, C-like control-flow statements, and a Shell variable that expands to the contents of a file so that a program can produce text that is used by Shell scripts.

The ready-to-use program and all C source code are included on disk. For IBM PC and direct compatibles.

Book & Disk (MS-DOS)   *Item #29-1*   *$39.95*

More C Programming Tools ...

/Util: *A UNIX-Like Utility Package for MS-DOS*

by Allen Holub

When used with the Shell, this collection of utility programs and subroutines provides you with a fully functional subset of the UNIX environment. Many of the utilities may also be used independently. You'll find executable versions of cat, c, date, du, echo, grep, ls, mkdir, mv, p, pause, printevn, rm, rmdir, sub, and chmod.

The */Util* package includes complete source code on disk. All programs and most of the utility subroutines are fully documented in a UNIX-style manual. For IBM PCs and direct compatibles.

Manual & Disk (MS-DOS)   Item #12-7   *$29.95*

NR: *An Implementation of the UNIX NROFF Word Processor*

by Allen Holub

NR is a text formatter that is written in C and is compatible with UNIX's NROFF. Complete source code is included in the *NR* package so that it can be easily customized to fit your needs. *NR* also includes an implementation of how -ms works. NR does hyphenation and simple proportional spacing. It supports automatic table of contents and index generation, automatic footnotes and endnotes, italics, boldface, overstriking, underlining, and left and right margin adjustment. The *NR* package also contains: extensive macro and string capability, number registers in various formats, diversions and diversion traps, and input and output line traps. NR is easily configurable for most printers. Both the ready-to-use program and full source code are included. For PC compatibles.

Manual & Disk (MS-DOS)   Item #33-X   *$29.95*

More C Programming Tools ...

Fractal Programming in C

by Roger T. Stevens

Fractals are the visual representation of "chaos," the revolution that is currently sweeping through all fields of science. *Fractal Programming in C* is a comprehensive "how-to" book written for programmers interested in fractals. Included are over 100 black and white pictures and 32 color pictures. All source code to reproduce these pictures is provided on disk, MS-DOS format. Requires PC or clone with EGA or VGA and color monitor; Turbo C, Quick C, or Microsoft C compiler.

Book & Disk (MS-DOS)   *Item #038-9*   *$39.95*
Book only   *Item #037-0*   *$24.95*

To Order: Return this form with your payment to **M&T Books**, 501 Galveston Drive, Redwood City, CA 94063 or **CALL TOLL-FREE 1-800-533-4372** Mon-Fri 8AM-5PM Pacific Standard Time (in California, call 1-800-356-2002).

☐ **YES!** Please send me the following: ☐ Check enclosed, payable to **M&T Books**.

Item#	Description	Disk	Price

Charge my ☐ Visa ☐ MC ☐ AmEx

Card No. _____ Exp. Date _____

Signature_____

Name_____

Address_____

City _____

State _____ Zip_____

Subtotal _____

CA residents add sales tax __ %_____

Add $2.99 per item for shipping
and handling _____

TOTAL _____

7026

M&T BOOKS